ROUTLEDGE LIBRARY EDITIONS:
TRANSPORT ECONOMICS

Volume 2

AIRLINE MANAGEMENT

AIRLINE MANAGEMENT

Business Management in Transport 3

W.S. BARRY

Routledge
Taylor & Francis Group
LONDON AND NEW YORK

First published in 1965 by George Allen & Unwin, Ltd.

This edition first published in 2017
by Routledge
4 Park Square, Milton Park, Abingdon, Oxon OX14 4RN
605 Third Avenue, New York, NY 10017

Routledge is an imprint of the Taylor & Francis Group, an informa business

British Library Cataloguing in Publication Data
A catalogue record for this book is available from the British Library

ISBN: 978-0-415-78484-9 (Set)
ISBN: 978-1-315-20175-7 (Set) (ebk)
ISBN: 978-0-415-79216-5 (Volume 2) (hbk)
ISBN: 978-0-415-79222-6 (Volume 2) (pbk)
ISBN: 978-1-315-21186-2 (Volume 2) (ebk)

AIRLINE MANAGEMENT

by W. S. Barry

London
GEORGE ALLEN & UNWIN LTD
RUSKIN HOUSE MUSEUM STREET

FIRST PUBLISHED IN 1965

PRINTED IN GREAT BRITAIN
in 10 *point Times Roman type*
BY UNWIN BROTHERS LTD
WOKING AND LONDON

CONTENTS

CONTENTS

PREFACE

At present we cannot generalise extensively from experience in the management of every sort of business. It is possible to form some notions that apply to a variety of industries; but a slender volume will cover this common ground, whereas many volumes would be required to encompass the differences.

By confining our study to a single industry, such as transport, we can generalise to a greater extent. We will find more in common, and fewer differences in principle and practice from one firm to another. The differences are likely to be even less within one section of an industry, such as the air section of the transport industry. But, however much there is in common from one airline to another, we must always bear in mind that there are still important differences.

All airlines are not brought into being under similar circumstances, nor do the environments, in which they continue, provide them with equal opportunities. Thus a profitable airline may be badly managed, and an unprofitable one well managed. The former may not make the most of the situation in which it operates, whereas the latter does so. Good management makes the most of favourable conditions, and minimises the effects of unfavourable conditions.

The variables in which airlines operate are geographical, economic, social and political. Geographical factors of location, distance, climate and physical features influence the costs of moving men and materials. Economic factors include prices of materials, level of wages, interest rates and taxation. Social factors include customs of working, holiday making, eating and drinking. Political factors include government policy on aircraft purchasing, route licensing and subsidies. This selection of variables is enough to indicate the differences in the situations of each airline, and to make us cautious in our judgement of the merit of any airline's management.

An important task in management education is to create a framework in which to fit what might otherwise remain a shapeless body of knowledge. This framework should assist the student by creating a pattern that makes it easier to remember much detail and to relate all the various portions of knowledge. It should enable a manager to make the most of his experience. Indeed I believe that it is not exaggerating to claim that whatever conceptual framework a manager acquires *controls his experience*.

I fashioned a framework of study for business generally in a previous volume, entitled *The Fundamentals of Management*. It was then used for studying the management of transport undertakings in a volume entitled *Managing a Transport Business*. It has been used again in this volume to study airline management.

The subject is approached from the point of view of *the relationships that managers maintain*. These relationships are broadly divided into: (1) external relations, between those inside a business and those outside it; (2) internal relations among those inside a business; and (3) the relation of ideas and aims within the individual manager. *External relations* are divided into those with customers (passengers, shippers and charterers), State, investors, suppliers, general public and competitors. *Internal relations* are examined firstly in the light of the essential relationship that distinguishes a manager. This is his relationship with the organisation that is instrumental to his purpose. Secondly, 'extra-to-authority' industrial relations are dealt with. Thirdly, the relations among general management and the six major management specialisations (finance, purchasing, production, marketing, personnel and research and development) are looked at. The part on the *individual manager* deals with certain integrating and disintegrating factors, brought to bear upon the individual, by the managerial task.

The section on organisation deals with elements under the hands of managers; with elements that make them managers. It deals with operatives, equipment and raw materials. It discusses the problems of division and co-ordination of elements *subordinate to management*. In the chapters on general and special management we are talking about *management itself*, and the way the overall managerial task is divided up. In a sense the two sections reflect the two great divisions in business: (1) the division of 'labour', and (2) the division of the 'headship' of business.

I hope this work will interest my co-workers, colleagues and friends in the many airlines that make up this fascinating industry. During the fifteen years that I have been a student of the air transport I have always been impressed by its international characteristics. The problems I have set out in this book are not particularly British or American or European. They are problems concerning the management of almost every airline in the world.

Gerrards Cross W. S. BARRY
April 1964

ACKNOWLEDGEMENTS

My colleagues in British European Airways in papers, and in discussion, supplied me with a number of the ideas in this work. My colleagues in the member airlines of the European Air Research Bureau and Mr Peter Cavanagh of Birkbeck College shared in the preparation of material on the training of non-technical personnel. Hugh Auld and John Crawford, while they were Research Fellows with BEA, supplied me with certain material.

Extracts from the Report of the Select Committee on Nationalised Industries (Report and Accounts)—The Air Corporations Act, 1949, a White Paper on the Financial and Economic Obligations of the Nationalised Industries, 1962, and the (Jack) Report of a Court of Inquiry, 1958, are reproduced with the permission of the Controller of HM Stationery Office. The Organisation for Economic Co-operation and Development allowed me to quote extensively from their two excellent reports entitled 'Issues in Management Education' and 'Development of a Body of Management Teachers'.

My thanks are due to a number of airlines for information on their organisation. Use has been made of illustrative material from American Airlines, Trans-Canada Air Lines,[1] Aer Lingus, Air France, Alitalia, British European Airways, British Overseas Airways, KLM Royal Dutch Airlines, Sabena, Scandinavian Airlines System, Swissair, Pan American Airways and United Airlines. I also gratefully acknowledge the contribution of ideas from H. Fayol, L. Urwick, E. F. L. Brech, A. J. Burkhart, T. T. Paterson, R. W. Revans and Jerry Ledgerer's Flight Safety Foundation. The International Civil Aviation Statistical Digests, the studies of the Civil Aeronautics Administration of the USA, and reports from the New York University 2nd Annual Air Transport Conference 1962, provided me with valuable information.

The University of London, The British Broadcasting Corporation and Messrs George Allen and Unwin kindly gave me permission to reproduce extracts from my own past works.

[1] Trans-Canada Air Lines changed their name to Air Canada in 1964. The former name has been used in this work when referring to circumstances before the change.

ACKNOWLEDGMENTS

SUMMARY

Part I

External Relations of Management

CHAPTER I
RELATIONS WITH CUSTOMERS: PASSENGERS, SHIPPERS AND CHARTERERS

Introduction. The distinction between 'customers' and 'consumers'. Airline 'customers' and 'traffic'. Various classes of passenger travel. Government intervention in management-customer relations. The preference of passengers for particular types of aircraft. The order of passenger satisfactions. Customer complaints. Aspects of service that customers comment on. What sort of people travel by air? Business passengers and holidaymakers. Special passengers. Languages and airline passengers. Passengers' fears. What sort of goods are sent by air? Shippers' requirements for freight services. Types of aircraft charters. Customer studies.

CHAPTER II
RELATIONS WITH STATE

Introduction. Legal rights to the use of the air. The 'Two Freedoms' and 'Five Freedoms' Agreements. General principles of sovereignty over airspace established by the Chicago Convention. States' bilateral agreements to establish rights to use the air. International Civil Aviation Organisation (ICAO)—a means of co-operation among States. The attitude of airline managements to the ICAO contribution to international air law. The conflict of laws: private and public international air law. International conventions. Domestic air law. The vesting of authority in organs of State. British Air Registration Board. State licensing of air services. The Civil Aeronautics Board of the United States. The British Air Transport Licensing Board. Governments and cabotage routes. National prestige. Government subsidies to national airlines. The interest of the State in the purchase of aircraft. The difference in governments' help to aircraft constructors in the early 1960's and the effect on the competitiveness of airlines. State financial control on aircraft purchases. States' attitudes to 'social' services. British Government's attitude to social services as stated in the 1958 Select Committee Report, and the White Paper 'Financial and Economic Obligations of Nationalised Industries 1961'. State and Air Traffic Control. State provision of airports. The attitude of States towards charging for the terminal and route services they supply.

CHAPTER III

RELATIONS WITH INVESTORS, SUPPLIERS, GENERAL PUBLIC AND COMPETITORS

Introduction. RELATIONS WITH INVESTORS. Investors and airline results. Statistical indices used in comparing airline results. Limitations of Statistical Indices from point of view of investors. RELATIONS WITH SUPPLIERS. Relations with aircraft constructors. The price of aircraft. Travel agents. RELATIONS WITH THE GENERAL PUBLIC. RELATIONS WITH COMPETITORS. Degree of competition. International Air Transport Association (IATA). The way in which airlines work through IATA. The attitude of airline managements to IATA. Competition and collaboration.

CHAPTER IV

ORGANISATION AND EXTERNAL RELATIONS

General view of organisation and external relations. Marketing departments. Travel agency sections in airline organisations. Agency and interline sales organisations. Tariff negotiations. Purchasing departments. Public relations. Organisation for dealing with customers' comments, complaints and claims. Relations with governments. Secretarial and legal branches. Finance departments.

Part II

Internal Relations of Management

CHAPTER V

ELEMENTS OF AIRLINE ORGANISATION

The distinction between a business and its organisation. Managerial process: activities of planning, motivating, controlling and contracting. The practicability of running an airline business without an organisation. The significance of the two concepts of 'business' and 'organisation' in running an airline. A brief review of the extent of contracting in airlines. A general view of the elements of airline organisation. Complexity of intentions in large-scale airline business. Complexity of the elements of airline organisation.

CHAPTER VI

THEORY OF ORGANISATION

Introduction. Factors influencing decisions on the alternatives of adding to organisation or contracting: costs, attitudes to organisation and contracting, availability of capital, availability of good managers, availability of operatives, availability of equipment, availability of raw materials, ideas on rate of growth, the concept of the optimum organisation. The matching of differing optima. The relation between the size of an airline 'business' and its 'organisation'. The variables influencing size of business. Approximate measures of sizes of airline business and organisation. The nature of work done within organisation. Factors influencing the 'order' in which tasks are brought into organisation. Factors affecting the proportions of the elements of airline organisation: measuring the elements in an airline organisation, the extent of organisation, the nature of the raw materials of an airline. The main sorts of airline contracting.

CHAPTER VII
COSTS AND SAVINGS OF ORGANISATION

The essential difference between having a job done within airline organisation, and having it done by a contractor. Two sorts of decisions to have jobs done within airline organisation. The concept of optimum organisation and moving average and marginal costs. Optimum organisation in existence and in utilisation. The savings of the optimum managerial structure. The advantages of the optimum financial structure. The optimum purchasing unit. The savings of optimum process of production. The optimum marketing unit. The effect of fluctuations in demand on costs and savings of organisation. The effect of steady trends in demand. The effect of cyclical trends in demand. The effect of seasonal changes in demand. The effect of erratic changes in demand. The effect of uncertainties (economic and political). The costs and savings of growth in airline organisation. The costs and savings of 'development' or 'innovation' in airline organisation. The effect of the scale of the airline industry on the cost and savings of individual airline organisations.

CHAPTER VIII
PRINCIPLES OF SUBORDINATION

The nature of subordination. The problems of subordination. Subordinating airline organisation to the business. Authority. Responsibility. Delegation. Delegation of authority—the critical act of management. The delegation of duties. Obtaining a 'fix' on a position in organisation. The importance of direct contact between superiors and subordinates. The ideal of concentrated authority. The effect of the authority of a number of specialists brought to bear on a general manager. The limitations on the span of control. The importance of tailoring comments and instructions to the characteristics and environment of the recipient. Purposefulness makes authority more acceptable. Participation makes authority more acceptable.

CHAPTER IX
OVERALL AND COMPONENTS ORGANISATIONS, AND THEIR GROUPS IN AIRLINES

The significance of the difference between 'component organisations' and 'groups' in the study of airline organisation. A summary of the bases of components of overall organisation. Overall organisation without components or groups. Components organisations based on manageability. The addition of organisation groups to components based on manageability. The inclusion in overall organisation of a component based on specialisation. Relationships among components and sub-components of overall organisation. General management and component organisations. The effect of having operatives located at some distance from the manager. The effect of operatives and managers working at different times. A summary of the variables found among overall and component organisations and their groups in airlines. Criteria of optimum divisions of overall organisation into components and sub-components in airline organisation. The distribution of the six fundamental business tasks in 10 airline organisations. The relationship with main domestic stations. The relationship with 'outstations'.

CHAPTER X

THE HUMAN ELEMENT IN AIRLINE ORGANISATION

The range of knowledge and skills required of 'non-technical' personnel. A classification of services performed by 'non-technical' personnel. 'Generalists' or 'specialists'? Operatives who do not make careers in airlines. Informal status symbols in airline organisation. Airline pilots and the professions. Pilots' associations. Attitudes to reporting dangerous incidents. Nostalgia for obsolete skills. The importance of small working units for morale. The skill of the maintenance engineer. The effect of change on 'non-technical' personnel.

CHAPTER XI

INDUSTRIAL RELATIONS

Introduction. The nature of industrial relations. The difference from airline to airline. Origins of industrial relations. Origins of airline industrial relations in Britain. The Institutions of the British airlines industrial relations machinery. Representation in the National Joint Council for (British) Air Transport. Constitutions. Powers of Industrial Relations Institutions of British Airlines. The significance of the terms 'Sectional', 'Local' and 'Joint' in British airline I.R. institutions. The difference between negotiation and consultation. Representatives and delegates. Elected and nominated members. Courts of Inquiry into Industrial Disputes. The Jack Report.

CHAPTER XII

THE NATURE AND TASK OF GENERAL MANAGEMENT

The distinction between general and special management. The organisation of Air France 1962. Choice of type of aircraft. Fleet Planning. Progress indicators. Efficiency indicators: general limitations of efficiency indicators, capacity ton miles (available tonne-Kilometres), CTM per employee, operating costs per CTM, Load Ton Miles (Tonne-Kilometre performed), load factor, passenger load factors, aircraft utilisation. General management and average length of haul. General management control of specialist representatives at international decision-making conferences.

CHAPTER XIII

FINANCE MANAGEMENT

Financial policy. Rigidity of airline financial structures. The working capital of airlines. Proportion between Loan and Share Capital. The significance of heavy interest charges. Depreciation and obsolescence. The economics of remedying obsolescence. Major categories of airline operating costs. The difference between 'operating' and 'total' costs. Major sources of airline revenue. Classification of costs for the purpose of route costing. The inherent difficulties in controlling costs in airlines. Costs of airport and navigational services. Financial accounting in an airline. Management accounting. Budgeting. Budgetary control (revenue and expenditure).

CHAPTER XIV

PURCHASING MANAGEMENT

The importance of skilful purchasing. The contract for the purchase of new aircraft. The major items of purchasing. The volume of purchasing. Categories of purchases. The aims of a purchasing organisation. The arguments for and against a single purchasing organisation. The tasks of a purchasing department in an airline. Airline planning and purchasing management.

CHAPTER XV

PRODUCTION MANAGEMENT

What is 'Production' in an airline? Airline products. Divisions of Production Management. Co-ordination of Production Management. Co-operation in the production field. Measures of production. Journey lengths and flight stages. The handicap of producing short-haul arrivals. MAINTENANCE CONTROL. The need for maintenance—preventive and remedial. Remedial maintenance and standby aircraft. Planning preventive maintenance. Making full use of organisation for maintenance. Limitations of a maintenance organisation. Compromises in maintenance planning. Inspection. State control on maintenance standards. 'Base' and 'on-line' maintenance. General ideas of 'airworthiness'. The effect of maintenance on utilisation. The balancing of hangars, workshops and stores. 'Main units' and 'components'. Maintenance by organisation or contracting. AIRCRAFT MOVEMENT CONTROL. Schedules Planning. Short-term operational control. Notams. Air Traffic Control. The economic disadvantages of air traffic control. Channels of communication between management and aircraft crews. Flight plans. In-flight communications. Establishing standards of performance. Maintaining standards of performance. Training. Reporting procedures. Analysis of delays in aircraft movements. Reporting accidents and incidents. PASSENGER AND FREIGHT CONTROL. Timetables. Route determination. Services extra to carriage. Bookings on other carriers. Reservations. Tariffs and rates. Tickets and waybills. Load control. Embarkation and disembarkation. Personal baggage handling. Communications along routes. Corrective procedures. Aircraft for freight-carrying. Pre-arranging loads.

CHAPTER XVI

MARKETING MANAGEMENT

The nature of a market. Physical limitations on marketing. Aims in marketing. Market potential. Economic limits on marketing. Theory of demand for air transport. The significance of IATA in marketing management. Divisions of the World Market. Airlines marketing agents. The division of the market into 'international' and 'cabotage' routes. Feeder services. Airline specialisation in particular markets. Progress indicators for marketing management. Marketing management and load factors. Marketing management and equipment. Price and the concepts of 'fares' and 'tariffs'. Price policies and marketing: relating prices to costs, discriminating markets by prices, changing prices to equate supply and demand, elasticity of the demand for air transport. Effects of competition and collaboration in marketing. Suggestions for opening up the market. Market research organisations. Marketing prospects for air freight. The problems of marketing freight services. The proper perspective for the transport of freight by air. The role of 'forwarders' in cargo marketing. Advertising. The organisation of marketing.

CHAPTER XVII

PERSONNEL MANAGEMENT

The role of personnel management. The work of an airline Personnel Department. Personnel problems characteristic of airlines. The wide variety of skills employed. The need to deploy simultaneously social and mechanical skills of a high order. The wide fluctuations in the amount of work to be done from one period to another. The geographical spread of employees. Airline staff abroad. The employment of foreign staff. An international outlook for home-based staff. The need to maintain a 24-hour service. The need to retire certain categories of staff at an early age. The need for a constantly effective disciplinary code. Differences in the nature of service in the air and on the ground. The economic vulnerability of an airline. The size of airlines organisations. Selection procedures in airlines. The costs of inadequate training. Training for cost control. The training and education of maintenance engineers. Training 'programmes' instead of 'courses' for 'non-technical' staff. Levels of training for non-technical staff. The way to construct a syllabus for training non-technical staff. The training and education of airline managers. The use of simulation exercises in management training.

CHAPTER XVIII

THE MANAGEMENT OF RESEARCH AND DEVELOPMENT

The fundamental role of research and development in airlines. The meanings attached to the terms 'research' and 'development' in aviation. Distribution of R & D activities in airlines. The decentralisation of R & D activities. Governments and R & D. Precepts for airworthiness governing aircraft development. Engineering R & D in airline organisation. Improving aircraft movement control. Improving passenger and freight control. Improving maintenance control. Market research. Research and development in the personnel field. Data processing. Development of clerical systems. Work study. New thinking in management.

Part III

The Individual Manager

CHAPTER XIX

THE INDIVIDUAL MANAGER

Managerial specialisation. Change and the individual manager. Pride in the system. The 'safety angle'. Professionalism. Conclusion.

APPENDIX I

NEW THINKING IN MANAGEMENT

Cybernetics. Decision Theory. Econometrics. Ergonomics. Group Dynamics. Heuristic. Information Theory. Input/Output Analysis. Management Science. Models. Operational (Operations) Research. Organisation Theory. Systems Analysis.

APPENDIX II

THE ORGANISATION STRUCTURE OF AMERICAN AIRLINES

FIGURES

TABLES

Part I

External Relations of Management

CHAPTER I

RELATIONS WITH CUSTOMERS, PASSENGERS, SHIPPERS AND CHARTERERS

Introduction

There is not any brand new idea on the dealings between airline managers and their customers that needs to be taught. As Dr Johnson said, 'People need to be reminded more often than they need to be instructed.' In describing and analysing the characteristics of passengers, shippers and charterers, this chapter does no more than sum up what every good manager knows already. Its real job is to bring managers back to the old simple principles which so many of us are too busy to see.

Every manager needs to remind himself, again and again, that customers matter most. Whether he be engaged on an engineering problem, or a flying problem or a finance problem, the customer is the only sure point of final reference. Every manager should be continually asking himself questions like these. How will what I am doing affect our customers? Am I making things better or worse for customers?

These questions cannot be answered properly unless managers take themselves back, time after time, from their specialist activities, to a consideration of people. They must learn to understand the human nature of the beings, whom it is their main purpose to serve.

The distinction between 'customers' and 'consumers'

Some managers believe that it is useful to distinguish between customers and consumers. The former are considered to be people who actually make the decision to use a particular airline. They are supposed to include travel agents, business houses, 'other' airlines, and at the end of the list, the man in the street. Only a small percentage of airline services are bought directly from the airlines who fly them.

It may be useful to classify the travel manager of a company as a customer, and the company representatives who actually do the travelling as consumers. But it is less useful to classify travel agents, and 'other' airlines as customers acting on behalf of consumers. The travel manager is a person who decides to pay out money to a particular airline. Agents cannot decide to pay out money, unless instructed by principals. This does not mean that the influence they exercise over the choice of their principals is unimportant, but that principals have a freedom of choice that remains important. The distinction between 'customers' and 'consumers' is useful only if it clearly separates those with power to choose from those who cannot.

Airline 'customers' and 'traffic'

(*a*) Airline customers may be classified as:
1. Passengers.
2. Shippers.
3. Charterers.

(*b*) The traffic they generate may be summarised as follows:

Passengers	Passengers. Free allowance baggage. Excess baggage. Hand baggage. Pre-booked excess baggage.
Shippers	Mail. Ordinary freight. Express freight.
Charterers	Bare hull charters. Aircraft and crew charters.

Various 'classes' of passenger travel

Airlines have, like rail and sea carriers, differentiated conditions of passenger carriage, to produce separate markets, based on the secondary intention of travellers. The names commonly applied to the various conditions are: 'first class', 'tourist', 'economy' and even 'austerity'.

Airlines have to judge carefully the value of these divisions of the passenger market. If they do not represent abiding features of demand, but rather artificially stimulated and temporary phenomena, then they may be more nuisance than they are worth.

Airlines are justified economically in differentiating markets if:

(*a*) Some passengers are persuaded to leave a less profitable, and enter a more profitable, market, and/or
(*b*) Some people are persuaded to fly, who would not otherwise have flown.

The 'extras-to-carriage' that are used to distinguish the various classes of passenger transport are:

(*a*) Separate compartments.
(*b*) More leg-room and elbow-room.
(*c*) Better food, and free drinks.
(*d*) A higher proportion of cabin attendants to each passenger.

If the technical difficulties in providing different classes of travel are considerable, they must be offset against additional revenue earned. Hitherto, airline organisations have not been sufficiently flexible to adjust rapidly to short term changes in demand for various classes. Managements have had to plan seating configurations that were best on average, knowing that at times this would cause loss of revenue. A particular seating configuration irrevocably built into an aircraft is too serious a risk, so most airlines have demanded some 'flexibility' in the design of their aircraft interiors. This may involve movable bulkheads and interchangeable seats. A promising development came in 1964 when BEA introduced in its Trident aircraft, passenger seats that are convertible in a few minutes from first to tourist class standards.

Demand for various classes of travel can be controlled within certain limits by altering tariffs.

Government intervention in management-customer relations

If governments provide some of the services associated with air transport they may influence the relations between management and their customers, for better or for worse. This is particularly the case with passengers. Their memory of a journey may be coloured by impressions of treatment at an airport. That treatment might have been at the hands of government and not airline employees. Many passengers fail to discriminate between them, and blame the carrier for everything that goes wrong.

Managements have to answer to their customers for the mistakes of government employees. Customers cannot be expected to regard government employees, providing airport services, as other than *agents* of the airlines. The only remedy for airline managements is to complain to the government for their employees' shortcomings. These complaints do not, however, carry much weight with the government because the airlines cannot apply the normal sanction of dismissing the agent who does not carry out his principal's wishes.

Governments also affect the relations between airlines and their customers to some extent by the way they treat people at customs and immigration examinations. Once again it is wise for airlines to accept responsibility for these inconveniences, and to keep exerting pressure on the authorities to mend their ways.

The preference of passengers for particular types of aircraft

Passengers' likings for particular types of aircraft are strong enough to attract them away from the services of one airline and towards those of another. There is evidence that on certain routes, many passengers transfer as each new type of aircraft arrives. What lies behind these preferences is obscure and probably irrational. For example, the fastest aircraft has a strong pull, even though its advantage in speed cannot be fully realised because of the time spent on embarkation and disembarkation.

The engine noise heard in the passenger cabin has some bearing on likes and dislikes. It is probably an unwelcome reminder for passengers that their lives depend upon the engines. It is interesting that the noise of engines has been replaced by music in some of the quietest aircraft. Vibration also causes uneasiness, and so does turbulence. Cabin pressurisation was a great advance in standard of comfort that created a gulf between pressurised and unpressurised aircraft.

There are grounds for believing that the look of an aircraft, whether it be streamlined or ungainly, influences traffic. Passengers also seem to notice technical details, like rate of climb. But whatever list we made would fail to answer the question. Why do some aircraft 'catch on' and others not? Why did the Comet prove so popular that it was able to overcome the disadvantages of high operating costs? The lesson has now been well learnt. Airline equipment is not just a matter of production costs, but also of passenger-appeal.

The order of passenger satisfactions

Doubt is not confined to passengers' reactions to the type of aircraft. Very few surveys of passenger satisfactions have been made. The few that have been completed covered too small a sample to be conclusive. They suggest, however, that the subject would repay study.

One of the soundest surveys was interesting not only because it confirmed the theory that passengers first and foremost want to arrive at their destinations on time, but also because it did not support beliefs currently held on the importance of such extra-to-carriage services as catering, cheap cigarettes, and so on. The last word will probably never be said on passenger preferences because the means of investigating lack precision.

But airlines must go on searching for the answer because the various items of satisfaction cannot be reconciled. For example, it is sometimes impossible to get an aircraft away on time and complete the catering services, so it is a question of doing one or the other.

The order of satisfactions may differ from one route to another.

On a holiday route incidental services may be more important than punctuality. On a business route punctuality and reliability may be all that matters. The order of satisfactions may also alter according to the time of a flight. Early morning and late night preferences may differ from those of mid-day. The order may also differ according to seasons and to whether passengers are catching connections.

If managements do not appreciate passengers' views, then money may be spent in an order of priority that does not coincide with that of the customer.

Customer complaints

When customers complain it is usually to the management. The two-way flow, of complaints and answers, forms a valuable link between management and customers. Apart from a small minority whom it is impossible to please, those who complain are worth listening to. Complaints come from the articulate, from those with the courage of their convictions, and from those who lead opinion. For this reason airlines do well to pay heed to them. Management can often create more goodwill by dealing sympathetically with aggrieved passengers, than by operating a number of uneventful flights.

Apart from the opportunities that complaints afford for creating personal relations, they also provide information on how to improve service, and hence to improve the general reputation of the airline. If complaints are analysed and classified over a period they form a valuable means of discerning trends in the quality of various services. Individual complaints taken in isolation can easily mislead the investigator as to their causes. But if complaints are dealt with in aggregate, it is possible to eliminate the occasional accident and to concentrate attention on the recurring issues.

Many complaints concern damage to or loss of personal baggage. Then they are accompanied by claims for compensation. One of the ways of damaging an airline's reputation is to treat complaints and claims as if they were unrelated. The natural suspicion, with which claims are regarded, must not be allowed to destroy the sympathy that is necessary in dealing with a complaint. In dealing with every claimant it is wise to treat him also as a complainant.

Aspects of service that customers comment on

The following are the aspects of service that evoke most comment from customers:

1. Standard and extent of advertising.
2. Treatment received from airline's agents.
3. The way baggage is handled (delays, losses, damage, etc.).

4. Excess charges for baggage.
5. Left luggage facilities.
6. Airport catering facilities.
7. Dealings with customs, immigration and health authorities.
8. Flight delays, diversions and cancellations.
9. Consequences of missing a flight.
10. Charges made for various services.
11. Information services (enquiry points and signposts).
12. Motor transport associated with the airport.
13. Manner of embarkation and disembarkation.
14. Treatment of special passengers.
15. Arrangements for catching connecting flights.
16. Failures to obtain seats on aircraft.
17. Aircraft interior appurtenances (public address system, heating, ventilation, noise, vibration, pressurisation, lighting, seating, luggage stowage and toilets).
18. Noticeable features of take-off, climb, cruising, descent and landing.
19. Cabin service (including quality of food, cigarettes and drinks).
20. Cleanliness and interior décor.

What sort of people travel by air?

There are a number of ways of classifying passengers. The following bases are commonly regarded as useful:

1. Frequency of travel.
2. Income.
3. Social 'class'.
4. Occupation.
5. Age.
6. Sex.

(*a*) *Frequency of travel*

The passengers on any airline flight may be categorised as:

1. Regulars—people who always fly by the particular airline.
2. Occasionals—people who sometimes fly by the particular airline.

   They may be subdivided into:

   Those who change to enjoy the special features of other airlines;

   Those who are indifferent to any feature except that of arriving on time. These people select their airline on the basis of schedules only.

3. First-timers by the particular airline.
   They will either:
   (i) Never fly by the particular airline again, or
   (ii) Become 'occasionals', or
   (iii) Become 'regulars'.
4. First-timers by any airline.
   These first-timers will in due course fall into one of the following groups:
   (i) They will never fly again by any airline, or
   (ii) They will never fly again by the particular airline, or
   (iii) They will become 'occasionals', or
   (iv) They will become 'regulars'.

This classification is significant for several reasons. 'Regulars' are valuable to any airline. Over a few years they may each spend hundreds of pounds. They deserve that little extra attention usually paid to the 'good' customer. Most airlines ask their employees to look out for regulars to see that they are not alienated by a moment's carelessness. In some ways 'regulars' are easy to deal with. They know their way around, make fewer demands on the 'enquiries' counter, do not lose themselves or become frightened.

The first-timer represents a challenge because he is uncommitted. His impressions are vivid; he is perhaps a little tense and worried, but ready to be won over by his new experience. He may even be less critical than the regular because he is not blasé, or bored; he probably will not be aware if something is not quite right because he has no comparisons to go by. But if things go badly he is not likely to be as understanding as the regular. However trite it may seem, airline employees must constantly be reminded that while 'regulars' may sustain the fortunes of the airline, the first-timers are the people who will cause them to grow.

(*b*) *Income*

Airlines must take account of the different spending powers of their passengers. The field of production that is usually referred to as 'services extra-to-carriage' is, within the limits of international agreement, characterised by the ability of people to pay more than just the bare minimum to travel by air from one place to another. Knowledge of the distribution of their passengers' income ranges enables airlines to make more intelligent decisions on quality of services. Knowledge of incomes also enables airlines to direct their marketing with greater precision. The importance of personal incomes is, of course, less in expense-account travel. There it is necessary to assess the prosperity of firms rather than individuals.

(*c*) *Social class*

Social class gives rise to a distinct set of problems. International carriers without a marked social stratification in their homeland, are at some disadvantage in that they do not so readily understand the problems. National differences in this respect are one reason why a nucleus of indigenous staff should be employed at each overseas base.

Some of the staff of one particular airline appeared to treat passengers of a lower class with condescension and those of a higher class than themselves with servility. In neither case did they give a warm and friendly impression. The management thought that the lack of warmth and friendliness in staff-passenger relations was caused by other factors as well.

The attitude of the staff towards passengers of various social classes was thought to be deeply rooted. It originated during their upbringing within the class structure of their country. One feature was the way in which a customer was judged by his accent and manner. As in most service industries, the customer was treated according to the social class to which the employee *thought he belonged.*

This 'class problem' was connected with the growth of the airline. In its early years the airline carried many fewer passengers. These passengers were generally of 'good' social class. Later, when more people could afford to fly, many passengers were middle and lower-middle class, as were most of the airline's employees. Some employees, particularly those who had been with the airline a long time, did not like this change.

Some passengers objected more to being treated with condescension than with servility. Some passengers expected servility and would resent any attempt at friendliness on the part of the employee. Servility, no matter how deplorable, was less of a problem than condescension towards the inexperienced passenger whose social class was equal to, or lower than, that of the employee.

(*d*) *Occupation*

Knowledge of the occupations of its passengers provides airlines with a means of identifying them in the population at large. This is particularly useful in considering ways of attracting businessmen to air travel, but its usefulness is not confined to business traffic. It may be helpful to know, for example, that a sizeable proportion of holiday traffic is composed of schoolteachers, or professional men. Then sales promotion efforts can be aimed directly at these people.

(*e*) *Age*

Age is important because it gives rise to a variety of human needs. Airlines must consider the problems of carrying babes-in-arms, school-children, the middle-aged and elderly folk. Each age must be provided for, even against a background of knife-edge economics, and critical operations.

(*f*) *Sex*

Statistics on the sex of passengers also help airlines to identify their market; and so to direct their marketing activities more precisely, to choose the right destinations to fly to, to sell the right liquor and cigarettes on board aircraft, and so on.

Business passengers and holiday-makers

Airlines usually consider business passengers and holiday-makers to be significantly different sorts of traffic. Characteristically, the former contains more regulars, and the latter more first-timers. Business traffic is usually spread more regularly over the year than is holiday traffic. Business men are usually more concerned with frequency of service, regularity and punctuality than are holiday-makers. However, it is wrong to make too much of the differences; it is more a matter of emphasis than clear-cut distinction. For example, business traffic may become seasonal in countries where winter air travel is undependable because of frequent cancellations of flights due to bad weather.

Travellers on business have been the largest source of demand for first-class seats, on some routes. But this situation can change suddenly if all business is affected by a general economic recession. Some airlines have had to make substantial alterations to seating configurations to adjust to a drastic change in the travel habits of business men.

The conclusions of a 1960 survey of *Britishers who take holidays in Europe* illustrates the sort of information airlines like to collect, about the *potential* holiday passengers:

1. He or she was usually from the more prosperous parts of society, but clerical and supervisory classes provided a growing section, particularly of young, unmarried girls. The older man and wife took holidays most frequently.
2. For the British holiday-maker the chief deterrent was cost, but even so he was willing to spend about £50 per head on his annual holiday.
3. The second most influential deterrent was the presence of young children in the family. The under-25s and over-45s were the tourists.

4. His, and particularly her, main incentive for taking holidays abroad was escape from the inhibitions of British society, but sunshine, change and usual tourist attractions were also incentives.
5. He relied heavily on travel agents both for holiday information and for his bookings, whether by means of an inclusive tour or independently.
6. He and she were keen readers of brochures and travel leaflets. In particular he displayed considerable ignorance at first about the costs of his holiday, and welcomed details of fares, prices, etc.
7. He and she took 10–14 days holiday when they went abroad, and mostly were free to take their holidays outside the July–August peak period.
8. The better-educated British tourist was ready to try new places and increasingly he was taking more than one holiday a year.

These people were regarded as potential airline passengers because they already took holidays abroad. It was assumed that there was less likelihood of attracting 'first-timers abroad' to travel by air. This assumption might have been wrong had there been a large section of people who were deterred from going overseas because of the discomforts of boat and train journeys.

If this information was accurate at the time it might not have remained accurate for long. In a swiftly changing social scene, airlines are unwise to rely on the results of any survey for more than a year or two. Such surveys are, however, important no matter how short-lived their conclusions. Getting to know one's potential customers is getting to know one's business.

Special passengers

A practice has grown up of discriminating certain passengers from others. The important, the powerful and the celebrated have been singled out and given extra attention. It is not always easy to explain why. In some cases there is an obvious commercial advantage in the publicity that can be obtained by making a little fuss over a famous person. In many cases the extra attention seems to be carried over from the days when colonial governors, and embassy staff were the most influential customers.

Some of these uncommercial practices lingered for two reasons. The first was that, in some parts of the world, airline officials were used as government representatives. Station officials were expected to observe the niceties of protocol and diplomatic etiquette while acting as hosts to their august passengers. Secondly, even where governments supplied their own official 'hand-shakers', airline officials became mixed up with the formalities. To this day airline officials occasionally mistake a government reception for an airline one.

Of recent years airlines have sought to escape from this dilemma by introducing a two-fold classification. Very important people must not be neglected, but should be handed over to their rightful owners at the earliest opportunities. Commercially important people are to be cherished as long as possible so that the airlines' persuasive influence can have maximum effect.

There are certain sorts of passengers that clearly need special attention, because without it they might get lost or suffer injury. Small children travelling on their own, invalids and old people are examples. The practice of discriminating on these grounds is less contentious than those described above. There is a danger of causing resentment among the majority of 'ordinary' passengers by creating a privileged minority, especially if that minority pays no more than the 'ordinary' traveller. This danger is less where the logic of the situation is clear to everyone.

Languages and airline passengers

It is difficult to generalise on the desirability of airline officials speaking the languages of their customers. At one extreme we might advocate that every passenger should have access to an official who can speak the passenger's own tongue. At the other extreme we might argue that the sort of people who travel by air are sufficiently cosmopolitan to follow the standard directions given them, and make their basic needs understood, whatever airline they fly by.

The argument cannot, however, be resolved simply on the grounds of basic needs. It is probably true that most passengers can 'get by' with any airline: but would they not feel *more comfortable*, and tend to travel by an airline employing a language with which they are familiar? So the question is really one of competition, and in practice most marketing men support efforts to increase the number of languages spoken in their airline.

It is one thing to see that the knowledge of every major language is represented somewhere among an airline staff. It is quite another to organise duties in such a way that the man with the right language is in the right place at the right time. For example, aircraft crews may be employed in a type of aircraft that flies to a dozen or more lingual areas. They must be rostered in accordance with the aircraft they are trained to operate, and this may sometimes conflict with language requirements. However, what has to be watched is that officials who underestimate the value of 'other' languages, do not brush aside the possibilities of using them, on the grounds of trivial inconvenience to operational procedures.

Often much more could be done to help passengers of different nationalities by the use of taped announcements, and leaflets printed in various languages.

Passengers' fears

Airlines have no means of knowing how many customers they lose because of fear of travel by air. Even people who have the courage to fly are beset by moments of uneasiness. Dangers are inherent in any form of transport, but few have been condemned for this reason alone. Throughout the ages men have been abandoning the slower in favour of the faster, even where the latter involves greater risk.

In the long run air transport will probably not be much affected by these fears. Statistics will undoubtedly indicate that travel by air is relatively safe, and that fears are irrational. But the long term view and overall statistics are not uppermost in the mind of the passenger who has an idea that his aircraft is in trouble. However ill-founded his fears are, the airline must deal with them.

Management must plan to allay individual fears, and to control group fear. They must plan to encourage the nervous, and comfort the fear-stricken and stop panics. Employees must be trained to avoid giving rise to unnecessary fears. They must be trained to recognise signs of individual fear so that they can behave sympathetically, and ease it. Above all they must be trained to sense the beginnings of group fear so that it can be dealt with before it gets out of hand. Sensible precautions taken openly, and in a matter of fact way, cause far less fright than strained whispers and covert moves.

What sort of goods are sent by air?

Goods that have a low value in relation to their bulk are not usually sent by air. For example, potatoes have such a low bulk value that the cost of carriage would usually exceed the price they would fetch in the market. Also goods that have a low value relative to weight are unlikely to be carried by air. Some forms of building stone would come into this class. Apart from these low value bulky and weighty commodities, airlines carry all sorts. However, air transport is particularly suitable for some commodities, and these comprise the majority of the goods traffic.

The smoothness and speed of air transport makes it particularly suitable for the carriage of livestock that would otherwise suffer from long and rough journeys. Smoothness brings traffic in fragile goods like eggs, which if committed to railways would have to be heavily crated. Air transport can also spare shippers the cost of crating easily damaged goods like washing machines and gowns. Precious metals and bearer securities are often sent by air to reduce the risks of theft. A small number of commodities are too rare to be stocked everywhere they may be needed in an emergency. They fall into two main classes: these involving human lives, and those involving expensive equipment. Highly specialised medical equipment comes into the first category, and ships' propellors and aircraft engines come into the second. The last big group of items that go by air are the perishable commodities. These include not only luxury items of food, but also newspapers, fashionable clothes, and so on.

The rate of growth of air freight indicates that there is no mass transfer of custom from surface transport to air transport, and that the latter will always have to sell hard on its good points. There is little reason to suppose that a landslide will suddenly occur, bringing goods of all varieties into the holds of aircraft.

Shippers' requirements for freight services

Some of the intentions of shippers are similar to those of passengers. Both shippers and passengers ask for safe arrivals at correct destinations on time. However, when a shipper entrusts goods to an airline his intentions are likely to be materially different from those of passengers in a number of ways. First, the shipper usually will not want his freight to make the return journey. Secondly, the arrivals he seeks to secure are just the first steps to another change that has far-reaching consequences. The essence of the undertaking from the shipper's point of view is the successful *transfer of possession.* This is what he is really aiming at, and arrival is a means to an end. So documentation is as important as careful handling, and bound up with the carriage of his goods are the shipper's contractual obligations, reputation and prosperity.

Thirdly, because shippers of freight regard their aim as that of producer-satisfaction rather than consumer-satisfaction, they usually try to achieve it at minimum cost, taking into account all circumstances. For this reason the rate structure is critically important. It is made even more so by the fact that shippers tend to assess the cost of air transport simply by looking at how much they have to pay to the carrier. They disregard the savings that can be made in other costs of handling, packing, storage and insurance. For many years to come it will be part of the job of salesmen to put shippers right in these calculations.

Broadly speaking airlines are meeting the demand for freight capacity in two ways. The first is by carrying freight in whatever space is available on passenger aircraft. The second is by carrying the traffic on all-cargo aircraft.

It is sometimes claimed that passenger aircraft give shippers the best service because they are 'free, frequent and fast'. The word 'free' is used to indicate that as space for freight is available on passenger aircraft whether it is used or not, it can be regarded as being produced at no cost, and therefore carriers are able to fix low rates. Then passenger services are at present much more frequent than all-cargo services, and finally the most modern, fastest aircraft are used for passenger and not all-cargo services.

On the other hand there are several drawbacks to the use of passenger aircraft for freight:

(*a*) The best timings for passenger services are not always the best for freight. Generally speaking passengers prefer to travel by day, and shippers to move their goods at night. This largely cancels the advantage of passenger services being frequent.

(*b*) The freight holds in passenger aircraft are small, and awkward to get at. Their physical limitations severely restrict the size and variety of articles that can be carried. In particular they prevent the carriage of large indivisible units of machinery.

(*c*) A passenger-aircraft freight service is unreliable because passengers and mail are given prior claims on whatever space is available. While this is an economic necessity for the airline, it may represent a serious risk for the customer.

(*d*) The position of freight holds in passenger aircraft prevents the introduction of cheap, mechanised methods of loading and unloading that could be reflected in lower charges for customers.

(*e*) The best embarkation points for passengers may not be the best loading points for cargo. In other words, it might be better in some areas to have separate passenger and cargo airports, the former situated for the convenience of a residential area, and the latter for the convenience of an industrial area.

(*f*) The outward-and-return pattern of passenger services is unlikely to be the ideal pattern for a freight service. Goods do not return in the same way as passengers do, nor is the goods traffic between two places even reciprocal. Freight services may ideally be roundabout services. It may even be profitable to develop air 'tramp' services on the model of those at sea.

The introduction of all-cargo services does not automatically overcome all the problems associated with carrying cargo on passenger services. Particularly in the early years of development all-cargo services would suffer severely from the limitations of the resources devoted to this section of the market.

Types of aircraft charters

The hiring of whole aircraft to carry passengers or goods usually takes one of three main forms. First, there are the 'journey' charters in which aircraft and their crews are hired to undertake particular journeys to particular places at particular times. For example, an agent may hire a whole aircraft and crew to provide the air transport for an inclusive tour. Or an aircraft may be hired to transport a school party or football team, and so on. Secondly, there are 'period' charters where aircraft and crews are hired by the week, or month, or for some other period on a 'dry' lease (without fuel) for unspecified journeys. Thirdly, there are 'bare-hull' charters in which the aircraft is hired without crew, and usually without fuel.

To all intents and purposes the charters that are with crew resemble the normal services of the hiring airline. For this reason management has to watch that charter standards do not depart too far from those of scheduled services and distort the image of the airline as a whole. At the same time airlines want to take every advantage of having a foot in a lower-priced market, by operating at lower costs.

The whole business of aircraft chartering is at a somewhat tentative stage. Very few companies have found it possible to reserve aircraft for charter work, so that negotiations often cannot be concluded until the last moment, when it has become quite clear that aircraft can be spared from scheduled services. Thus relations between airlines and charterers suffer from the uncertainty that bedevils the relations between airlines and shippers, where passengers take priority over freight.

Customer studies

We need to be reminded that it is necessary *to study to please* customers. Customers are not pleased automatically, or by accident. Systematic efforts must be made to get to know what sort of people they are. Otherwise airlines will go on making the mistakes that are characteristic of superficial acquaintanceships.

Unless airlines study the habits, tastes and fashions of customers, their services will be based upon hearsay and the prejudices of officials. Unless employees are sympathetic with the problems of their customers, they will not have the patience to deal with them. Sympathy can come only through knowledge and understanding.

These studies should be conducted professionally. They call for the expertise of social scientists. Their conclusions should be arrived at by the new techniques that hold promise of a rigorous approach to such studies.

CHAPTER II

RELATIONS WITH STATE

Introduction

That the relations between airline managers and government officials are important is indicated by the fact that most countries have departments of state dealing exclusively with the transport industry. Many of them have even hived off the aviation section of the industry to be dealt with by a Ministry of Aviation. The legislatures of almost every country with an airline have been involved with 'air' legislation: the judiciaries of these countries have also been concerned with the evolution of air law. The executive arms of government have been concerned with the negotiation of treaties for traffic rights, the provision of navigational aids, and airports. All in all, the state contributions and restrictions upon airline operation are powerful and extensive.

The activities of states, both at home and abroad, are an important part of the environment in which an airline manager works. These activities become a framework, which the airline manager must at first try to shape to his own purpose, and within which he must finally work. He must try to persuade state authorities to do the right things, because in the end the decisions of state will circumscribe his own endeavours.

Legal Rights to the use of the air

When national representatives met in 1944 (Chicago Convention) to attempt to sort out questions of rights to the use of the air, there were three schools of thought:

(*a*) There were those who believed that the airspace of the entire world should be free to all users. Thus there would be no national or private rights to preclude anyone using certain airspace.

(*b*) There were those who believed in freedom of the air within certain defined limits. Thus no nation or private individual would be able to preclude certain types of flight.

(*c*) There were those who believed that each nation should exercise complete sovereignty in the airspace over its territory.

In the end the doctrine of inviolable state-ownership of airspace was accepted. Henceforth the airspace over the territory of any State could be used only with the permission of that State. There was to be no freedom akin to that of the freedom of the sea.

The 'Two Freedoms' and 'Five Freedoms' Agreements

The Chicago Convention confirmed the complete sovereignty of States over their airspace, but by two further agreements, viz.

(*a*) The International Air Transport Agreement (Five Freedoms, or Transport Agreement), and
(*b*) The International Air Services Transit Agreement (Two Freedoms, or Transit Agreement),

there was an attempt to obtain international agreement on the way the sovereignty would be exercised. Some contracting States made a *general grant of five privileges* to all other contracting States. The 'Five Freedoms' were:

(i) The privilege to fly across their territory without landing;
(ii) The privilege to land for non-traffic purposes;
(iii) The privilege to put down passengers, mail and cargo *taken on* in the territory of the State whose nationality the aircraft possesses;
(iv) the privilege to take on passengers, mail and cargo *destined for* the territory of the State whose nationality the aircraft possesses, and
(v) The privilege to take on passengers, mail and cargo *destined for* the territory of *any other contracting State* and the privilege to put down passengers, mail and cargo *coming from* any such territory.

Other contracting States were not prepared to make *a general grant* of more than the first two transit privileges, hence the two agreements. Some of the original signatories of the 'Five Freedoms' Agreement subsequently denounced it, so that the 'Two Freedoms' Agreement became more the widely adhered to.

General principles of sovereignty over airspace established by the Chicago Convention

The most definitive statement of principles emerging from the 1944 Chicago Convention was made in Part I of the Convention itself. In it every contracting State recognises that each State has complete and exclusive sovereignty over the airspace above its territory. No *scheduled international air service* is permitted over or into the territory of contracting States without that State's permission, although non-scheduled flights into or in transit non-stop across a State's territory, and stops for non-traffic purposes, are permitted without the prior consent of the State concerned, subject always to the right of that State to require the aircraft to land. Non-scheduled flights may also take up or set down passengers and cargo from foreign territories, subject to certain limitations.

Every contracting State reserves the right, for reasons of military necessity or public safety, to restrict or prohibit flights over defined areas, provided that the restriction or prohibition applies equally to its own civil aircraft which are engaged in international scheduled airline services. States may oblige offending aircraft to land at designated airports in their territory.

A scheduled international air service was defined in 1952 by ICAO as 'a series of flights that possess all the following characteristics:

(*a*) It passes through the airspace over the territory of more than one State;
(*b*) It is performed by aircraft for the transport of passengers, mail or cargo for remuneration, in such manner that each flight is open to members of the public;
(*c*) It is operated so as to service traffic between the same two or more points, either:

  (i) According to a published timetable; or
  (ii) With flights so regular or frequent that they constitute a recognisable systematic series.'

States' bilateral agreements to establish rights to use the air

The failure of the Chicago Conference to establish a general 'freedom of the air', and the failure of the five 'privileges' to command general support, and the restrictive nature of Part I of the Convention left only one hope for a *permanent* basis for international scheduled flights. This was that the nations would agree on a multilateral exchange pattern, capable of being modified as the need arose. This the representatives at Chicago failed to do.

The industry was thus left with the necessity of bilateral exchanges. The piecemeal exchanges of traffic rights among sovereign States betray something of the nature of horse-trading. And through them governments have also acquired power to approve the fares fixed by airlines at IATA conferences, by making their approval of fares a condition before negotiating international agreements.

International Civil Aviation Organisation (ICAO)—a means of co-operation among States

ICAO was created to carry out certain proposals made at the 1944 Chicago Convention. It became a specialised agency in relationship with the United Nations Organisation. The proposals were embodied in 96 articles, covering in the main:

(*a*) General privileges of and restrictions on the conduct of contracting States were established. For example, as mentioned above, every State was to have complete and exclusive sovereignty over the airspace above its territory. No scheduled international air service was to be operated over or into the territory of a contracting State without its previous consent. This provision put the ultimate control of international air transport firmly in the hands of State authorities.
(*b*) It was agreed in principle to adopt international standards for air navigation.
(*c*) Member States were to provide route equipment to help aircraft navigation.
(*d*) Contracting States agreed to reduce hinderances to swift passage, occasioned by entry formalities, such as those required by customs and immigration authorities.

The Organisation has a Headquarters in Montreal. Its constituent parts are:

(*a*) A *legislature*, called the Assembly. This meets about once every three years, and decides issues by majority of the single votes of each state.
(*b*) An *executive*, called the Council. This is a permanent body responsible to the Assembly. It was originally composed of 21 contracting States, but an amendment to the Convention in 1962 raised the number to 27. It is elected by the Assembly for a three-year term.
(*c*) *Standing Committees.* Work is delegated by the Council to five committees: Air Navigation, Air Transport, Legal, Joint Support of Air Navigation Services, and Finance.
(*d*) A Secretariat with sections corresponding to each Council Committee.

The Organisation can add to the 96 Articles of the Convention by adopting Annexes to the Convention. By 1962 there were 15 such Annexes. Representative bodies of ICAO are shown in Fig. 1, the structure of the ICAO Secretariat in Fig. 2 and a Schedule of Annexes to the Convention as at January 1, 1963, in Fig. 3.

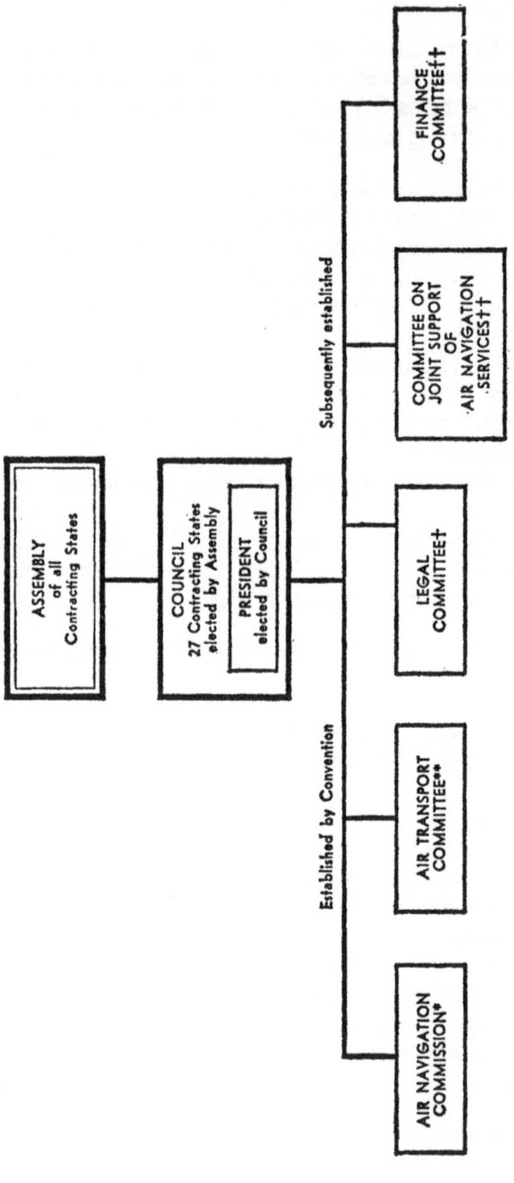

FIG. 1. *Representative Bodies of ICAO*

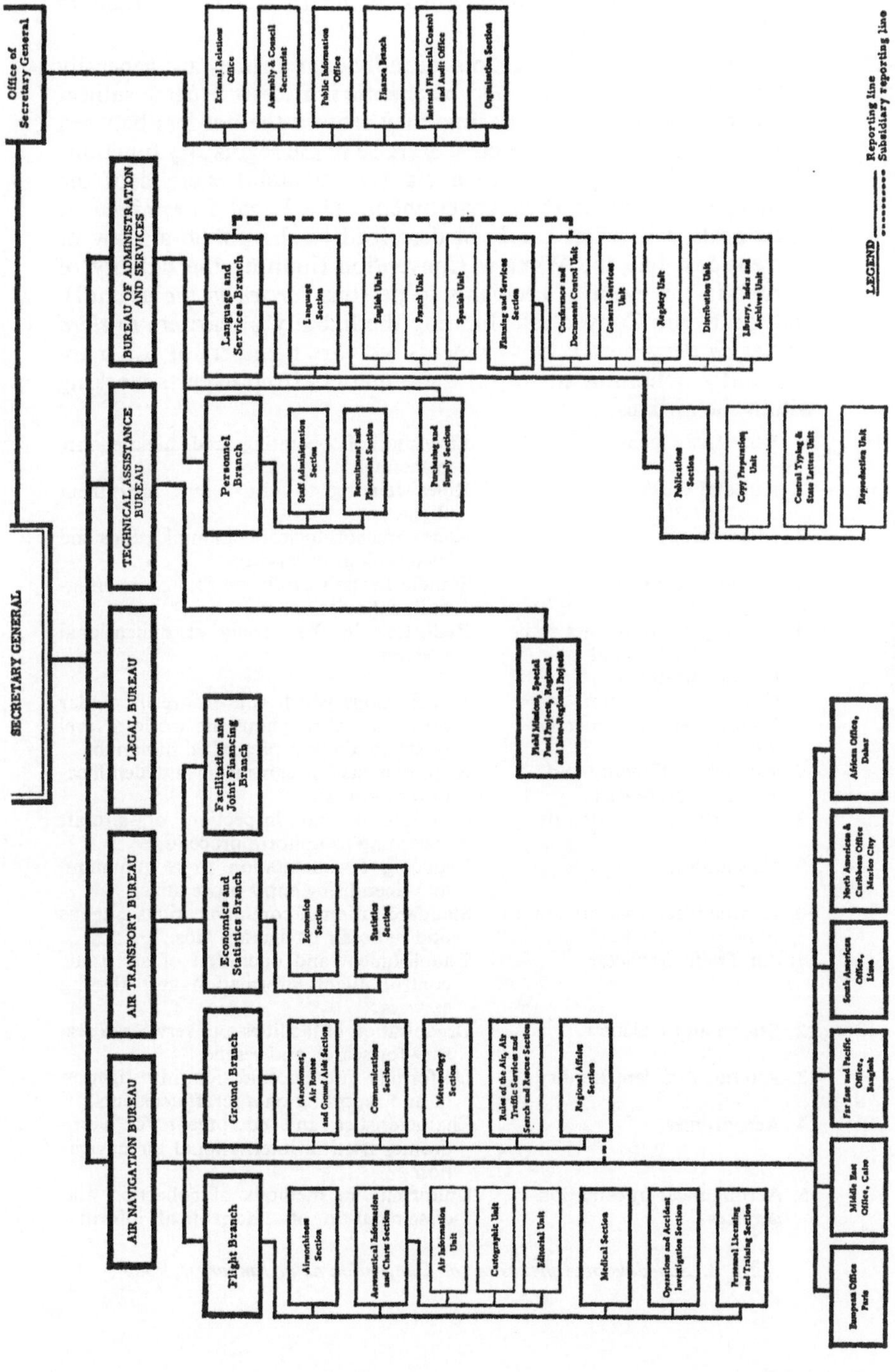

FIG. 2. *Structure of ICAO Secretariat*

The attitude of airline managements to the ICAO contribution to international air law

ICAO limitations on the freedom of individual airlines are generally welcomed. The situation would be chaotic if aircraft became subject to different regulations every time they crossed the borders between sovereign States. So the collective exercise of the regulatory functions of ICAO makes it possible to avoid the unilateral exercise of the regulatory powers of each government. The Legal Committee of ICAO deals with what has been described as the public air law of conventions, like the Warsaw Convention (limiting the liability of carriers in the event of accidents to persons *carried in the aircraft*), and the Rome Convention (limiting the liability of carriers *to third parties on the ground*). Governments who are members of ICAO are constantly obtaining advice on these matters from experts working within the airlines.

1. Personnel Licensing	Licensing of operating and maintenance personnel.
2. Rules of the Air	Rules relating to visual and instrument flight.
3. Meteorology	Codes, meteorological communications and meteorological services.
4. Aeronautical Charts	Standardisation of charts for use in international aviation.
5. Units of Measurement to be used in Air-Ground Communications	Reduction in the variety of dimensional systems.
6. Operation of Aircraft—International Commercial Air Transport	Specifications which will ensure in similar operations throughout the world a level of safety above a prescribed minimum.
7. Aircraft Nationality and Registration Marks	Requirements for registration and identification of aircraft.
8. Airworthiness of Aircraft	Certification and inspection of aircraft according to uniform procedures.
9. Facilitation	Reducing documentation to a minimum, and liberalising entry procedures.
10. Aeronautical Telecommunications	Standardisation of communications systems and radio air navigation aids.
11. Air Traffic Services	Establishment and operation of air traffic control, flight information and alerting services.
12. Search and Rescue	Organisation of facilities and services necessary for search and rescue.
13. Aircraft Accident Inquiry	Uniformity in the notification, investigation of and reporting on aircraft accidents.
14. Aerodromes	Characteristics and equipment for aerodromes used in international air navigation.
15. Aeronautical Information Services	Uniformity in methods of collection and dissemination of aeronautical information.

FIG. 3. *Schedule of Annexes to the Convention as at January 1, 1963*

The conflict of laws: private and public international air law

Most countries have a separate set of rules applying to cases that *concern individuals* as distinct from States, and involving the laws of a foreign country. These rules are sometimes referred to as *private* international law. It is often necessary to decide which of several national legal codes should be used to resolve a particular issue. The claims made for the appropriateness of this or that national law led to the notion of the 'conflict of laws'. Thus the term 'conflict of laws' has become a way of expressing the idea of a private international law that, in fact, involves many national legal systems, governing cases concerning individuals.

So-called *public* international law is based on the consent of those it governs, and springs in the main from treaty or convention. It reduces the area in which the conflict of laws applies. The most important sources of international air law at the moment are the Warsaw Convention of 1929, and the Chicago Convention of 1944. These Conventions seek to provide a universal code of rules to eliminate problems of jurisdiction and choice of law.

International conventions

(*a*) *The Geneva Convention of 1948*

This Convention was designed to secure international recognition of property and other rights in aircraft, so that, when an aircraft crossed the frontier, the holders of such rights would still be protected. The Convention was expected to prevent investment in new aircraft from being discouraged by the uncertainty of the legal situation. By July 1963 this Convention had been ratified or adhered to by twenty-one States.

(*b*) *The Rome Convention of 1952*

This accepted the principle of absolute liability of the aircraft operator for damage caused to third parties on the surface, but placed a limit on the amount of compensation. It also provided, for the first time, international agreement to the compulsory recognition and execution of foreign judgements. By July 1963 fourteen States were party to this Convention.

(*c*) *The Protocol of Amendment (1955) to the Warsaw Convention of 1929*

The Legal Committee of ICAO inherited the task of revising this Convention, which *inter alia* limited the liability of the air carrier to passengers and consignors, except where there is gross negligence, to a maximum of 125,000 gold francs. The Amendment doubled this limit of liability. The (Hague) Protocol came into effect between the ratifying states in August 1963.

(*d*) *The Tokyo Convention of 1963*

This Convention provides that the State *in which the aircraft is registered* has jurisdiction over acts committed on board. It ensures that offences are not unpunished because they are committed outside of any nation's jurisdiction. Aircraft commanders and others are empowered *to prevent acts committed on board*, that may jeopardise the safety of the aircraft or persons or property therein, or good order and discipline on board, *and to disembark* the persons concerned. In the case of an expected or actual unlawful and forcible seizure of an aircraft in flight by a person on board, the States that are party to the Convention are obliged to take all appropriate measures to restore control of the aircraft to its lawful commander or to preserve his control of it. Twelve ratifications were required to bring the Convention into force.

Domestic Air Law

Domestic air law is as important as international air law to an airline manager. The laws of his own country may extend to other countries, that are dependent or protected, and to the airspace over the territory of these countries. Territory will include those waters regarded by public international law as being within the sovereignty of the adjacent land. The laws of his own country may apply to persons and aircraft of his nation, wherever they may be.

The ordinary laws of his land will have considerable influence over his conduct as a manager, particularly where contractual relations are involved. In most countries, however, an additional body of domestic air law has grown up to deal with the new problems created by the advent of the aeroplane. In many countries considerable power to make regulations governing air transport has been delegated by the legislature to a minister or some aviation organisation. Air Law in Britain, for example, is dominated by a few Statutes passed since 1930, and much use is made of delegated legislation. The Civil Aviation Act, 1949, gives the Minister responsible for aviation wide powers to make regulations to implement the policies of the Act. This British Act charged the minister with the duty of 'organising, carrying out and encouraging measures for the development of civil aviation'. In the United States federal regulations under the Civil Aeronautics Act, 1938 was to be exercised by the Civil Aeronautics Board in accordance with the broad aims of 'the encouragement and development of an air transportation system properly adapted to the present and future needs of the foreign and domestic commerce of the United States, of the postal service, and of the national defense'.

It is not possible to do more here than briefly illustrate the detail, and great variety of 'domestic' regulations governing the management of airlines. Part of the British Air Navigation Order, 1954, covering the operation of aircraft, regulates the actions of pilots of aircraft. It requires pilots to check aircraft instruments and visibility before flight; it requires commanders to peruse load sheets and accept responsibility for their being correct; it requires commanders to keep a record of defects, and so on.

Many airlines owe their existence to legislation vesting in them powers to provide air transport. The British nationalised air corporations were established by an Air Corporations Act, 1949. The Trans-Canada Air Lines Company was incorporated by the Trans-Canada Air Lines Act of 1937.

Finally, much domestic air law gives effect to the internationally agreed regulations that have come to be regarded as public international air law. For example, in Britain the Air Navigation (Investigation of Accidents) Regulations 1951 conform to those of ICAO, and implement provisions of the Chicago Convention for foreign representatives to partake in investigations concerning their aircraft. The Civil Aviation Act, 1949, mentions the Rome Convention on Surface Damage, 1933. A section of the Air Corporations Act, 1949, is in accordance with the 'Two Freedoms Agreements'. The Air Navigation Act, 1920, was passed to give effect to the Paris Convention, 1919; effect was given to the Warsaw Convention, 1929, so far as international carriage was concerned, by the Carriage by Air Act, 1932, and so on.

The vesting of authority in organs of State

When we talk about government control of air transport we can mean one of two things. First, we may be talking about influences, in the shape of party political doctrines. These conflicting pressures may produce an atmosphere of uncertainty and rapid changes that destroy the foundations of sound business management. British airlines, both nationalised and private, that operated for two decades in the constantly shifting polemics of socialist and conservative parties, deserved the sympathy of their sternest critics. Pro-nationalisation arguments were soon succeeded by pro-independence doctrines. Air corporations were split up, reunited, redivided, and then soon threatened by reamalgamation. They were exhorted to carry the flag, buy British, make profits and run social services in a bewildering succession of government pronouncements. These changes and threats of change did not do very much to ease the problems of airline management.

Secondly, in talking about government control we may be talking about the permanent, consistently directed control of organs of state like the Civil Aeronautics Board of the USA, the Secretariat-General of Civil Aviation of France, the Luftfahrtbundesamt of West Germany, and the Air Registration Board of Great Britain. These institutions tend to take on a life of their own, and at best to assume the sturdy characteristics of professional, incorruptible civil services, and at worst to degenerate into arbitrary bureaucracies that bedevil the industry.

British Air Registration Board

The Government of the United Kingdom vested part of its authority and control over civil aviation to an organ known as the 'Air Registration Board'. It was originally provided for by the Air Navigation Act, 1936, as a non-profit making corporation, registered under the Companies Act, 1929, and limited by guarantee. Under Section 7 of the Civil Aviation Act, 1949, the Minister may, *by order delegate* to the ARB; a body made up of:

(*a*) Persons substantially representative of the interests concerned with civil aviation (and in particular of operators, constructors and insurers of aircraft); and
(*b*) Two persons appointed by the Minister, one as being an independent person and the other as being a person who has had not less than five years' professional experience as a pilot of a civil aircraft, such of the *administrative functions of the Minister*, as the order specifies.

The main work of the ARB may be summarised as follows: (1) it represents Great Britain at ICAO meetings; (2) it draws up national specifications for air frames and engines; (3) it issues certificates of airworthiness; (4) it conducts examinations of engineers and pilots for licences; (5) it publishes technical information booklets; (6) it maintains a register of civil aircraft.

In general, then, the ARB aims to ensure the fitness (and legality) of aircraft, and the men who fly and maintain them. The British Government, by the same Act (Civil Aviation Act, 1949), delegated another part of its control, i.e. over airports, to a Minister of Aviation. By the Civil Aviation (Licensing) Act, 1960, it delegated yet another part, i.e. powers over the routes that airlines fly, and the prices they charge, to an Air Transport Licensing Board. There are many countries in which more than one organ of government are involved in aviation; for example, in West Germany the Luftfahrtbundesamt fills a similar role to that of the British ARB, and licensing is done by a Government department.

State licensing of air services

State authorities 'create' international airline routes by obtaining and granting 'rights to fly', through a series of agreements with other States. They negotiate for rights to fly routes *on behalf of* their own national airlines, giving away as little as possible to other national airlines. This puts State authorities in powerful positions, *vis-à-vis* their national airlines. They are in a position to alter the course of negotiations either indirectly by procedural means, or directly by deciding whether to negotiate or not.

Some governments take the view that it is for their national airlines to decide what they want, and for the government to aim at getting as near as possible to the targets set by airlines. This leaves the initiative and the decision on national aspirations with airlines. This is, however, impracticable in those countries where two or more national airlines are permitted to fly on the same routes. The horse-trading of bilateral negotiations seldom results in any significant departure from the principle of each pair of national carriers sharing 50-50 on a route. This means that if two or more airlines of one country want to operate over the same route, they must divide their country's share. The job of dividing the national share is normally given to a government licensing authority. The British Air Transport Licensing Board is an example of such a body.

Government 'licensing' occurs even where carriers have a 'national monopoly' over certain routes. For example, Air France was guaranteed a minimum annual route mileage by the Government in 1948. At the same time the Secretariat-General of Civil Aviation was empowered to authorise independent companies to engage in:

(i) Regular service over routes not served by Air France;
(ii) Unscheduled freight and cargo transport;
(iii) Charter and taxi services;
(iv) Seasonal air traffic.

The Civil Aeronautics Board of the United States

The Federal Aviation Act, 1958, although regulatory in nature, included two positive features. It emphasised the objectives of promoting, encouraging and developing civil aeronautics, and it enabled subsidies to be paid to airlines. It left the ownership, management and operation of all airlines in private hands.

The Civil Aeronautics Board is the licensing authority for both domestic and international carriers. It has considerable power to initiate proceedings to expand routes, but much less authority to contract them. However, in 1963 it began exploring the question of excessive competition on domestic and international routes. The Board cannot compel carriers to merge, but it can impose conditions before approving requests for mergers, and it can even refuse to allow a merger to take place. Much of the Board's regulatory powers derive from the need for most types of agreements between air carriers to be filed with the Board for approval.

The dominant theme in the licensing powers assumed by the US Government is the placing of national interests before those of the business interests of individual carriers. The licensing power is not meant to restrict service to the community, but to expand it; it is not meant to support monopoly in the interests of business, but to oppose it for the protection of the consumer. The ability to pay subsidies for uneconomic services is a *sine qua non* in the pursuit of this policy.

The British Air Transport Licensing Board

The British Government established an effective means of limiting the routes over which each of its national airlines flies, with the passing of the Civil Aviation (Licensing) Act, 1960. The Act was designed to cover (i) any flight in any part of the world by an aircraft registered in the UK, and (ii) any flight beginning or ending in the UK by an aircraft of such foreign States *as may be prescribed.* It made the holding of an 'air operator's certificate' (certifying that the operator is competent to ensure safety), a condition of the grant of an 'air service licence' (the airline's authority to operate aircraft on particular routes).

The Act provided for applications for licences to be made to an organisation to be called the Air Transport Licensing Board. The Board was to take into account, in deciding whether or not to grant the licence, (*a*) whether having regard to his financial resources and experience and his ability to provide satisfactory equipment, organisation, and staff, the operator is competent to run the service concerned, (*b*) any proposed limitation of liability for loss of or damage to persons or property, (*c*) the terms and conditions of service of his employees, (*d*) the existing or potential need or demand for the proposed service, (*e*) the adequacy of similar authorised services, (*f*) the extent to which the proposed service would duplicate or materially divert traffic from another authorised service, (*g*) any expenditure incurred or contract made in connection with the operation of air transport services by anybody (including the applicant) under a licence already granted, and (*h*) proper objections and representations. Every air service licence was to contain a provision as to the tariff to be charged in respect of the service.

Governments and cabotage routes

Cabotage is a word originally used for the practice of 'coasting', and then for 'coastal-trade' by sea. In air transport it means trading, or carrying traffic solely within the territory of one State. The Chicago Convention of 1944, Article 7, reserves the right to any contracting State 'to refuse permission to the aircraft of other contracting States to take on its territory passengers, mail and cargo carried for remuneration or hire and destined for another point on its territory'. Article 2 defines 'territory' as 'the mother country, colonies, territorial waters adjacent to, and the territories of protectorates'.

In many countries the fares charged on cabotage routes are subject to government approval. By and large governments and airlines are able to agree on fares, but every so often airlines are obliged to charge fares they would not have freely chosen. Fares on cabotage routes may be agreed by governments at a lower level than for international routes of the same distance. For example, for many years London to Malta had lower fares than London to Rome. The grip of individual governments on cabotage routes is weakened by certain poaching devices. Sometimes airlines issue tickets to an intermediate point and then other tickets to the final cabotage point.

National prestige

Most international airlines are, to a greater or lesser extent, regarded as means of promoting national prestige. Many small nations are prepared to see their airlines make losses while they fly on the major air routes of the world. New nations may be expected to place the creation of a national airline high on their list of priorities.

The furtherance of national prestige may influence the decisions of airline managements in two main directions:

(*a*) As to the routes they fly—unprofitable routes are justified on the grounds that it is important to carry the flag on them;

(*b*) As to the aircraft they buy. Some national airlines tend to buy home-produced aircraft.

Arguments for flying routes for prestige, or for buying home-produced aircraft, are not always government inspired. In Britain BEA had a buy-British policy that was not imposed by government. BOAC had a carry-the-flag policy that was not imposed by government: it was a management policy. The government appeared to sympathise with these policies, and there was evidence that BOAC was asked by individual members of Parliament to fly certain routes. But BOAC were strong enough to resist pressures from MPs, had they wished to do so.

It is tempting for airline managements to use national prestige to justify continuing to fly a route at a loss. They set up a route expecting commercial gain, and are then reluctant to dismember the organisation when it fails to come up to expectations.

Managements may yield in the first place to pressure from a nearby manufacturer to buy his aircraft. In some ways life can be a lot easier in dealing with a manufacturer on one's own door-step. Then, if the purchase turns out to be a costly one, the operator may seek shelter behind arguments for buying home products.

Not all governments look in a kindly manner upon the argument that national prestige justifies an airline's being unprofitable. The moves to reorganise KLM, that were started in 1963, were inspired by the Dutch Government's determination to make the business pay, and reject any excuse that KLM was an international status symbol for the Netherlands.

Government subsidies to national airlines

The way in which governments help their national airlines varies from one country to another. The most common forms of help are as follows:

(*a*) By providing loans free of interest;
(*b*) By meeting part of the cost of purchasing aircraft;
(*c*) By making grants towards the cost of developing new aircraft;
(*d*) By making grants towards the cost of pilot training;
(*e*) By manipulating mail carriage rates;
(*f*) By exempting from or rebating landing fees and other airport service charges;
(*g*) By exempting from or reducing taxation;
(*h*) By making grants for flying routes that are considered strategic or social necessities;
(*i*) By making outright payments to meet annual losses.

In the United States the federal government pays subsidies to create various types of air service 'required by the public convenience and necessity'. Although neither the Federal Aviation Act, 1958, nor its predecessor, the Civil Aeronautics Act, 1938, mentioned the word subsidy, innumerable day-to-day decisions of the Civil Aeronautics Board clearly involve it, and the Reorganisation Plan No. 10 of 1953 separated subsidy from mail pay. The CAB is responsible for the payment of subsidies and for justifying them to the Appropriations Committees of Congress. The Postmaster-General pays the mail rates established by the Board. It is claimed that subsidies are paid not to make good the deficiencies of airlines, but the inherent deficiencies of certain routes in their ability to produce adequate revenue. In fact, by the early 1950s most of the domestic trunk lines were profitable enough to do without subsidies. Nevertheless, in 1963 the bill for subsidies was 86 million dollars, mostly for shorthaul local services.

The interest of the State in the purchase of aircraft

Some governments ensure that if they become involved in war, they have the means of manufacturing their own aircraft. The industry may be geared to military orders, but supported by orders for civil aircraft. Civil and military contracts may help each other. Large scale production, making possible a spreading of the extensive overheads associated with aircraft manufacture, may reduce unit costs. Governments sometimes encourage military and civil customers to compromise on specifications so that military and civil aircraft types are sufficiently similar to enable manufacturers to enjoy economies of large-scale production.

The military orders of some governments are enough to support, by themselves, healthy manufacturing industries. Airlines may obtain economically-priced aircraft from these countries. This, by itself, is not so very important, as stated in Chapter III. But considerable benefits come from the development achieved during intensive military flying programmes.

The history of the Boeing 707 illustrates this point. The prototype first flew in July 1954. Soon afterwards the United States Air Force gave the Boeing Airplane Co. an order for about 400 of the type to be used as jet tanker-freighters, known as KC.135s. The first production model was handed over to the government two and a half years later. The design, construction and development flying that the company did on the military version enabled them to offer civil aircraft on the data of actual flight performance. This is more convincing than estimates and expectations. Furthermore, in 1955 Boeings obtained permission to continue to rent Government land, buildings and equipment for the construction of the Boeing 707.

Where their orders are not enough, by themselves, to support healthy manufacturing industries, governments may subsidise military production and thus indirectly assist civil air transport, or assist it directly by subsidising civil production.

Even if a government wishes to promote the production of a certain manufacturer it may not have the power to enforce its wishes. This may be because it lacks 'legal' powers, or cannot give economic backing to its policy. It may also be because the government cannot command the expertise equal to that of the airlines, and is thus weak in argument.

The differences in governments' help to aircraft constructors in the early 1960s and the effect on the competitiveness of airlines

United States

(*a*) The government provided money for basic aeronautical research, through the National Aeronautics and Space Administration.
(*b*) The three fighting services spent money on research and development, conducted by aircraft constructors.
(*c*) The government placed orders for military transport aircraft, sometimes ahead of civil orders. The military orders, which were big enough to make the price of civil versions cheaper, were:

Boeing Stratocruiser	approx. 850
KC.135 (Boeing 707)	400
Douglas DC6 series	200
Lockheed Constellation	250
Convair series	300

Russia

Under the communist system the government fully controlled both aircraft construction and operation, so that in theory the two could be closely integrated.

France

(*a*) The government provided money for basic aeronautical research through the Direction Technique et Industrielle de l'Aeronautique and l'Office National d'Etudes et de Recherches Aeronautiques.
(*b*) The government was empowered to make loans to aircraft constructors.
(*c*) The government was empowered to remit certain levies on aircraft constructed for export.

Netherlands

(*a*) The government assisted aircraft construction through the Netherlands Board for Aircraft Development.
(*b*) The government advanced money occasionally, in the form of interest-free loans (to be repaid by production levies) for the design, construction and development of aircraft.

Italy

Up to 1960 there was little evidence of the government helping Italian aircraft constructors.

Japan

When aircraft production began again in 1952 the government came forward with offers of loans and defence contracts.

General Situation

(*a*) Many governments provide some money for basic aeronautical research.
(*b*) Some governments directly subsidise the development of civil aircraft.
(*c*) Many governments indirectly assist civil aircraft production with defence contracts.

Significance of differences

(*a*) In general the differences in the amount of help given to aircraft constructors are probably more closely related to the size of countries rather than the policies of particular governments. Most governments believe they should help: some are more able than others to do so effectively.
(*b*) Help given to aircraft constructors can affect the economics of airlines in two obvious ways. It can cheapen aircraft, and thus reduce overheads: this advantage is not very significant. It can reduce the costs of development for airlines: this advantage can be considerable.
(*c*) The competitive position of airlines is not, however, affected unless *either* the country with the greatest advantage (in terms of aircraft costs), refuses to allow airlines of other countries to buy at the same price as the national airline buys at, *or* a government of a country without the greatest advantage forbids its national airline to buy any but home-produced aircraft.

State financial control on aircraft purchases

Aircraft purchasing policy cannot be free of the influence of those who provide the money needed to buy modern aircraft. The metal airframe, bigger capacity, and higher power have progressively weakened the independence of 'operators'. If a State subsidises an airline, or controls its borrowings, it can prevent the airline from obtaining money for purchases it does not approve. In Britain, the Treasury must approve any borrowings of the nationalised air corporations. The Treasury requires to be satisfied on the following points, before approving loans for the purchase of new aircraft:

(*a*) That the routes on which it is proposed to fly the aircraft will provide traffic to fill them;

(*b*) That there are good prospects of obtaining IATA agreement on a fare structure needed to operate the aircraft successfully;
(*c*) That the aircraft, themselves, are good enough to compete with alternative types;
(*d*) That the timing of the order is right, having regard to all the other demands on the Treasury;
(*e*) That the proposed manufacturer of the aircraft is in a sound financial position;
(*f*) That where a demand is made for the purchase of a foreign aircraft there is no alternative British aircraft available.

If an airline is not free to choose its own aircraft, the skill of its management may not prevail against the handicap of poor equipment. An airline may be well-managed and yet make losses because of State control on the vital decision on the type of aircraft to buy.

States' attitudes to 'social' services

It is sometimes argued that because, one way and another, airlines enjoy considerable State protection, they are under an obligation to their own nations. For example, government grants of traffic rights are said to provide monopolistic environments in which it is easier to make profits, and, therefore, it is reasonable to expect airlines to provide some uneconomic, or 'social' services, for the good of the nation. For this reason some governments have refused to subsidise airline losses caused by their operating social services, while an airline enjoys, on balance, profits from flying on commercially sound routes.

Government refusal to subsidise social services in these circumstances does not mean that a subsidy is not paid. The unprofitable services, and consequently the communities they serve, are subsidised out of airline profits. This means that passengers on 'busy' routes are subsidising small outlying communities for the purpose of their social and economic preservation, or betterment. Secondly, there is little evidence that government grants of traffic rights create monopolistic situations in which it is easy to make profits. Competition among airlines on international routes is too fierce for easy profits, and domestically airlines face severe competition from road and rail.

On the other hand, it is difficult to discover how much subsidy should be paid, if any. The costs of running social services are not easily isolable. They are often inextricably interwoven with all the other costs. Their effect is obscure and it becomes difficult for shareholders, government, or even management to judge the efficiency of the commercial core of the airline.

British Government attitude to social services as stated in the 1958 Select Committee Report, and the White Paper 'Financial and Economic Obligations of Nationalised Industries 1961'

The 1958 Select (Parliamentary) Committee said that they could not accept the arguments of the then Ministry of Transport that the State-protected British European Airways owed a debt to the community. It recommended that the management of the airline should press the Minister to 'order' them to carry on providing the social services, and thus discontinue an ill-defined situation. The Government were advised to respond with a grant from monies authorised by Parliament in the Annual Government Departments' Estimates.

The British Government White Paper on the Financial and Economic Obligations of the Nationalised Industries, 1961, Cmnd. 1337, said, among other things, that 'although the industries have obligations of a national and non-commercial kind, they are not, and ought not, to be regarded as social services absolved from economic and commercial justification'. On the other hand 'they cannot be regarded only as very large commercial concerns which may be judged mainly on their commercial results: all have, although in varying degrees, wider obligations than commercial concerns in the private sector. The object of these proposals is to find for each industry or Board a reasonable balance between these two concepts.'

Is it practicable for airline management to strike a reasonable balance between these two concepts? Who is to decide what is reasonable and what is not? Will the meaning of reasonable be stretched with every turn in the fortunes of an airline?

State and Air Traffic Control

Even on domestic routes, unless an airline has a monopoly of the skies, which is unlikely except in communist countries, its management requires the help of a lawful authority to control air traffic, to avoid collisions. Safe flying depends to a great extent on good navigation, which in turn depends on installations up and down a country, that override the power of numerous interests and local authorities. Often it would not be fair to charge all the cost of State navigational aids to civil aviation, as they are provided partly for military traffic, and partly to keep civil and military traffic apart. The inability of an airline to protect its own aircraft is, of course, even greater beyond its own national boundaries. The individual State has no authority to control traffic beyond its boundaries and regulations inevitably become a matter for international agreement.

State provision of airports

In most countries the central government, or local authorities, are concerned with providing airports. National authority over airport management tends to follow logically from the need for national, and even supra-national air traffic control. Governments' involvement varies, in fact, from ownership and administration (as with London Heathrow) to powers of inspecting and regulating privately owned airfields. Between are 'independent' airport authorities, working under government charters.

There are reasons why airlines should not provide and operate their own airports. First, separate airports for each airline would be wasteful and chaotic. The alternative of several airlines using a terminal controlled by one of their number has obvious disadvantages. It is desirable to have a neutral authority if competitors are to share an airport. Secondly, airports disturb neighbouring communities, and some of the problems are best resolved by an authority armed with legal powers. Land may have to be purchased compulsorily, business interests damaged and compensated, wayleave rights created and so on.

The influence resulting from government ownership and administration of airports may, however, be anything but desirable. Civil Service procedures seldom go happily with the cut and thrust of business, and there are strong arguments for the creation of independent, businesslike authorities to administer the major airports of a country.

Article 15 of the Chicago Convention was designed to prevent governments from discriminating in favour of certain airlines by making different conditions or charges for the use of airports. It reads as follows:

'Every airport in a contracting State which is open to public use by its national aircraft shall likewise, subject to the provision of Article 68, be open *under uniform conditions*[1] to the aircraft of all the other contracting States. The like uniform conditions shall apply to the use, by aircraft of every contracting State, of all air navigation facilities, including radio and meterological services, which may be provided for public use for the safety and expedition of air navigation.

Any charges that may be imposed or permitted to be imposed by a contracting State for the use of such airports and air navigation facilities by the aircraft of any other contracting State *shall not be higher*,

(*a*) As to aircraft not engaged in scheduled international air services, *than those that would be paid by its national aircraft* of the same class engaged in similar operations, and

[1] Author's italics throughout.

(*b*) As to aircraft engaged in scheduled international air services, than those that would be paid by its national aircraft engaged in similar international air services.

All such charges shall be published and communicated to the International Civil Aviation Organisation: provided that, upon representation by an interested contracting State, the charges imposed for the use of airports and other facilities shall be subject to review by the Council, which shall report and make recommendations thereon for the consideration of the State or States concerned. *No fees, dues or other charges* shall be imposed by any contracting State *in respect solely of the right of transit* over or entry into or exit from its territory of any aircraft of a contracting State or persons or property thereon'.

The services provided by States are usefully regarded as coming under two heads:

(*a*) Airport services, which include provisions for landing and parking aircraft, space for storage and maintenance, space and sometimes assistance with the handling of passengers and freight, and other special services such as policing.
(*b*) Air navigation services, which include weather information, aircraft guidance and separation services. Essentially these are provided to fulfil the responsibility of governments for the safety of aircraft and persons and property on the ground. For some purposes they are classified as approach, landing and take-off phase on the one hand, and the en-route phase on the other.

The attitudes of States towards charging for the terminal and route services they supply

Most governments have to face the problem of deciding how much the air transport industry shall contribute to the cost of the terminal and route services they supply. Unfortunately the airline revenues that governments approve on the one hand do not always influence them in considering the levies they make on the other hand. Indeed the department of government that approves fares is in some cases not the same department that charges for airport and navigational services. Airlines are thus sandwiched between a closely regulated revenue framework and the unchallengable decisions of government on charges.

Very few governments consult airlines before they alter these charges, and some of them do not give much notice of alterations proposed. For example, international airlines serving German stations were informed on March 9, 1962, that their landing fees would go up by 35 per cent on April 1, 1962. International airlines using

United Kingdom airports were told in September 1960 that the landing fees would go up by 33⅓ per cent in the following March.

In the majority of cases governments aim to recover the costs of airport service from the airlines, passengers and other users. An increasing number of them are also seeking to recover expenditure on navigational services. The economic argument for their doing so is based upon two assumptions: first, that the benefits of air transport are confined to airlines, their customers and airport concessionaires, and secondly, that the costs of government services truly represent the degree of diversion of scarce resources from other employment in the community. Some authorities challenge these assumptions on the grounds,

(*a*) That air transport brings benefits to a wide section of all communities by stimulating industry, trade and tourism, and
(*b*) That the industry often makes use of derelict land, and gives employment in areas of unemployment.

Economic arguments of this sort do not seem, however, to carry much weight with governments. In the final analysis most of them must yield to political pressure. In most countries this means that more and more of the costs of government provisions are imposed upon the industry.

CHAPTER III

RELATIONS WITH INVESTORS, SUPPLIERS, GENERAL PUBLIC AND COMPETITORS

Introduction

Management's 'external' relations with four sets of people are dealt with in one chapter, whereas customers and the State each had chapters to themselves. This is reasonable. Relations with customers, and State authorities dominate the airline business. It has long been axiomatic that in business the consumer is sovereign: airlines are no exception. But in the airline business, if consumer is Sovereign, the State is Consort. The situation is more complex for international airlines that must work with many sovereign States.

Airlines are not subjected to such an extent to investors, suppliers, general public and competitors. With these it is more a relationship of equals. Even where the State is an investor, the management-investor relationship is conducted within the conventions of financial accountability. The general public is a force to be reckoned with, but one that can take action only through customers and State. Suppliers and competitors are businesslike in their dealings unless the State compels them to be political.

All this does not mean that relations with investors, suppliers, general public and competitors are unimportant. All it means is that the relations with these four are more characteristic of business generally. Thus they are bound by laws of contract, private and public nuisance, company administration and so on.

Relations with investors

If an airline is privately owned, relations with its investors in the long run are not markedly different from those found in other sorts of business. Management is under an obligation to the investors. The latter have a right to expect certain standards of conduct from the airline. Management must take precautions to safeguard the money entrusted to it: management must ensure that the airline can pay a fair return for the use of the money: management must keep faith with investors by informing them fully on what is happening to their money. In the short run any airline has to give priority to safety measures, even where these conflict with the interests of investors. But the relations between a private airline and its investors are clearly governed by the obligation to give a fair return on money invested.

If an airline is partly or wholly state-owned the position is not nearly so clear. An individual investor thinks of returns in the form of hard cash. Governments talk of returns in the form of abstractions, like national prestige, and social services, as well as cash.

However, private and public investors are agreed that a critical feature in their relations with airline managements is that of knowing what is going on. Annual statements of profit and loss have too often proved misleading. The airline business is essentially long term. The difficulty is in discerning long-term trends by analysing short-term situations. In other words it is difficult for airline managements to be frank with their investors. They are not always sure what is happening themselves.

Investors and airline results

The Report from the Select Committee of the House of Commons of the British Parliament on the Air Corporations (HMSO), 1959, throws light on the difficulties investors have in judging airline results. The Committee examined the reports and accounts of the airlines, on behalf of the nation investor, to draw conclusions as to whether the airlines were well managed.

The Committee stated that statistics, comparing the results of international airlines, supplied *a useful guide* to the performance of the Corporations they were investigating, as long as a number of qualifications were made. The judgement of the two Corporations was made in the following terms.

'BEA have been achieving a satisfactory passenger *load factor* on international routes. *Aircraft-utilisation* has been low because the Corporation is a short-haul operator, but there is room for improvement. Operating costs, in terms of *capacity ton-miles*, which are not strictly comparable with those of longer-haul operators, have not improved recently as much as they have in the case of most other airlines. BOAC's passenger load factor has been satisfactory; this may have been partly at the expense of aircraft utilisation, which has been low but is now improving. Operating costs, per capacity ton-mile, have been high.' (My italics.)

This statement reveals an attempt to get behind the financial results expressed in terms of profit or loss, to find out why the profit or loss occurred, and to find out how much managements were responsible. The 'investors' were prepared to believe that financial results were not wholly dependent on the quality of management: good management may produce a loss, and bad management may produce a profit. With bad management the loss would have been worse, and with good management the profit better. The Committee pointed out that the hands of managements were tied in such matters as fares to be charged, safety standards and legal requirements, places to which they fly, choice of aircraft and so on. The Committee concluded that *the competitive position of an airline can be affected by management only in such things as quality of service, the reputation for efficiency and punctuality, and the speed of flights: and the best way of winning traffic from competitors is by flying better aircraft than they have.*

The Committee goes on to say that it would not be fair to make mangement fully responsible for the aircraft they buy because 'the success or failure of these aircraft is in the long run dependent, not only on the airline itself, which makes the choice, but on the manufacturer; and in evaluating the results achieved by the Corporations, account should be taken of the extent to which their aircraft have lived up to expectations'. This appears to be an unsatisfactory position from an investor's point of view. If what the Select Committee said is taken at face value, there is very little they can hold managements responsible for. And, of course, there is no getting away from the fact that airline managements have less freedom than those of most other industries.

Investors should look then to the skill with which management deals with the restrictions of IATA, ICAO, Government, suppliers and so on. External relations are tremendously important in the airline business. One airline may passively accept all that these outside bodies cause it to suffer; another may fight back. One airline may grouse as an unwilling victim; another may bend its energies to see that IATA, ICAO, Government and suppliers behave favourably towards its interests. A supine management in the airline business is defeated from the beginning.

Statistical Indices used in comparing airline results

In making *their* comparisons of the results of a number of international airlines the Select Committee used the following criteria:

(*a*) Total capacity ton-miles.
(*b*) Total revenue.
(*c*) Revenue ton-miles (total, passenger, mail and freight).
(*d*) Overall load factor.
(*e*) Available seat-miles.
(*f*) Passenger miles flown.

(*g*) Passenger load factor.
(*h*) Passengers carried.
(*i*) Number of employees.
(*j*) Operating cost per capacity ton-mile.
(*k*) Utilisation of aircraft.
(*l*) Capacity ton-miles per employee.
(*m*) Ratio between capital employed and traffic revenue.
(*n*) Profit or loss (excluding income tax, subsidy, interest and dividends, and proceeds of retirement of operating property and equipment).
(*o*) Profit or loss as a percentage of total revenue.

The significance that these criteria have for airline management is dealt with in later sections. The Committee obtained its statistical information (*a*) from airline annual reports and (*b*) from the annual statistical bulletin published by ICAO.

Limitations of Statistical Indices from point of view of investors

The Select Committee pointed out the limitations of using statistical indices to compare the performances of airlines. First, it is difficult to obtain figures to cover exactly the same period or even similar periods for all airlines; one airline may, for example, include two Easters in its financial year. Secondly, in the year selected for comparison it is possible that one or two of the airlines were operating in exceptional circumstances; they may have been introducing new aircraft.

Statistical indices, to some extent, reflect the scale of operation. A small airline will not be able to enjoy the economies of large-scale operation. Some may be working below their optimum technical size. On the other hand, because of all the external controls on an airline business, by way of traffic rights and international price fixing, the scale of operation of an airline is a matter that lies largely outside the control of individual airlines. Scale of operation depends partly on marketing opportunities. These are not so great for some airlines as for others. Some United States airlines have very restricted competition on big domestic air routes. Other airlines, like KLM, have virtually no domestic market. In the international market the national airline of the country where most traffic is generated tends to get the biggest share of the traffic. The airlines of highly populated countries are more sure of their markets.

Efficiency of effort (proportion of input to output) may be expressed by costs per ton and seat-miles flown and sold. But in the airline business this ratio is largely determined by factors other than the quality of management. Because every journey, irrespective of its length, gives rise to broadly similar efforts in selling, ticketing, reservation, maintenance, embarkation and disembarkation, costs per mile tend to vary inversely with the length of journey. The shorter the journey the higher the cost per mile flown, because the fixed costs of efforts in marketing and production are spread over fewer miles. Therefore, an airline with relatively short average journey lengths must face higher costs per mile flown, all other things being equal, than an airline with relatively long average journeys. So airline managements face unequal tasks, and this should be taken into account in judging managements by efficiency. The following table illustrates the differences in the tasks facing various airlines whose average passenger journey lengths in one year were as shown.

TABLE 1. *Annual average passenger journey lengths in statute miles of certain selected airlines*

BEA	Swissair	SAS	Air France	TWA	PAA	KLM	BOAC
329	489	671	763	893	1306	1313	2929

Relations with Suppliers

The over-riding importance of aircraft purchases tends to draw attention from the number and variety of airline suppliers. They include building contractors, office furnishers, clothing manufacturers, stationers, caterers, vehicle manufacturers, fuel companies, travel agents, other airlines, airport and navigation authorities. The proportion of total annual expenditure that is for the supply of equipment and contractor's services is usually high. Fig. 41 shows a typical airline in which aircraft purchases account for 12 per cent of the total annual expenditure, fuel and oil 9 per cent, maintenance and overhaul equipment, materials and contracting 8 per cent, commission to travel agents 7 per cent, landing fees to airport authorities 6 per cent, payments for supply of capital 6 per cent, payments for accommodation 3 per cent, passengers' meals 3 per cent, and other costs 6 per cent. In fact the direct labour costs were 40 per cent, and the remaining 60 per cent represented the purchase of indirect labour and materials. Several major airlines each have over 5,000 suppliers, and are placing between fifty and one hundred thousand purchase orders a year.

This volume of purchasing activity involves not only many suppliers but also many officials in an airline. Some airlines group most of the officials responsible for buying into one organisation. The advantage of this is that an airline thereby develops considerable expertise in the buying processes. The people who do the buying know the law of contract, prices and discounts obtaining in the market, lead times and reliability of suppliers. The suppliers know they are dealing with expert buyers and the relationship is professional.

Other airlines spread their buying among the other functional departments. Thus a property branch deals with building contractors, a passengers' services branch with caterers and so on. It is claimed that the advantage of this is that there is no intermediary between the people who know what they want and those who can supply it. The relationship is that of consumer and producer, rather than that of trader with trader. The buyer is not an expert in the process of buying, but he is an expert in what he wants to buy.

However, there is little doubt that the expertise of a professional buyer is as important as the expertise of an accountant, a salesman, or a personnel officer. With most 'middlemen' he fills a gap between one extreme and another. The airline business is certainly in need of these middlemen between the airline operating expert at one extreme and the producing expert at the other. The middleman buyer is able to temper the demands of airline experts to make the most of the market, and to influence the processes of manufacture to accord more with the needs of his airline.

In the next two sections some of the problems in dealing with aircraft constructors and travel agents are mentioned because they are characteristic of the industry.

Relations with aircraft constructors

Airline managements' relations with aircraft constructors are usefully considered under four heads:

(*a*) Specification.
(*b*) Design.
(*c*) Construction.
(*d*) Development.

At the specification stage the airline is shopping around, and clarifying its ideas. Specification may be concerned with only minor alterations to an off-the-peg aircraft, or with a tailor-made aircraft at the other extreme. The design stage is critical in that the major crystallisation of thought occurs here, and stamps the character of the rapport between customer and supplier. Co-operation between the two parties is probably less fruitful at the construction stage, and becomes very important again at the development stage. These four stages are not, of course, clearly divided in time; they occur in a logical order, but they overlap to some extent. The main significance of the distinction, from the point of view of management is that each step calls for different treatment.

The price of aircraft

There is no easy way of assessing whether the price proposed for a new aircraft is reasonable or not. There are checks of a broad kind, e.g. by detailing proposed standards of performance; by evaluating innovations in design; by probable weight and by certain statistics about cost per pound, etc. Perhaps the best protection against unreasonable charges is the measure of competition among aircraft constructors. Prices are to some extent competitive. If aircraft constructors put up their own money they usually strive to be competitive in a world market. If a government puts up money the constructor may be feather-bedded into a take-it-or-leave-it attitude.

The market for aircraft is 'imperfect', in the sense that the price at which aircraft are bought and sold is not always widely known. So it is possible, for example, for home buyers to pay less than foreign buyers, and second buyers to pay more than first buyers.

Constructors tend to protect themselves in their contracts (*a*) by 'escalator' clauses, that automatically raise the price of aircraft proportionately with increases in wages, and the prices of raw materials, and (*b*) by charging heavily for modifications called for after construction has begun. The following table shows the way the cost of one type of aircraft rose above the initial contract price for one airline.

TABLE 2. *The final price showed an increase of approximately 30 per cent over initial contract price*

	Per cent
Initial contract price	100
Wages awards made during period of construction	8
Alterations before completion	4
Radio, navigational equipment, passenger cabin furnishings	8
Modifications:	
(*a*) Mandatory—anti-corrosion	3
engines (including up-rating)	3
other	2
(*b*) Non-mandatory—brakes	0·25
seat rails and all-up weight	0·25
other	1
	129·50

Despite the fact that aircraft may represent up to 90 per cent of the capital investment of an airline, the annual costs of depreciation, and interest, if any, may still not be a large proportion of total annual costs. Thus marginal differences in the purchase price of aircraft are not usually of great significance. A 10 per cent increase in purchase price might well result in an increase of no more than

1 per cent of aircraft operating costs. The difference between a 'good' buy and a 'bad' one is not so much a question of a few thousand pounds in purchasing price, but rests on considerations such as the way the aircraft performs (fuel consumption, etc.) and the extent to which the aircraft attracts customers.

Travel Agents

Travel agents supply a selling-service to airlines. The latter sell a great number of tickets *through* travel agents. To the airlines this is part of their marketing arrangements. But to the travel agents the job of *selling airline tickets* is their production: their marketing arrangements are concerned with *selling their services as a go-between*, to both airlines and customers. Agents' production expenses consist of office rents, representatives' wages and so on. Their marketing expenditure is confined to the outlay on drawing attention to their names and extent and quality of services. Agents' revenues come from their principals, the airlines, and not directly from travellers. They are custodians of the monies collected from travellers, and earn for their services a fixed percentage of monies collected on behalf of their principals.

The relationship between airlines and travel agents is influenced partly by the fact that IATA airlines may not market through agents other than those approved by IATA. The conditions of approval, including general reputability and financial standing, and the conditions for retaining a licence, establish a code governing the conduct of both agents and airlines. This code is designed primarily to prevent one airline from seeking an unfair advantage over another, and to prevent an agent from playing off one airline against another, and to control the financial stakes that airlines have in agents' businesses by limiting periods of credit.

The main problem from the point of view of an individual airline is that the spirit of fair shares for all, implicit in IATA regulations, is difficult to reconcile with an aggressive commercial attitude proper to an airline. No self-respecting marketing manager can stomach the thought of one of 'his' agents being completely indifferent as to which airline's tickets he sells. Airlines individually would like to see agents fiercely partisan (as long as it is in their favour), but collectively they react to the dangers of such a situation. In the long run the industry could not stand by and allow one airline to monopolise its retail outlets. For any airline to attempt to do so is self-defeating. The only practicable approach for the individual airline is for it to address its persuasive messages directly to the customer, so that he goes in and demands to travel SAS or Swissair, or whatever it is.

The effectiveness of travel agents depends partly on the skill of their staff. Some of the training in the skills necessary to make a good job of selling airline tickets should come from the airlines, as it is impracticable to delegate it completely in such a rapidly developing industry.

Relations with the 'general public'

Probably no two airlines have similar ideas on what is expressed by the English term 'general public'. To find common ground we would have to resort to saying that the term acknowledges the existence of people, other than customers, who are interested in, and affected by, the activities of airlines. Opinions range from the need for some such term to recognise the existence of 'potential' customers to the need to recognise the interests of certain people who are never likely to travel by air. By holding the first opinion 'public relations' comes to be regarded as a close partner, if not a subsidiary, to advertising. By holding the opinion at the other end of the range an airline may come to occupy a rightful and responsible place in a community.

If 'public relations' are restricted to oblique addresses to likely customers they tend to arouse the suspicions of people who earn their living from the more open forms of advertising. For example, newspapers are watchful to see that free advertising is not obtained under the guise of public relations. The doings of airlines, and particularly national airlines, often make good news, so airlines receive a number of mentions anyway. Any attempt to force the pace in such favourable circumstances is likely to earn a smart rebuff. The delicacy of the situation is eased for many airlines by the fact that they advertise considerably in the national dailies. It often happens, however, that 'foreign' airlines also spend a lot of money advertising in national dailies, so the latter must take care to see that they do not jeopardise this revenue through the public relations activities of the national carrier.

To escape from this narrow interpretation of public relations, some airlines have allowed it to encroach on other well-defined relations. For example, one airline has said, 'Company public relations policies and practices are aimed at obtaining and retaining the goodwill, confidence, understanding, approval and support of those "publics" upon whom the company depends for its sales, labour, facilities, supplies, money and moral support.' Another has said that because it is a national airline, accountable to its parliament, a whole nation of 'investors' must be regarded as its general public. Such wide interpretations are apt to provoke opposition from within the organisation. Industrial relations experts may be suspicious of a public relations role covering the passing of information to employees. Purchasing officers may resent public relations dealings with suppliers. Finance officers may dislike public relations versions of accounts and statistics, and so on.

There is no need for public relations men to wander like a lost tribe in the wilderness. The industry has a 'general' public not covered under the specific heads of suppliers, agents, employees and so on. They are those people whose standards of living are affected, favourably or adversely by the activities of an airline. There are people whose economy hangs on the thread of an air service. There are people who have had to alter their whole way of living because an airline has put on a night-tourist flight. There are people who cannot sleep at nights because of the noise of jets at take-off. These and many other sorts of people have *the right to be specially considered* in the deliberations of airline management. If they have to suffer from any act of management then they have a right to an explanation.

This outlook is exceptionally important while air transport is regarded as primarily benefiting the small minority that can afford to travel by air, and the even smaller minority that ships goods by air. It is also important to remember that any one person may represent the interests of customers on one occasion and those of the general public on another. Both these terms describe 'roles' rather than separate persons.

Relations with Competitors

Degree of competition

The degree of competition among airlines on any one route is a product of a number of variables and limitations, the most important of which are:

(*a*) The number of airlines flying on a route may vary from one, in the case of certain domestic monopoly routes, to about twenty flying on trans-Atlantic routes;
(*b*) The airlines flying on a route may operate quite independently, or some of them may operate under a 'pool' (sharing) agreement;
(*c*) The airlines operating on a route may be of different nationalities, or they may include two or more airlines of the same nationality;
(*d*) Many international airlines are nationalised; almost all are supported or protected in some way by their Governments;
(*e*) The way airlines go about their business can materially affect goodwill, and their competitive positions;
(*f*) Tariffs are fixed by agreement in IATA;
(*g*) Certain operating standards are ensured by ICAO regulations;
(*h*) Rights to fly are settled by governmental bilateral agreements.

International Air Transport Association (IATA)

IATA was formed in 1945. It is an association of airlines, unlike ICAO which is an association of governments. An airline is eligible to be a member of IATA if it is licensed to provide *scheduled* air service, by a government eligible for membership of ICAO (apparently 'any nation willing to subscribe to the Chicago Convention'). It is officially claimed that its work begins only after governments have decided what companies they wish to license, and how they wish to exchange traffic and other rights between them. But from that point on the activity of IATA spreads through virtually every phase of air transport. The terms of reference set out in the Articles of Association are:

(*a*) To promote safe, regular and economical air transport for the benefit of the people of the world, to foster air commerce and to study the problems connected therewith.
(*b*) To provide means of collaboration among the air transport enterprises engaged directly or indirectly in international transport services.
(*c*) To co-operate with the International Civil Aviation Organisation and other international organisations.

The interests of IATA appear to coincide to a large extent with those of ICAO. The former regards its *operational* task as that of ensuring that aircraft can fly with a maximum of safety, comfort and efficiency and under well-defined and universally understood rules and procedures. It regards its *commercial* objective as the point where people and their goods can move to anywhere from anywhere else on the global network as simply as though they were taking a trip on a single airline within a single country. These two aspects are also the concern of the Air Navigation Commission and the Air Transport Committee respectively of ICAO. The Legal Committee of IATA holds a watching brief over the work of the ICAO Legal Committee.

The most distinctive work of IATA is as follows:

1. Interline agreements: standardisation of forms, procedures, landing agreements, and other factors, making possible the quick and easy exchange of traffic between airlines.
2. The negotiation of international tariffs and rates.
3. The provision of a clearing-house for the settlement of airlines' accounts with each other.

The way in which airlines work through IATA

IATA's *legislature* is the Annual General Meeting, in which all members have an equal vote, and in which many decisions must be by unanimous votes. Many of its decisions are subject to the approval of governments. Its *executive* is called the Executive Committee, which is elected. It has a *judiciary* consisting of a Court which may impose fines for breaches of regulations. It has its own *police* in the shape of a Chief Enforcement Officer with a staff of approximately 10 inspectors. Alleged breaches of regulations are reported to the Director-General, who heads up the *Secretariat.* The Director-General may refer cases to a Commission that sits three or four times a year. Airlines that do not pay their fines may be expelled.

The Executive Committee, composed of Presidents of 18 of the world's leading airlines, delegates much of its work to five committees: Finance, Legal, Technical, Traffic Advisory and Medical. Members of IATA committees are nominated by individual airlines, but once appointed they represent the whole industry.

Tariffs and rates are negotiated through Traffic Conferences. The delegates to Traffic Conferences act for their own airlines only. Traffic Conference decisions are subject only to the approval of governments and not the Annual General Meeting or Executive Committee. There are three Conference Areas:

No. 1. Western Hemisphere, Greenland and Hawaiian Islands;
No. 2. Europe, Africa and the Middle East (including Iran);
No. 3. Asia, Australia and islands in the Pacific.

The attitude of airline managements to IATA

Most managements regard IATA as a logical necessity. It does not appear to them to impose an unnatural relationship. If there were no IATA, airlines would have to have regular meetings under another name, because it is impracticable to have more than one fare between any two points. The existence of IATA is indeed an expression of the fact that there cannot be unregulated competition in air transport. IATA is a creature of necessity; it is not an instrument of choice.

Although IATA includes in its ranks a number of airlines that are preoccupied with the need to prevent fares being lowered, because their operating costs are high, it is by no means a foregone conclusion that the rule of unanimity in voting will enable them to succeed. An airline that is asking for fares to be lowered is in a fairly strong position. If such a carrier is denied lower fares there is always the possibility that if it wants them badly enough it will go off on its own and somehow operate them. In 1963, even after Atlantic fares had been agreed at the annual conference, an American carrier threatened the whole edifice of IATA by going back on the agreement, at the instigation of the American CAB, and charging lower fares. Only the sharp reaction of the British government saved a tariff war that might well have badly shaken the working relationships built up within IATA over a number of years. Managements have to collaborate if there is to be any order in an international industry, and IATA, despite its imperfections is workable.

Competition and collaboration

The strains in interline relationships that come to light through IATA are, however, only a part of a pervasive problem. Recurrent themes, in any discussion on the dealings among the world's airlines, are those of competition and collaboration. Life would be simpler for airline managers if we could do away with one or the other. Then they could be single-minded in their approach to their job, and not be worried by having to balance skilfully between the two opposing forces. But neither can be done away with if we are to keep a healthy airline industry: competition must temper collaboration.

In the interests of the peace of mind of individual managers it is a problem that must be dealt with by clear definition, and considerable understanding.

The fundamental need for collaboration is more clearly understood than that of competition. Airlines have to share terminals, and their equipment; they have to share airspace, and navigation aids; they even act as agents for each other, in the handling of precious customers. And it is these last who act as the most powerful binding force of all. Passengers and shippers tend, wistfully, to regard air transport as an integrated industry rather than as a collection of competing airlines. Collaboration can, of course, be objectionable to them if it means an international conspiracy to keep air fares artificially high, but by and large collaboration appears to be beneficial.

Competition, on the other hand, commands no such universal respect from the customer, or common understanding from airline management. It has too many meanings. At one extreme it can mean a belief that the prosperity of one airline can be secured only at the expense of others. Although this is not true, because airlines can 'create' new traffic, that has not been 'diverted' from any other airline, nevertheless the airline business is often conducted as if it were true. A second meaning of competition is that of drawing as many as possible from a common supply of customers, of which there are plenty for all. This is a difficult view to accept, because *at any given moment* the supply of customers is limited. This view of competition is practicable only in the long run. But it leads to a third point of view that is tenable in the short run. This is the sort of competition we get among regiments in the same army—competing to do better than each other, but always in the complete acceptance that they are working to the same end. And so it is with airlines. Pride of airline is good; it gives mettle to management and improves the morale of men.

CHAPTER IV

ORGANISATION AND EXTERNAL RELATIONS

General view of organisation and external relations

It is salutary to pause, before becoming involved in the intricacies of internal relations, to discover how much of airline organisation is directly concerned with external relations. A close study of airline organisation reveals that a considerable part of it works immediately for the benefit of other parts. A great deal of activity is concerned with internal relations. The product of one component of organisation becomes an element in another. Organisation appears to be pre-occupied with the problems of its own survival. So to put the matter into perspective this section ends with a brief review of the parts that deal with the sorts of people referred to in the preceding chapters.

If we look first at customers we come up against an important characteristic of the industry. At present passengers form a large proportion of airline customers. Passengers are the raw materials of an airline organisation, and as such they are mixed up in the process of production. This means that even those components specialising in 'production' have to concern themselves with people. Thus, despite the intricacies and introspective tendencies of airline organisation, only a relatively small part is not immediately concerned with external relations. It has been estimated that only about a quarter of the staff of most airlines never deal with customers. Of the quarter who are not, there are many who deal regularly with suppliers, government officials and so on.

The table opposite indicates the extent to which divisions of business organisation (i.e. finance, purchasing, production, marketing, personnel, research and development) cater for airline external relations, and the extent to which special divisions have to be created.

Marketing departments

The Personnel Statistics in Appendix 14 of the 1962–63 Report and Accounts of British European Airways show a total of 1,750 sales

TABLE 3. *The external groups associated with airlines and the organisations dealing with them*

EXTERNAL GROUPS	ORGANISATIONS DEALING WITH THEM
Customers	Production: Passenger and Freight Control Marketing Customer relations Claims and insurance
States	Secretarial and legal Tariffs negotiation Government relations
Suppliers	Finance Purchasing Production Research and Development Agency and Interline Sales Secretarial and legal
Investors	Finance Secretarial and legal Public relations
General Public	Public relations Secretarial and legal
Competitors	Production: Passenger and Freight Control Marketing Tariffs negotiation Prorating Secretarial and legal

staff in a total airline strength of 16,000. The total number of staff engaged on marketing (including sales planning, advertising, tariffs negotiation, etc.) did not exceed 2,000, as against nearly 6,000 employed on passenger and freight control, and nearly 4,500 on maintenance. The revenue per marketing employee was approximately £25,000, against about £3,100 per airline employee. The amount spent on sales and publicity in the year was approximately 10 per cent of total costs. Seventy per cent of the 10 per cent was spent on agents' commission, and a further 17 per cent on advertising and other publicity. The remaining 13 per cent of total sales costs was for pay and allowances of selling staff. Pay and allowances for the whole airline constituted 40 per cent of total airline costs.

These figures indicate the extent to which this airline relied on Agents (both travel agents and other carriers) for maintaining good relations with its customers. The situation differs, of course, from airline to airline. Some have much larger marketing organisations and depend very much less on the services of agents. If an airline does most of its selling through agents, then it must have a very competent nucleus of marketing staff to handle relations with agents.

Travel agency sections in airline organisations

Many airlines, particularly in Europe, employ someone of managerial status to supervise relations with travel agents. 'Agency' sections act as watchdogs within airlines to see that the interests of agents are not overlooked, and that agents are kept informed on all matters that concern them. Agency managers tend to act as liaison officers when relations are smooth, and as mediators when interests are in conflict. Sometimes Agency Sections provide special facilities such as direct telephone lines for bookings, and arrange special flights to introduce agents to new routes. They also concern themselves with the standard of training of clerks employed by travel agents, and are often instrumental in obtaining airline help in this respect.

Agency and interline sales organisations

Airline organisations often reflect the fact that travel agents are not the only agents through which airlines sell tickets and space. The proper and equitable treatment of both travel agents and other airlines (acting as selling agents) is ensured by putting the conduct of relations with both under the same manager. Agency and Interline managers usually have the responsibility for planning and recommending the extent of and conditions governing sales through travel and airline agents. Their duties may include:

(*a*) Handling agency matters with IATA;
(*b*) Developing co-operative marketing arrangements with travel agents and other carriers;
(*c*) Helping sales representatives to obtain more business from agents;
(*d*) Ensuring that agency and interline interests are considered in reservations, advertising and training;
(*e*) Analysing revenues and costs attributable to agency and interline sales.

Tariff negotiations

The complicated fare-structure for world airlines must be handled with considerable expertise. For this reason many airlines have set up Tariffs sections in their marketing organisations to represent them at IATA and other inter-airline negotiations. These sections often put into negotiable terms (usually involving compromise) the ambitions of their marketing colleagues. They may also provide a service giving special quotations in the case of complex itineraries, and charters. They may also provide tariffs data for inclusion in timetables, advertising literature and so on. They may negotiate the proration of passenger and baggage revenue with other carriers, and maintain official relations with regulatory bodies on tariff matters.

Purchasing departments

The subject of purchasing is dealt with at length later. All we need do here is to note that its importance is reflected in the prominence given to purchasing components in overall organisation. The differences in the extent to which purchasing is centralised in one department, or dispersed among several may be the product of different circumstances or faulty organisation in some airlines. There may be similar causes of differences of levels at which purchasing is specialised. For example, while Trans-Canada Air Lines make purchasing a first-line managerial specialisation, many others do not.

Public Relations

Most airlines believe that a good 'public opinion' is important to them. As we have seen they are not agreed on whom should be regarded as general public. Nevertheless, most of them make some organisational provision for dealing with whatever comes within the particular airline definition. In general these organisations:

(*a*) Recognise that public relations cannot be monopolised by a small section of the overall organisation;
(*b*) Aim to win consideration for the public relations aspects of all airline planning, motivating, controlling, and contracting;
(*c*) Aim to promote and maintain a uniformly high standard in all airline dealings with the general public;
(*d*) Aim to channel certain dealings (for example, with the press) through a single section of organisation;
(*e*) Aim to keep management informed of public reactions to their decisions.

Public Relations branches of airline organisation are sometimes divided up into sections that specialise in dealings with the press, in dealings with public figures (members of government, etc.), and in dealings with broadcasting authorities (radio and television). Other divisions are made on the basis of the way information is supplied (e.g. written material, photographs, exhibitions, talks, etc.). All these divisions have in common the aim of releasing and distributing information in a manner that at least will not do any unnecessary damage to the airline's reputation.

Organisation for dealing with customers' comments, complaints and claims

Many airlines employ an official who specialises in dealing with customers' comments, complaints and claims. Some of them separate the responsibility for dealing with claims by placing it under an official who is an expert in insurance.

Customer relations sections usually have to reply or draft replies to all letters addressed to an airline head office. This is a rough-and-ready way of selecting for special attention those letters purporting to be of company-wide significance, or to be addressed to a senior official. Additionally, branch offices may be asked to forward any correspondence addressed to them, but judged to be of company-wide significance. Customers-relations sections usually keep records, analyse and classify the types of comments and complaints received to provide management with a picture of trends in customer opinions.

Claims, or insurance sections, investigate customers' statements of loss or damage and assess their claims. Sometimes these sections are empowered to settle claims up to a substantial figure. The manner in which aggrieved customers are dealt with can make a considerable difference to the goodwill of the airline.

Relations with governments

The following is an example of the responsibilities given to a sub-component of airline organisation that has to deal with state authorities.

(*a*) To act as company representative in dealings with the State Air Transport Authority on all matters except tariffs, schedules, accounting and finance matters.
(*b*) To act as company representative in dealings with the State Airport Authority on terminal buildings on matters of a policy or non-technical nature.
(*c*) To act as company representative in dealing with sundry ministries (e.g. Trade, Health, Home Affairs, Foreign Affairs and Revenue).
(*d*) To act as company representative in dealings with Postal Authorities concerning the carriage of mail.
(*e*) To act as company representative in dealing with the department of State conducting the negotiations of bilateral traffic agreements, and to act as a member of the national delegation in such negotiations.
(*f*) To apply for company route licences and to co-ordinate all the company's activities to secure them.
(*g*) To co-ordinate all the company's activities related to the application of other carriers for route licences.

Such an organisational sub-component may be included in a marketing component, or it may be included in an administrative or service component, or it may be a separate section reporting to the General Manager.

Secretarial and legal branches

The importance of secretarial and legal branches is usually crucial in airline organisation for a number of reasons.

(*a*) Many airlines have 'constitutions' that are at least partly framed by governments. Nationalised airlines usually owe their existence to a piece of legislation. The latter then becomes a charter of operations. Partly government-owned airlines usually have written conditions attaching to government participation; privately-owned airlines are usually circumscribed in their activities by various government controls. Secretarial and legal branches often have the responsibility of ensuring that their airline works within the bounds of these constitutional enactments.
(*b*) The problems associated with crossing many national boundaries call for an expertise that is difficult to acquire outside of an airline. The expertise involves questions of international air law, and domestic air law.
(*c*) International airlines have to conclude a number of formal agreements that require careful drafting and perusal on behalf of particular carriers.
(*d*) On a number of occasions airlines are placed in the position of suitors, who have to press claims for 'rights' of various kinds, before tribunals empowered to hear and judge claims. Airlines are also required on occasions to defend their actions before tribunals empowered to establish blame.

Finance departments

Among the specific responsibilities of the finance department of a particular airline are listed:

(*a*) To supply the financial and accounting data, statements, reports and statistics required by the President, the Board of Directors, inter-company and government agencies, and for special hearings and commissions.
(*b*) To represent the Company in contacts with outside auditors.
(*c*) To participate in the Company's representation before the parliamentary committee constituted to review the affairs of the Company; and to prepare the information necessary therefore.
(*d*) To ensure conformity of the Company's financial, accounting, and statistical policies, methods and transactions with applicable government statutes and regulations.

Part II

Internal Relations of Management

CHAPTER V

ELEMENTS OF AIRLINE ORGANISATION

The distinction between a business and its organisation

An organisation may be usefully regarded as distinct from the business it serves. Not every business requires an organisation for its success. Many sorts of business can be conducted with various forms of organisation. Organisation is something added to and separable from business itself.

The reason for the existence of a business lies in the opinion of the community it serves. When this community ceases to want what the business produces the business must discontinue. But the organisation that served the business could then be used for some other business.

Organisation is an instrument. It is an instrument, used by a manager, to achieve the intention of the 'head' of the business. By definition a manager is a man who acts *through an organisation*. If someone commands and uses an organisation he should be regarded as managerial. Without an organisation he should not be regarded as managerial.

Basically the head of a business intends to sell something 'created' by the process of changing what is already there. His intention may or may not be achieved by the managerial use of organisation. The managerial process involves the four major activities of planning, motivating, controlling and contracting.

(*a*) *Planning*

A plan is a managerial notice, issued beforehand, of some intended schemes or proceedings. It may indicate the relations of objects or events, and their timing, placing, etc.

Planning is usually carried out in three stages:

First the intention is considered; this involves collecting, analysing and digesting relevant facts.

Secondly, all alternative courses of action to achieve the intention are considered; this involves estimating the probable results of each alternative.

Thirdly, the best courses of action are chosen; this involves a weighing of probable results of various alternatives.

A plan must take account of the fact that, almost always, besides achieving the intention of the business, the performance of an organisation will have to satisfy other requirements. For example, all organisational performance may have to conform to agreements made with trade unions, or to the laws governing income tax.

In any business considering alternative courses of action to achieve an intention calls for *imagination*. It requires mental consideration of actions of events not yet in existence. However much business turns to scientific method and automation, it is difficult to escape the conclusion that planning will always remain essentially a human activity. Plans must continue to germinate in human minds, and the process of germination cannot be forced by artificial means beyond a certain point. Ideas germinated in the human mind are developed into detailed alternatives.

The main problem in airline planning is the difficulty in estimating the results of each alternative. It is possible to predict results only if we have an understanding of all the variables at work in the business situation. In some situations we do have an understanding of the variables at work. The interplay of heat and pressure on the behaviour of metals in a certain gas may be predicted by the application of a scientific law, or equation. Few if any businesses are like this. The variables at work are only discerned vaguely. There is no doubt about the truth of this proposition in the airline situation. Even if we were able to identify all the variables at work in the airline situation, it would be impossible to predict their behaviour accurately because:

(i) Certain situations can be foreseen on a statistical basis only. For example, it may be possible to forecast a percentage loss of aircraft through crashes, but it will not be possible to forecast the day or month of a disaster.
(ii) The airline situation is a competitive one. We can never be certain of the results of any plan because of the uncertainty of competitors' reactions to any move.

Having said this we must remember that plans have more chance of being good if:

(i) The variables in the airline situation are identified. The process of detection must therefore be continued unremittingly.
(ii) The airline's knowledge of variables is kept up to date by taking into account the moves of competitors.

Because of the difficulty of estimating results, plan-changing becomes as important as plan-making, and this fact should be reflected in the organisation. Thus 'operations' branches are often charged with the responsibility of re-shaping plans to meet short-term situations.

(*b*) *Motivating*

The managerial activity of 'motivating' includes all the efforts that are made to get things moving in an organisation, in accordance with the plan. In an airline this involves issuing a great number of rules and regulations that tell people what to do, and what not to do. It includes verbal and written instructions, temporary and standing orders. It includes teaching people to do the right thing, and even persuading them by precept and incentive; it includes inspiring them by tradition and example.

(*c*) *Controlling*

In the 'controlling' activity a manager first compares the performance achieved with what was planned. If there is any deviation from plan he measures it. He then has to make a decision on whether to alter his plan, or to re-motivate his organisation, in order to close the gap between actual and planned performance. The control activity may call for an accurate and swift 'feed-back' on what is happening. In airlines this involves various monitoring and inspection procedures. Budgetary control summaries and data processing, are other examples of 'feed-backs'. Corrective procedures may involve issuing fresh instructions and even admonishing people for their mistakes.

(*d*) *Contracting*

The activity of 'contracting' is that of *drawing people together* for a mutual undertaking. An undertaking is *mutual* if the interests of those concerned are reciprocal. This involves the idea of a return made for something given. The activity of 'contracting' is essentially based upon the agreement of equals, and not as in the case of 'motivating', upon the authority of a superior. Contracting includes commercial agreements such as buying and selling, agreements on the way business will be conducted, and agreements among specialist managers in large organisations.

The practicability of running an airline business without an organisation

At the time of writing Cyprus Airways' services were provided 'in co-operation' with British European Airways and Olympic Airways. The aircraft used on the Nicosia to London, Beirut, Tel Aviv and Ankara routes were Comets owned, flown and maintained by either BEA or Olympic Airways. Cyprus Airways did not have the usual airline's flying, maintenance, development, personnel or purchasing organisations.

The business intention of Cyprus Airways was similar to that of any other airline, i.e. to sell 'arrivals' by air. In order to achieve this intention they assigned their traffic rights to other airlines, in return for a royalty on revenues earned from the possession of these rights. The royalties covered the costs of the general management, finance, passenger and freight control and marketing organisations of Cyprus Airways and yielded a small profit in addition. The Republic of Cyprus was a member of the International Civil Aviation Organisation, and Cyprus Airways was a member of the International Air Transport Association.

Would Cyprus Airways still have been regarded as an airline if the General Manager had handed over his accounting to a firm of professional accountants, his marketing to a sales agency, and his passenger and freight handling to other agents? Would the top man still have been able to call his business an airline, if he had been sitting in an office all by himself, just dealing with a number of contractors? Would he not have turned himself into a travel agent?

The answer is that, even by doing away with all organisation, he would not have turned himself into a travel agent. Cyprus Airways would remain an airline because its intention would still be to sell 'arrivals'. A travel agent could not have this intention because he has no 'arrivals' to sell. A travel agent cannot choose to produce his 'arrivals' within his own organisation or by buying them in. In other words the travel agent does not plan a process of production, or a buying programme to provide so many arrivals per month, and then set out to sell this number. He is merely an intermediary. Somebody comes along with a request; he enquires to see if the request can be met.

Cyprus Airways, even without an organisation, would still have traffic rights, without which no arrivals can be produced. They would still be able to reverse the decision to do business without an organisation, and buy a fleet of aircraft to run their services.

The significance of the two concepts of 'business' and 'organisation' in running an airline

What we have been looking at, in this hypothetical development of Cyprus Airways, is an extreme situation in which the use of organisation as an instrument of doing business is completely abandoned in favour of the alternative of doing business by contracting.

The significance of the two concepts of 'business' and 'organisation' is that they draw attention to the fact that organisation is not a *sine qua non*. Business can be conducted successfully without it. There are two ways of running an airline, by organisation and by contracting. One of the important skills called for, in airline general management, is the ability to strike the right balance between the alternative methods.

It is important to examine organisations critically, in the light of their degree of organisation (i.e. ratio of organisation to contracting), because there are inbuilt tendencies to become more and more self-contained. These tendencies may derive from fear of being let down by contractors, or from the empire building of ambitious airline officials. In looking at any organisation chart we must constantly bear in mind that it does not give a complete picture of business activity. What it does not show may be more important than what it does show.

A brief review of the extent of contracting in airlines

Most airlines engage heavily in contracting in their marketing activities. Travel agents play such an important part in the airline business, that it has been found necessary to subject them, as airline organisations are, to the authority of IATA.

Most airlines contract heavily in the maintenance aspect of production. Little actual repair is done. Maintenance is largely by replacement of defective parts with manufacturers' spares. Even complete engine overhauls are often carried out by manufacturers.

The handling of passengers and freight is contracted to a considerable extent. Many airlines have handling agents all over the world, a number of them being other airlines. Most airlines at some time or other have to supplement their own aircraft and crews by chartering from other operators. These and many other ways of contracting serve to limit the extent of airlines' organisations.

A general view of the elements of airline organisation

The intention of the owners or Board of Directors of any business is fundamentally to sell, at a profit, something they have created, by the process of changing the existing condition of materials or people. Businesses can change the condition of materials by altering shape, physical structure, chemical composition, time and place of availability. The condition of people can be changed by making them happier, warmer, better fed and so on. The change that airlines make is in place: they take people and their goods to places where it is better for them to be. The intention to change the place of people and goods covers both the organising and contracting activities of an airline. There must be a plan to cover both organising and contracting activities, but the subsidiary plans of individual managers may apply only to their organisations (Fig. 4).

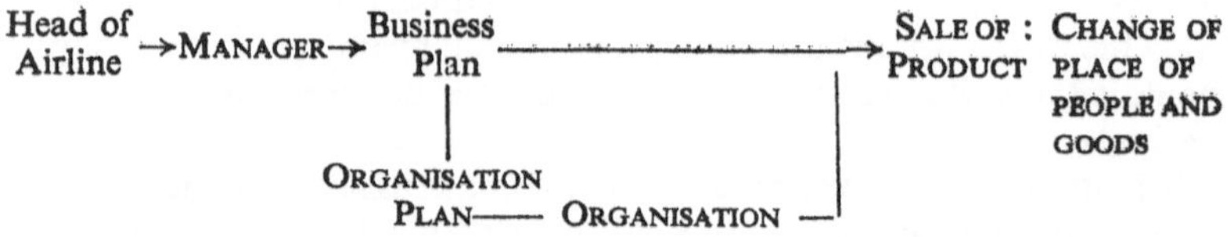

FIG. 4. *A general view of the elements of airline organisation*

A manager's organisation consists of three physical elements. First, there are *operatives* who are the persons who handle the various sorts of airline equipment, and its raw materials. Secondly, there is the *equipment* that is the agent for bringing about change. Aircraft are an obvious example of this. Thirdly, there are the *raw materials* that are the object of change. In the case of an airline, people and their goods are the raw materials. People and their goods are what an airline works on to bring about a change in place.

Besides these physical elements an airline organisation, like any other business organisation, requires three link elements. First, a manager must be linked to his organisation by the *expression of ideas,* in the form of commands, persuasion or inspiration. Secondly, operatives must *exercise skill* in the use of equipment. Thirdly, equipment must effect *physical change* on raw materials.

Complexity of intentions in large-scale airline business

An airline, as a whole, can be regarded as satisfying one large intention. This overall airline intention is the product of a number of component intentions which intermingle and follow one another in an intricate way. Component intentions arise for three main reasons. First, a business must satisfy many other requirements besides its business intention. For example, an airline may not be able to sell passenger arrivals without filing tax returns, or giving its workpeople good conditions, or proper training. Secondly, equipment and raw materials make demands upon an organisation as a consequence of their use. For example, aircraft cannot be flown without adequate maintenance. Thirdly, there is a fundamental, natural pattern of tasks for an airline as for any other business. This encourages managerial and operative specialisation, if the tasks are dealt with in organisation. Specialist managers develop intentions that are subsidiary to the main intention of the airline.

The sequence of tasks that brings about managerial specialisation, and the development of subsidiary intentions is given opposite.

Although these tasks are fundamental, they are fundamental to business and not to organisation, i.e. they do not all have to be carried out by organisation. Some may be carried out by contracting.

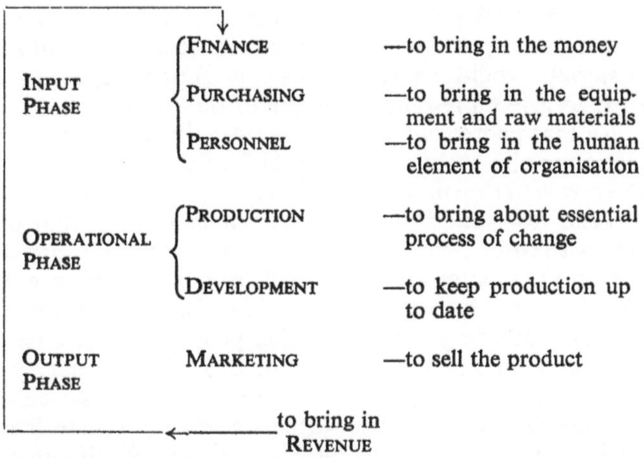

FIG. 5. *The sequence of tasks that bring about managerial specialisation*

Complexity of the elements of airline organisation

We have already seen that the general view given, of the elements of airline organisation, over-simplified the situation by referring to an *overall* intention, and omitting to mention the complexity of *subsidiary* intentions. The development of subsidiary intentions was partly ascribed to the managerial specialisations based on the six fundamental tasks of business. In fact, of course, most airlines do not have just one manager; they have several. They usually have at least one general manager in charge of a number of specialist managers.

By definition each manager must have an organisation, so there are as many organisations within an airline as there are managers. To help further analysis the general manager's organisation will be referred to as the *overall organisation* and his subordinate managers' organisations as *component organisations.*

There is no difficulty in applying the foregoing analysis of the elements of organisation to single components, where we have a manager directing the work of operatives. Each such component can be clearly seen to have its own type of operatives, its own equipment, and its own raw materials. For example, a foreman in the welding shop of a maintenance base, will have his skilled craftsmen, using welding equipment to repair unserviceable gear coming into the shop. The difficulty comes when we try to analyse in this way the overall organisation of an airline general manager.

It is tempting to say quite simply that the operatives in the overall organisation of an airline are the numerous men and women exercising a wide range of skills, from those of pilots, engineers and salesmen to aircraft cleaners. Equipment would then cover such various items as airport buildings, maintenance hangars and aircraft. Raw materials would be passengers and freight. But this is too unrealistic to give more than a glimpse of the truth.

The idea that people and freight are the only raw materials of the organisation is obviously an over-simplification. The operatives in a maintenance department may rarely see a passenger or a piece of freight. Their raw materials are unserviceable aircraft; they exercise their skill with equipment to change these raw materials into serviceable aircraft. The latter are 'produced' by the maintenance department, to become the equipment of the flight department. The product of a marketing department, i.e. people who have been sold tickets, become the raw materials of the flight department.

How then can our analysis of the elements of organisation accommodate these facts? There are a number of subordinate managers in an airline organisation: there are many sorts of equipment, raw materials and products: yet from the point of view of the business there is only one sort of product—that of 'arrivals'. Out of this assortment of operatives, equipment, raw materials and products, which belong to the general manager's organisation?

To describe a general manager's organisation adequately we must say that the human element consists of subordinate managers as well as operatives. Also we must add that the terms 'equipment' and 'raw materials' often refer to temporary rather than permanent roles. An aircraft is at one time a piece of equipment and at another time a raw material. Finally, a general manager's overall organisation has many secondary products that are not for sale. Some of these products are transferred to other organisation components, and some of them are outputs like annual report and accounts, and income tax returns, that do not bring in revenue. An overall organisation is a constantly changing phenomenon, with components feeding into one another, and with human beings and materials becoming different elements as they move from one component to another.

CHAPTER VI

THEORY OF ORGANISATION

Introduction

A theory of airline organisation should take account of the following four main groups of factors:

1. Factors influencing the choices that managers make between the alternatives of doing work with airline organisation, or putting it out to contractors, up to the limits imposed by size of business.
2. Factors limiting the size of an airline organisation by limiting the size of business.
3. Factors affecting the order in which activities are brought into organisation.
4. Factors affecting the proportions of the elements of organisation.

Factors influencing decisions on the alternatives of adding to organisation or contracting

The main factors are:

(*a*) Costs.
(*b*) Attitudes to organisation and contracting.
(*c*) Availability of capital.
(*d*) Availability of good managers.
(*e*) Availability of operatives, equipment and raw materials.
(*f*) Ideas on rate of growth.
(*g*) The concept of the optimum organisation.

Costs

In considering costs we must take into account the concept of *optimum* organisation, and the varying optima of its different parts. The forces determining optimum airline organisation operate to produce differences in costs of organising and contracting. An explanation of how this causes costs to differ from one organisation to another is given in Chapter VII.

Attitudes to organisation and contracting

Most managers have conflicting ideas on the advantages and disadvantages of organisation, and their attitudes result from the balance. Ideas that doing business by organisation is inherently better than doing it by contracting are largely based on the apparent advantages of authority. Pride of command, impatience with delay, desire for security are all ingredients in the feelings that sustain a preference for the authority that goes with organisation.

One of the errors in thinking about the alternatives of doing business by contracting or by organisation is akin to the philosophical error of dualism. We conceive two things that simply co-exist and have no other relation. But an airline and its contractors do not simply co-exist; nor, if it adds another part to its organisation, does that part simply co-exist with the parts that were already there. New relations are created by both contracting, and adding to organisation.

Decisions to organise or contract are often influenced by a subconscious regard for the difference in the two sets of relations. Contractual relations may be regarded as less complicated than organisational relations as the cardinal feature in the former is simply approval of a product. On the other hand, organisational relations may be regarded as complex. They involve all the intricacies dealt with in this volume.

Availability of capital

The task of raising capital influences the initial size and growth of airline organisation. The risks that prevail in the industry discourage the supply of equity capital or even fixed-interest bearing capital from private sources. Thus, in general, only if an airline is sustained by government subsidy to even out shortfalls in revenue, or if investors' funds are guaranteed, or if government itself provides capital at a reasonable price, can its organisation grow large.

Airlines do not have to commence business with such big organisations, as do railways or canal companies. Indeed most of the world's major airlines have grown from quite small beginnings, or are the result of the amalgamation of a number of small airlines. But usually airlines have not been able to rely on profits as the only source of additional capital, and they have had to expand organisation by fresh borrowings.

Availability of good managers

It is reasonable to suppose that the growth of some airline organisations has been restricted by a lack of good managers. Their enthusiasm and vision sustained many managers during the lean early years of the industry, but the continued inability of some airlines to pay proper salaries must have over-strained many loyalties.

Availability of operatives

On a number of occasions the expansion of individual airlines has been hampered in the short term by shortages in particular categories of operatives. At one time it may be that there are insufficient trained pilots, and at another time that there are too few skilled engineers. Less obvious shortages may occur in the ranks of salesmen, catering staff and so on.

Availability of equipment

On occasions an expansion in airline organisation must wait upon the arrival of some new equipment. This is a common experience when airlines come to consider increasing the size of their fleets. No airline willingly risks the addition of obsolescent aircraft to its fleet, and most will prefer to postpone expansion to ensure their obtaining the most up-to-date aircraft.

Availability of raw materials

In the long run the amount of traffic available for carriage will regulate the size of organisation for the whole industry. But in the short run and for the individual airline the relationship between traffic trends and organisation size may not be apparent.

Ideas on rate of growth

Some managements have theories on an optimum rate for the growth of organisation, and consequently tend to restrict growth to this 'most efficient' rate. This optimum rate may not coincide with the natural growth of traffic. Views on what is the most efficient rate vary from airline to airline.

This is not surprising as the different circumstances of airlines probably, in fact, give rise to differing optimum rates of growth. Such factors as existing size of organisation, the balance of processes, and degree of co-ordination, would all affect the ability to increase organisation without causing confusion.

We might expect, in general, that the optimum rate of organisational growth in airlines, where a high degree of planning and control is necessary, would be lower than in other industries where the processes of production are fairly simple, and where there is not the same interdependence of functions.

The concept of the optimum organisation

An organisation of optimum size, working at full capacity, *would have lowest average costs per unit of production, taking into account all costs to be covered in the long run.* The concept can be applied to overall organisation, and to its components. If an overall organisation is at optimum size an increase or decrease in any part of it will increase total costs per unit of production. However, an overall organisation that is at optimum size may contain components, none of which are at optimum size. In other words the optimum size of an overall organisation may be attained by a compromise in which the size of each component suffers some divergence from optimum in order to accommodate it with other components.

Let us assume that a certain overall organisation attains its optimum size at a production rate of one hundred units a month. It does not follow that the financial, purchasing, production, marketing, personnel and development components will attain their optimum sizes at this rate. For example, the average costs per unit of production of borrowing money, safeguarding assets, dealing with investors and so on, may well reach their lowest at a rate of a thousand units a month. On the other hand at a rate of a hundred a month the purchasing department may be running into supply shortages, and the production department may be incurring abnormal maintenance costs. But the marketing department might be able to reach lowest average costs by selling two hundred a month.

This concept is not concerned with questions of selling price. In the airline business, with its IATA control on prices, these need not coincide with average costs. Optimum organisations need not emerge, because demand is so limited. To secure additional sales an airline must usually attract customers from its competitors by spending more on display, and it may decrease the profit by expanding to optimum size.

The matching of differing optima

There is no reason to suppose that in airline organisation all the special functions of management, and the three physical elements will reach their optimum size at the same total output of passenger and freight arrivals. General management, therefore, faces serious problems in trying to match the different optimum sizes of different parts of the overall organisation.

The view is held among airline managers that the production process optimum is larger than can be managed by the optimum managerial unit. They believe that large staffs and fleets may bring operating economies that are more than offset by loss of efficiency in management. For this reason some managements tend to restrict the growth of organisation by resorting to charter. Alternatively organisations are broken up into a number of companies to deal with various aspects of airline work.

The optimum financial structure may be larger than that required by the optimum scale of production for some types of airline business. The history of failures of small independent operators in Britain in the early 1960s tends to support this idea.

The marketing optimum for airlines is usually larger than is needed for the optimum scale of production. Because of this airlines rarely attempt to do all their own marketing, but hand part of it to travel agents, acting for a number of transport operators.

The relation between the size of an airline 'business' and its 'organisation'

The limits of airline organisations are determined by the size of their business. Size of business is largely determined by the demand for arrivals of passengers and freight by air, and marginally by the demand for extra-to-carriage services (such as doing maintenance work for other airlines). The limits are, therefore, not static but grow and shrink roughly with size of market.

In principle an airline organisation should grow to a size at which its rate of production can maximise the profit to be obtained *solely in organisation.* Both organisation and contractual activities may bring profit to an airline business, and each should be fixed at a level to bring maximum profit.

Thus the relation between the size of an airline's 'business' and its 'organisation' is not a simple one. The biggest airline businesses do not necessarily have the biggest organisations. Airline organisations do not always grow at the same pace as the businesses themselves.

Another way of looking at this is to say that the maximum size of organisation (where the maximum position is judged from the standpoint of profitability) varies, relative to the amount of contractual activity from airline to airline. The maximum size of organisation *for any given size of business* will depend upon relative costs of contracting and organisation.

The variables influencing size of business

First the size of the market, in the area in which an airline operates sets a limit to the size of its business. The size of the market may be expressed as demand per period for arrivals of all forms of traffic at destinations or at transit points on the airline's routes. Only where an airline has a monopoly on its routes is it likely that the size of its business will approximate to the size of the market. In a monopoly it is possible, in the short run, for airline business to be controlled at a level below that of size of market, leaving some demand unsatisfied.

The area over which an airline operates, or the routes over which it flies, are regulated by its rights to do business. These rights are almost always controlled by government.

With competition airline business approximates to the share of the market that it has gained. This share is the result of the interaction of the activities of all competitors on the routes. An airline's business may be controlled at a level lower than the share of market it has gained, leaving some demand for its products unsatisfied.

Approximate measures of sizes of airline business and organisation

An approximate measure of the size of an airline business is the revenue it earns during a certain period. It is imperfect because fares per mile are not the same on all routes. Some routes pay better than others, so revenue passenger miles per period may be considered to be a better measure.

An approximate measure of the operatives employed is the average of employees per period. It is imperfect because it does not distinguish between experienced and inexperienced workers, between the lowly paid and highly paid or between management and operatives. In some ways the wages bill would be a better measure. An approximate measure of the amount of equipment used is the figure of capacity ton-miles. By using these admittedly imperfect measures over a number of airlines we may reasonably conclude from their comparative positions that the relationship between size of airline business and organisation is not direct.

TABLE 4. *Airline Business and Organisation Ratios 1962*
(*Source:* Airline reports and ICAO statistical digests)

	Sabena	QEA	Swissair	SAS	BEA
Size of Business:					
Total revenue	1·0	1·2	1·4	1·8	1·8
Revenue passenger miles	1·0	1·1	1·2	1·6	1·9
Size of Organisation:					
Number of employees	1·0	0·6	0·7	1·2	1·5
Capacity ton-miles	1·0	1·4	1·3	1·8	1·6

	KLM	BOAC	Air France	TWA	PAA
Size of Business:					
Total revenue	2·2	3·4	4·1	5·3	6·6
Revenue passenger miles	2·0	3·2	3·6	6·6	8·4
Size of Organisation:					
Number of employees	1·6	2·0	2·3	1·9	2·1
Capacity ton-miles	2·1	4·6	3·8	7·8	9·1

Of the ten selected airlines Sabena had the smallest business in 1962, as indicated by total revenue and revenue passenger miles. Using Sabena as a basis for comparison we can see that size of business is not directly related to size of organisation. For example PAA employed only twice the number of staff, but nine times the amount of equipment employed by Sabena, to produce eight and a half times the number of revenue passenger-miles.

The nature of work done within organisation

A manager has been defined as a man who acts through an organisation. So far we have considered what takes place within organisation as something different from management. We have regarded what a manager does as different from what his organisation does. Managers plan, motivate, control, and contract, whereas operatives use equipment to change raw materials. The distinction is made between the manager who does the thinking, and the organisation that does the physical work.

This is a reasonable approach because a man who introduces an organisation to his business usually believes he has a comparative advantage in thinking and comparative disadvantage in doing. This belief is probably justified in most men who have enough initiative and intelligence to run a successful business in the first place.

In fact, planning, motivating, controlling and contracting are not always carried out by managers: they are sometimes performed by an organisation. Nor is physical work always carried out by organisation: it is sometimes done by managers. Managers do not always relegate all the physical tasks associated with their work, especially if they involve highly developed skills. Thus a chief pilot, or chief medical officer, or chief instructor may relegate to organisation many of the administrative tasks associated with management, and continue to exercise his particular skills. Other examples of the managerial processes being exercised within organisation are where the General Manager has special Planning and Inspection Branches within his organisation.

This ability of a manager to relegate, within certain limits, managerial processes to organisation, provides us with a second alternative to organisation. It has been argued that contracting is an alternative to organisation as a way of doing business. We must now add that the manager doing it himself is a second alternative to doing business through organisation.

Factors influencing the 'order' in which tasks are brought into organisation

The advantage to be gained from bringing them into organisation differs from one activity to another. Airlines tend to bring in first the activity which yields the maximum advantage, and then that which is the next most advantageous, and so on. Thus, if more were to be gained by bringing engine-overhauls than, say, the overhaul of a flight-system into organisation, then there would be a tendency to bring engine overhauls in first.

It does not always work this way. Most airlines will be tempted to give priority to flying because it appears more 'businesslike' to have their own flying organisation. Many young nations insist on their national airlines having their own aircraft fleet and crews, regardless of cost. Then again the powerful advocacy of a special manager with a relatively weak case may prevail over a stronger case less powerfully argued.

The tasks that the individual manager performs through an organisation *instead of doing them himself*, are usually delegated in accordance with the principle of comparative advantage.[1]

Factors affecting the proportions of the elements of airline organisation

Measuring the elements in an airline organisation

The only practicable way of measuring the elements in an airline organisation is by the money spent on each during an accounting period. Thus we might analyse airline expenditure as in Table 5.

The main problem is what to regard as the cost of bringing raw materials into an airline organisation. In a manufacturing company these are easily identified as buying costs plus any transport charges.

But an airline does not have to *buy* passengers or freight in order to effect a change in their condition. A manufacturing company usually becomes the owner of its raw materials before processing them, but not so with an airline. Passengers and freight are presented free-of-charge in the sense that there is no payment for change of ownership, because this does not occur.

There are, however, other costs of bringing passengers and freight into airline organisation. Publicity must be given to the means by which passengers and freight are presented for carriage by air. Some airlines may have to provide ground transport. Most airlines have to incur the costs of 'storage', represented by seat reservation systems, and warehouse space.

The extent of organisation

The extent of organisation determines the proportions of the costs of bringing elements into use. The more organised a business is, the higher are operatives' wages and equipment costs, in relation to the

[1] *Managing a Transport Business*, p. 50. W. S. Barry, Allen & Unwin, 1963

TABLE 5. *Analysis of Airline Expenditure*

			Percentage of total annual expenditure
MANAGEMENT		Salaries, pensions, other expenses	5
ORGANISATION	OPERATIVES	Wages, pensions, etc.	31
	EQUIPMENT	*Capital equipment*, depreciation of aircraft, airport buildings, maintenance equipment, offices, compensation, renewals, insurance, etc.	
		consumable equipment, fuel and oil, tyres, printed material, food, etc.	38
	RAW MATERIALS	Passengers and freight, publicity, seat reservations, costs of storing freight	2
CONTRACTING		Maintenance work, marketing, passenger and freight handling, aircraft charter, etc.	15
FINANCIAL		Interest on capital	9
			100

cost of raw materials. Contracting can influence these proportions in two ways. Contracting may *reduce* costs of bringing operatives and equipment into use, and secondly may *increase* the cost of bringing raw materials into use. In airline organisation the costs of bringing operatives and equipment into use are more variable than those of bringing raw materials into use.

The nature of the raw materials of an airline

It is possible to vary the degree of finish of airline raw materials only within relatively narrow limits. It is possible to vary expenditure on operatives and equipment considerably by, say, doing all aircraft and building maintenance under contract, and even chartering aircraft and crews. But the degree of finish that a contractor can give to passengers or freight cannot give rise to such big variations *from the point of view of the carrier*. A furniture dealer's raw materials may vary in state from rough-sawn timber to completely finished chairs and tables. If he buys rough-sawn timber and manufactures furniture in his own workshops, the raw material costs will be low relative to the cost of labour and equipment. If he buys ready-made furniture, raw material costs will be high in relation to labour and equipment costs.

The most a carrier can do to obtain 'more finished' raw materials is to contract the job of getting passengers and freight on board its aircraft. In this way it then deals with 'processed passengers'. The job of processing will have been done by a contractor, and the price charged by the contractor, or handling agent, may be regarded as a cost of raw materials for the airline. In many airlines the cost of passenger and freight handling does not represent more than 20 per cent of total costs. This indicates the extent to which the proportion of operative and equipment costs to raw material costs can be altered by increased costs of raw materials.

The main sorts of airline contracting

The main sorts of contracting by airlines may be summarised as follows:

(*a*) Manufacture of capital equipment (offices, hangars, workshops, stations, aircraft, communications equipment).
(*b*) Maintenance of equipment (building maintenance, overhaul and repair of aircraft, etc.).
(*c*) Temporary additions to equipment (bare-hull aircraft charter).
(*d*) Temporary additions to operating strength (chartering aircraft and crews).
(*e*) Processing raw materials (carriage by other operators, passenger and freight handling, etc.).
(*f*) Marketing through travel agents.

CHAPTER VII

COSTS AND SAVINGS OF ORGANISATION

The essential difference between having a job done within airline organisation, and having it done by a contractor

To have a job done by a contractor is essentially to have a job done by another firm's organisation. If an airline decides to have its aircraft engines overhauled by a manufacturer, instead of overhauling them in its own workshops, it is in fact deciding that the manufacturer's organisation can do a better job than its own can do.

Without legal limitations, traditions or personal preferences it would be reasonable to suppose that the judgement of the performance of the manufacturer's organisation is based on 'cost'. The costs that are compared are disbursements on elements of airline organisation against a lump-sum price charged by a manufacturer.

The price charged by the manufactuer may or may not approximate to his average, or even his marginal, costs in the short run. But frequently a contractor's costs are lower than those of an airline, for doing a particular job, and it is this difference we set out to explain in this chapter.

Two sorts of decisions to have jobs done within airline organisation

If an airline weighs the pros and cons of having a job done within its own organisation, or within the organisation of a contractor, in considering the first alternative it much reckon either (i) to utilise existing elements of organisation more, or (ii) to add to existing elements of organisation.

(*a*) *Greater utilisation*

Assuming that 'avoidable' costs represent costs of *use of organisation*[1] a decision to utilise existing elements of organisation will cause an increase in avoidable costs.

(*b*) *Adding to the elements of organisation*

Assuming that 'unavoidable' costs represent the notional costs of having *organisation available for use*, a decision to add to the elements

[1] See *Managing a Transport Business*, p.65.

of organisation will cause an increase in unavoidable costs, and then to avoidable costs as newly available elements are brought into use.

The concept of optimum organisation and moving average and marginal costs

Implicit in the concept of optimum organisation is the idea that organisations may not be, and probably are not, at optimum. We would not expect an organisation's position, relative to the optimum, to remain stationary over a long period of time. An airline organisation would probably be moving towards or away from it.

Optimum organisation has been defined as that having lowest average costs of production per unit. Therefore, as we move step by step away from the optimum we would expect average costs to rise. This means that each step, away from optimum, costs more than the preceding step. The costs of each step may be referred to as marginal costs. Movement towards or away from optimum results in decreasing or increasing marginal costs, and hence average costs.

One of the factors influencing decisions on the alternatives of organising or contracting is that of costs. Changes made in an organisation affect its average costs. They will be increased or decreased by adding to organisation because it will be taken farther away from or brought nearer to its optimum.

Optimum organisation in existence and in utilisation

In defining optimum organisation one of the conditions given, for having lowest average costs of production, was its working at full capacity. Only if an optimum organisation works at full capacity will it have lowest average costs. Thus an optimum organisation can exist without attaining its supremacy if it is not fully utilised.

We now have two reasons why changes in the amount of work done in organisation give rise to changing costs. First, a change in the amount of work done in organisation may bring an organisation nearer to, or take it further away from the optimum size. Secondly, whether the organisation is at optimum size or not, a change in the amount of work done by it may bring an organisation nearer to, or take it further away from maximum utilisation.

The savings of the optimum managerial structure

In a small airline the manager has various functions to perform. He must possess or obtain capital. He must choose routes to operate, and negotiate for them; he must choose aircraft. He must buy materials and hire operatives, supervise operations and control development. He must plan and control marketing. Few men can do all these jobs well. The characteristics of a human being may make him a good financier but a bad salesman, or a good production planner but a poor innovator. Only if a number of managers are brought together and set to work on tasks they are good at, do we get well-balanced management.

When management is divided into, say, higher management planning, and junior management supervising, rare and expensive abilities are not so often wasted on routine work. The manager who specialises in, say, cargo sales is able to increase his knowledge of that particular task. A large management structure makes it economic to employ certain service subcomponents such as legal, organisation and methods, security branches and so on.

On the other hand, where a managerial structure is large enough it may be economic to do away with the divisions created by specialisation. One of the most important changes of recent years has been the amalgamation of administrative processes by putting a whole series of systems on to electronic computers.

Beyond a certain point the gains from managerial specialisation diminish. Decisions take longer to make; communication becomes more difficult; co-ordination becomes less efficient.

The advantages of the optimum financial structure

By financial structure we mean more than the amount of money invested in an airline. An airline's financial structure is determined by the proportions of certain features; liquid to fixed assets, reserve to contingencies, interest payable to operating expenditure, and so on.

The optimum financial structure is one in which critical proportions are right. It is also one in which the ratio between capital employed and scale of operations is right.

The savings of an optimum financial structure lie mainly in the probabilities of obtaining capital more cheaply and in maintaining assets through difficult times. The costs of not being at optimum lie mainly in the risks of not surviving periods of poor traffic, and consequent capital loss.

With an optimum financial structure an airline will be able to exploit natural growth in traffic, or take advantage of new equipment, such as blind landing aids or X-ray apparatus for diagnosing metal fatigue.

The optimum purchasing unit

(*a*) *The economies of large-scale buying*

A large purchasing unit can buy supplies (e.g. office equipment, furnishings, fuel and oil, food, etc.) in large single orders. This puts it in a strong bargaining position and enables it to buy cheaply. A large unit can afford to employ expert buyers, and assist them with up-to-date information. A large unit can afford to spend more time preparing detailed specifications for large orders. A large unit is more able to ensure that equipment is fully tested before it goes into service.

(*b*) *The dangers of large-scale buying*

Mistakes made in large-scale buying are big. If an airline buys twenty aircraft it may get each aircraft more cheaply than a single aircraft bought by a small airline. But if the aircraft turn out to be unsuitable, the loss for the larger airline will be much greater. A mistake in purchasing a large number of aircraft may be more difficult to rectify than a mistake in purchasing a single aircraft. It may be possible to resell a single aircraft without serious capital loss. To resell a number of aircraft may be more difficult to accomplish without suffering heavy loss.

The savings of optimum process of production

(*a*) *Operative specialisation*

The advantages of operative specialisation are considerable. The cost of training and paying a pilot is so great that an airline cannot afford to waste any of his skill. More machinery can be used when operatives specialise. If men specialise in loading, they can use fork-lift trucks, loading pallets and so on. With operative specialisation there is less time spent in going from one task to another. If clerks check passengers in and then escort them to the aircraft, they may waste time in walking from one point to another. The production process should therefore be sufficiently large to obtain the maximum profitable operative specialisation.

(*b*) *Amalgamation of processes*

Sometimes it is advantageous to do away with the divisions created by specialisation. One large machine may take over what was done by a series of manual or small machinery operations. An airline with a big enough process of production can support a computer to handle its reservations procedures, and interpret its statistics.

(*c*) *The large machine*

In many cases large machines are less costly than small ones. Advantages derive from the fact that containers increase their capacity with the cube of the dimension, whereas the area of the walls increase as the square of the dimension. This is particularly important where an object has to be moved against the resistance of water or air. Rate of production should be high enough to obtain the economies of large machines.

(*d*) *The balance of production processes*

Units of various elements of airline organisation become fully utilised at different rates of production. For example, there may be an aircraft carrying 120 passengers who are checked-in by clerks who can deal with 50 passengers each over the check-in period. Two aircraft docks able to deal with the maintenance of 20 aircraft may have to be provided for 18 aircraft and so on. A big airline may reach a rate of production high enough to provide a multiple of all the various maximum outputs.

(*e*) *Beyond the optimum process of production*

Beyond a certain point there is little to be gained from further operative specialisation, as problems of co-ordination, frustration and boredom increase. Secondly, the economies of large machines are offset by the problems of accommodation. For example, a dis-economy in increasing the size of aircraft is the need to lengthen and strengthen runways. Thirdly, the advantages of balance of production processes can be secured at a lowest common multiple.

The optimum marketing unit

(*a*) *The economies of large-scale selling*

Selling is said to be large-scale if a large *number* of sales are made. Small-scale selling is to a small number of buyers. Airlines may:

(i) produce on a large scale and sell on a small scale;
or (ii) both produce and sell on the same scale, large or small;
or (iii) produce on a small scale, and sell on a large scale.

An airline with a large fleet, used solely on a government trooping contract, is producing on a large scale and selling on a small scale. A large scheduled airline both produces and sells on a large scale. A one-aircraft charter airline both produces and sells on a small scale. The one-aircraft scheduled airline produces on a small scale and sells on a large scale. The proportion of selling costs to total operating costs varies from one situation to another.

All airlines having to sell on a large scale have common problems. A big number of salesmen are required to deal with customers, scattered throughout the length and breadth of a country. A large sales force is costly and difficult to utilise to the full. For this reason the size of airline sales organisations is usually smaller than optimum. Hence we have the extensive use of travel agents, who can fully utilise their selling resources by selling for a wide variety of enterprises engaged in the travel business.

The situation is not quite the same as that referred to by economists as 'vertical disintegration' in selling. In a number of industries marketing is taken over by specialist firms who *buy* producers' *whole stocks*. In these industries the optimum marketing organisation is too big for the individual enterprise. For example, in agriculture large specialist marketing organisations are created to handle the produce of numerous small producers.

In industries in which products are standardised it does not matter to the producer whether his product is mixed in with all the others in the industry. Airlines are not in this position. They seek to brand their products, and to compete in quality against the products of rival airlines. For this reason they seek to attach individual travel agents to their interests in a variety of ways, but do not make the agent 'buy' stocks, and shoulder marketing risks.

(*b*) *The advantages of a marketing organisation specialising in one product*

Airlines, then, usually hand a large part of their marketing task over to specialist marketing organisations. These contractors are, however, specialists in *marketing* in a certain field. They are seldom specialists in *air transport*, and even more rarely are they specialists in the product of an individual airline. There are many advantages to be gained by specialising in the marketing of a single commodity, and most airlines obtain these by having their own highly specialised marketing units in large centres of population.

The effect of fluctuations in demand on costs and savings of organisation

Fluctuations in demand may be considered under the following headings:

(*a*) Steady upward or downward trends.
(*b*) Cyclical trends.
(*c*) Seasonal changes.
(*d*) Erratic changes.

The effect of steady trends in demand

Steady upward or downward trends are not easy to follow closely. Airline organisations cannot be built up or dismembered at steady rates. If the trend of demand could be illustrated by a smooth curve, organisation adjustment to the trend would have to be illustrated by a series of steps, in the general direction of the curve. So that even upward trends in demand give rise to extra costs as airlines do not usually wait for demand to outstrip supply before adding to organisation.

The effect of cyclical trends in demand

The demand for air transport is affected by the succession of ups and downs that occur in national economies. During a long period of growth in traffic a setback may be no more than a temporary slowing up of rate of growth. The effect of a 'boom' or 'slump' in one country is difficult to assess in an airline whose traffic is derived from a number of countries. It is difficult to find out whether a national 'boom' or 'slump' has proportionate effect on air traffic. Claims are made that demand for air transport is sensitive to changes in prosperity. The truth of these claims is by no means certain, but it is reasonable to expect that air transport would be one of the first industries to suffer, as it is still regarded as something of a luxury.

Airlines cannot rely on being able to adjust organisations to cyclical changes, and their long-term plans must take account of the necessity to live through short periods of under-utilisation, or under-capacity.

The effect of seasonal changes in demand

Most airlines experience changes in demand from one period to another. Traffic changes from summer to winter, from weekend to weekday and from day to night. Airlines tend to equip themselves to deal with peak traffic, to avoid losing any. They then seek to reduce costs by 'creating' more traffic to fill off-peak capacity.

The root of the problem of seasonal changes in demand lies in the inability of airlines to accumulate stocks of their product. Most manufacturing industries that face seasonal demand equalise the rate of production at the mean rate of consumption, accumulate stocks at times of high demand and reduce stocks at times of low demand.

The effect of erratic changes in demand

In the long run erratic changes in demand increase costs of organisation. Airlines minimise the occasions on which they cannot meet a sudden call for extra aircraft, by equipping themselves with standbys. In the short term, where aircraft are in reserve, a sudden demand for more seats can, of course, produce savings in organisation.

Demand is often more erratic in the charter market than in the market for scheduled services. Partly for this reason many airlines employ their aircraft only marginally on charter work.

The effect of uncertainties (economic and political)

The main uncertainties in the airline business are:

(*a*) The fares and rates that will be agreed for particular routes.
(*b*) The granting or withholding of rights to fly to particular destinations.
(*c*) The precise bargain that is struck in the negotiation of traffic rights.
(*d*) The disturbance of services through political or industrial unrest.
(*e*) The concerted activities of a number of airlines operating on a route, resulting in excess capacity.

The effects of uncertainties are often not so adverse for small, and large, airlines as for medium-sized ones. Small airlines have a resilience from their ability to survive on small returns, and to slip into the margins of markets. Big airlines probably have staying power, despite their heavy organisational commitments, because of financial reserves or government backing. Medium-sized airlines often have the worst of both worlds in that they have sunk a fair amount of capital in their businesses, but have not been able to accumulate adequate financial reserves or win government protection.

The costs and savings of growth in airline organisation

In periods of growing demand savings may be achieved by increasing the use of organisation without increasing certain costs. Where no growth is in prospect extra traffic can be obtained only at the cost of attracting customers from other airlines. Sooner or later a point will be reached where the extra cost of attracting traffic exceeds the savings of increased use of organisation.

A phenomenon observed in many industries is the tendency for firms to fail at a critical size. It may be at a point where the firm has ceased to be easily manageable and has not yet become technically viable. It is reasonable to suppose that the same situation exists among airlines, and that it may account for the failure of a number of organisations as they begin to grow. The problem of organisational growth is partly that of minimising the costs incurred at the critical size.

One way of avoiding the costs of critical size of organisation is to jump from small airline organisations to large airline organisation by the process of amalgamation. The growth of British independent airlines was achieved in this way. This method of growth in size of organisation has the added advantage of avoiding costs of competing for customers.

The costs and savings of 'development', or 'innovation' in airline organisation

New men, new equipment, and new procedures are brought into organisation to produce savings in the long run. In the short run, development often gives rise to costs rather than savings. For example, operating costs may rise temporarily when a new aircraft is introduced. Aircraft components are examined frequently in their early life, just to be on the safe side. As experience grows and parts can be trusted not to fail, the aircraft can spend more time in the air and less in the hangars. Operatives must be trained on new equipment, and this further cuts into production time. If new aircraft are delivered in a peak operating period, and come into full service in a slack season, further losses will be incurred.

The following table shows an expected improvement with experience in overhauling two types of aircraft engines:

TABLE 6. *Expected Improvement with Experience in Overhauling Two Types of Aircraft Engines*

AVON ENGINE		TYNE ENGINE	
Months of Operation	*Hours use between overhauls*	*Months of Operation*	*Hours use between overhauls*
8	1000	6	400
10	1300	16	800
13	1600	23	1000
23	2200	26	1200
32	2500	30	1400
37	2800	34	1600
41	3100	43	1800
46	3450	49	2000
50	3700	55	2200
54	4000	61	2600
		73	3000

The effect of the scale of the airline industry on the cost and savings of individual airline organisations

So far we have looked at the effect of various aspects of individual airline organisations upon costs of production. Operating costs depend, however, not only upon the size of individual airline organisations, but also on the total size of all organisations engaged in the industry. For example, as the airline industry grows it is likely to be able to buy its aircraft more cheaply, as aircraft manufacturers may then enjoy economies of large-scale production. The more airlines there are in the industry the more will be spent on fundamental, industrial and operational research. The larger the industry the more it may influence ground transport to serve its needs; and the more it will encourage the learning of skills of the industry.

On the other hand, as the air transport industry grows, diseconomies are likely to arise. Thus as more and more aircraft are brought into operations, and existing airports become too small, additional airports must be built in less convenient areas, and so on.

CHAPTER VIII

PRINCIPLES OF SUBORDINATION

The nature of subordination

Subordination becomes necessary as a business grows, and its work has to be shared by a number of people. A number of people must be reduced to order. They cannot be allowed to behave in accordance with individual whims. They must be arranged so that some take precedence over others. Some will be more important than others so they are 'ranked'. Those of lower rank must obey those of higher rank.

In airline organisation the order, which produces effective subordination, is made more clear by rank titles, and insignia on uniforms. The terms used in airlines as in other forms of human organisation, to describe the ideas involved in *subordination* are:

(*a*) Authority.
(*b*) Responsibility.
(*c*) Delegation.
(*d*) Duties.

The problems of subordination

The problems of subordination spring, of course, from the nature of man himself. Most people at some time or another become insubordinate, either because they feel compelled to avoid the hardships of doing what they have been told to do, or to enjoy the pleasures of doing what they have been told not to do. The effect of influences, that can be brought to bear to prevent insubordination in general, cannot be predicted with certainty for the individual human being. The larger the number of human beings considered, the more surely can we predict that good working conditions and fear of dismissal or demotion will encourage them to conform, but we would be unwise to rely on such an effect on an individual human being.

Subordinating airline organisation to the business

An organisation has been defined as 'an instrument used by a manager to achieve the intention of the "head" of the business'.

As an airline organisation grows and settles down subtle changes may take place in its purpose. At first it may be well-adapted or 'tuned' to the intention of selling arrivals by air at a profit. Then it may add to the idea of arrival by air, a panoply of extra-to-carriage services. It may abandon the aim of profit, and substitute the aim of providing a 'social service', or 'carrying the flag', or some other non-profit-making consideration. The original airline *business intention* is in this way replaced by an airline *organisation intention.*

This again illustrates the fact that an airline organisation is usefully regarded as something distinct from the business it serves. An organisation has a life of its own, and its members naturally seek to maximise their own safety, comfort and prosperity.

An airline organisation is not successfully subordinated unless it is compelled to remain instrumental to the intention of the head of the business. One of the greatest difficulties airline boards and top managers face is the tendency for organisation to substitute its own aims, especially as there are so many apparently strong reasons for diluting simple business aims.

Authority

A subordinate is someone who is controlled, who is dependent, and who is obliged to render certain services to his superior. A superior's right to control is called his authority. Authority is variable in that it may be great or little. Authority includes the idea of the role of an author. It implies originating and giving existence to things and situations. A man with authority is one who gives rise to actions. His decisions are acted upon.

Authority must be exercised within an organisation to secure concerted action. Where, as in airline organisation, there is necessity for quick and co-ordinated decisions, authority must be strong.

A manager has been said to contract for, plan for, motivate and control the performance of his organisation. In order to motivate and control he must exercise authority. By exercising authority he gets things done through other people. By exercising authority he causes tasks to be completed through organisation. The tasks, or work that a manager passes on to other people, are referred to as *duties*, because they become actions or conduct due to him as the superior. Whatever tasks are left for the manager to do himself are also referred to as duties, because he owes their completion to the business.

There are two widely recognised sorts of authority. There is *personal authority* and *formal authority*. The former a man obtains from his own experience, knowledge and personality. The latter derives from the office a man holds. A large airline organisation calls for such considerable expertise that personal authority is a force worth considering alongside that of formal authority.

There are the usual bases of industrial authority in airlines. Men accept authority because they are paid to do so, or because they hope for promotion, or because they enjoy the work. On the other hand, they may be prevented from flouting authority by fear of reprimand or dismissal. The strength of authority is usually dependent upon the degree of acceptance as fashioned by these internal influences. In airlines authority is strengthened because the 'zone of acceptance' does not depend entirely on internal influences. Industrial sanctions are often reinforced by legal sanctions. For example, a pilot not only has to obey his company's regulations, but also State regulations.

It is not easy to give a theoretical explanation of the authority of an aircraft commander. This type of authority has been referred to elsewhere as 'situational'.[1] Aircraft commanders often exercise, during periods of command, authority that extends over organisational superiors, with greater formal authority. Command, or 'situational' authority, is a temporary addition to the formal authority exercised in an organisation, and situational authority is continuously supported by formal authority. A superior subject to command authority, is, in fact, subject to his own ordinance, or to that of his superior. An airline chairman who obeys the orders of an aircraft captain while on board his aircraft, is conforming to his own regulations giving captains certain powers while on service.

When a captain relinquishes command he loses formal authority and is left only with personal authority. This is, of course, considerable in the case of a man with great experience and knowledge.

Responsibility

The word responsibility is related to 'respond', which means to answer. Responsibility is answerableness. Once a person accepts a command or instruction, issued by a superior possessed of the necessary authority, the former becomes *responsible* for completing a *duty*. He must answer to his superior for the efficient performance of the duty. The term duty embraces the idea of responsibility. A duty is a task that has to be performed with responsibility. Any responsibility involves duties.

The amount of responsibility in an organisation is added to with every instruction that is received. If a manager instructs an aircraft captain to do something, and the captain in turn instructs his first officer to do it, the captain remains responsible to the manager,

[1] *Managing a Transport Business*, p. 72.

while the first officer is responsible to the captain. Responsibility cannot be shed by passing on a duty to a subordinate.

Delegation

The word 'delegate' is derived from a root meaning to send as representative. A representative is a person *with power to act for another*. In delegating a manager may entrust his representative in organisation with power to act in two ways:

(i) To perform duties himself.
(ii) To exercise authority to make others perform duties.

In talking about delegation it is important to be clear whether delegating *duties*, or delegating *authority*, or both, are referred to. The delegation of duties is dealt with later. We consider next the supremely important problems of delegation of authority.

Delegation of Authority—The Critical Act of Management

In the conduct of international affairs, in the functioning of national political institutions, and in the employment of military organisation, *balance of power* has long been regarded as an issue of critical importance.

In the industrial field thought has been given to problems epitomised by such terms as 'centralisation' and 'de-centralisation'. Useful studies of the distribution of power, were conducted on Britain's nationalised industries. The mammoth British Transport Commission was bedevilled throughout its existence by questions of balance of power. It is perhaps too dramatic to suggest that the giant was torn asunder by contrary pulls but the weakness of the whole exposed it to a statutory *coup de grâce*.

If universities had devoted as much time to studies of power in business, as they have to power in politics and armies, we might be wiser now. As it is we must grope our way through the difficulties of large business organisation armed only with a few crudely fashioned concepts.

The number of human beings in an organisation grows as more work is undertaken, and it has to be shared more widely. To deal with extra work an organisation grows in two directions, usually more or less at the same time. In the language used to talk about organisation charts we can say that:

(*a*) Organisation grows downwards as additional levels of authority are created;
(*b*) Organisation grows sideways as additional components are created;

Thus:

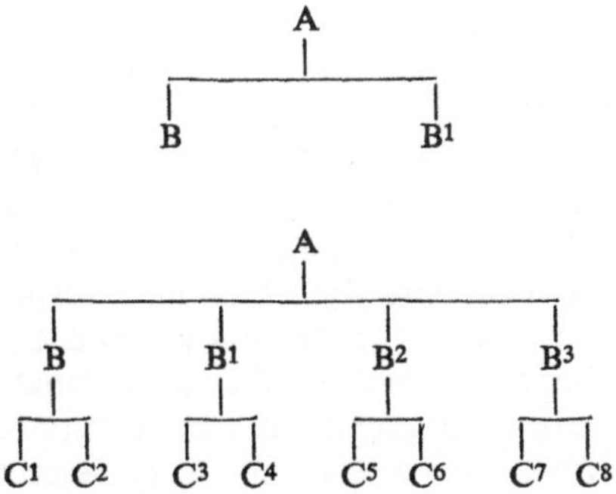

may grow to

FIG. 6. *Growth of organisation sideways and downwards*

Some have a naïve approach to the problems of power in industry. They talk as if industrial authority were somehow free of the aberrations, that afflict authoritarian, oligarchical, and democratic government. Some, at the top of vast industrial empires, do not appreciate that the authority they give to their subordinates can be abused.

With every act of delegation of authority, the amount of authority is added to. Every increase in the ability to initiate calls for a compensating ability to control. Otherwise the authority that is delegated can get out of hand.

It is reasonable to suppose that authority got out of hand in some of the major world airline organisations, when the only cure for their ills was draconian. The root and branch reconstructions in recent years should not have been necessary had authority been well balanced.

There are many ways in which the balance of power in an airline can be wrong. Here are some of them:

(*a*) A managing director may give so much authority to his departmental heads, that he is no longer able to control them. If authority is uncontrolled it may not be bad, but there is always the danger that it will be exercised in accordance with the opinion of the individual, and no other.
(*b*) A managing director may delegate too little authority so that he is overwhelmed by the need to make minor decisions.
(*c*) A managing director may give too much authority to one component of organisation.

For example, if a chief maintenance engineer is given too much authority the airline may find that scheduled services are being built around the convenience of the engineer rather than the needs of the customer. Or if a chief pilot is given too much authority the airline may find that its commercial activities are hampered by the operational standards of pilots, and so on.

The delegation of duties

Once a manager delegates some of the work, for which he is responsible to the business, to a subordinate within his organisation, a difference occurs between the amount of work he does personally and the total amount of work for which he is responsible. The tasks which he does personally are his duties, and the tasks that are delegated to a subordinate become that subordinate's duties.

Where someone in an organisation has no subordinates his duties and responsibility are co-extensive. But a manager's responsibility is not co-extensive with his duties. For example, the responsibility of a managing director of an airline is as follows:

Total responsibility for efficient operation of the airline	=	Duties of managing director of the airline	+	the sum of duties in all posts subordinate to the managing director

A first stage delegation of a duty duplicates responsibility; a second stage delegation of a duty triplicates responsibility, and so on. So delegation of duties increases the amount of responsibility in an organisation, but it also increases the sum of duties because delegation produces need for the managerial activities of planning, motivating, controlling and contracting.

Obtaining a 'fix' on a position in organisation

The simplest method of describing an organisation is by means of a conventional organisation chart as illustrated in Fig. 7.

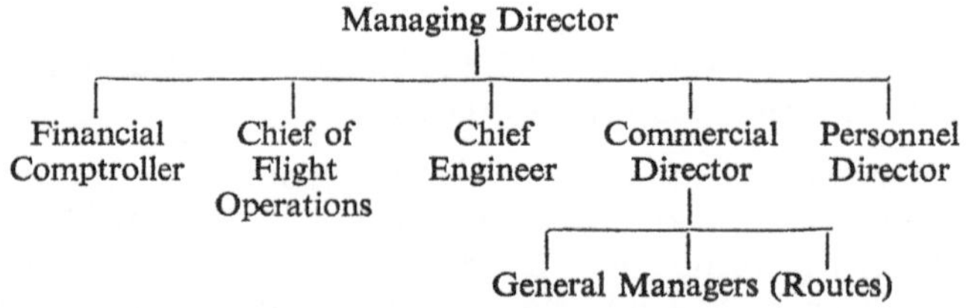

FIG. 7. *Illustration of conventional organisation chart*

The vertical alignment shows superior-subordinate relationships, and the horizontal alignment shows posts at the same level of authority. The continuous lines are said to show a 'chain of command'.

Successful subordination depends upon management's being able to define the position of each member of the organisation. A fairly accurate 'fix' can be obtained for each post by stating:

Taking the Commercial Director (Fig. 7) as an example:

(*a*) The person (or persons) to whom the holder is responsible:	Managing Director
(*b*) What the holder is responsible for (general area of responsibility):	Efficient marketing
(*c*) The holder's subordinates:	General managers (routes)
(*d*) The holder's own duties:	Planning, integrating and controlling performance of general managers (routes)
(*e*) Colleagues:	Financial Comptroller, Chief of Flight Ops., Chief Engineer, Personnel Director

The importance of direct contact between superiors and subordinates

There are reasons for believing that problems of subordination increase as the amount of direct contact between superiors and subordinates decreases. A superior who frequently meets his subordinates face-to-face will probably discover a number of useful facts about their individual reactions to instructions. He will probably learn that some require to be handled differently from others, that some are slower on the uptake, but slower to forget and so on. He will probably hear quickly of personal problems that threaten the efficiency of a subordinate.

Direct contact between superiors and subordinates is difficult in some components of airline organisation. For example, a flight manager may meet each pilot in his flight only once every few weeks. Pilots arrive at an airport when they are due to begin planning a flight, and leave the airport as soon as they have completed the formalities at the end of the service. Their managers have little opportunity for even a few minutes quiet talk. Similarly, a manager of a maintenance branch may have few opportunities of talking to his supervisors on night shift, as most of his work has to be done at a desk in the day-time. The managing director of an airline cannot frequently meet and talk to his overseas representatives. The geographical distribution of staff, and the giving of a twenty-four-hour service are the basic factors contributing to these difficulties.

The ideal of concentrated authority

Ideally authority should be concentrated in as few hands as possible, at each level of organisation, to reduce problems of co-ordination. Also ideally one man should serve only one master.

In airlines, because of the need for much specialisation, it is difficult to keep the first split in authority down to the six fundamental tasks of finance, purchasing, personnel, production, marketing and development. The list of people reporting directly to the Director General of a major world airline is as follows:

3 Assistant Director Generals (Technical, Economic and Secretary)
5 Directors (Financial, Personnel, Flight Operations, Engineering and Commercial)
2 Managers (Ground Telecommunications and Fleet Planning)
1 Senior Medical Officer

The effect of the authority of a number of specialists brought to bear on a general manager

The ideal of one man serving only one master cannot be practised where it is necessary to bring the authority of specialists to bear upon a general manager.

This is a common situation in airlines, where a number of managers control the activities within particular areas. For example, Air France may have an area manager to look after all the airline's interests in, say, Europe. But, because of the highly specialised nature of airline work, the Area Manager (Europe) must accept the rulings of the Commercial, Financial, Personnel, Flight Operations and Engineering Directors, upon matters that concern their respective departments. The position of general (area) managers is not made easier by the fact that specialist or 'functional' managers may give their rulings through many 'sub-specialists'. Area managers may feel they have dozens of masters, and that their situation is bewildering. This danger can be reduced by controlling the number of specialists who exercise such authority.

The limitations on the span of control

There is a limit to the number of subordinates that any man can control. This limit varies according to the work involved, the ability of the superior, the inter-action of the work of his subordinates, and their abilities, and the time available for control.

There is little doubt that ideas on the limits of span of control are often disregarded in airline organisation, under the pressure of the distribution of staff in time and space, and the considerable expertise that the airline business requires.

In 1962 the managing director of one of the biggest airlines had 38 officials reporting to him. It would have been difficult to prove that 38 was in fact too wide a span of control. But this number was a product of history rather than the result of a decision consciously based on the factors mentioned above.

The importance of tailoring commands and instructions to the characteristics and environment of the recipient

Commands or instructions are seldom completely effective, or completely ineffective. The perfect command that everyone can understand, and the abysmal command that nobody at all can understand probably exist only in the imagination. Most instructions are well understood by some and less well understood by others.

Instructions must sometimes be made to suit the circumstances of the giver. For example, an aircraft commander could not be expected to give long-winded, patient explanations every time he gives his first-officer an order. But as a general rule a manager, in giving instructions, must take one of two lines:

(*a*) The circumstances of the receiver must be adjusted to accord with the complexity of the instruction; or
(*b*) The complexity of the instruction must be adjusted to accord with the circumstances of the receiver.

These two precepts have innumerable applications, and some very important ones in airline organisation. For example, management must ensure that they recruit, for certain jobs, staff intelligent enough to understand complicated instructions, say in a reservations or station manual. When a co-pilot is being given orders in the control cabin, besides the orders being simplified and standardised, he is assisted by a drill card from which he can read as the orders are given. A group of operation controllers may be given a soundproof room to assist them and so on. On the other hand, instructions given in English over radio-telephone to a French-speaking pilot must be spelt out as simply and clearly as possible.

A subordinate must be able to understand an instruction he is expected to obey. An instruction is a sort of communication, and the aim of communication is to pass *understanding*, not just words, from one person to another. One of the commonest causes of failings to convey understanding from one person to another is to assume that the recipient will take more for granted than he, in fact, does.

Purposefulness makes authority more acceptable

If a subordinate fully understands the purpose of an order, and is convinced of its necessity, he is less likely to need being prodded by sticks or tempted by carrots into obeying it. Unless blind obedience is called for, it is also desirable for a subordinate to be able to deviate from an instruction if circumstances make it impracticable to obey it strictly. He is better placed to deviate if he is aware of the purpose of the instruction.

Participation makes authority more acceptable

It is generally believed that if subordinates are allowed to share the authorship, implicit in the exercise of authority, they are more ready to accept it. This idea lies at the roots of many democratic institutions, and there is no reason to suppose that it could not be equally effective in industry. Thus one of the arguments for joint consultation is that it reinforces industrial authority, as it enables subordinates to help frame the regulations they are expected to obey.

CHAPTER IX

OVERALL AND COMPONENT ORGANISATIONS, AND THEIR GROUPS IN AIRLINES

The significance of the difference between 'component organisations' and 'groups' in the study of airline organisation

Component organisations may be traced from detailed organisation charts. Every branch on a well-constructed chart should represent a component organisation. The bases of components may often be distinguished through the titles of their managers, but sometimes supplementary information is required. Since organisation charts are based upon divisions of the *human element* in organisation, groupings of equipment or raw materials in an organisation with operatives ungrouped, will not be reflected in these charts. Thus the fact that an organisation is dealing with two sorts of raw materials with the same operatives and equipment is not revealed.

A summary of the bases of components of overall organisation

The basic reason for components in business organisations is manageability; there is an effective limit to the number of operatives and operations that can be controlled by one man.

Components also take account of specialisations which may increase the efficiency of the organisation and may exist without components. Or the components may set up specialisations between intermediaries and physical elements which again may increase the efficiency of the organisation. But sometimes components exist solely for manageability, and as a workman cannot push a wheelbarrow of more than a certain size, so a manager may divide his organisation and insert intermediaries between himself and his operatives to reduce the number of authority links attaching to any one person. Or the nature of the equipment and raw materials may be such that certain groupings of operatives are necessary or desirable to operate them, even if there is no specialisation.

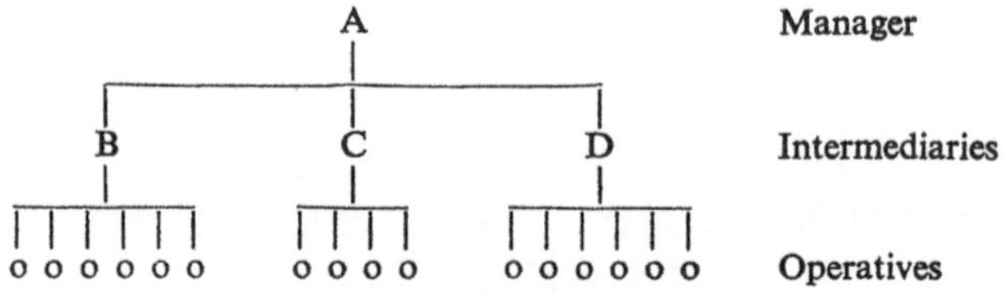

FIG. 8. *Components of overall organisation*

It is, of course, impossible to say what the basis of division into three components is in Fig. 8.

(i) If the operatives do not specialise in equipment or raw materials —then they are grouped (*a*) for ease of handling by the manager[1] (through intermediaries) or (*b*) because of managerial specialisation[2*] or (*c*) because of demands of equipment or raw materials.[3]
(ii) If the operatives do specialise, but the managers do not—then they are grouped (*a*) to specialise in equipment[4] or (*b*) to specialise in raw materials[5] or (*c*) to specialise in both equipment and raw materials[6] (where equipment specialises in raw materials).
(iii) If both managers and operatives specialise, the component will take account of managerial and operative specialisation in either (*a*) equipment,[7] (*b*) raw materials[8] or (*c*) equipment and raw materials.[9]

Sometimes these possibilities can be distinguished simply through the titles of the managers (see examples); often supplementary material is required to reach an answer.

Examples of titles of managers:

1 B.C.D. = shift 1, shift 2, shift 3, foremen.
2* B.C.D. = Purchasing, Production, Sales managers.
3 B.C.D. = Crew A, Crew B, and Crew C captains.
4 B.C.D. = milling, light turning, heavy duty shop supervisors.
5 B.C.D. = fine cloth, rough cloth, Harris Tweed uniform cutting supervisors.
6 B.C.D. = steel drilling, iron drilling, copper drilling foremen.
7 B.C.D. = Vanguard, Comet, Trident maintenance supervisors.
8 B.C.D. = financial, management, audit, accounting managers.
9 B.C.D. = goods, passenger and charter fleet managers.

Overall organisation without components or groups

It is possible to have an airline run with the minimum of organisation. For example, the proprietor of an airline may employ a manager

* Specialisation can also be in equipment and operatives.

who has no more organisation than one pilot, one aircraft and a number of passengers for a single route. We may describe the business diagrammatically thus:

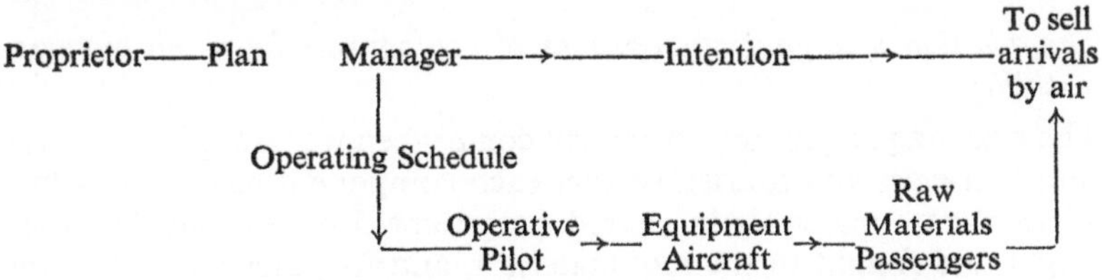

FIG. 9. *Overall organisation without components or groups*

In this case maintenance would be done by contracting. Selling would be contracted to agents, and so on.

It is not necessary to illustrate the simplest organisation by referring to flying. We might have used a sales organisation illustrating an airline that contracted its flying to another operator.

Component organisations based on manageability

The first step in complexity may come by employing a number of pilots, and flying a number of aircraft. It is simpler if all pilots and all aircraft are interchangeable, i.e. there is no specialisation in the use of equipment, and if passengers are indifferent as to which aircraft they go by. The picture may then be as in Fig. 10.

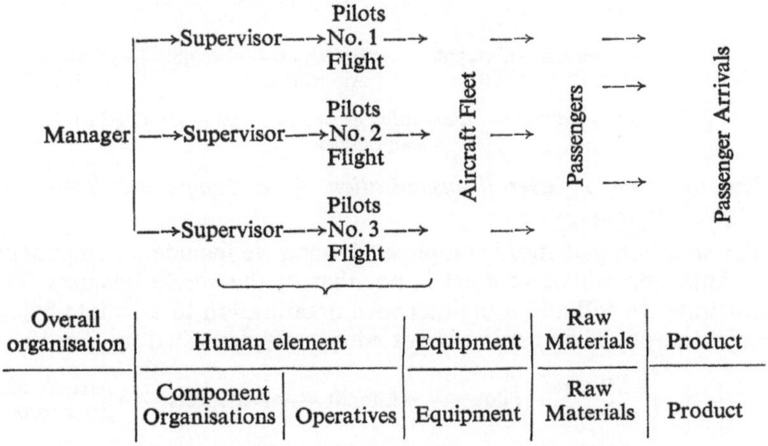

FIG. 10. *Component organisations based on manageability*

The pilots have been divided into flights to make them more manageable. The number of authority links attaching to the manager has been thereby reduced.

E

Note that in this illustration the three divisions of operatives share the use of ungrouped equipment, that in its turn is used to carry ungrouped raw materials, i.e. passengers.

The addition of organisation groups to components based on manageability

The next stage of complexity might come when we 'group' passengers into first-class and tourist, so that each component has to carry two sorts of raw materials in shared (ungrouped) equipment. We then might add freight to the raw materials, and freighter aircraft to the equipment, and specially trained freighter pilots to the operatives. The overall organisation now has components, and organisational groups of equipment and raw materials.

The picture at this stage is, however, still fairly simple, as the products of the component organisations are still the products of the business. Thus:

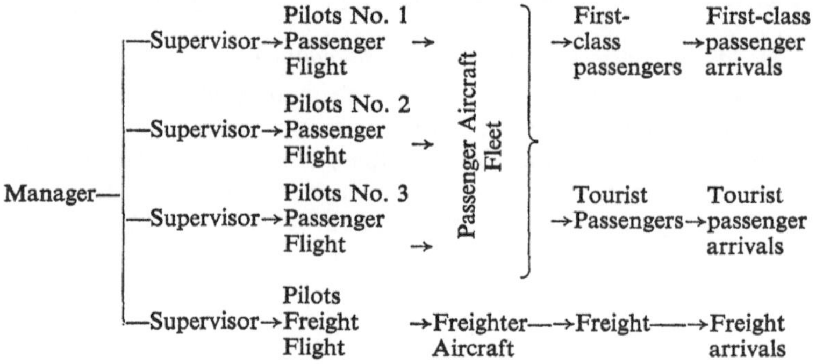

FIG. 11. *Addition of organisation groups to components based on manageability*

The inclusion in overall organisation of a component based on specialisation

The situation gets more complicated when we include a component organisation whose product is not that of the whole business. To illustrate we will add a maintenance organisation to a simple flying organisation. The position is not adequately described by Fig. 12.

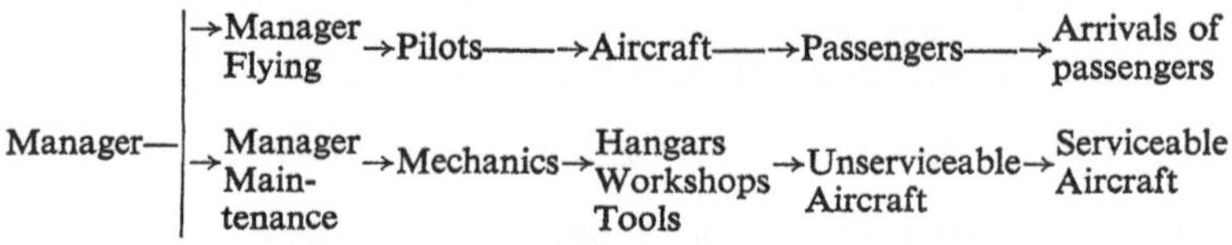

FIG. 12. *Inclusion in overall organisation of a component based on specialisation*

Serviceable aircraft are products of the organisation, of the maintenance manager, but they cannot be regarded as the product of the overall organisation since they do not leave the business and become exchanged for revenue. Nor would the general manager regard his raw materials as unserviceable aircraft. The situation must be presented as shown in Fig. 13.

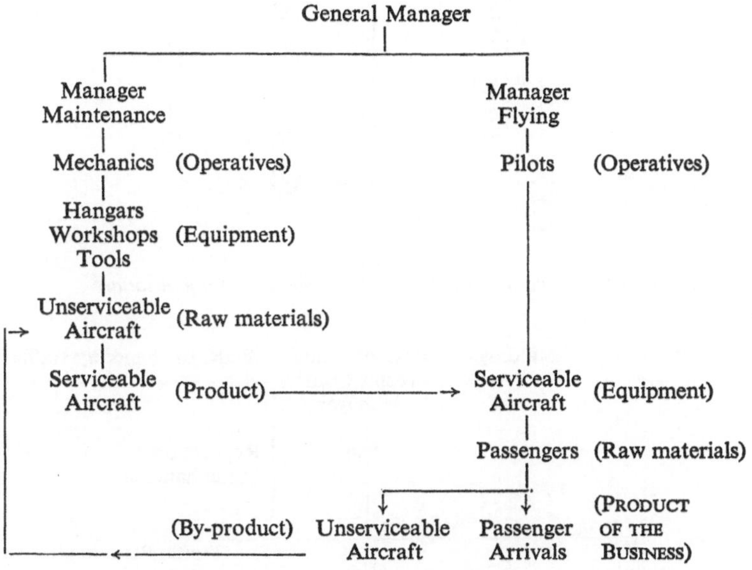

FIG. 13. *Illustrating the relationship between flying and maintenance components of an airline organisation*

Relationships among components and sub-components of overall organisation

Fig. 14 shows only the relationships among components and does not reveal relationships among components *and* sub-components.

We have already seen that the management 'process' consists of the activities of planning, motivating, controlling and contracting. None of these activities can be effective for long without a 'feedback' from the organisation. So there is a two-way link between a manager and his organisation.

Fig. 15 illustrates feedbacks from sub-components to a manager, and shows an inter-relationship of sub-components.

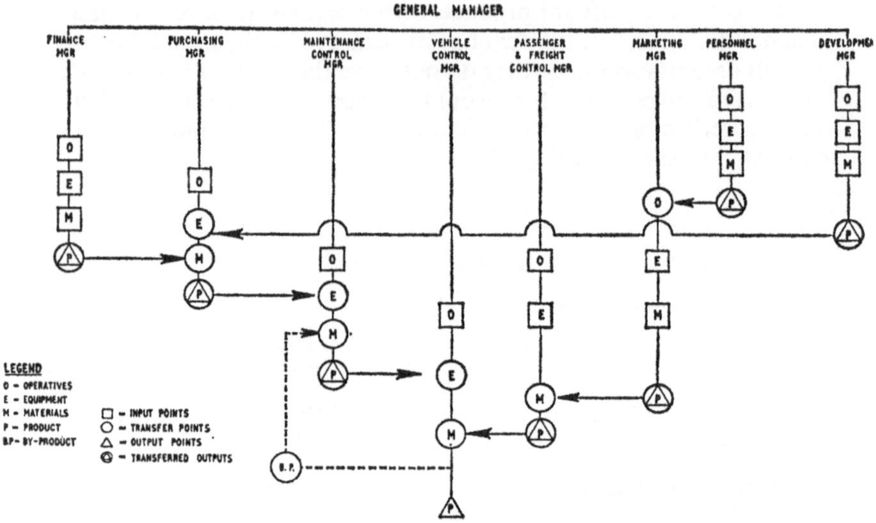

FIG. 14. *Illustrating inter-relations of components of organisation*

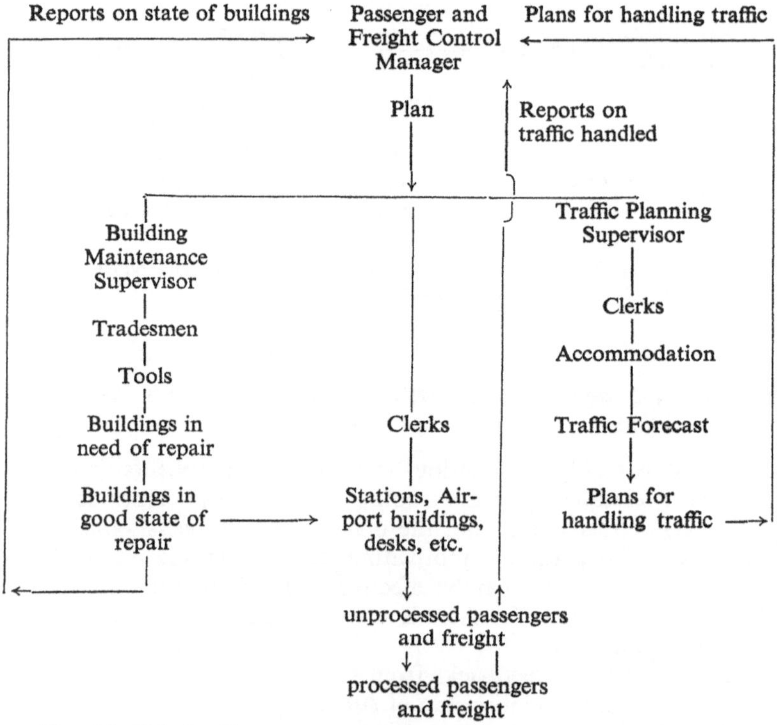

FIG. 15. *Relationships among components and sub-components of overall organisation*

TABLE 7. *Identifying elements of component organisations in the airline illustrated in* FIG. 14, *and showing the products of each organisation*

BRANCH OF SPECIAL MANAGEMENT	OPERATIVES	EQUIPMENT	RAW MATERIALS	PRODUCT
Finance	Clerks	Accommodation, office equipment	Stocks of money	Money distributed
Purchasing	Clerks	Accommodation, information, new designs, storage space	Money	Equipment required by maintenance dept.
Maintenance Control	Mechanics	Hangars, workshops, tools	Unserviceable aircraft	Serviceable aircraft
Vehicle Control	Pilots	Aircraft	Passengers and freight	Arrivals of passengers and freight
Passenger and Freight Control	Clerks	Stations, air-port buildings, desks, etc.	'Unprocessed' passengers and freight	'Processed' passengers and freight
Marketing	Sales Assistants	Sales offices, counters, etc. Entitlements to travel	Potential customers	'Booked' customers
Personnel	Personnel Assistants	Office, records, etc.	Applicants for employing in marketing	Employees in marketing divisions
Development	Assistants	Drawing offices, laboratories, etc.	Existing equipment	New designs

The situation depicted by Fig. 14 is over-simplified in a number of ways, among them:

(*a*) The role of the Finance Manager has been assumed to be only that of providing money for the use of the Purchasing Manager.

(*b*) The role of the Purchasing Manager has been assumed to be only that of buying equipment for the Maintenance Control Manager.

(*c*) The role of the Personnel Manager has been assumed to be only that of recruiting and training personnel for the Marketing Manager.

(*d*) The role of the Development Manager has been assumed to be only that of providing new ideas to the Purchasing Manager to become part of his buying 'equipment'.

(*e*) We have supposed a single component for each special manager, whereas for example the Vehicle Control Manager possibly has a number of sub-components as shown in Figs. 10 and 11.

(*f*) We have supposed that component organisations achieve their intentions without having to satisfy other requirements. We have already seen how *a business*, besides selling a product, must file income tax returns, obey labour laws and so on. Similarly *component organisations* have obligations. For example, it is obviously wrong to imagine flying passengers from one airport to another without its giving rise to consequential requirements. Traffic rights must be obtained, fares fixed, landing fees paid, fuel obtained, passengers' luggage dealt with, and so on.

(*g*) The by-product of vehicle-movement is not only unserviceable aircraft. Could an airline regard its business as complete when passengers, with baggage, are spewed on to the concrete runway? However unwelcome are the by-products of arrival, airlines have to concern themselves with the carriage of baggage and conduct of passengers, through customs and immigration to a ground vehicle. We might take the view that it is the passenger and freight handling organisation that delivers the product.

If we wanted to be more realistic we would have to include at least the sub-component organisations shown in Table 8. Many important ones have been excluded only because there is not space to deal with them all.

General management and component organisations

A general manager may be regarded as one who co-ordinates the activities of two or more component organisations based on the six fundamental business tasks of Finance, Purchasing, Personnel, Production, Development and Marketing. Thus a manager who co-ordinated Finance and Purchasing would by definition be a General Manager.

In Fig. 16 the General Manager is linked by eight authority links to the component managers. The component managers give rise to 28 'first-order' association links.

If as in Fig. 17 a 2nd-order General Manager is created to co-ordinate the activities of the managers of two former component organisations, six things happen:

(*a*) The two former component managers become sub-component managers. From being 2nd-order managers they have become 3rd-order managers. So to some extent their tasks lose status in the eyes of the organisation.

TABLE 8. *Sub-component organisations*

Special Management organisation	**Subsidiary 'Branch' organisations**	**Based on demands of**
FINANCE	(i) Revenue (ii) Expenditure	raw materials
	(i) General Accounts (ii) Budgets (iii) Costing	product
	(i) Typing (ii) electronic data processing	equipment
PURCHASING	(i) land and buildings (ii) aircraft and spares (iii) food (iv) ground vehicles (v) office equipment	product
	(i) buying by special contract (ii) buying by normal contract	equipment
MAINTENANCE	(i) Section 1 (ii) Section 2 (iii) Section 3, etc.	manageability
	(i) Viscount (ii) Comet (iii) Vanguard	raw materials
	(i) hangars (ii) workshop	equipment
	(i) repair and overhaul (ii) inspection	product
AIRCRAFT MOVEMENT CONTROL	(i) Flight 1 (ii) Flight 2 (iii) Flight 3, etc.	manageability
	(i) Viscount (ii) Comet (iii) Vanguard	equipment
PASSENGER AND FREIGHT CONTROL	(i) Shift 1 (ii) Shift 2 (iii) Shift 3	manageability
	(i) passengers (ii) freight	product
	(i) lost baggage (ii) enquiries (iii) complaints	by-products
	(i) town terminal (ii) airport (iii) cabin	equipment
MARKETING	(i) Area 1 (ii) Area 2 (iii) Area 3, etc.	raw materials
	(i) passengers (ii) freight	raw materials
	(i) counter sales (ii) telephone sales	equipment
PERSONNEL	(i) hourly-paid staff (ii) weekly-paid staff, etc.	raw materials
	(i) recruitment (ii) training (iii) industrial relations	product
DEVELOPMENT	(i) Viscount (ii) Comet (iii) Vanguard (iv) Trident	raw materials
	(i) airframe (ii) engines (iii) radio, etc.	raw materials

(*b*) As sub-component managers they are now subject to a general manager having to exercise only two authority links.

(*c*) The 1st-order General Manager is now required to exercise only seven authority links.

(*d*) 1st-order association links have been reduced from 28 to 21 in accordance with the formula $\frac{1}{2}n(n-1)$ where n=no. of managers of component organisations.

(*e*) One 2nd-order association link has been added to make a total of 22 for the overall organisation against the previous 28.

(*f*) Authority links for the overall organisation have been increased from eight to nine.

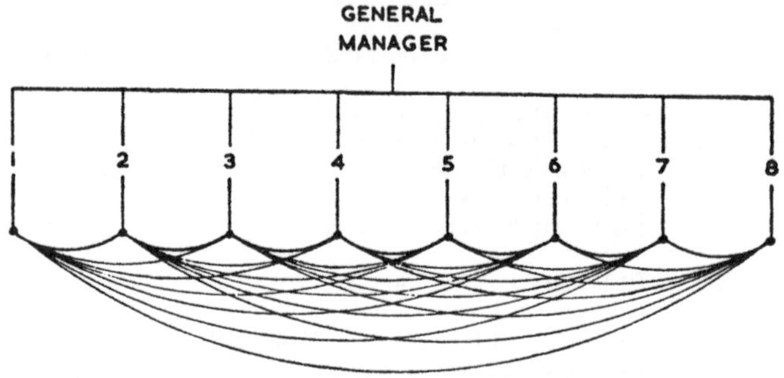

FIG. 16. *General management and 1st-order association links*

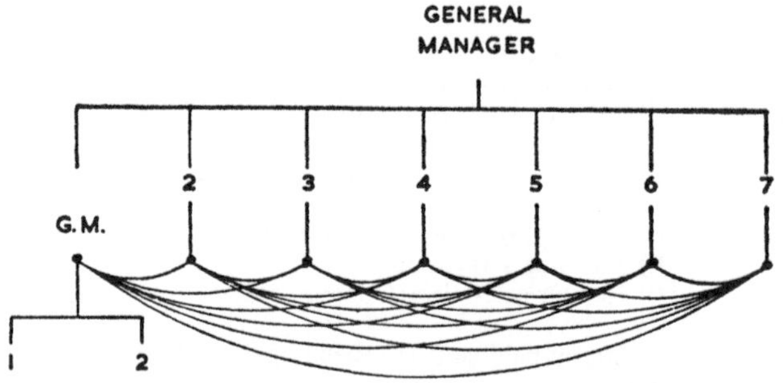

FIG. 17. *General management and 1st- and 2nd-order association links*

The effect of having operatives located at some distance from the manager

If a manager sends a number of operatives to a place where it is impracticable for him to supervise them, then he may have to appoint an on-the-spot supervisor. If the operatives had remained at hand he could have managed them, but because of the distance between two groups he cannot do so. A manager may plan for and motivate the distant group, but the feed-back will probably be too weak for effective control. Someone may have to oversee and check their work.

If an overall organisation with two components (say production and sales) were established with operatives from each component, in six distant places, the organisational structure might be depicted as in Fig. 18. The features of this situation are:

(*a*) There are direct links of authority from the production and sales managers of the component organisations to each of the respective managers of the sub-component organisations.

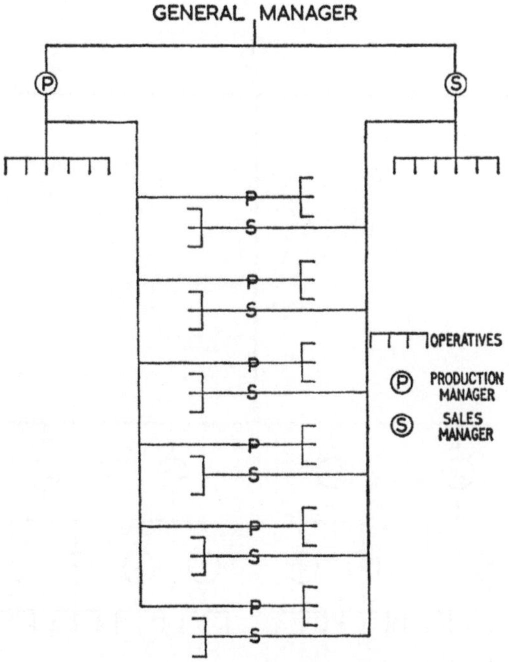

FIG. 18. *General management at the centre*

(*b*) The association link between production and sales manager in each of the six locations away from H.Q. are controlled at the level of the General Manager of the overall organisation.

(*c*) Thus while the General Manager has only two authority links, he is concerned with co-ordinating the work of sub-component organisations in six localities.

An alternative form of organisation would be as in Fig. 19.

The features of this situation are:

(*a*) The production and sales managers of the component organisations have lost their direct authority links with the respective sub-component managers. The component managers' authority must now be exercised, in principle, via the General Manager of the overall organisation, and the general managers of sub-component organisations. In practice component managers may short-cut this circuit in the exercise of their authority.

(*b*) The General Manager of the overall organisation now has six more authority links, but does not now have to concern himself with co-ordinating the activities of sub-components in the six localities.

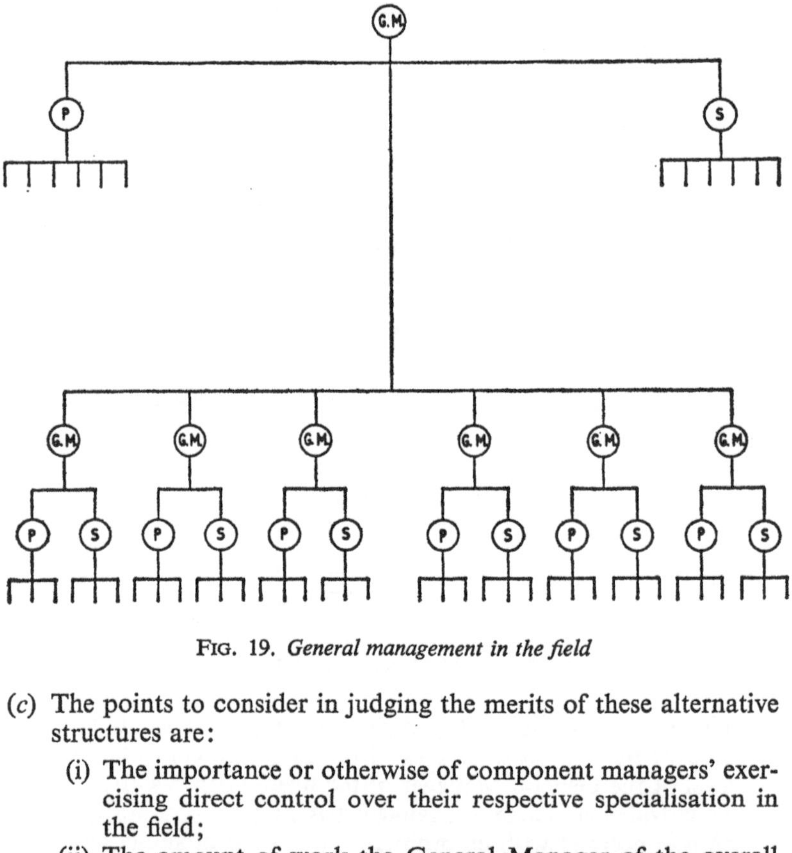

FIG. 19. *General management in the field*

(*c*) The points to consider in judging the merits of these alternative structures are:

(i) The importance or otherwise of component managers' exercising direct control over their respective specialisation in the field;

(ii) The amount of work the General Manager of the overall organisation would be involved in, to co-ordinate the activities of sub-component organisations in each location;

(iii) The amount of work involved for the overall General Manager in exercising of authority over six additional component general managers.

(*g*) If the six additional authority links proved too much of a burden for the overall General Manager he could reduce them by placing an intermediary between himself and the six. One effect of this would be to make the official authority channel between specialists even lengthier.

The effect of operatives and managers working at different times

If the manager of a component organisation requires a number of his operatives to work at times when it is impracticable to supervise them, then he may have to appoint 'shift' supervisors. 'Time' sub-component organisations are created much in the same way as 'local' sub-components. The differences are:

(*a*) 'Time' sub-components find delays in access to higher authority greater than those suffered by 'local' sub-components. A shift at 22.00 hours may have to wait until 09.00 hours on the next day for fresh instructions. But a local office, a thousand miles away from headquarters, by using telecommunications may suffer no more than a few minutes' delay by reason of distance alone.

(*b*) A 'time' component's antecedents may not be accessible. When a shift goes off duty, it takes the history of its operations with it, except for the entries that are made in its log.

A summary of the variables found among overall and component organisations and their groups in airlines

(*a*) The total numbers of component and sub-component organisations, and the ratio of the two. These variables depend on general management's judgements on what is the best organisational structure, and on the amount and sort of work that is done (i) by organisation and (ii) by contracting.

(*b*) The total number of input, transfer and output points and the ratios among them. These variables depend on the natural sequence of business tasks and management views on the need for 'independence' of components and sub-components.

(*c*) The representation of the six major business tasks in component and sub-component organisations. These variables depend on management views on the relative importance of the tasks in the business.

(*d*) The location of general management *vis-à-vis* special management, in the overall organisation. These variables depend upon the relative claims of authority and expertise in the conduct of airline business.

(*e*) The location of planning components within the overall organisation. These variables depend on management views on the importance of planning in various aspects of the airline business.
(*f*) Spans of control, and number of levels of authority. These variables may be the result of historical accident, or depend upon opinions of management.

Criteria of optimum divisions of overall organisation into components and sub-components in airline organisation

Criteria for the optimum structure of an airline organisation cannot be isolated from criteria of success of the business. This follows from the nature of organisation as an instrument for a purpose. Therefore criteria for optimum structure must include at least the following:

(*a*) The degree to which it satisfies the intention of the business.
(*b*) The degree to which it satisfies other requirements (i.e. legal, social, etc.).
(*c*) Costs of satisfying these needs, especially compared with the alternative of doing business by contracting.
(*d*) The matching of expertise with the needs of the various business tasks.
(*e*) The matching of authority with the needs of the managerial process.

The distribution of the six fundamental business tasks in ten airline organisations

Figs. 20 to 29 show the distribution of the six fundamental business tasks among the component organisations into which each of the overall organisations have been divided. In deciding whether or not to include a task, obviously being performed within a component, but appearing to be relatively unimportant, obviously the author had to exercise personal judgement. Some of the inclusions and the omissions are arguable, but these marginal uncertainties need not invalidate the general conclusions that are drawn.

Firstly, it is clear that managerial specialisation in components is more marked in some tasks than in others. All the airlines illustrated specialised in some aspect of production, almost all in finance, personnel and marketing, fewer in purchasing, and least in research and development. Two airlines dealt with production (passenger and freight, maintenance, and aircraft movement control) in three separate components. Five airlines dealt with passenger and freight, and aircraft movement control in one component, and with maintenance in another. Three airlines dealt with all three aspects of production within one component.

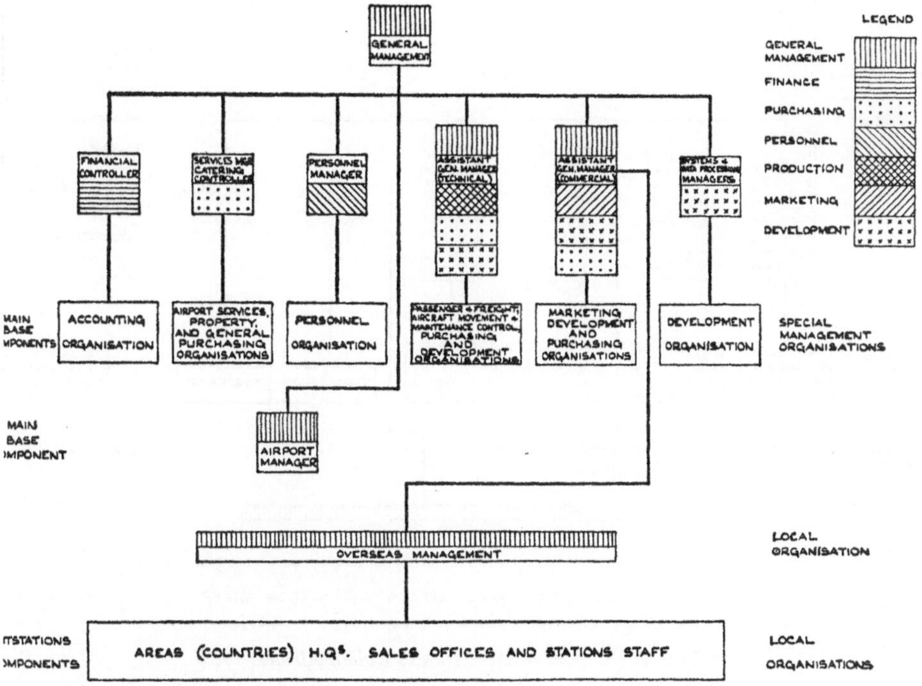

FIG. 20. *Organisation—Aer Lingus Irish International Airlines 1961*

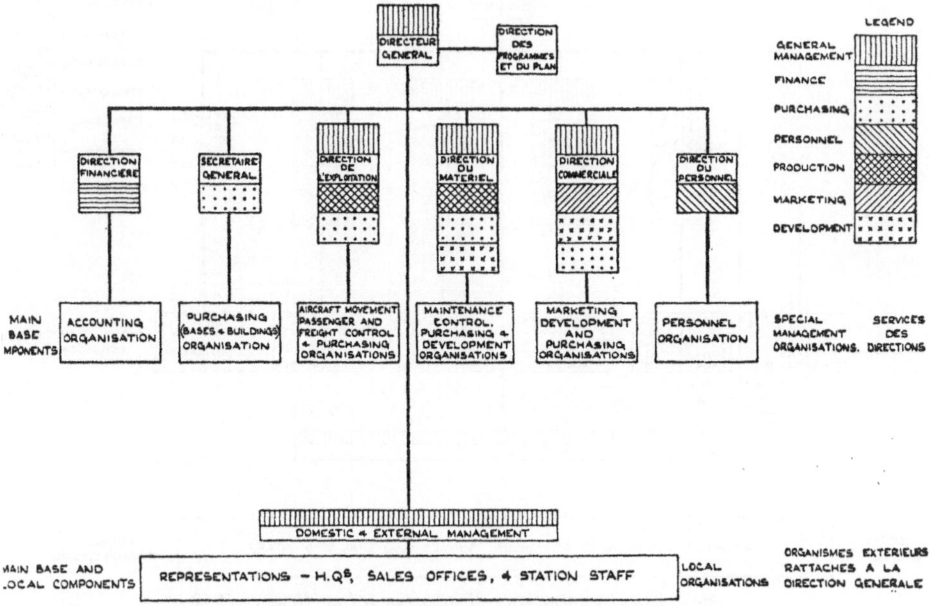

FIG. 21. *Organisation—Air France 1961*

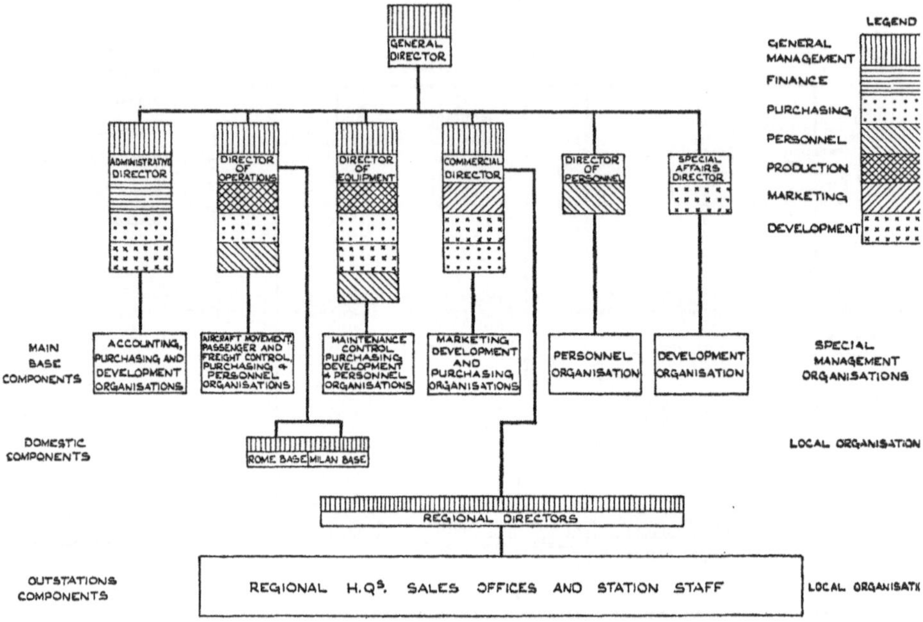

FIG. 22. *Organisation—Alitalia Italian Airlines 1961*

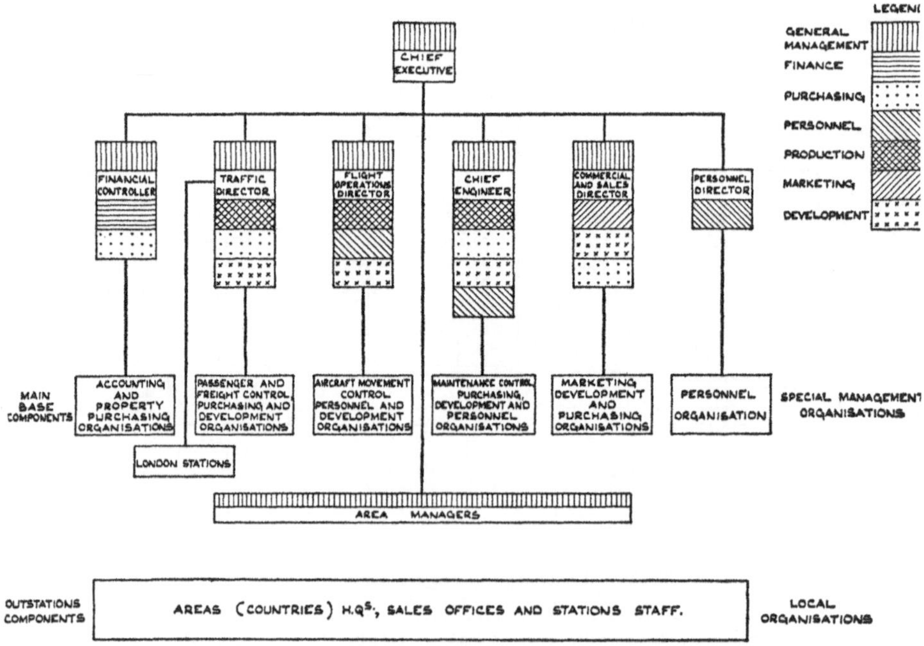

FIG. 23. *Organisation—British European Airways 1962*

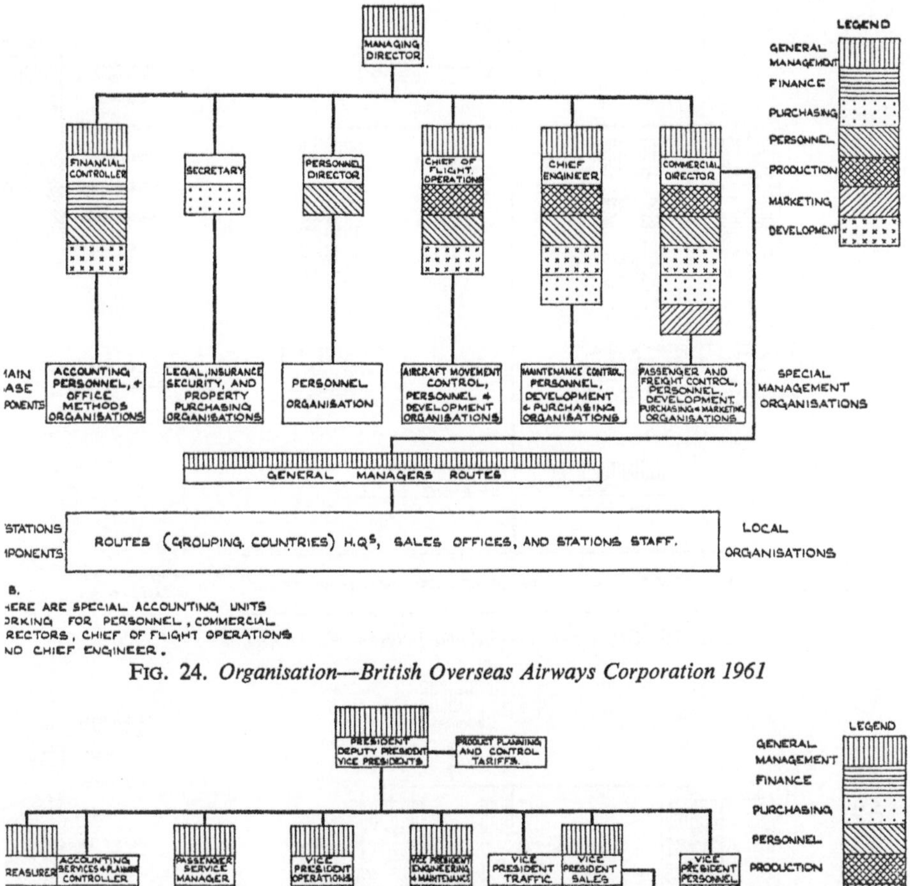

FIG. 24. *Organisation—British Overseas Airways Corporation 1961*

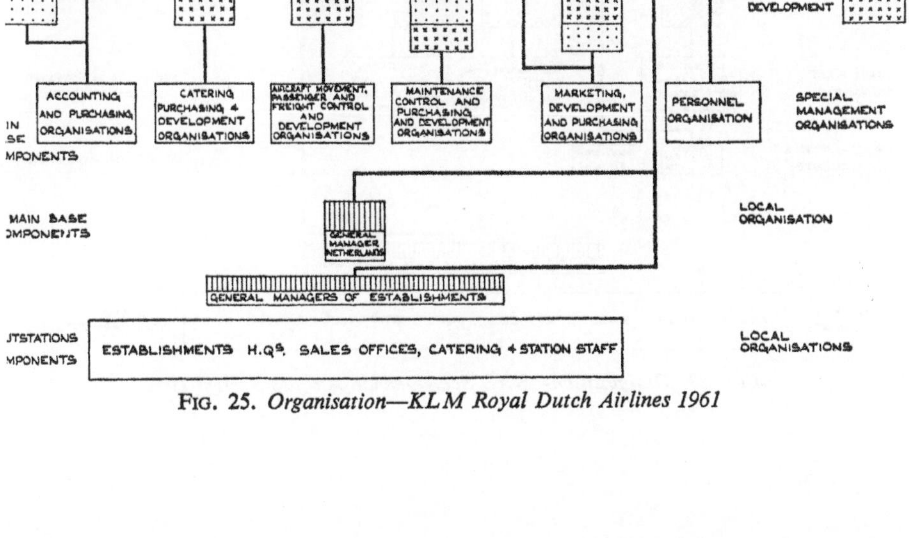

FIG. 25. *Organisation—KLM Royal Dutch Airlines 1961*

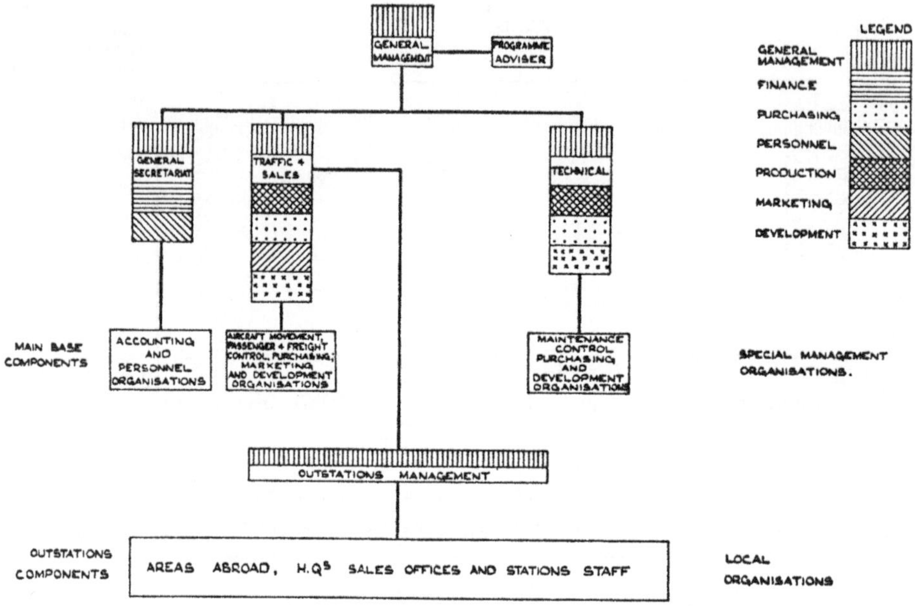

FIG. 26. *Organisation—Sabena Belgian World Airlines 1961*

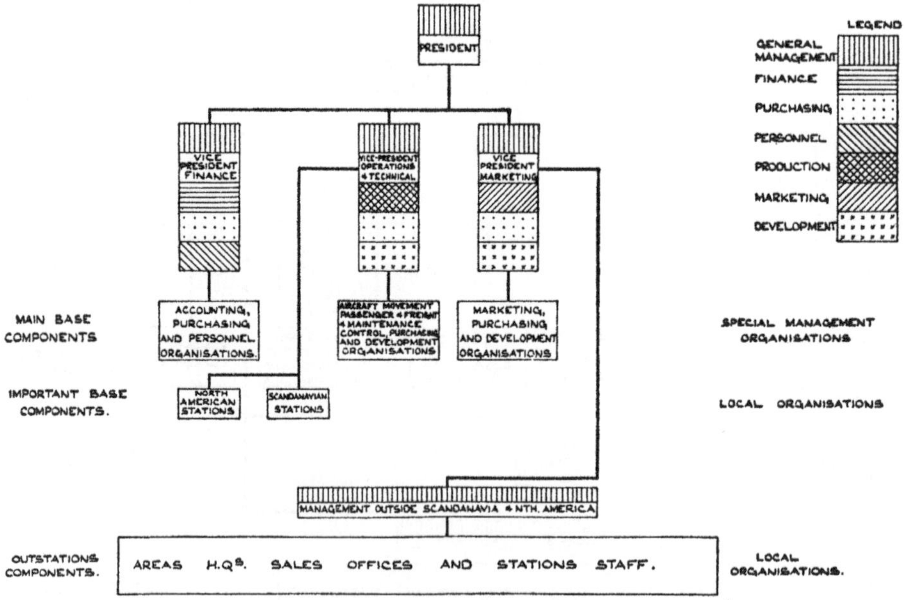

FIG. 27. *Organisation—S A S Scandinavian Airlines System 1962*

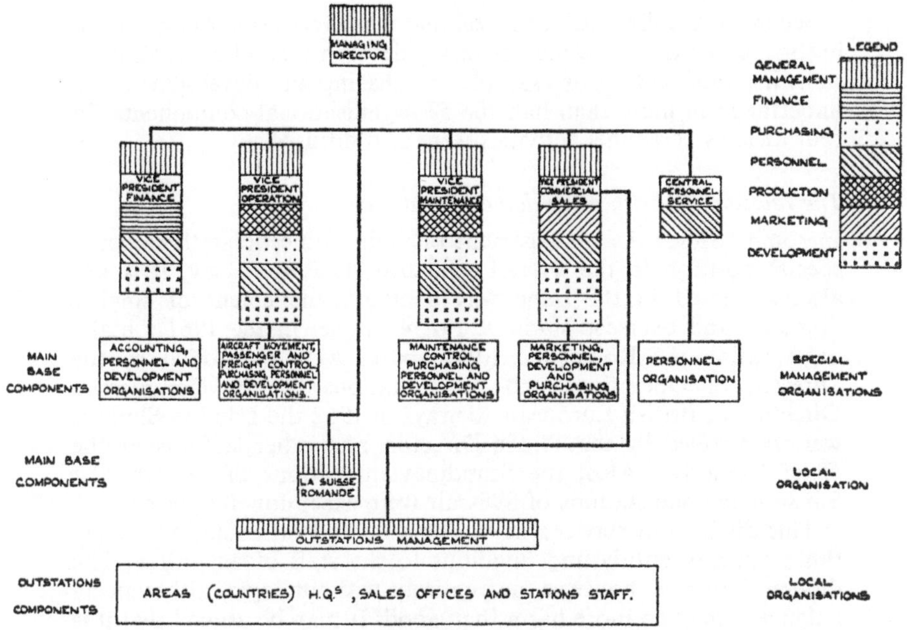

FIG. 28. *Organisation—Swissair 1962*

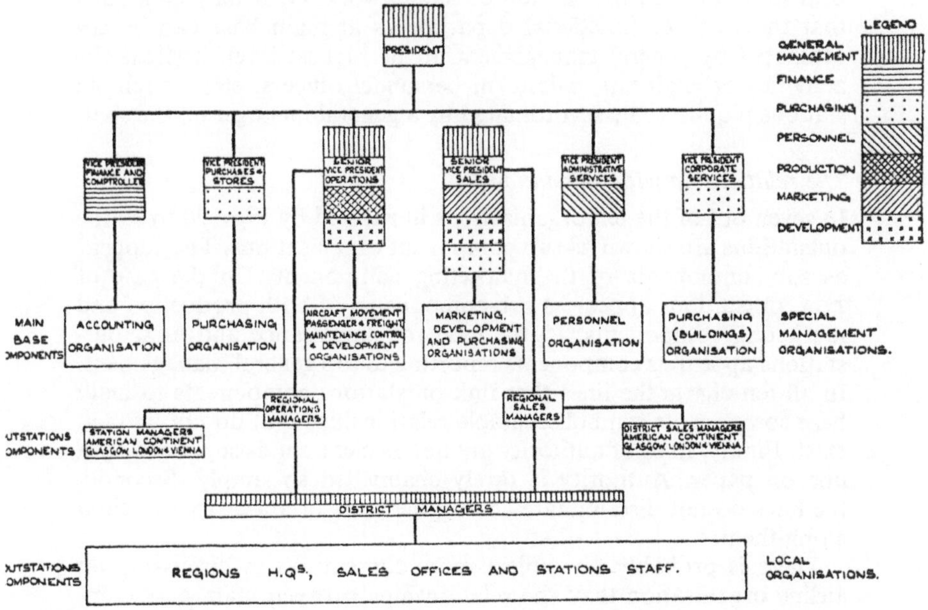

FIG. 29. *Organisation—Trans-Canada Air Lines 1961 re-named Air Canada in 1964*

Secondly, the illustrations reveal that managers primarily specialising in one of the fundamental tasks, develop secondary specialisations in other tasks. For example, purchasing and development are undertaken in more than half the 53 organisational components. In four airlines personnel activities were also diffused.

The relationship with main domestic stations

In some airlines the management of main domestic stations has a special position in the overall structure. That is to say, it is not always treated in the same way as the management of smaller domestic and overseas stations. For example, in the 1961 Alitalia organisation the Rome and Milan bases were controlled by the Director of Operations and other stations by the Commercial Director. In British European Airways in 1962 the London Stations were controlled by the Traffic Director, and other stations by the Chief Executive. Also, the Scandinavian stations of SAS and La Suisse Romande stations of Swissair were exceptionally placed.

This distinction between main domestic and other stations sometimes appears untidy and invidious to the staff of an airline. The differentiation is, however, not entirely without logic, although on balance it may do more harm than good. It may be argued that it is necessary to bring the expertise of certain functional departments to bear more directly on the hub of the network. Or it may be argued that the work of functional departments at main base can be coordinated by general management at the highest level, whereas the activities of engineers, salesmen, personnel officers, etc., at remote stations require to be co-ordinated by a general manager on the spot.

The relationship with 'outstations'

In seven out of the ten organisations illustrated by Figs. 20 to 29 the outstations are shown as sub-component organisations. They appear as sub-components of the marketing components. In the case of TCA, outstations appear as sub-components of both production and marketing components. In the cases of Air France and BEA, outstations appear as components reporting to top general management. In all ten charts the lines that link outstations components to main base components symbolise simple relationships that do not, in fact, exist. Firstly, lines of authority are not as clear cut as suggested by a line on paper. Authority is rarely channelled so simply. Secondly the lines do not discriminate among the sorts of authority exercised along them.

There is probably no subject more contentious in discussion on airline organisation than the relationships between main base components and outstation components. The subtleties and nuances in these relationships are manifest in the following statements (author's italics) made by six well-known airlines.

Company A

'Countries overflown or served are divided into *Areas*. These have a double role. Firstly they *represent* the company by seeing to the sale of tickets, sales promotion, publicity and public relations. Secondly, they have *executive responsibility* for certain station services, flight and ground personnel. Two areas *control* fleets that enable them to *operate effectively* on decentralised networks.'

Company B

'The manager or official-in-charge of a station abroad is invariably a member of the Commercial Department and is, therefore, *primarily responsible* to the Commercial Director. There are, however, two Regional Managers controlling all stations in certain areas. The managers or officials-in-charge of stations within these regions are *basically responsible* to the Regional Managers. At most of the on-line stations, however, the Engineering, Operations and Accounts Departments have *representatives* of their own. Whilst these three officers are responsible to their respective departmental heads, they are for *day-to-day administration* under the control of the manager of the station. Consequently, the manager is also responsible to a certain extent to these departmental heads.'

Company C

'Around the nucleus of the central management are the Regional directors and representatives, at home and abroad, *each responsible* for the Company's activities within his own area. The Commercial Department is *alert to maintain* the closest and most efficient co-operation between sales considerations, the operating departments and the regional direction at home and abroad.'

Company D

'The actual performance of a large proportion of the company's activities take place in establishments spread all over the world. These activities involve not only the handling of passengers and freight, the technical handling of the aircraft and the catering work at the various stations along the routes, but especially the sales, which for the greater part are effected outside of the homeland. In every establishment the *general management and responsibility* rests with the General Manager of the establishment. For each separate function he *comes under* the function management concerned at Headquarters (e.g. under Marketing for the sales function, under the

Operations Division for the handling functions, etc.) and *above* the local function supervisors in his establishment.'

Company E

'With one exception overseas organisations, whether individual divisions, regions or districts, *report directly* to the Vice-President, Marketing but *administratively* through the Vice-President Sales.'

Company F

'The staff (including accountants, salesmen, dispatchers, mechanics, etc.) of all offices abroad report to the Traffic and Sales Department. The advantage is that the whole staff of any representation reports solely to the local representative ('has the boss on the spot'). It is obvious, however, that they have to *follow working instructions* from their respective services at headquarters (which should reach them, in theory, through their boss, i.e. the local representative).'

The qualifications and hedging that may be found in these statements reflects the uncertainties that surround this important aspect of airline management.

CHAPTER X

THE HUMAN ELEMENT IN AIRLINE ORGANISATION

The range of knowledge and skills required of 'non-technical' personnel

We may refer to 'non-technical' personnel as those not engaged in flying, aircraft maintenance or in vocations like accountancy, law, etc. This is an ill-defined group whose skill is commonly under-rated. They are engaged among other things in passenger and freight control, and marketing.

The range of knowledge and skill of these operatives is ideally as follows:

Background knowledge of the industry and its environment.
  Aviation history and politics; IATA, ICAO and SITA; Airport authorities; Air traffic control; Aerodynamics; Meteorology.
Background knowledge of the particular company's business.
  Company history; company organisation; network geography; technical equipment and processes; airline economics; revenue accounting.
Conditions of employment.
  Conditions and privileges; recognition of ranks; selection, training and promotion procedures; Trade Unions.
Practical skills common to all non-technical operatives.
  Timetables; route construction; communications; other airlines' procedures; space control; emergency procedures.
Practical skills required by operatives dealing with passengers.
  Ticketing; tariffs; passenger handling; baggage handling; services extra-to-carriage; reservations.
Practical skills required by operatives dealing with cargo.
  Air waybills; rates; cargo handling; service extra to carriage; securing space.
Practical skills required by operatives doing aircraft and load handling.
  Load and trim sheet; mechanics of loading.
Social skills.

Dealing with the general public; dealing with agents; advertising, publicity and sales promotion; dealing with staff.

These operatives work in five main localities:

(*a*) Cargo offices in towns.
(*b*) Sales offices in towns.
(*c*) Passenger terminals in towns.
(*d*) Cargo areas at airports.
(*e*) Passenger handling areas at airports.

A classification of services performed by non-technical personnel

Although the industry has been able to standardise much of its terminology, it has not succeeded with the naming of jobs. A reservations clerk in one company is a telephone sales clerk in another, and a passenger agent in another. Even within one organisation there may be local variations; a reservations clerk in one district may be called a distribution, servicing, check-point, or pre-flight clerk in another, depending upon particular emphases in duties. In order to avoid confusions arising from such differences in job titles, management should aim to group these operatives under as few as possible headings which describe the services they provide. Such a classification might be as follows:

TABLE 9. *Classification of services performed by non-technical personnel*

PASSENGER	CARGO	
Sales promotion		Marketing
Passenger Sales	Cargo sales	
Seat procurement	Space procurement	Production
Space Control		
Passenger Service	Cargo Handling	
Aircraft and Load Handling		

In some circumstances these services may be provided by the same people. For example, in a small sales office there may be one person dealing with both passenger and cargo business; or cargo sales, and space procurement might be combined. Again, there may be some sub-division, with separate groups handling counter, postal and telephone sales; or a large cargo unit may be divided into import and export sections. Despite such local variations the services listed above are the main ones on which the 'non-technical' personnel are employed. Operatives are not recruited 'off-the-street' for all these classes of work. Previous sales experience is generally required for sales promotion staff; space control people are normally recruited from among those with a background of seat or space procurement; and in only some airlines is there 'direct entry' to aircraft and load handling.

'Generalists' or 'specialists'?

The selection standards of 'non-technical' personnel depend, among other things, on the individual airlines' personnel policy. The problem to be resolved is whether an airline is to go for 'specialists' or 'generalists' or, to put it another way, how versatile the airline wants its staff to be. Specialisation makes it possible to modify, perhaps to lower, an airline's entry requirements, and training can be streamlined (though not necessarily shortened). Generalisation, on the other hand, makes for flexibility in staffing and offers to individuals better career prospects. Many of the tasks to be performed in an airline are essentially very simple. They could be performed by people of less ability than are generally employed on them. Indeed, they sometimes are, by temporary staff taken on for seasonal work. However, this throws an additional burden on the supervisor, because he is not only called on to cope with anything out of the ordinary, but also has to spend more of his time in 'quality control'. The routine nature of many individual tasks means that airlines must provide for job rotation, or job mobility, because only in this way can they offer able employees the variety of work necessary to maintain their interest.

Operatives who do not make careers in airlines

The overall wastage among operatives, which commonly runs from 10 per cent to 20 per cent per annum, gives a misleading impression of the situation in most airlines. Usually an airline has a solid core of 'career' men, and a substantial fringe of short-service staff.

Some sections, for example, cabin service and passenger escort, are staffed by young women of marriageable age who do not stay for more than a few years. Most airlines engage temporary staff on a seasonal basis to carry out single tasks such as routine check-in work.

The main problems management faces with this sort of staff are those of ensuring that they do not lower the general standards of training and recruitment, and at the same time to see that time spent on training is not disproportionate to the total length of time spent in airline employment.

Informal status symbols in airline organisation

W. Karraker, a member of the Air Line Pilots' Association of the USA, in his address to the 2nd annual Air Transport Conference at New York University 1962, told of an experiment he conducted in 1954 to test the influence of informal status symbols. On a six-day flight from New York to Buenos Aires and back he had a co-pilot who had been a major in the Army Air Corps during World War II. From the beginning of the flight Karraker manoeuvred him into every informal status symbol normally restricted to the Captain. Whenever they went through a door Karraker held it open and persuaded the co-pilot to go through first. When the stewardess brought lunch to the cockpit Karraker insisted that the co-pilot ate first. At overnight stops Karraker threw his cap on the hotel bed away from the window, thereby pre-empting the co-pilot's usual resting place. Karraker was check pilot at the time so he asked the co-pilot to fly from the left-hand seat of the aircraft for the entire southbound portion of the flight. Karraker told how by the middle of the second day the co-pilot was in complete command of the aircraft, and it was quite a job to get back control from him.

When Karraker was flying DC-6s between New York and Puerto Rico there were usually five in the crew: captain, first officer, flight engineer and two stewardesses. Over a period of time he kept track of crews arriving and departing in taxis from the hotel at Puerto Rico, and found that in 8 out of every 10 such taxis the crew sat according to status; the captain in the right rear seat, the co-pilot left rear, the senior stewardess centre rear, flight engineer right front and junior stewardess centre front, beside the driver.

Airline pilots and the professions

To emphasise the need to maintain strict standards, pilots sometimes refer to their job as a profession. They may hope to acquire some of the traditional status of the learned professions of the law, church and medicine. But it is as well to remember that these three occupations are called professions because those who practise them make a public avowal of faith in certain principles. The lawyer's belief in the rule of law, the doctor's belief in the sanctity of human life, and the churchman's belief in God, are uncompromising to a degree that a pilot could not maintain in, say, his belief in promoting safety.

The professional man vows to uphold his ideals through thick and thin, and these vows may sometimes prove to be incompatible with the daily compromises necessary in the rough and tumble of business. Pilots should not be encouraged to take a 'holier-than-business' attitude to their daily work. Good doctors, clergymen and lawyers are more single-minded in their pursuit of ideals than business men can ever hope to be. And society demands a higher-than-business standard of them. This is illustrated by the contempt in which the lawyer turned business hireling is held.

It is safer for pilots to regard their job as a craft that is exercised for profit, but which demands exceptional skills in pursuit of the perfection aimed at by good craftsmen.

Pilots' Associations

The Air Line Pilots' Association of the USA, besides having the role of a Trade Union, has a Committee of Professional Standards, charged with raising the standards of flying. The British Air Line Pilots Association, while being an active Trade Union, still finds time to think about operating procedures. In Britain there is also a Guild of Air Pilots and Air Navigators that is concerned with vocational standards.

These associations may lobby for stricter licensing laws, and so ensure that no-one is allowed to fly until *fully* qualified. This prevents a man from beginning to fly commercially with the minimum qualification, and completing his qualification by experience on-the-job. On the other hand, there will never be the need for pilots' associations to fill the same role as say a Bar Association, as in aviation the State has always made stringent laws, and eliminated the unfit. Airline managements have themselves insisted on the highest standards from applicants, and have thus left less work for pilots' associations to do in the way of raising standards.

Pilots' associations should very properly be given a say in the making of flying regulations. Otherwise there is a danger in their assuming the role of defending counsel for all pilots in breach of regulations that have been imposed upon them.

Attitudes to reporting dangerous incidents

Because the activities of airline organisation are widespread, managements rely on staff, for feedbacks on the safety and efficiency of operations. Pilots complete 'voyage' reports on difficulties encountered en route. Technical log books record irregularities in the performance of equipment. Station logs report troubles that have occurred during embarkation or disembarkation.

The reliability of these feedback depends upon the attitude of those reporting. Staff must believe that frankness 'pays', in the long run; they must be keen to co-operate in endeavours to improve standards. Their frankness and keenness will in turn depend upon the wisdom with which rewards and punishments are meted out.

There were some disasters in the United States in the late 1950s that prompted Congress to create the Federal Aviation Agency. The early activities of this Agency frightened pilots and caused them to dry up as sources of information on 'near-misses'. Indeed the Agency were able to announce a significant reduction in near-misses, as a result of fewer reports coming in.

Nostalgia for obsolete skills

It is a common experience among people who acquired a considerable skill and then gave up practising it, to feel a strong urge to renew their fading skill. Actors who have been away from the stage for some years, or teachers from their classrooms, or accountants from their books, are among those who feel the pull of past skill. In most cases this sort of person is able to return at least for brief periods to enjoy a little exercise. The opportunities for practice still exist because the skills still exist, and it is a matter of adjusting personal circumstances.

Airlines may be regarded as somewhat exceptional in the wide variety of skills they employ, and in the complexity of some of them. It would not be surprising to find a number of airline executives yearning to regain lost skills. But what is more important is that there are many very skilled operatives with nostalgic longings for skills that have become or are becoming obsolete.

The rapid technological advances that have occurred in aviation have rendered obsolete the skills of innumerable men in mid-career. The use of metal for airframes affected woodworkers; the advent of turbine engines affected those skilled in the maintenance of piston engines; the advent of transistors has affected the radio-mechanic trained to deal with valves. But nowhere is this more striking than with pilots at the coming of automation.

The best example of this was the automatic pilot. For years after its introduction it was almost a ritual for many pilots to fly by hand during climbs, descents and in turbulent weather. This was despite the fact that auto-pilots were able to hold steadier flight paths in all these circumstances, and that, in rough air, automatic flight imposed 7 per cent less stress on airframes.

Those pilots who use automation as fully as they can in the interests of safety, efficiency and passenger comfort have to depend upon training periods for maintaining manual flying efficiency. This means that management must ensure that lack of practice on the line must be offset by increased training for as long as manual skills are called for on occasions.

The importance of small working units for morale

It is reasonable to suppose that operatives work with better morale in small working units. Good morale in business is a spirit engendered by the business that raises men's conduct above the level of their conduct as individuals. Bad morale makes them do bad things that they would not do as individuals. Good morale makes them do good things that they would not do as individuals. Large working units tend to be impersonal, and the individual loses the feeling that his conduct has any effect on the whole unit.

In some of the world's major airlines big working units are found where good morale is of prime importance. In one company in 1962 one flight manager in New York had over 600 pilots reporting to him. In many companies flight managers have to control over 100 pilots. Large working units are also commonly found among cabin staff organisations. One airline has adopted the device of breaking-up 100-strong 'flights' of cabin staff by appointing a number of 'aunts' and 'uncles', without organisational status, who are expected to work informally among groups of 25 cabin staff.

The skill of the maintenance engineer

Views on the training and education needed by maintenance engineers, differ from airline to airline. On the one hand we have maintenance organisations staffed almost wholly by men whose training is limited to that of the skilled mechanic, and on the other, organisations employing hundreds of engineers with academic qualifications.

The productivity of maintenance workers varies from airline to airline. In 1960 the productivity of American workers was over double that of British maintenance engineers. This may reflect the capital invested per head, but it may also reflect differences in skill.

In considering the right balance of qualifications in a maintenance organisation the critical features are:

(*a*) Aircraft are designed to fly near to the limit of their capabilities, to avoid unnecessary weight;
(*b*) Because aircraft must be capable of adjusting to a variety of conditions, control systems are complicated, and provide plenty of room for failure;
(*c*) Because airlines do not make much money the engineer cannot always be 'erring on the safe side';
(*d*) Maintenance usually constitutes about one-fifth of total expenses;
(*e*) The amount of time spent on maintenance may vary from one-third to one-half of the life of aircraft;
(*f*) Airlines may spend up to 30 per cent more money on maintenance than on depreciation of aircraft and spares.

The effect of change on 'non-technical' personnel

The airline industry has been a rapidly changing one, and these changes have affected non-technical personnel no less than flying and aircraft maintenance personnel. There has been a continual need for retraining existing staff, as well as training newcomers. This considerable burden cannot be eased by regarding training as something that occurs only on classroom courses. Most training should take place on the job. Most airlines cannot afford to have their staff away from their jobs for lengthy periods, to enable them to attend classroom courses. The airline industry offers exceptional opportunities for developing on-the-job training because of the considerable fluctuations that occur in workload.

CHAPTER XI

INDUSTRIAL RELATIONS

Introduction

The 1961–62 Annual Report of Qantas Airways says, *inter alia*:

'Staff decreased by 283 during the year due mainly to careful economy in the replacement of terminating employees, including 84 retirements. Because of the downturn in traffic and the substantial reduction in the Company's earnings, 69 staff became surplus to requirements and it was unfortunately necessary to retrench them.

With the exception of one major dispute over the redundancy issue, which resulted in a loss of 1,000 manhours, satisfactory industrial relations prevailed throughout the year. Total time lost as a result of stoppages was limited to 27,000 manhours, compared with 39,000 manhours lost in the preceding year. Progress was made on the agreement with the Australian Federation of Air Pilots which was subsequently signed on June 27, 1962, by the Company and representatives of the Federation, and later certified by the Commonwealth Conciliation and Arbitration Commission.'

At March 31, 1962, Qantas employed 6,604 staff at 55 points in 27 countries throughout the world. Included in this total were 893 locally appointed employees at overseas stations. In the same year KLM reported: 'The number of employees decreased from 18,065 at the end of 1961 to 16,728 at the end of 1962. This reduction of staff took place within and beyond The Netherlands and involved both flying and ground personnel. To a large degree, the reductions were effected through normal labour attrition and by restricting to a minimum the replacement of employees who left the Company.

The 1962 wage agreement concluded with the recognised Dutch trade unions for the ground staff was approved by the Government Mediation Board. A collective agreement expiring on July 1, 1963, was concluded with the Association of KLM Pursers and Stewards;

this agreement too was approved by the Government Mediation Board.

The Joint Consultation Committee and its sub-committees were elected on November 28, 1962, and formally installed in December. The positive influence which this Committee also exerted on the atmosphere within the Company during 1962 is most gratifying.'

These extracts illustrate the important aspect of airline management relations that is covered by the term industrial relations. They throw light on the character of these relations varying from differences to disputes and to agreements. They refer to the manner in which the issues between employers and employees are resolved, in terms of negotiation, consultation, mediation, conciliation and arbitration. They point to the fact that employers and employees have created organisations to handle these relations. The industrial relations branches of airline personnel departments, and workers' associations at shop floor level are joined to the big employers' federations and trade unions respectively. Each of these works through the voluntary or state organs of conciliation and arbitration. Courts, Commissions and Government Mediation Boards are all part of the industrial relations scene.

The extracts also reveal one of the burning issues of the industry as well as the more common issues of wages, hours of work and so on. The industry's economic ups and downs have threatened the security of employment of large numbers. Both employers and employees have made mistakes in the handling of what is referred to as redundancy, or retrenchment and even 'early retirement'.

The organisations set up to deal with airline industrial relations, although often founded on good intentions, have almost always disappointed those who hoped for trouble-free relations. But a lot has been learnt. It has been discovered that industrial relations is not a field for the 'good-hearted' amateur. Industrial relations management requires as much skill and experience as any other specialist management.

The nature of industrial relations

Industrial relations are between employers and employees. Employers are often represented by personnel managers, and employees by trade union officials. The conduct of industrial relations is governed by constitutions and rules of procedure. Meetings of the two sides are carefully arranged, regulated and minuted. The relations are conducted within certain institutions with various names (like committee, panel and council). The restraints in procedure are regarded as inherently conciliatory. The aim of the relations is to obtain agreement on issues that affect both sides. If the conciliatory procedures fail to achieve agreement there is resort to arbitration.

The differences from airline to airline

The managements of most of the world's major airlines are involved in 'industrial relations'. Most of them have permanent 'machinery' for dealing with workers' demands for increased pay and better working conditions. Most of them have procedures for dealing with disputes between employers and employees.

Constitutions, and rules of procedure, differ from airline to airline. The number and nature of industrial relations institutions vary widely. The degree of autonomy of the 'machinery' differs. But there are certain constitutional principles common to many that are illustrated by the British situation.

International airlines are brought together by their having to observe labour laws, and industrial relations conventions of the different countries to which they fly.

Origins of industrial relations

The origins of industrial relations in airlines reflect the political, social and economic conditions of their mother countries, and of those to which they fly. These origins may be classified as:

(*a*) By accord; where both parties seek the benefits of conciliatory procedures;
(*b*) By compulsion; where dissenting employers or employees have not been able to resist pressure from the other side;
(*c*) By compliance with national code; where an industrial code is established by law for all industries;
(*d*) By compliance with industrial code; where a code is established by law for a particular industry.

Origins of airline industrial relations in Britain

The origins of airline industrial relations in Britain are in the Civil Aviation Act, 1946, requiring the industry:

(*a*) To establish machinery to regulate terms and conditions of employment;
(*b*) To discuss matters affecting the safety, health and welfare of workers in the industry, and other matters of mutual interest;
(*c*) To establish procedures for settling differences.

These three obligations may be referred to briefly as obligations:

(*a*) To negotiate.
(*b*) To consult.
(*c*) To seek arbitration, if necessary.

The Institutions of the British airlines industrial relations machinery

The whole machinery may be referred to as the 'National Joint Council for Civil Air Transport'. This title is also used for the plenary assembly of representatives.

The constituent institutions are:

The Council (the plenary assembly).
The Standing Joint Committee.
Sectional Joint Panels (12 in number).
Local Panel Committees.
Local Joint Panel Committees.
The Secretariat.

Representation in the National Joint Council for (British) Air Transport

The following employers were represented on the Employers' side of the NJC in 1963:

British European Airways.
British Overseas Airways.
Independent Operators.

The following trade unions were represented on the Employees' side of the NJC:

Amalgamated Engineering Union	(AEU)
Amalgamated Society of Woodworkers	(ASW)
Association of Engineering and Shipbuilding Draughtsmen	(AESD)
Association of Supervisory Staffs, Executives and Technicians	(ASSET)
British Airline Pilots' Association	(BALPA)
Clerical and Administrative Workers' Union	(C & AWU)
Electrical Trades Union	(ETU)
Merchant Navy and Airline Officers' Association	(MN & AOA)
National Association of Clerical and Supervisory Staffs	(NACSS)
National Society of Coppersmiths, Braziers and Metal Workers	(NSCBMW)
National Society of Painters	(NSP)
National Union of Furniture Trade Operatives	(NUFTO)
National Union of General and Municipal Workers	(NUGMW)
National Union of Sheet Metal Workers and Braziers	(NUSMWB)
National Union of Vehicle Builders	(NUVB)
Radio Officers' Union	(ROU)
Transport and General Workers' Union	(TGWU)

Constitutions

'Constitutions' usually attempt to embody, in a single or small number of documents, fundamental activities and institutions.

Constitutions are not always wholly or even partly written. Conventions established by the spoken word, and custom and usage can sometimes work as effectively as a written constitution.

De Tocqueville, in his *La Democratie en Amerique*, refers to a constitution as 'an instrument of special sanctity, distinct in character from all other laws, and alterable only by a peculiar process'.

This is true of constitutions of industrial relations. They are difficult to alter. For example, the Constitution of the British National Joint Council for Civil Air Transport has not been altered substantially since it was written in 1946, although both sides have agreed for many years that it needs revision.

The Constitution of the British NJC was embodied in two documents:

(*a*) Headed: National Joint Council for Civil Air Transport Constitution and Rules of Procedures.

(*b*) Headed: Constitution, Functions and Rules of Procedure of Local Committees—UK Establishments.

This Constitution:

Enshrines obligations laid upon airlines by statute;
Establishes rights of membership of the Council;
Lays down rules of conduct of the business of the Council;
Establishes a procedure for the settlement of differences;
Establishes the institutions of Sectional Joint Panels,
  Local Panel Committees and Local Joint Panel Committees;
Enables *ad hoc* committees to be appointed;
Provides for the financing of the institutions;
Provides means of amending the constitution.

Powers of Industrial Relations Institutions of British Airlines

The National Joint Council

Although in theory plenary powers are vested in the NJC, this body is too unwieldy to act quickly, so much of its power is delegated.

The Standing Committee of the National Joint Council with 6 members a side, has power to;

Determine conditions of employment common to employees covered by more than one panel in the industry;

Act as arbitration board for differences referred to it by Sectional Joint Panels;
Act in all other matters requiring the authority of the Council, and calling for quick action.

Sectional Joint Panels

Each Panel has plenary powers:

To *negotiate* and *settle* terms and conditions of employment of peculiar interest to employees covered by it;
To refer differences either to the Council, or to an outside arbitrator (Ministry of Labour or Industrial Court);
To act as an arbitration board for differences referred to it by local panel committees.

Local Panel Committees

have power, restricted as follows:

(*a*) To *consider* and *decide* matters of local concern;
(*b*) To refer differences to the Employers' Head Office, to a National Sectional Panel, or to the Council;
(*c*) they may not *make decisions*
Contrary to national trade questions, such as wages and like subjects; or
On wide questions of policy going beyond the base concerned, but may *discuss* such matters and refer them to either a National Sectional Panel (Joint Sectional Panel) or to the NJC.
(*d*) To *consider* particularly the following matters:

PRODUCTION MATTERS

Maximum and most efficient use of vehicles, plant and machinery;
Upkeep and conservation of jigs, tools, gauges and fixtures;
Improvements in methods of working to secure better results and/or higher or better production;
Efficient use of the maximum number of productive hours;
Elimination of defective work, unnecessary journeys and waste;
Efficient use of materials supplied and intelligent salvaging of discarded parts;
Proper use of safety precautions and devices, and the furtherance of all steps designed to reduce and prevent accidents.

WORKING CONDITIONS

Ventilation of offices, hangars and workshops;
Sanitary and cloakroom facilities;
First-aid arrangements;

Catering arrangements;
Protective clothing;
Transport to and from work;
Any matters which are related to the general welfare of staff, but which do not come within the scope of Union agreements.

Local Joint Panels

have the same powers as Local Panel Committees in respect of matters that are of common concern to employees of more than one Local Panel Committee.

The significance of the terms 'Sectional', 'Local' and 'Joint' in British airline IR institutions

Sectional (National)

'Sectional' panels are institutions providing for the sectional interests of certain occupational groups. The twelve British national panels, and the unions represented on them are:

Pilots	BALPA
Navigating and Engineering Officers	MNAOA
Radio	ROU
Supervisory, Engineering and Technical	ASSET, AEU, ETU
Draughtsmen, Planners and Tracers	AESD, ASSET
Engineering and Maintenance	AEU, ASW, ETU, NUSMW & B, T & GWU, NUGMW, NUFTO, NUVB, NSP, NSCBMW
Surface Transport and Goods Handling	T & GWU
General Service Workers	T & GWU, NUGMW
Catering	T & GWU, NUGMW
Clerical and Clerical Administrative	C & AWU, NACSS
Monthly paid grades M1–4	AEU, AESD, BALPA, C & AWU, ROU, NACSS, ASSET, NUGMW
Monthly paid grades M5–6	AESD, ASSET, BALPA, C & AWU, NACSS, NUGMW

Local

'Local' panels provide for the interests of each occupational group employed at each station, base or establishment. Thus there are several clerical and clerical administrative local panels in the London area.

Joint

'Joint' panels represent the interests of two or more occupational groups working in the same locality.

The difference between negotiation and consultation

In industrial relations negotiation usually means a process involving the need to reach agreement. Negotiation usually concerns issues of pay and physical conditions of work (hours, holidays, etc.). Consultation is a process of discussing and does not involve a need for the two sides to agree. Basically it is a formal channel, through which management may obtain the views of employees, before making up their minds on a course of action. Where consultation is practised management may go against the views of employees, but they should not make up their minds before hearing those views.

Some airline industrial relations institutions combine within one institution the processes of both negotiation and consultation.

The British NJC makes negotiation exclusively a matter for national sectional institutions, so that local institutions engage only in consultation.

Representatives and delegates

It is useful to distinguish the meaning of these two words. Representatives weigh up the merits of cases and *decide for* the people they represent. They are not ciphers; they are allowed to exercise their own judgement in deciding whether to support or contest proposals. Delegates must express the views of the people who appoint them. They are committed before discussion to a line of conduct preconceived by their principals. Their authority to act needs continually renewing with changing situations. In industrial relations institutions we may often find that representatives on one side face delegates on the other side.

Elected and nominated members

Elected membership of industrial relations institutions normally applies to employees only. It gives a democratic flavour to employee representation, but makes representatives more open to popular pressures. Elected representation may also cut across union loyalties.

Nominated membership usually involves nomination by Trade Unions. Nominated members may be less representative of the wishes of employees than they are of the wishes of unions. On the other hand there are advantages in a situation in which employers have to deal with only one other side. It is difficult to settle disputes where unions and employees do not agree.

Nominated or elected members of industrial relations institutions on the employees' side may be (*a*) full-time trade union officials (usually sitting on the Council and Joint Sectional Panels of the British NJC), (*b*) part-time officials of the unions (sometimes sitting on Joint Sectional Panels and Local Panels of the British NJC), (*c*) members of unions, and (*d*) interested staff members who are not members of unions. This last is, however, quite exceptional as employees who are interested in representing their fellow workers are interested enough to join Trade Unions.

Courts of Inquiry into Industrial Disputes; The Jack Report

In Britain the Industrial Courts Act, 1919, empowers the Minister of Labour to refer Trade disputes to a Court of Inquiry. In 1958 the Minister directed a Court under the Chairmanship of Professor D. T. Jack 'to enquire into the causes and circumstances of the dispute' between the Employers' and Employees' sides of the NJC for Civil Air Transport. The Court had power to compel witnesses to give evidence on oath, and to produce documents.

The conclusions of the Court revealed the limitations of the industrial relations institutions of the British airlines. They suggested that the restraints in procedure were not as inherently conciliatory as was generally thought. In fact the procedures can be abused to delay and even frustrate the settlement of difficulties. The mere existence of industrial relations machinery does not mean that it will be used. It is difficult for it to withstand the disruptive influence of militant elements. This is true the whole world over. The militant group in Britain happened to be the Shop Stewards' Committee. Industrial relations machinery is not an open sesame to good management-worker relations. The machinery needs to be handled by highly skilled, professional men. And industrial relations procedures are no substitute for firm management and strong leadership. The Court said:

'In our examination of the problem which was referred to us we are emphatically of the opinion that it is imperative to re-establish the authority of the National Joint Council. This is partly a matter of individual behaviour and partly a matter of machinery. We have been forced to the view that in the past there has been inadequate responsibility and leadership at various levels on both sides and that this has given scope and encouragement to certain militant elements whose activities have brought discredit to the existing constitutional arrangements. In particular we think it important that the shop stewards and their committees should have their powers more clearly defined and circumscribed and that they should be given no encouragement, whether by management or by the unions which they serve, to exceed their proper functions. This may appear, to some extent at least, to be a matter of machinery but it is also a matter of the way the machinery is used or misused and it is in that connection that proper responsibility and leadership are so very vital.'

CHAPTER XII

THE NATURE AND TASK OF GENERAL MANAGEMENT

The distinction between general and special management

The term 'general management' as it is normally used in business means a particular sort of management. It means management that is different from special management. General and special are distinguished by the former having breadth and the latter depth. General management is defined by three characteristics; its responsibility for more than one kind of variable business effort; its duty to optimise the results of more than one kind of variable business effort; its duty to judge an optimum position from specialist claims.

Special management is defined by the two characteristics; its duty to maximise the result of only one kind of variable business effort; its duty to advocate a maximised specialist effort.

Airline management is usually specialised as follows:

Finance (including accounting, auditing, EDP, etc.).
Purchasing (including contracts, suppliers, property, catering, etc.).
Production: I. Passenger and freight control.
II. Aircraft Movement control.
III. Maintenance control.
Marketing (including advertising, sales promotion, selling, etc.).
Personnel (including manpower control, industrial relations, training and education, etc.).
Research and Development (including commercial, traffic and engineering research and development).

The organisation of Air France 1962[1]

The Board of Directors is composed of 16 members: 4 public servants, either active or retired, represent the government; 4 persons,

[1] 'Air France 1962'—Brochure published jointly by Air France's Public Relations Division and the Advertising Section of the Commercial Division.

not associated with the government in any way, but appointed by the Ministry of Public Works, Transport and Tourism (2 of whom represent the Chambers of Commerce); 4 non-governmental shareholders; 4 staff representatives. The Chairman of the Board has a Special Assistant.

The Managing Directorate. The Managing Directorate is formed by:

The Managing Director;
The Deputy Managing Director, General Secretary;
The Deputy Managing Director, Technical;
The Deputy Managing Director, Economics;
A General Inspector is attached to the Managing Director.

The General Secretariat. The General Secretariat is placed under the direct control of the Deputy Managing Director, General Secretary. Its functions are manifold and include: claims and insurance; verification that the agreements entered into with firms having an Air France participation are implemented; general organisation of labour structures and methods; operation and control of vehicles; maintenance and supervision of premises; printing and reproduction of documents.

The Commercial and Sales Division. The Commercial and Sales Division determines, orientates and controls the Company's commercial policy. It guides and supervises the local Regional offices and provides them with the instruments for their commercial activity.

It comprises various specialised units: commercial agreements, fares and regulations, market surveys, sales promotion and publicity, problems concerning offices and reservations, passengers sales, freight, mail. Sales Inspectorates, each special to a particular geographic area, are responsible for checking the implementation of policies and for co-ordinating the commercial problems inherent in their areas.

The Personnel Division. The Personnel Division works out the Company's policy with regard to its personnel, sets up the appropriate means for applying this policy, controls its implementation and assists the various Departments with their personnel problems. It lays down regulations concerning personnel administration: status, salary, etc. It selects applicants and devises training and development programmes for staff. It also endeavours, in so far as possible, to provide housing assistance and to keep the staff informed on the Company's activities.

The Finance Division. The Finance Division is responsible for defining the Company's financial and accounting policy. It draws up and publishes the accounting programme, centralises the accounting results and prepares the corresponding documents, ensures revenue accounting, manages the finances and deals with tax problems, acts

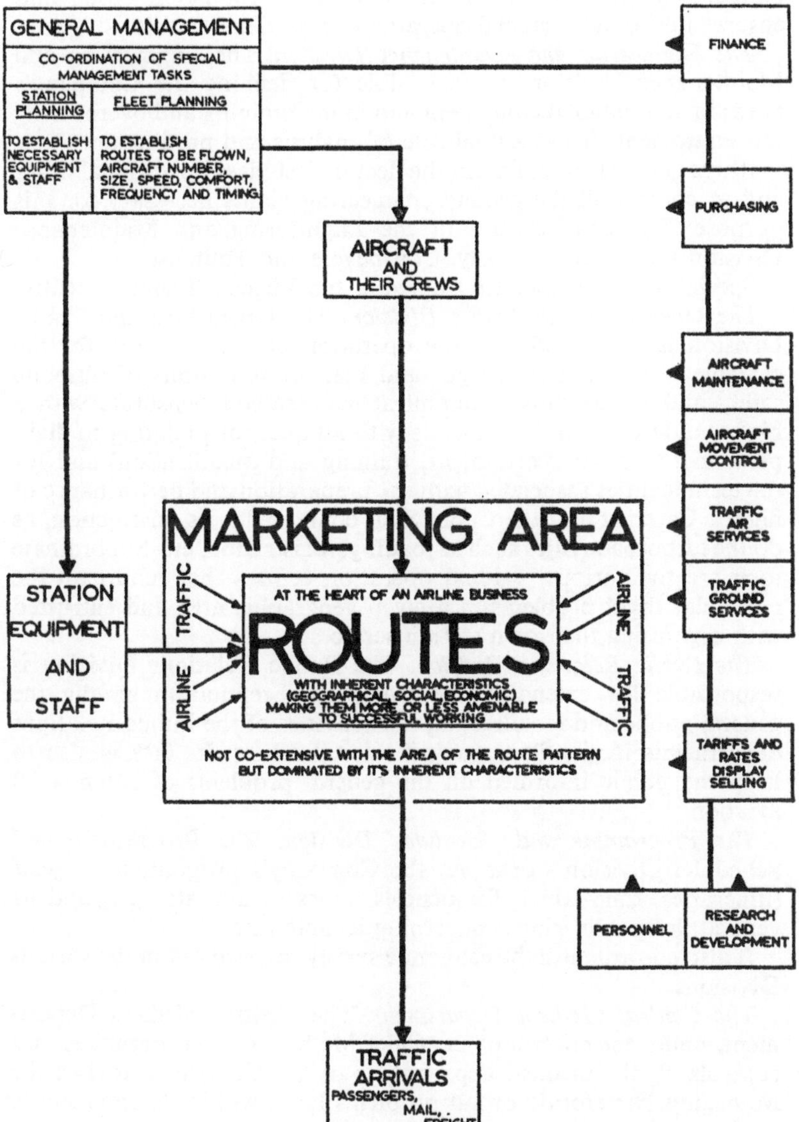

FIG. 30. *The General Management Task in an Airline*

in sales and orders placed with foreign suppliers, centralises the budget estimates of all the divisions and production costs, and ensures the sound financial operations of all departments.

The Engineering and Maintenance Division. The Engineering and Maintenance Division is responsible for defining the Company's needs in aeronautical equipment and in maintaining and overhauling this equipment. It has a dual role of analysis and production.

Its main task is to maintain the fleet in first-class operational order and to control all the ground engineering plants necessary for this purpose. The chief centres of the Engineering and Maintenance Division are situated at Orly, Courbevoie and Toulouse.

Specialised personnel are trained at the Vilgenis Training Centre.

The Operations and Traffic Division. The Operations and Traffic Division is responsible for the operation of the fleet and for the carriage of passengers, freight and mail in conditions of absolute safety and in the most economical manner commensurate with a high standard of service. It deals with all questions relating to flight personnel (such as recruitment, training and qualification) and for the technicalities associated with the preparation and performance of flights. Catering and the Cabin Staff come under its jurisdiction, as do the airport activities such as loading, registration, etc. Subordinate to it are the various regional operation centres that report on the particular flight problems in a given geographic area and entrusted with organising their own station services.

The Public Relations Division. The Public Relations Division is responsible for extending the Company's reputation among the general public and for directing the activities of the Public Relations departments in the Company's Regional offices. Its task is also to keep the public informed on the general problems of commercial aviation.

The Programme and Schedules Division. The Programme and Schedules Division works out the Company's programme projects (itineraries, time-tables, frequencies, types of aircraft . . .) and its general, long-term plans concerning its activities.

It also co-ordinates the economic surveys carried out in the various Divisions.

The Central Medical Department. The Central Medical Department, under the control of the Chief Medical Officer, organises and controls all the medical departments of the Company, advises the Managing Directorate on all problems lying within its competence and maintains contact with national and international medical bodies.

Regional Offices. The territories flown over or served by Air France are divided geographically into 34 regions. The regional offices have a dual role. On the commercial side they 'represent' the Company, sell air transport facilities and provide the various ancillary services (sales promotion, publicity, public relations). Wherever necessary they perform the same services on behalf of foreign or independent carriers in accordance with commercial agreements. On the technical side the regional offices look after all the airport services in their particular area and provide all necessary supervision and assistance for aircraft, both on the ground and in the air. In addition, aircraft fleet, to operate decentralised networks, are attached to the head regional offices in Algeria and the West Indies.

6 Regional Offices for Metropolitan France.
12 Regional Offices for Europe.
3 Regional Offices for North Africa.
4 Regional Offices for Central, West and East Africa and Madagascar.
6 Regional Offices for Asia and the Pacific.
3 Regional Offices for the Americas.

Choice of type of aircraft

The 1958 Select Committee of the British Parliament said, 'the actual process of choosing a new aircraft is at the heart of an airline's operations'. The type of aircraft flown has such a profound influence on the profitability of an airline that its choice must be made by top management. The importance of the issue is well demonstrated by the history of competition between BEA and Air France on the London–Paris route in which:

(*a*) Both began flying Dakotas.
(*b*) BEA went ahead with Vikings.
(*c*) Air France went ahead with DC4s.
(*d*) BEA went ahead with Elizabethans.
(*e*) BEA went further ahead with Viscount 700s.
(*f*) Air France drew level with Viscount 700s.
(*g*) BEA went ahead with Viscount 800s.
(*h*) Air France went ahead with Caravelles.
(*i*) BEA drew level with Comets.

The various responsibilities for the purchase of aircraft come under the following main heads:

(i) Deciding when new aircraft will be required, having regard to the sort of aircraft that competitors are buying, and the need to remain competitive in type;
(ii) Detailed specification of requirements in terms of operating costs, speed, weight, etc.;
(iii) Deciding whether to buy a developed or an off-the-peg aircraft to meet the requirements;

(iv) Choosing a manufacturer having regard to government policies, fiscal policy and spares position, etc.;
(v) Approving detailed designs and drawing up contract with manufacturer;
(vi) Finding the capital to invest at the right time and at the right price;
(vii) Collaborating with the manufacturer at all stages of construction;
(viii) Providing for a development programme.

The first four of these responsibilities may be regarded as the critical ones that must be dealt with at the highest level, and the second four may be left to be dealt with by various specialist managers.

The general management of an airline may decide to buy a 'new' aircraft (i.e. one that is recently designed and untried) for a number of reasons. First, there may be a need to catch up with the performance of a competitor's 'foreign' aircraft, when the airline's government will not permit the purchase of a 'foreign' aircraft and while no home manufacturer yet produces an aircraft equal to the foreign one in question. Secondly, an airline may be able to spring a winner on the industry with a new aircraft that may afford them a two to three year period of superior equipment.

There are, of course, considerable risks involved in commissioning new constructions. There are the risks that in the end operating costs will be higher, that unforeseen delays may occur, and that when the new creation finally arrives it will already be outdated. Usually several years elapse between the ordering and completion of 'off-the-drawing-board' purchases, and the customer airline in its anxiety to keep right up to date with the design may keep changing its mind and calling for alterations. During the period that BOAC was waiting for the Britannia it made the aircraft:

(*a*) Over 50 per cent heavier;
(*b*) Bigger overall, with twice the payload capacity, and three times the number of seats;
(*c*) A long-range aircraft;
(*d*) A turbine instead of a piston-engined aircraft.

Fleet Planning

Close in importance to the choice of the type of aircraft is the planning of the use to be made of the aircraft fleet. The allocation to routes of the right aircraft with the right frequencies at the right times is a heavy responsibility that must also be shouldered at the highest level of airline management. The detailed consideration of the many variables that must be taken into account to reach an optimum solution is, in many airlines, made the task of a separate component of organisation, whose manager acts in a staff role to the general manager.

The following variables bear upon the problems of deploying aircraft (and complementary operatives and equipment), to bring about the necessary changes in raw materials (passengers and freight) with maximum profit.

For the whole route structure

(i) The total number, sizes and types of aircraft in the fleet;
(ii) The configuration of various aircraft types (ratios of seating of various classes);
(iii) Maintenance requirements;
(iv) Needs for standby aircraft;

And from route to route

(v) Demand for passenger seats and space for freight;
(vi) Demand for various classes of travel (e.g. 1st and tourist);
(vii) Demand for a certain frequency of service;
(viii) Demand for certain arrival and departure times;
(ix) Amount and type of competition from other carriers (type of aircraft, frequencies, timings, etc.);
(x) Tariffs and rates;
(xi) Operating costs;
(xii) Available crews;
(xiii) Equipment capacity (airports, reservations systems, etc.);
(xiv) Rate of aircraft physical 'write-off'.

The sort of problems that have to be faced in the task of reconciling these variables are:

(*a*) It is usually impracticable to confine an aircraft to one route. The seating configuration will, therefore, usually have to be a compromise among the optima of a number of routes. It may not be the best type for more than one route.
(*b*) Demand may be heavy at the same time of the day on a number of routes. The problems of satisfying peak demands are complex.
(*c*) Because operating costs differ from route to route, a route that gives the most revenue may not yield the greatest profit. This gives rise to considerations of service against profitability.
(*d*) Best times for picking up traffic may be inconvenient for crewing and maintenance.
(*e*) Competitive timings may produce highest operating costs.
(*f*) To satisfy demands for air transport at certain times may saturate the capacity of airports, air traffic control or reservations systems.

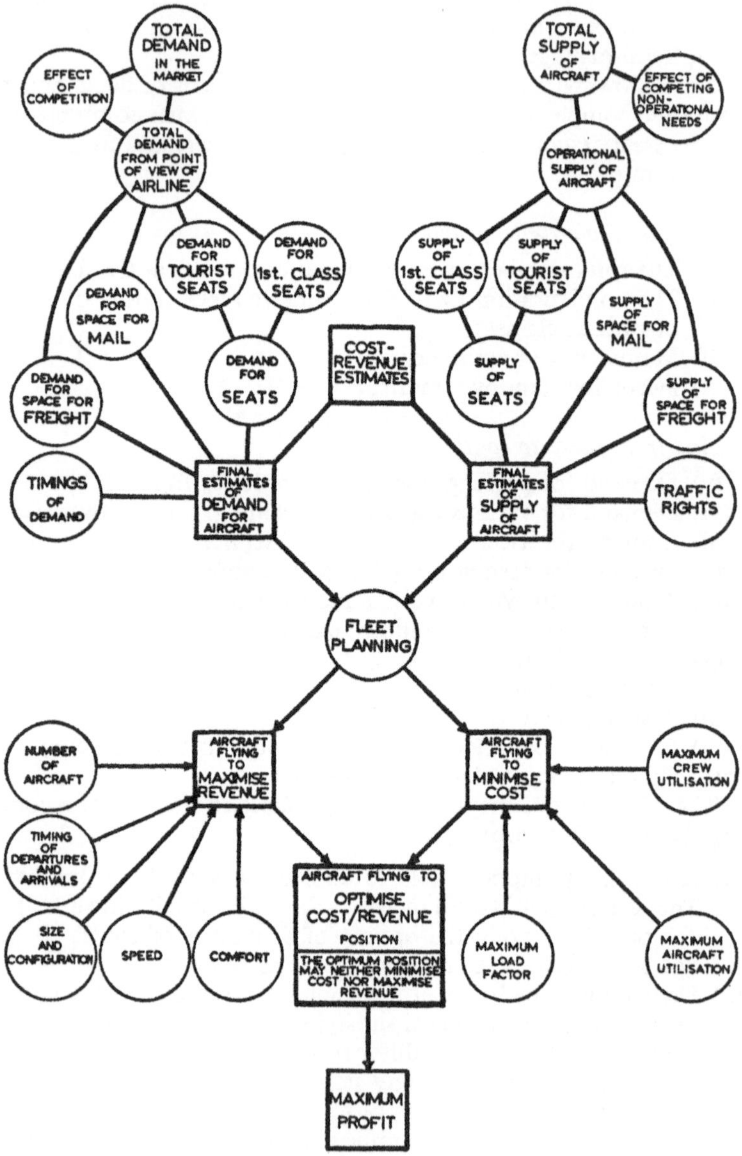

FIG. 31. *Fleet Planning seen as the attempt to balance supply and demand at levels that will give maximum profit*

Progress Indicators

One of the signs that general managements look for, in considering the state of their airlines, is something they may refer to rather loosely as 'progress'. The progress of an airline is seen as a number of 'more-or-less' conditions of the present, compared with similar conditions in the past. For example, does the airline carry more or less traffic than last year? Are the load factors up or down? Are the revenue and expenditure more or less? Is the profit or loss higher or lower? No boardroom is complete without certain 'how-goes-it' charts. The charts shown in Figs. 32–38 are similar to those used in the boardrooms of many airlines.

This historical approach tells management something about what is happening, but tells them little about why it is happening. Nevertheless, this is a good beginning. General management can tell someone to go and find out the why, the when, the where and the which.

The 'more-or-less' is not always a matter of efficiency. The picture of 'more-or-less' traffic does not *by itself* tell whether they were carried more or less efficiently. The output of more passengers may call for a more than proportionate input of airline organisation, in which case efficiency will be less. Conventional how-goes-it charts do, however, sometimes indicate progress in efficiency. For example, charts showing load factors show the ratio between utilisation of equipment and output; revenue and expenditure charts show comparative inputs and outputs over time; profit and loss histories show the accountants' answers to the periodic differences between inputs and outputs.

Efficiency Indicators

The general limitations of efficiency indicators

When we say that something is *efficient* we mean that it *is capable of producing a desired effect*, and that it is not unequal to a task. At any given moment being efficient depends on someone's decision as to what is a desired effect. Over a period being efficient may depend additionally on efforts made to reach a required standard. The shooting efficiency of a soldier at any moment depends on a decision, say, that he should be accurate up to 100 yards. He cannot alter his ability at a moment's notice, but someone in authority may alter his efficiency in an instant, by saying a soldier must shoot accurately up to 150 yards. The soldier may, however, be able to raise his ability to the required standard after a week's training. There cannot be a state of efficiency without someone having declared a standard or a target.

Efficiency indicators point out by how much something has not

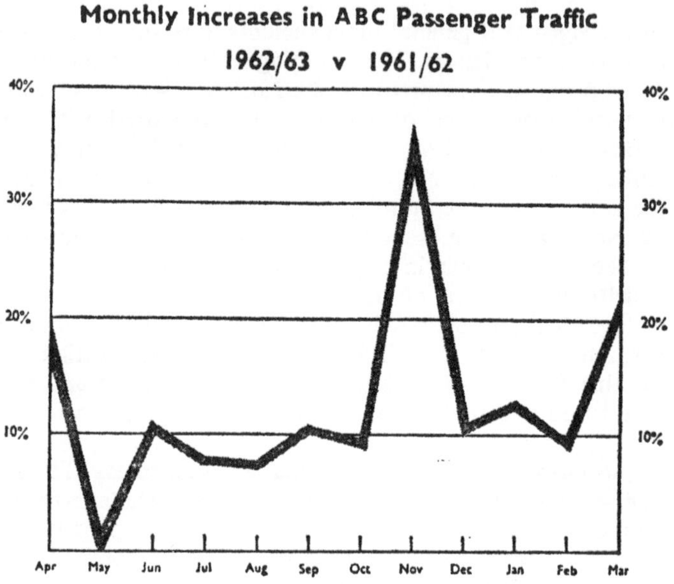

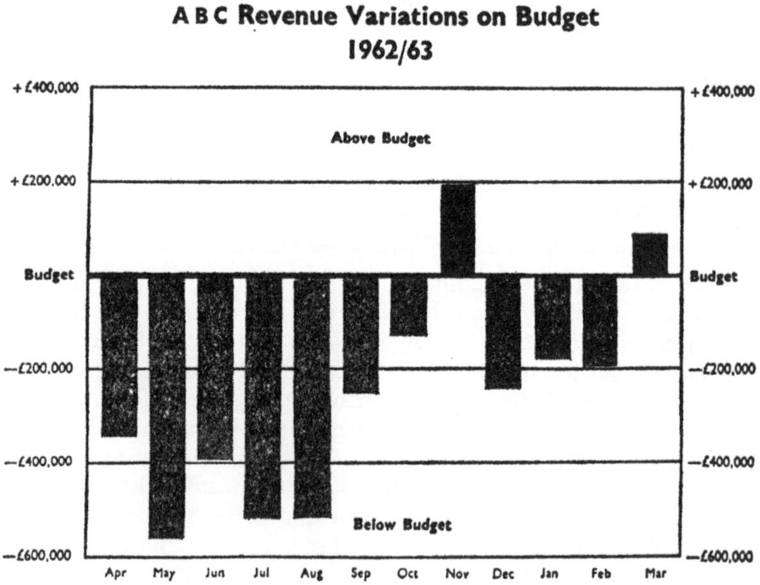

FIG. 32. *Progress Indicators: Monthly increases in ABC Passenger Traffic ABC Revenue Variations on Budget*

reached a standard. For example, the indication that load factor is 55 shows that it is, say, 5 points short of the desired 60.

The usefulness of efficiency indicators depends, therefore, on the usefulness of the standards set. If a load factor of 60 is regarded as desirable, and an aircraft proves capable of producing it, this standard is not necessarily the best for the business. Airline approaches to the problem of setting standards reflect the use of the

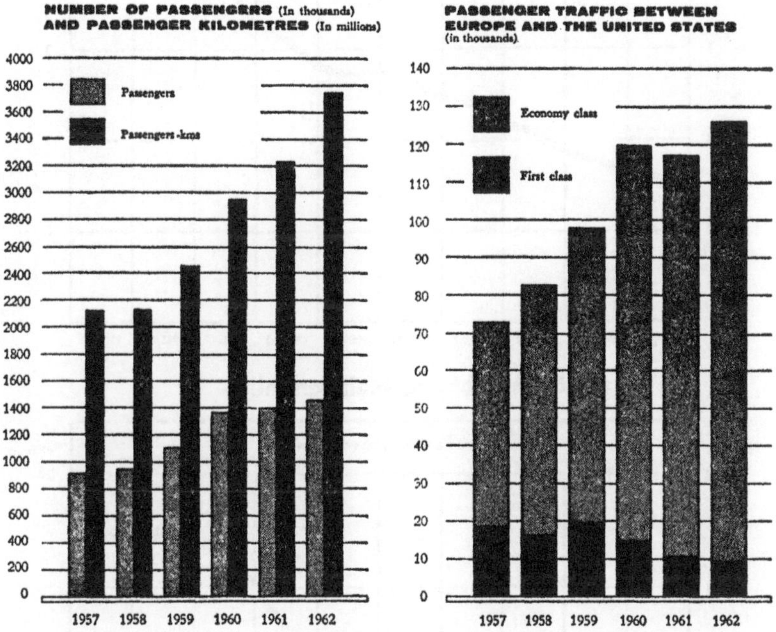

FIG. 33. *Progress Indicators: Number of passengers and passenger kilometres Passenger traffic between Europe and the United States*

term 'efficiency' to express the ratio of the output of a machine to the input of power. But airline managers cannot be as precise as an engineer, talking about fuel of a known quality and an engine of known capacity. The input of an engine may be regarded simply as the petrol it uses and output as the horse-power derived from it. There is not a single input for an airline (any more, in fact, than there is for an engine); there are many inputs. So airline management, short of accepting a money measure for the whole lot, and relying solely on a profit and loss account, is obliged to isolate certain inputs (just as the engineer may isolate fuel, and ignore all the work

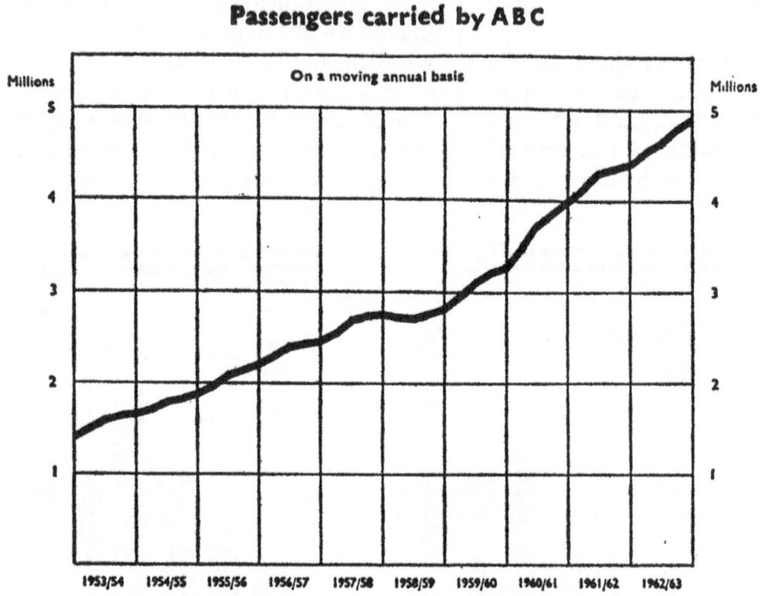

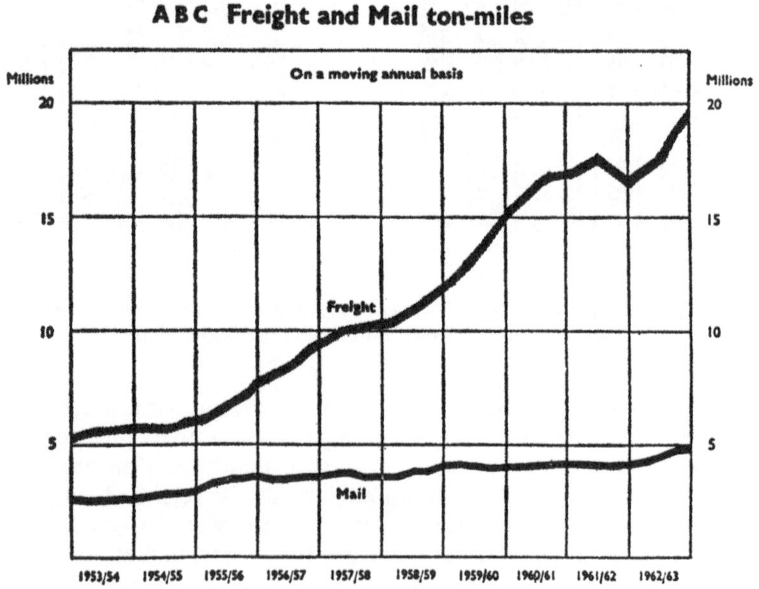

FIG. 34. *Progress Indicators: Passengers carried by ABC*
ABC Freight and Mail ton-miles

ABC Capacity and Revenue Load ton-miles

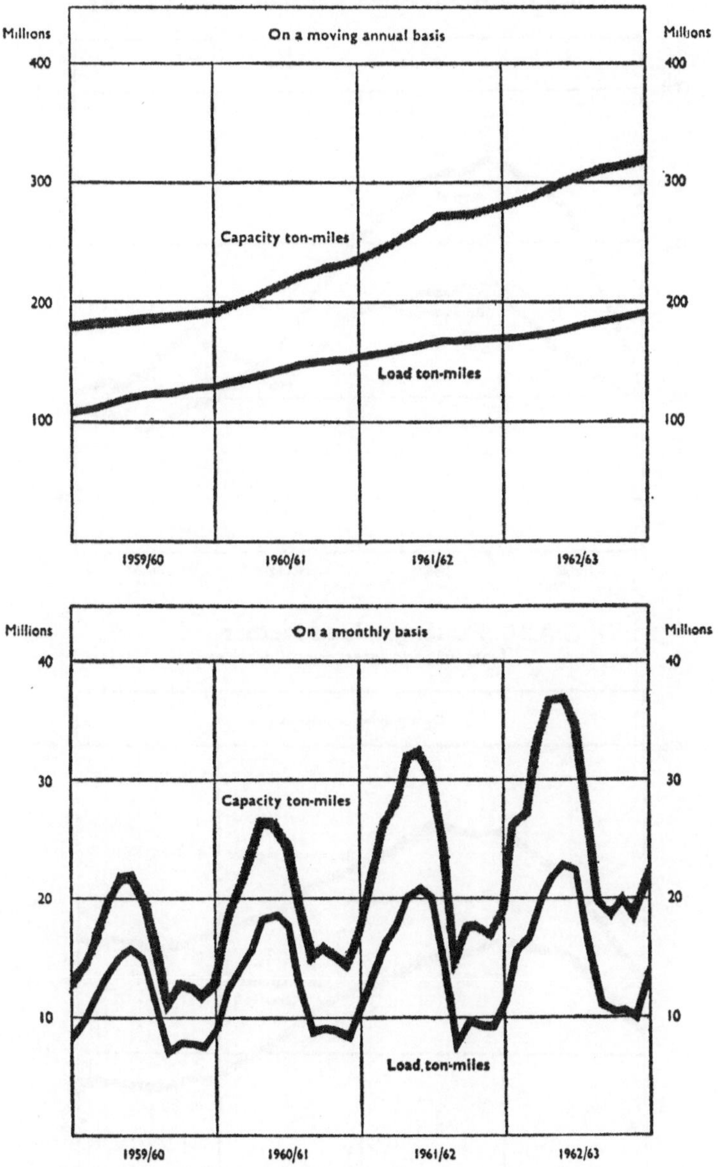

FIG. 35. *Progress Indicators: ABC Capacity and Revenue Load ton-miles*

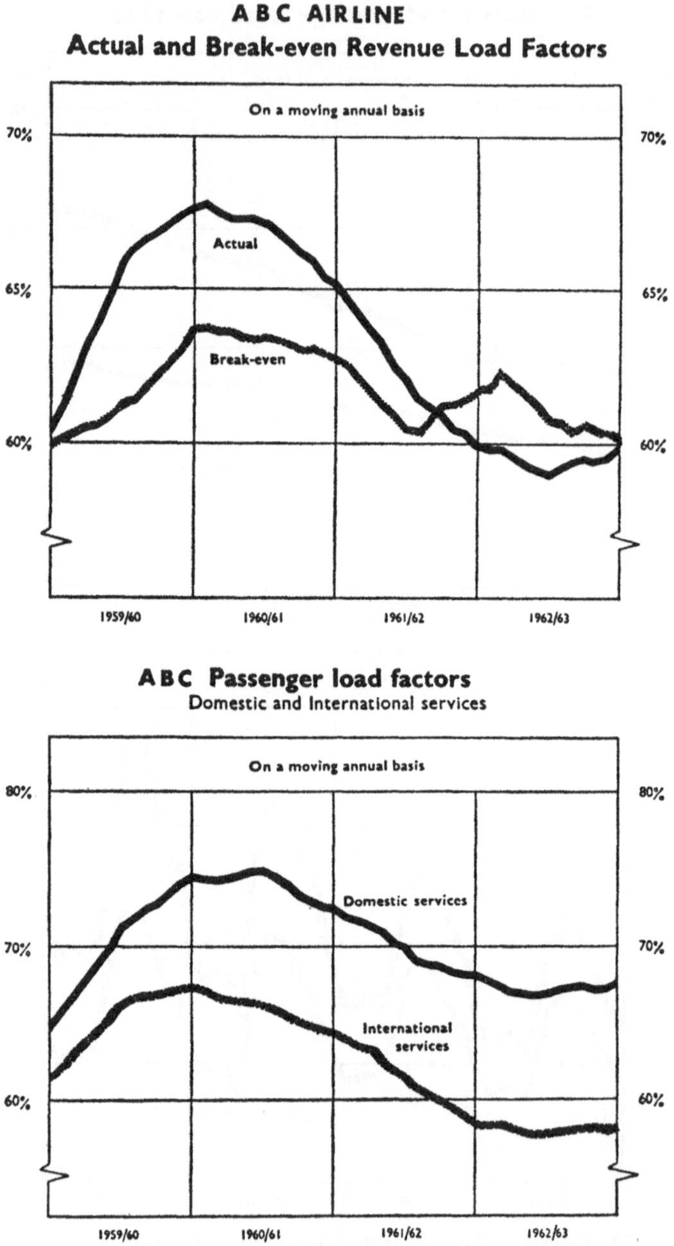

FIG. 36. *Progress Indicators: ABC Airline Actual and Break-even Load Factors ABC Passenger Load Factors*

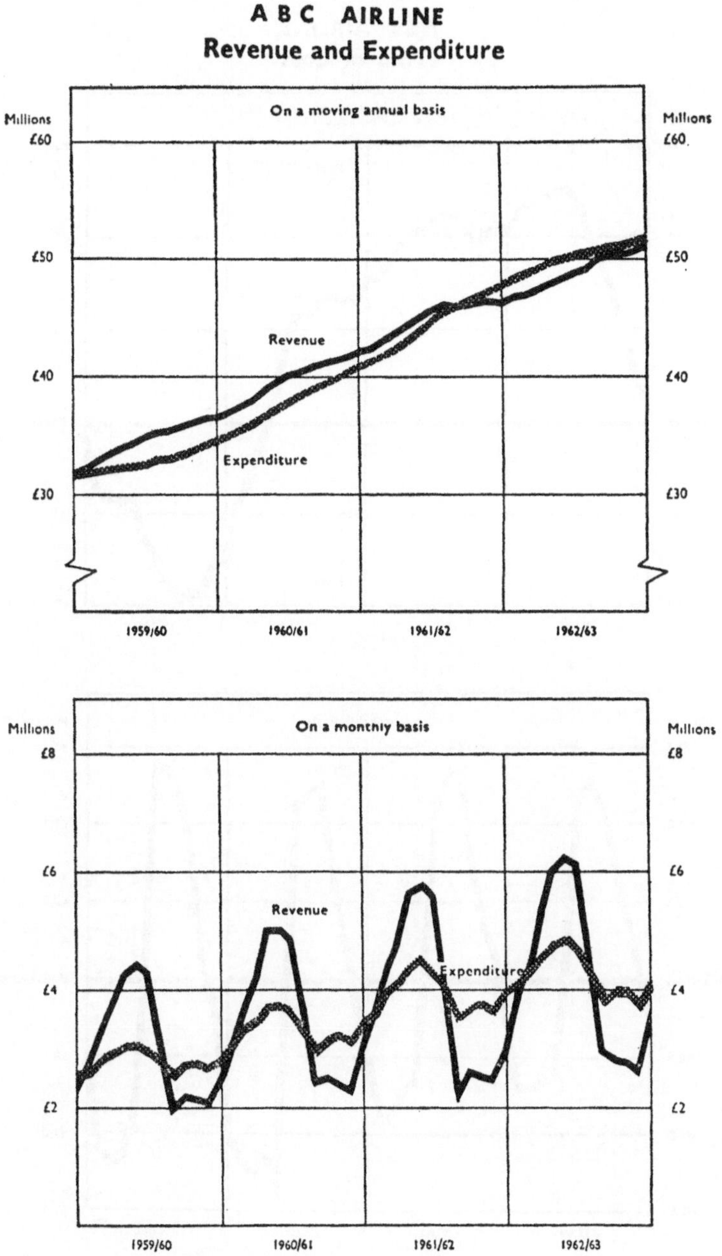

FIG. 37. *Progress Indicators: ABC Airline Revenue and Expenditure*

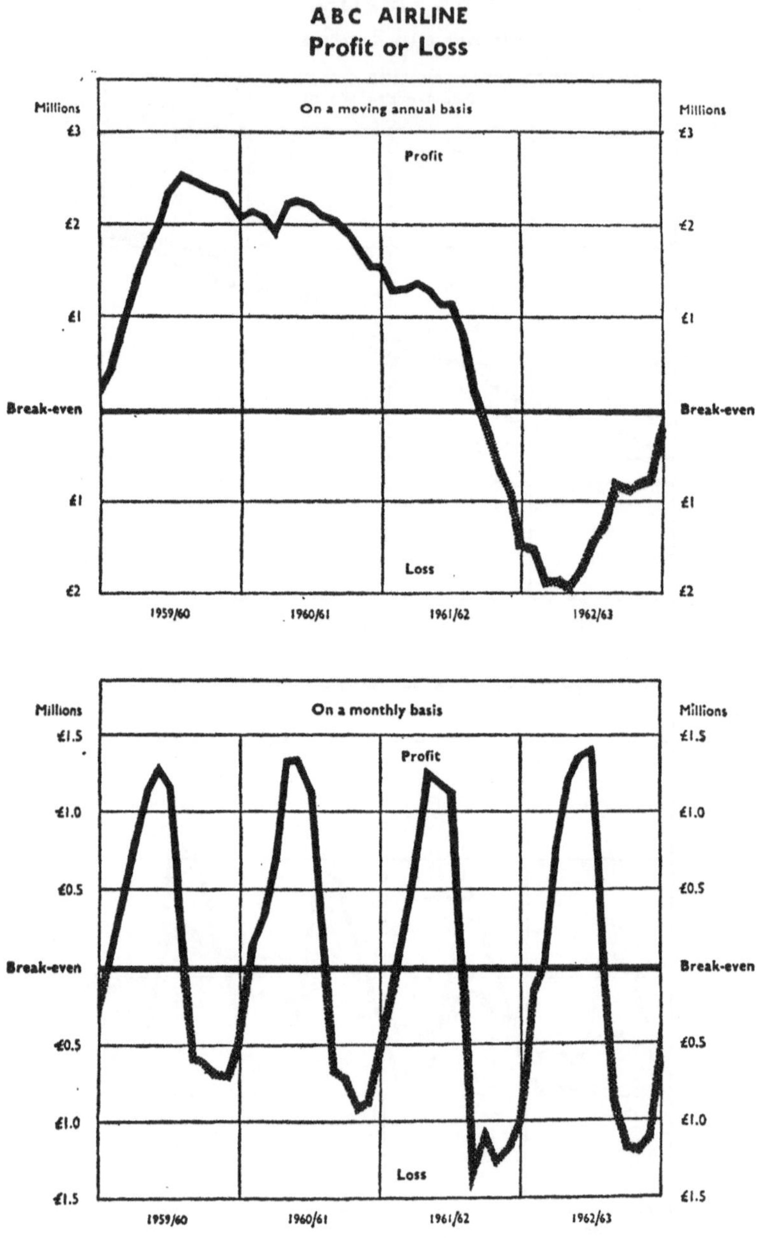

FIG. 38. *Progress Indicators: ABC Airline Profit or Loss*

of construction, maintenance, etc.), and establish hypothetical standards by which to determine their efficiency.

The measurement of an input by the amount of it that is used up seems sound. However, there are problems in practice. How much of an aeroplane is used up in flying a mile? A load factor may show how many seats are being *used*, but not how much they are being *used up*. This is a simple illustration of an intricate problem.

Problems spring from the fact that an input occurs as soon as an element of organisation is made *available for use*. An aircraft represents an investment, and a 'using up' of funds whether it is used or not. When an element of organisation comes to be used a fresh *input* must be made to provide for running costs. When an aircraft is put into use it will incur crewing and fuel costs, landing fees and so on. Airline managements, conscious that idle men and equipment are not producing anything, tend to regard 'utilisation' not as a fresh input, but as a *representation of output*. Then it is a short step to using primary inputs and utilisation as quantities for establishing 'desirable' ratios, and to using ratios of the actual quantities as indicators of variations from these hypothetical standards.

The use of the term 'outputs' *from the point of view of the whole business* should be confined to *revenue earning changes*, such as carrying passengers or freight from one point to another. For some purposes we might also consider non-revenue obligations such as presenting accounts, paying income tax and paying interest on capital, but generally outputs must bring returns to the business. Confusion originates in the use of the term 'output' for the changes brought about by components of organisation to provide an element for another component. These are referred to as *transferred outputs* in an earlier chapter, dealing with organisational groups.[1] From a business point of view these transfers are better referred to as 'utilisation' rather than 'outputs'.

Interposing the idea of utilisation between those of input and output gives rise to the possibility of establishing further hypothetical standards from ratios of utilisation to output. An attempt has been made to develop a range of possibilities, some of them tenuous, in Figures 39 and 40.

After this critical look at efficiency indicators we can acknowledge the usefulness of the light they throw on airline performance. Analysis of anything as complicated as an airline must depend upon the purpose in view. Different analyses can be equally correct, but useful for different purposes. For example, in considering the extent to which the elements of organisation are being employed, the important distinction is between the whole amount available, and the part employed. In considering the extent to which the employ-

[1] See Chapter IX, pp. 130–134.

ment of the elements is productive, the important distinction is between the total of elements employed, and the part earning revenue.

Capacity Ton-Miles (Available tonne-kilometres)

The CTM index is used as a measure of production. It can be misleading unless it is understood that by 'production' is meant 'process of production' and not 'product'. The latter is better measured by the load ton-miles index dealt with in a later section. The capacity ton-miles produced by a flight are the capacity for payload of the aircraft, measured in Short Tons (2,000 lb.) multiplied by the miles flown. Thus an airplane which has a capacity for payload of five tons produces 1,000 CTM on a flight of 200 miles.

A similar index, used widely outside of America and the British Commonwealth, is that of 'Available tonne-kilometres', defined in ICAO statistics as the sum of the products obtained by multiplying the number of tonnes available for the carriage of revenue load (passengers, baggage, freight and mail) on each flight stage, by the stage distance.

CTM per employee

This is the ratio of the number of CTM and the average number of employees during a certain period. It is sometimes used to indicate the output achieved by staff. It can be misleading if the assumption, that all the output of a business is achieved by its organisation, is allowed. This is one reason why it is important to distinguish between a business and its organisation.

All airlines achieve some output from contracting work out. Organisations can never be credited with the whole result. In fact, CTM per employee is to some extent an indicator of degree of organisation. For example, a certain airline used to have all its apron services at its main base carried out by the airport authority. The airline then took all the staff employed on this work into its own organisation. This they estimated would save money, although CTM per employee dropped, because the same amount of business was now being done by a larger organisation. Conversely the same amount of work was being done with less contracting.

A second danger in the use of CTM per employee arises if another element of organisation, i.e. equipment, is ignored. An increase of equipment in organisation, with a less than proportionate increase in operatives, will often increase CTM per employee. It is illogical to regard this solely as an operative achievement. A good deal of credit should go to management if such a change is successful in reducing unit costs.

	CLASSIFICATION	INPUTS	UTILISATION	OUTPUTS
THE RELATIVELY PERMANENT ELEMENTS OF AIRLINE ORGANISATION OPERATIVES AND EQUIPMENT SINCE THEY ARE NOT READILY DISPENSED WITH THEY MUST BE UTILISED	PERSONNEL	Number of employees on payroll Hours of work available Personnel costs (wages etc)	Number of employees working regularly Hours of work achieved	
	AIRCRAFT	Number of aircraft in fleet Number of aircraft hours available Number of aircraft miles available Aircraft capacity for payload in tons a) with zero fuel. b) with maximum fuel. Number of aircraft seats available Aircraft costs (standing charges)	Number of aircraft used in service Number of aircraft hours flown on service Number of aircraft miles flown on service Aircraft capacity achieved in tons Number of seat miles flown Mean block speed Capacity ton miles achieved Number of flights Number of take-offs and landings	Revenue passenger miles flown Mail ton miles flown Revenue freight ton miles flown Revenue load ton miles flown Number of seat miles sold Revenue load ton miles flown
	MAINTENANCE ACCOMMODATION AND EQUIPMENT	Number of units of accommodation (hangars, workshops, docks etc) Number of items of equipment (test beds etc) Amount of space in square or cubic feet Hours use available Cost (depreciation and insurance)	Number of units of accommodation in use Hours of aircraft maintenance achieved Number of items of equipment in use Number of maintenance checks Amount of space in use Hours during which accommodation and equipment is used	
	ROUTE ACCOMMODATION AND EQUIPMENT	Number of units of accommodation (passenger buildings, freight sheds etc) Number of stations. Number of miles of route Number of items of equipment Amount of space in square or cubic feet Hours use available. Cost (depreciation and insurance)	Number of units of accommodation in use Number of items of equipment in use Amount of space in use Hours during which accommodation and equipment is used	Revenue load ton miles Load tons embarked and disembarked
	HEAD OFFICE AND CENTRALISED SERVICES ACCOMMODATION AND EQUIPMENT	Number of units of accommodation (offices, drawing offices etc) Number of items of office equipment Amount of space in square or cubic feet Hours available for use Cost (depreciation and insurance)	Number of units of accommodation in use Number of items of office equipment in use Amount of space in use Hours during which accommodation and equipment is used	
PART OF THE AIRLINE BUSINESS DONE BY CONTRACTING	SUPPLIES AND SERVICES PURCHASED AS REQUIRED FOR USE DURING YEAR	Cost of - chartering aircraft and crews, fuel and oil, landing fees etc, materials, payments to contractors, payments to handling agents, commission to travel agents, advertising and publicity		
THE RAW MATERIALS OF AIRLINE ORGANISATION	TRAFFIC PRESENTED FOR CARRIAGE	Number of passengers for carriage Number of tons of mail for carriage Number of tons of freight for carriage Number of tons of originating load Intended journey lengths		Number of revenue passengers carried Mail tons carried Freight tons carried Revenue load tons carried

OUTPUTS ARE DIRECTLY RELATED TO SUPPLY OF TRAFFIC-UTILISATION IS NOT-OUTPUT MAY BE LOW WHILE UTILISATION IS HIGH

TOTAL COST OF INPUTS — TOTAL COST OF UTILISATION — TOTAL TRAFFIC REVENUE

TOTAL EXPENDITURE — TOTAL REVENUE

FIG. 39. *Indices of airline inputs, utilisation and outputs*

INPUTS	UTILISATION	INDICES
Number of employees on payroll.	Capacity Ton Miles.	C.T.M. per employee.
Personnel costs (wages etc.)	Capacity Ton Miles.	Employee costs per C.T.M.
Number of hours of work available.	Number of hours of work achieved.	Percentage utilisation of personnel.
Number of aircraft in fleet.	Number of aircraft used in service.	Percentage utilisation of fleet.
Number of aircraft hours available.	Number of aircraft hours flown in service.	Fleet utilisation time factor.
Number of aircraft miles available.	Number of aircraft miles flown in service.	Fleet utilisation distance factor.
Aircraft hours maintenance accommodation and equipment available	Aircraft hours use of main-tenance accommodation and equipment achieved.	Utilisation of maintenance accommodation and equipment time factor.
Cost of maintenance.	Capacity Ton Miles.	Cost of maintenance per C.T.M.
Amount of space available for maintenance.	Capacity Ton Miles.	Maintenance space per C.T.M.
Number of stations.	Capacity Ton Miles.	C.T.M. per station.
Number of miles of route.	Capacity Ton Miles.	C.T.M. per route mile.
Number of miles of route.	Number of take-offs and landings.	Average stage length.
Hours use available route accommodation and equipment.	Hours use achieved route accommodation and equipment.	Route accommodation and equipment utilisation time factor.
Cost of route accommodation and equipment.	Capacity Ton Miles.	Route costs per C.T.M.
Number of employees H.Q. and centralised services.	Amount of space in use H.Q. and centralised services.	Space per employee in H.Q. and centralised services.
Cost of H.Q. and centralised services.	Capacity Ton Miles.	Cost of H.Q. and centralised services per Capacity Ton Mile.
H.Q. and centralised services hours of available accommoda-tion.	H.Q. and centralised services hours use achieved accommoda-tion and equipment.	H.Q. and centralised services utilisation time factor.
Cost of supplies and services contracted.	Capacity Ton Miles.	Cost of supplies and services contracted per C.T.M.
Number of passengers for carriage and intended journey lengths.	Number of seat miles flown.	Passenger load factor.
Originating load in tons X intended journey lengths.	Capacity Ton Miles.	Revenue load factor.
INPUTS AND UTILISATION	**UTILISATION**	**INDICES**
Total expenditure.	Capacity Ton Miles.	Cost per C.T.M.
Total expenditure.	Number of aircraft hours flown on service.	Cost per revenue flying hour.
Total expenditure.	Number of aircraft miles flown on service.	Cost per revenue flying mile.
OUTPUTS	**UTILISATION**	**INDICES**
Load Ton Miles.	Capacity Ton Miles.	Revenue load factor.
Revenue passenger miles flown.	Number of seat miles flown.	Passenger load factor.
Total revenue.	Capacity Ton Miles.	Revenue per C.T.M.
Total revenue.	Number of aircraft hours flown on service.	Revenue per revenue flying hour.
Total revenue.	Number of aircraft miles flown on service.	Revenue per revenue mile flown.
INPUTS	**OUTPUTS**	**INDEX**
Number of employees on payroll.	Total revenue.	Revenue per employee
OUTPUTS	**OUTPUTS**	**INDICES**
Total revenue.	Load Ton Miles.	Revenue per Load Ton Mile.
Traffic revenue.	Load Ton Miles.	Traffic revenue per Load Ton Mile.
INPUTS AND UTILISATION	**OUTPUTS**	**INDEX**
Total expenditure.	Total revenue.	Profit or Loss.

RATIOS OF INPUTS, UTILISATION AND OUTPUTS THAT MAY BE USED AS INDICATORS OF THE WAY AN AIRLINE BUSINESS IS PERFORMING

FIG. 40. *Ratios of inputs, utilisation and outputs that may be used as indicators of the way an airline business is performing*

Operating costs per CTM

This is generally used for comparing the operating costs of airlines. Operating costs cannot, however, be regarded as reliable indicators of managerial ability (as distinct from its efficiency in the sense of ratio of ability put in to product put out), because some costs cannot be influenced by managerial ability. Operating costs are affected by certain factors that lie outside the control of individual managements. For example, they may be compelled to buy aircraft that are uneconomic; they are not wholly responsible for the routes they operate, the average distance of haul, wage levels and so on. There was a flare-up in 1963 over the racial policies of the South African government. South African Airways lost heavily by having to fly to Europe via Las Palmas in the Canary Islands, a detour of about 2,000 miles. BOAC was threatened overnight with the loss of Nairobi as a stop-point, and consequently an uneconomic, if not physically impossible, London–Johannesburg Comet service. The Comet could just cover the very long Khartoum–Salisbury leg of the journey with a depleted passenger load and heavy extra fuel supplies, but it was not worthwhile with the loss of the Nairobi traffic.

Load Ton-Miles (Tonne-Kilometres performed)

The LTM index is the product of revenue loads in tons and the standard distance over which they are carried. The capacity ton-miles of a flight are the amount an aircraft *is able to carry* multiplied by the distance over which it flies. Load ton-miles show *the amount of capacity on offer that was filled.* Load ton-miles are a measure of the profitable amount of work an airline has done. CTM show the amount of work done: LTM show how much of the work has been useful in carrying passengers and freight.

A similar index, used widely outside of America and the British Commonwealth, is that of 'Tonne-Kilometres performed', defined in ICAO statistics as the sum of the products obtained by multiplying the number of tonnes of revenue load carried on each flight stage, by the stage distance.

Load Factor

A ratio that interests general management is that of LTM to CTM. It is called the load factor and is officially defined as the percentage relationship of revenue load *carried* to capacity *provided.* It tells management how much that is being used is wasted, but not how much is being wasted because it is not used.

Passenger Load Factors

Passenger load factors indicate percentage relationship of

(i) Number of passengers × the number of miles each flew; and
(ii) Number of aircraft seats that were available × the number of miles they were flown, during a certain period.

Table 10 shows, for example, that over all the miles that all the SAS aircraft were flown, during a certain period, each seat was occupied for 55·7 per cent of those miles; or in other words, on average over each mile flown during a certain period 55·7 per cent of an aircraft's seats were occupied.

TABLE 10. *An example of passenger load factors for various airlines during a certain period*

SAS	KLM	Sabena	Swissair	TWA	BOAC	PAA	Air France	BEA
55·7	59·5	60·0	61·7	62·9	63·3	67·0	68·5	68·5

The passenger load factors shown for Air France and BEA were generally agreed to be satisfactory for the period. That is to say these two airlines were considered to have achieved a hypothetical standard of efficiency during the period, in the aspects indicated by this particular ratio. These aspects may be classified according to argument in the previous section as (i) *utilisation*, and (ii) *output*.

The distinction here is between *process of production* and *product*. The former may be doubled without affecting the latter. The latter may be increased without anything having been done to the former. The distinction may also be regarded as between *production effort* and *marketing success*.

Passenger load factors may indicate an unbalance between *production effort* and *marketing success*, but they do not reveal whether it is practicable to strike a balance by raising the number of seats sold to equal the number on offer, or by reducing the number of seats on offer. In other words a poor load factor does not enable general management to conclude that the efforts of production management are excessive or that the efforts of marketing management are too weak. Furthermore, a 'high' load factor does not tell general management whether the production and marketing are both at too low a level. A good load factor would not reveal that aircraft were not spending enough time earning money. Most of its seats might be occupied during every mile flown, and yet the airline remain inefficient, because it was not flying a sufficient number of miles. A poor load factor can be improved by withdrawing aircraft from service.

Aircraft utilisation

The indicator showing how much time aircraft are gainfully employed is usually labelled 'aircraft utilisation'. Usually 'aircraft utilisation' shows the average of hours of earning by all aircraft per day (on all days when they are available for service, or are unavailable only by reason of routine maintenance). The aircraft utilisation indices for various airlines over a certain period are shown in Table 11.

TABLE 11. *Aircraft utilisation—average hours per day during 1962*

BEA	Air France	QEA	TWA	SAS	Swissair	PAA	BOAC
4·71	4·87	5·33	5·93	6·12	6·27	7·30	8·10

In considering aircraft utilisation, general management must bear in mind the average length of flight of the airline.[1] For a short flight, the more or less fixed time spent embarking and disembarking passengers, loading and unloading treight and refuelling, is comparatively long. The time spent on these tasks increases proportionately as the number of landings and take-offs increase per given mileage. Furthermore, passengers on long journeys are usually willing to fly on during the night, whereas passengers on short journeys need inducements to travel at night. Night-time is bad for getting people to begin or end a journey, but all right for journeying through.

General management and average length of haul

It is sometimes argued that the management of airlines carrying traffic short distances is more difficult than that of airlines carrying traffic long distances. Carrying traffic is a 'haul', so we have 'short' and 'long' hauls, and the intermediate 'medium' hauls. Short hauls are regarded as under 1,200 miles, long hauls as over 2,500 miles, and medium hauls between the two. The difficulties of managing short hauls should not be exaggerated into a belief that short hauls cannot be made to pay under any circumstances.

Short hauls are necessarily *expensive*, but not necessarily *unprofitable*. This is because shortness of haul affects both the supply and demand for air transport. And the results may be contrary. Undoubtedly supply problems are greater but demand may be greater than for long hauls; the disadvantages for supply may be more than offset by the advantages for demand. For a true assessment of difficulties of managing short hauls, we have to examine their effects on both costs and revenues.

[1] See pages 70–71.

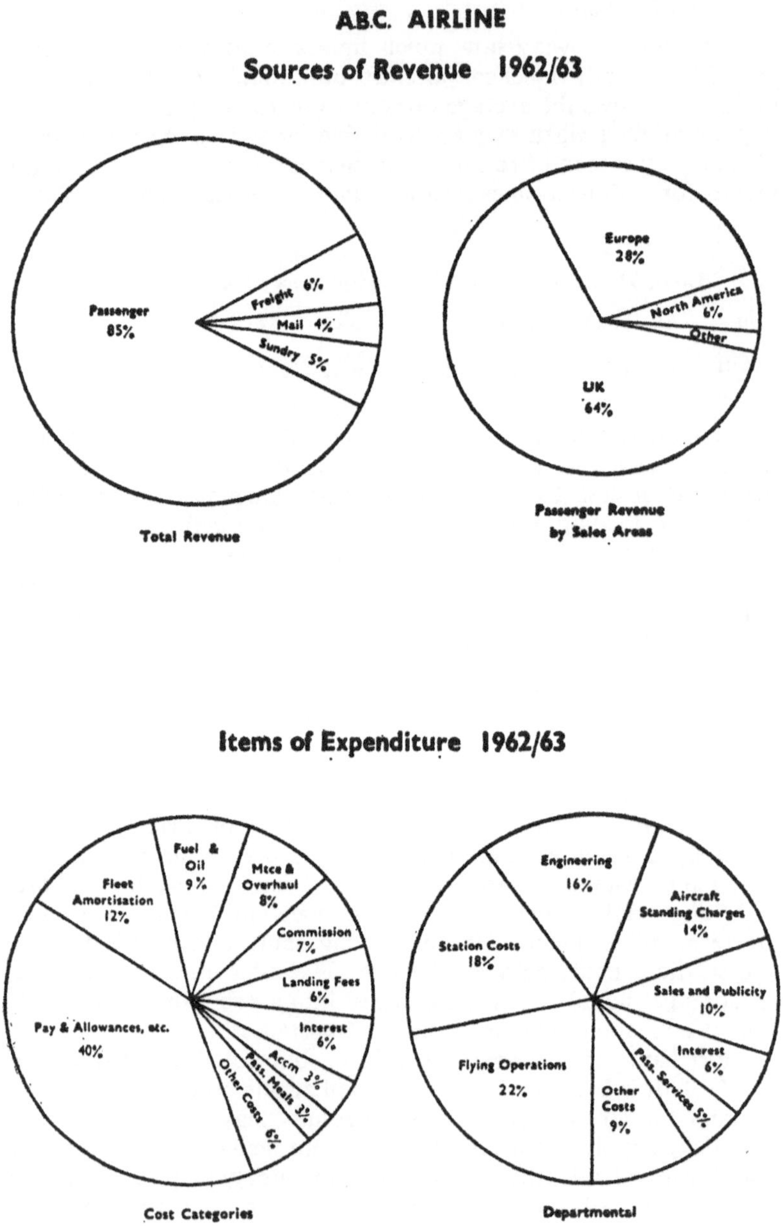

FIG. 41. *Efficiency Indicators: ABC Airline Sources of Revenue Items of Expenditure*

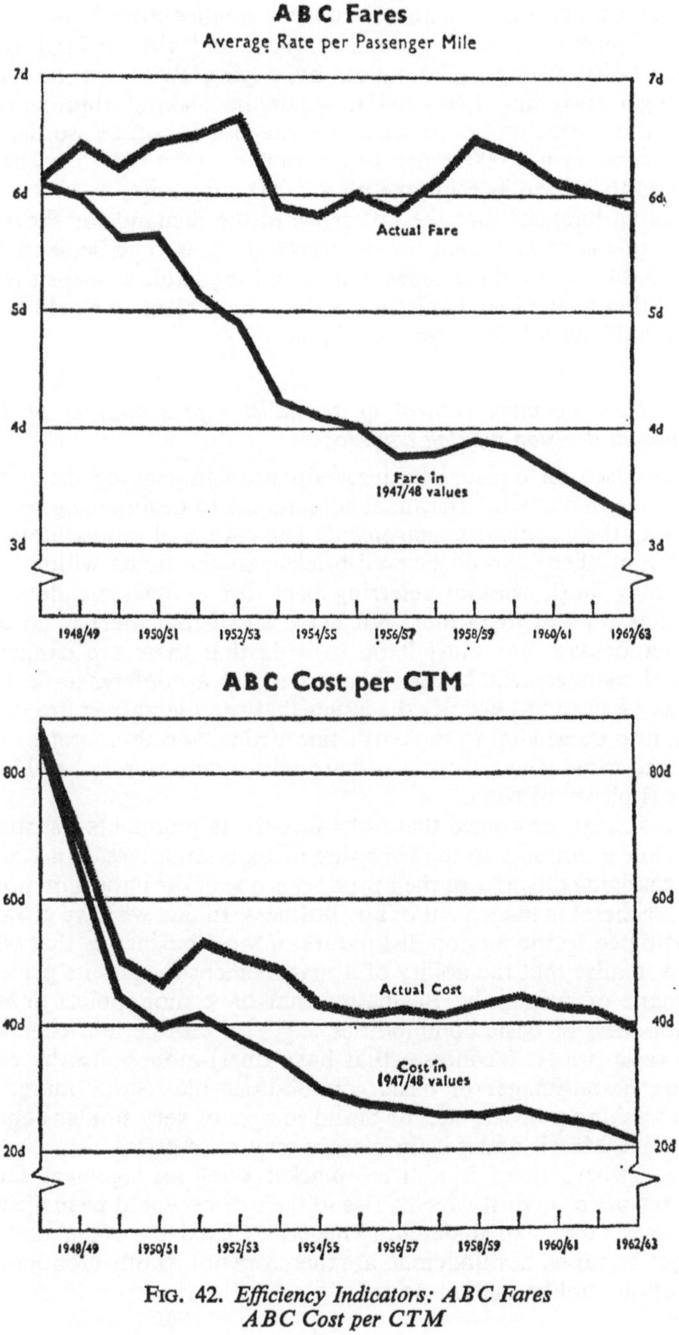

FIG. 42. *Efficiency Indicators: ABC Fares*
ABC Cost per CTM

On short hauls each customer makes a smaller contribution to the costs of terminals, other ground services, and aircraft landings. A passenger travelling 2,000 miles, by paying twice the fare of a passenger travelling 1,000 miles, would be making approximately twice the contribution to these overheads. In other words, two passengers on a 1,000 miles trip would be required to make the same contribution as each one on a 2,000 miles trip.

It often happens that the difference in the demand for short and long hauls is greater than the difference in fares. The demand for a short haul may be three times that for a long haul, whereas the fare is half that of the long haul. So the short haul revenue would be one and a half times that of the long haul.

General management control of specialist representatives at international decision-making conferences

Airlines face an unusual business situation in sending their representatives to many international conferences to negotiate agreements affecting their general management. The choice of representatives is important. They should be well-briefed on the limits within which they may work without referring back for a fresh mandate. The freedom allowed them must not be so small that there is no room for manoeuvre, nor must it be so wide that there are dangers of general management being embarrassed by a conference decision. It may be useful to classify the issues that representatives are to deal with, into those vital to the particular airline, and those not so vital, and into those where there is little room for compromise, and where there is plenty of room.

It is sometimes argued that IATA fare-fixing represents a surrender of airline autonomy to the bartering of representatives. It is claimed that changing the price of their product is one of the important powers of the general management of any business. In fact we have grown so accustomed to the monopolist nature of most businesses that we no longer realise that the ability of a management *to raise* its price is a hallmark of monopoly. Businesses that have monopolies or near-monopolies, of basic commodities, e.g. ICI with certain chemicals, may raise prices. Businesses that have quasi-monopolies by establishing brand-images of basic commodities like Stork margarine, OMO washing powder, etc., or brand images of very similar commodities like Morris and Austin motors may raise prices.

Only where there is a 'free' market does management face a 'market-price' against which a rise in their price would be ineffective, but which they can undercut. The prices fixed by IATA, that can neither be raised nor undercut, are therefore not wholly monopolistic nor wholly unlike market-prices.

CHAPTER XIII

FINANCE MANAGEMENT

Financial Policy

A typical policy of a manufacturing company may be set out in terms like these:

(*a*) To meet all operating costs from its own resources (either reserves or current earnings), avoiding short-term borrowing;
(*b*) To increase its capital when it is necessary to finance expansion or development, and to maintain ordinary share capital at not less than three-quarters of the total issue;
(*c*) To depreciate plant and equipment at a prudently high rate, and to maintain reserves adequate to meet all forseeable contingencies;
(*d*) To distribute by way of dividends and interest not less than 70 per cent of profit in each year's operation.

The financial policy of most airlines could probably be expressed in broadly similar terms, touching on the normal commercial issues of short-term borrowing, raising capital, depreciation, reserves and the distribution of profits. Detailed consideration of airline financial policies must, of course, be affected by the characteristics of the industry.

Trans-Canada Air Lines have stated their financial policy as follows:

(*a*) To be accountable to stockholders for its acts, as would any private corporation;
(*b*) To establish a fair scale of charges;
(*c*) To give an equitable return on the capital invested; and
(*d*) To remain financially secure so that it does not become a drain on the national purse.

Sometimes financial policy is dictated to some extent by the instrument by which an airline is formed. For example, the financial policy of the British nationalised air corporations is partly laid down by the provisions of the Air Corporations Act, 1949. The Act expressly enables them to borrow temporarily, by way of overdraft or otherwise, and to raise capital for certain purposes by fixed interest loans. The Act also provides for reserve funds and the application of revenue.

Where a government has a general authority over the activities of its national airlines, financial policy may be partly determined by government decree or direction. The British Treasury in 1963, in accordance with government views on the financial and economic obligations of nationalised industries, set a target of 6 per cent as an equitable return on capital invested.

Rigidity of airline financial structure

Table 12 illustrates the difficulties that are characteristic of the financial position of many airlines. Column A typifies the structure of numerous manufacturing companies, compared with the structures in Columns B and C, derived from the accounts of two major world airlines. The percentages shown against assets are approximately those of each item as a proportion of the total value of assets.

TABLE 12. *Comparison of typical financial structures of manufacturing companies and airlines*

	Manufacturing Co. A		Airline B		Airline C	
	£000	%	£0,000	%	£0,000	%
Fixed Assets						
Plant and buildings	2,500	64·50	8,100	85·00	9,000	72·20
Trade investments			450	4·75	1,235	10·00
Current Assets						
Stores			65	0·65	115	0·90
Raw materials	500	12·50				
Work in progress	250	6·25				
Finished stocks	300	7·75				
Debtors	180	4·50	775	8·00	1,995	16·00
Cash	175	4·50	125	1·60	115	0·90
Total	**3,905**	**100·00**	**9,515**	**100·00**	**12,460**	**100·00**
Current Liabilities						
Creditors	200	14·00	1,200	124·00	2,620	118·00

The percentages shown against current liabilities are approximately those of the item as a proportion of current assets.

The financial structure of an airline may be regarded as rigid if the proportion of fixed to total assets is high. Businessmen are generally agreed on the need for fine adjustments of the balances among the various types of assets and liabilities. The area for adjustments becomes smaller as the proportion of fixed assets rises.

It is normally regarded as important to provide funds to meet liabilities as and when they fall due. Fixed assets cannot be regarded as being available to meet these liabilities, except when a business is being wound up. The financial stability of an undertaking tends to be measured, therefore, by the ratio of current liabilities to current assets. This view should, however, be modified when we are considering the balance sheets of airlines whose finances are underwritten by government guarantees.

The balance sheet of Pan American Airways, as at December 31, 1961 (see Table 13) shows current assets standing at approximately 163 million dollars and current liabilities at 109 million. This is a better position than that of the airlines illustrated in Table 12, but still not good. Fixed assets are nearly 72 per cent of the total.

The working capital of airlines

'Working capital' is the term usually used to describe the excess of current assets over current liabilities. James P. Mitchell of the Chase Manhattan Bank[1] argued that because of the relatively short period in which aircraft are depreciated (seven to ten years), an airline operating *at no worse than breakeven* accumulates substantial amounts of cash in relation to its total revenue. He believed that a large part of the cash asset, created by depreciation policy, should be used to amortise (by repayment) the loans raised to pay for the equipment that is being depreciated. He further argued that limitations should be put on the use of such cash for the purchase of further capital assets. In other words, working capital should not be used to finance re-equipment programmes.

The Chase Manhattan Bank attempted to establish as a condition for lending to airlines, the preservation of sufficient cash to meet a month's operating expenses, apart from all other demands on working capital. The Bank also expected to be able to limit the amount of working capital used to *hire* capital equipment, and the amount of cash paid out in dividends.

In business generally, a substantial amount of working capital is regarded as necessary for financial stability, although no hard and fast rules can be framed to establish this requirement precisely. It is clearly true, however, that in any business, beyond a certain point investment in fixed assets will reduce the proportion of current assets below the level of safety. In this way, even a profitable airline can become insolvent. If its management is tempted to buy from profits more aircraft in times of exceptional demand, when demand slackens it may be left with fixed assets it cannot use, and with insufficient capital to meet current obligations. Table 14 shows the changes in the working capital of Pan American during 1961.

[1] New York University, Air Transport Conference, 1962.

TABLE 13. *Balance Sheet—December 31, 1961—Pan American Airways*

	$000
ASSETS	
CURRENT ASSETS:	
Cash	42,074
Short-term cash investments (at cost)	27,690
Notes and accounts receivable:	
United States Government	20,070
Foreign governments	3,645
General traffic	23,201
Associated companies	3,204
Other	9,182
Stock of National Airlines, Incorporated	8,347
Flight equipment expendable parts	15,020
Miscellaneous materials and supplies	7,879
Short-term prepayments	1,852
Other	775
Total current assets	162,939
INVESTMENTS AND SPECIAL FUNDS:	
Stock of associated companies (at cost—estimated equity based on their books value: $33,000,000)	19,149
Non-current advances to associated companies	2,301
Advances on equipment purchase contracts	10,624
Other	11,896
OPERATING PROPERTY AND EQUIPMENT (at cost):	
Flight equipment	483,824
Ground property and equipment	52,265
Land	5
Construction work in progress	3,004
Total operating property and equipment	539,098
Less Reserves:	
Depreciation:	
Flight equipment	172,974
Ground property and equipment	27,596
Maintenance of flight equipment	7,201
Total reserves	207,771
Operating property and equipment—net	331,327
DEFERRED CHARGES AND SUNDRY BALANCES RECEIVABLE	34,911
	$573,147

	$000
LIABILITIES AND STOCKHOLDER EQUITY	
CURRENT LIABILITIES:	
Current notes payable—to banks	29,700
Accounts payable and accrued liabilities	43,366
Accounts payable—associated companies	1,546
Collections as agent—traffic and other	4,960
Accrued taxes	1,449
Unearned transportation revenue	28,014
Total current liabilities	109,035
LONG-TERM DEBT:	
Notes payable to banks and insurance companies	243,950
Convertible subordinated debentures	46,970
DEFERRED CREDITS:	
Deferred Federal income taxes	16,575
Other	5,899
RESERVE FOR SELF-INSURANCE	10,000
STOCKHOLDER EQUITY:	
Capital stock—$1 par value per share	6,753
Other paid-in capital	72,694
Retained earnings	62,640
	142,087
Less: Treasury stock (at cost)	1,369
Stockholder Equity—net	140,718
	$573,147

SHARES OF CAPITAL STOCK:	
Authorised	10,000
Issued	6,753
In treasury	94
Reserved for conversion of debentures	1,566
Reserved for options not yet issued	300
Under option, reserved	121

TABLE 14. *Pan American World Airways, Inc.—Changes in Working Capital in 1961*

Working capital, January 1, 1961		$31,500,000
Increase in working capital, 1961:		
Earnings	$8,900,000	
Depreciations and amortisation	59,100,000	
Book value of property sold and retired	19,000,000	
Other changes in working capital	2,900,000	
		89,900,000
		121,400,000
Decrease in working capital, 1961:		
Purchase of aircraft and other property	25,200,000	
Advances on purchase contracts	10,700,000	
Decrease in long-term debt	26,300,000	
Dividends	5,300,000	
		67,500,000
Working capital, December 31, 1961		$53,900,000

Proportion between Loan and Share Capital

Long-term liabilities, such as debentures, are normally referred to as 'loan capital' in Britain, and as 'debt capital' in the US. The proportion between loan or debt capital, and share or equity capital is usually regarded as significant, even by those airlines financed wholly by loan capital. Debenture holders are creditors (or senior lenders), while shareholders are proprietors. The importance of this distinction is that creditors must be paid, but proprietors are not entitled toa penny unless profits are earned. In bad times an airline with a high proportion of loan capital is in a more vulnerable position than an airline with a high proportion of share capital, since the former must continue to reduce its resources by paying large amounts of interest, while the latter has a smaller burden of interest, and can conserve its resources by paying no dividends.

The financial structure of the United States domestic trunk airlines in 1962 was estimated to be:

(*a*) Equity capital (including deferred stock) approximately $1·1 billion.

(*b*) Loan capital approximately $1·7 billions (i.e. a loan-equity ratio of about 1·5 : 1).

(*c*) Working capital approximately $220 million (i.e. just a little more than one month's operating expenses).

(*d*) Cash accumulation—assuming breakeven load factors (i.e. depreciation earned but no additional income) approximately $300 billion.

This structure was regarded as top-heavy because of the disproportionate amount of loan capital. Improved earnings were needed for equity financing to reduce loan capital to bring loan and equity into better balance.

The significance of heavy interest charges

Interest charges in 1961 on the loan capital of United States domestic trunk and international carriers was about $75 million. Interest paid by British carriers in the same period was about £9 million. These charges had to be deducted from any profit, or added to any loss on Operating Accounts. As operating profits, if any, were small, at best only a small net profit was available for distribution, and at worst operating losses were augmented.

Interest charges are a burden that must be borne in both good and bad years. It is sometimes argued that this is psychologically bad for employees, whether they be managerial or operative. If a business is financed wholly by equity capital, with no fixed interest to pay, all operating surplus is regarded as profit. Even if a business has only a small operating surplus, it has made some profit. But an undertaking financed wholly by loan capital has its operating profit reduced by interest.

The profitability of a business does affect the morale of both management and men. But the problem is that the operating surplus of most airlines is not large enough to attract equity capital. Airline equities have been notorious for selling at below book value. In 1961 the Civil Aeronautics Board of the USA estimated that a return of ten and a half per cent on investment would be needed for the Big Four domestic carriers to attract equity capital.

The British Government in 1962 fixed a target of 6 per cent for return on the capital invested in one of its nationalised carriers. This was to include the fixed interest, currently averaging at about 5 per cent payable on the Government loans with which the airline was financed. Thus the government enabled the airline to regard all operating surplus as profit, and to enjoy the psychological advantages of equity financing. It did not, of course, thereby remove the obligation to carry over the fixed interest burden from a bad year to the next year.

Depreciation and obsolescence

The *depreciation* policy of an airline represents an attempt by its management to allocate to successive financial periods the asset costs proper to them, and to anticipate the replacement of assets, by retaining sums that will be ultimately required for this purpose. Assets are said to be depreciated over the number of years in which it is planned to accumulate sufficient cash to equal the original or expected replacement cost. This number of years is usually based on what is regarded as the 'normal' life of an asset. 'Normal' life is limited by ordinary wear and tear.

Unfortunately it often happens in air transport that assets are rendered *uneconomic* by a new invention or other improvement, before the completion of the 'normal' life period. This risk is called *obsolescence*, and it creates serious difficulties for airline managements.

In the fifteen years following the end of the Second World War the average cruising speed of commercial aircraft increased from about 150 m.p.h. to about 600 m.p.h. And in 1960 airlines faced the prospect of increases up to 2,000 m.p.h. within the following fifteen years.

Progress between 1945 and 1960 was achieved by major airlines buying and selling several successive types of aircraft. For example, in America DC-3s were superseded by DC-4s and they in their turn by DC6s, DC7s, Constellations and then Super-Constellations. This crown of achievement in piston aircraft soon fell to the Boeing 707 jets. In Britain, Dakotas were succeeded by Vikings, Elizabethans, Viscount 700s, 800s, Vanguards, Comets and Tridents. It was claimed by United Airlines that up to 1962 none of its aircraft had ever worn out and been replaced by a similar aircraft. Nor had any of United's aircraft ever reached an age where it was more costly to keep it in repair than to scrap it, and buy a new one of the same type. The replacement had always been an improved type.

The practice among major carriers has been to write-off aircraft over a period of seven years to a residual value of 25 per cent. That the rate has been standardised among a number of airlines using a variety of aircraft means that managements are not exercising individual judgement. They may be looking for safety in what everyone else is doing, and think that if the policy is mistaken all airlines will be in similar positions.

There is a fallacy in this thinking. A standard rate does not represent a common policy, as it must be related to different types of aircraft. The two main factors that should influence judgement on this issue are:

(*a*) How long the airline will be able to go on using the aircraft they have bought; and
(*b*) The price at which they will be able to sell them when they can no longer use them.

The dangers of a standard rate were illustrated by the failure of several airlines to make adequate provision for the replacement of their aircraft. BOAC asked the British Government for permission to write-off some £50 million in the 1961–62 financial year. This could not be regarded as even an *exceptional* depreciation process, as they had not put this amount aside. The request meant either a write-off as a dead-loss, or an increase in accumulated deficit.

The number of years an airline can continue to use a particular type of aircraft profitably is not likely to be determined simply by the time it takes to wear out. Aircraft do not wear out. Their efficiency is not allowed to diminish. Indeed they are likely to be better aircraft at the end of ten years than at the beginning. An aircraft's 'life' and 'identity' are notional. An aircraft in ten years' time will be a different 'bundle of components' with the same registration number.

The profitable use of aircraft is likely to be *immediately* affected by alternatives offered from time to time. That is to say, there is really no long-term prospect for an aircraft. A splendid machine can be rendered obsolescent in a short time by the design, construction and introduction to service of a new aircraft. It may be a matter for management foresight but sometimes it is good or bad fortune whether an aircraft is made obsolescent shortly after its purchase, or a long time after purchase. BOAC's Britannias were obsolescent almost as soon as they came into service.

An airline's rate of write-off may, therefore, appear sound for years and then suddenly be invalidated. Airlines with Constellations in the mid-1950s had a second-hand market for them. They could sell them at written-down value. Then the bottom fell out of the second-hand market. Nobody wanted piston-engined aircraft. They all wanted turbo-prop or jets.

The economics of remedying obsolescence

By definition it cannot be economic to go on using an obsolescent aircraft. In the language of economics 'obsolescent' does not mean worn out. It does not mean no longer usable in the physical sense. It means no longer usable in the economic sense. In other words obsolescence is a state that ends the life of the aircraft (or any other equipment) *from the point of view of a particular airline management.*

In the simplest terms an aircraft becomes obsolete as soon as it becomes less profitable to fly than the aircraft that could be bought as an alternative. The mere fact of the existence of another aircraft that could be flown more profitably is of no economic significance unless it can be bought. An aircraft may become comparatively unprofitable by a falling-off in earning powers because traffic is attracted to alternative aircraft. This causes a rise in costs per ton-mile. Or the aircraft may become comparatively costly because new aircraft (say as a result of increased speed and consequent higher use) can produce cheaper seat-miles.

It follows that there is no cost of obsolescence apart from its occurrence, i.e. there is not economic cost in remedying it. The coming of obsolescence causes loss, but once this loss is incurred, the remedy of disposing of aircraft does not involve considerations of cost. The main task facing finance managers is to do all the calculations necessary to detect obsolescence. It is not always immediately apparent that one aircraft type has become less profitable than another. Doing the calculations is not a science; diagnosis of the situation is an art, involving assumptions. What should management do when obsolescence occurs? There is no question of continuing to operate the aircraft, or other equipment. It has become unusable economically and should be discarded. There is a temptation to 'recoup' by continuing to work obsolescent equipment so that its initial cost can be spread over a greater number of years. This might correct an inadequate allowance for replacement. The depreciation cost per seat-mile flown by a particular aircraft might be reduced by continuing to use it after it had become obsolescent. But either the overall cost per seat-mile would be increased or revenue would be decreased. Even if depreciation costs of obsolete aircraft are spread over the whole of the incorrectly estimated life, it still pays to discard them because depreciation costs are usually a small proportion of overall costs. (Table 15.)

TABLE 15. *Annual depreciation of Flight Equipment provided by various airlines, expressed as percentage of total costs*

Years	SAS	BOAC	Quantas	TWA International	PAA Atlantic	KLM
1951	6·4	7·4	8·0	9·4	10·4	11·7
1957	9·7	7·3	10·0	8·3	10·9	11·8

The data on which the diagnosis of obsolescence should be based are illustrated in Table 16.

TABLE 16. *Illustration of data that forms the basis for diagnosing aircraft obsolescence*

Year	Planned Depreciation	Residual Book Value	Depreciation cost per flying hour	Depreciation costs in pence per seat-mile	Other airline costs per hour	Other airline costs in pence per seat-mile
	£	£	£		£	
1	120,000	960,000	60	0·24	910	3·64
2	120,000	840,000	60	0·24	910	3·64
3	120,000	720,000	60	0·24	910	3·64
4	120,000	600,000	60	0·24	910	3·64
5	120,000	480,000	60	0·24	910	3·64
6	120,000	360,000	60	0·24	910	3·64
7	120,000	240,000	60	0·24	910	3·64
8	80,000	160,000	40	0·16	910	3·64
9	80,000	80,000	40	0·16	910	3·64
10	80,000	Nil	40	0·16	910	3·64
	£1,080,000 = original cost of aircraft					

Aircraft (i) flies 2,000 hours per annum.
(ii) flies at speed of 600 m.p.h.
(iii) carries 100 seats.
(iv) produces 60,000 seat-miles per hour.
(v) assuming other airline costs remaining constant over the life of the aircraft.

Other data required: current market price of aircraft being examined for obsolescence.

How is it that an obsolescent aircraft can be worth anything? The answer is that obsolescence is a state that ends the life of an aircraft *from the point of view of a particular airline*. The airline with the aircraft can no longer operate it profitably, but another airline may be able to do so. The conditions that render an aircraft obsolete for one airline may not apply to all airlines. For example, another airline may not have competition from the new alternative, nor do the sort of work in which it has a comparative advantage. Thus a new aircraft can push an old aircraft off some routes, and leave it usable on other routes.

Major categories of airline operating costs

By placing all expenditure in one of the following categories management would obtain a feedback on cost changes. Such feedback is an essential for financial control.

Unavoidable aircraft charges

(*a*) Depreciation.
(*b*) Insurance.
(*c*) Uninsured loss.

Maintenance of aircraft

(i) *Unavoidable costs*
   (*a*) Staff (pay, allowances, pensions, etc.).
   (*b*) Accommodation (hangars, workshops, offices).
   (*c*) Plant and equipment.

(ii) *Avoidable costs*
   (*a*) Extra labour.
   (*b*) Materials.
   (*c*) Payments to contractors.

Flying Operations

(*a*) Crews (pay, allowances, pensions, etc.).
(*b*) Fuel and oil.
(*c*) Landing fees.

Charter of aircraft and crews

Passenger and cargo air services

(*a*) Cabin staff (pay, allowances, pensions, etc.).
(*b*) Insurance.
(*c*) Meals and other passenger costs.

Passenger and cargo ground services

(*a*) Staff (pay, allowances, pensions, etc.).
(*b*) Accommodation (offices, counters, sheds, etc.).
(*c*) Ground communications.
(*d*) Payments to handling agents.

Marketing

(*a*) Staff (pay, allowances, pensions, etc.).
(*b*) Display (posters, letters, etc.).
(*c*) Payments to travel agents.

Technical training

(*a*) Proportion of unavoidable aircraft charges (see 1).
(*b*) Maintenance of aircraft (see 2).
(*c*) Flying operations (see 3).
(*d*) Ground accommodation and equipment.
(*e*) Staff costs.

Head Office and Centralised Services

(*a*) Specialist managers (with deputies and secretaries).
(*b*) Special management departments.
  (i) Finance.
  (ii) Personnel (including Industrial Relations, Training and Education, Welfare, etc.).
  (iii) Research and Development.
(*c*) Centralised Services.
  (i) Public Relations.
  (ii) Stationery, Printing and Property.
  (iii) Ground Communications.
  (iv) Medical Services.
(*d*) Accommodation.

The difference between 'operating' and 'total' costs

Operating costs are the costs of acquiring, maintaining and using elements of organisation, plus contracting costs. In the case of an airline financed wholly or partly by fixed-interest bearing loans, total costs equal operating costs plus finance charges, or interest on loans.

Another way of looking at this is that operating costs are incurred after capital has been invested in assets; they begin when money is converted into equipment, raw materials, etc. Finance charges begin as soon as money is borrowed, and continue even if the money is not converted into equipment, etc. There would be no distinction between 'total' and 'operating' costs as defined above in an airline financed wholly by equity capital. The distinction is made then to separate and draw attention to the cost of debt financing.

Major sources of airline revenue

The major sources of airline revenue may be classified as follows:

Traffic revenue.
(*a*) Passenger.
(*b*) Excess baggage.
(*c*) Mail.
(*d*) Commercial freight.
(*e*) Charters.
Commissions.
Incidentals (training, overhauls, etc.).

Classification of costs for the purpose of route costing

Airline managements often run into difficulty in trying to establish the cost of a single route. Sometimes the best they can do is to determine the costs of a group of routes. For the purpose of route costing the following classification is helpful.

First, there are those avoidable (variable) costs that increase directly with the amount that a route or group of routes is used. Thus an increase in flying hours on a route would bring about extra costs incurred solely for that route, e.g. maintenance, fuel and oil, and landing fees.

Secondly, there are those unavoidable (allocated) costs, that can be attributed in their entirety to a particular route or group of routes. For example, the depreciation costs of aircraft used exclusively on the route or routes, and the crewing costs of those aircraft would be allocated.

Thirdly, there are those unavoidable (apportioned) costs that are a portion of a total of costs covering a number of routes or groups of routes, and are reasonably attributable to each. Thus parts of the total cost of a station may be attributable to a number of routes.

Fourthly, there are those largely unavoidable (overhead) costs that do not directly pertain to routes (e.g. Head Office and Centralised Services) and must be shared arbitrarily. The arbitrary

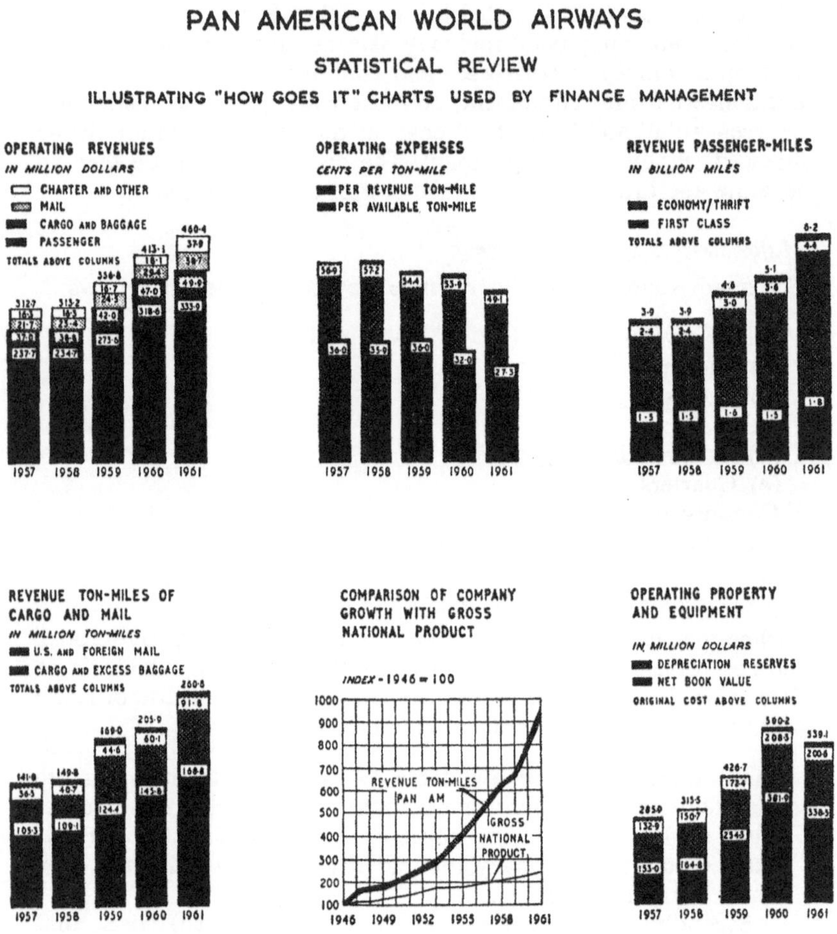

FIG. 43. *Pan American World Airways—Statistical Review*

nature of this device is demonstrated by the fact that if a route or group of routes ceased to be operated, it is unlikely that total overheads could be reduced by an amount equivalent to the proportion charged to that route or group of routes.

The inherent difficulties in controlling costs in airlines

The Finance Manager of an airline faces two particular handicaps in his task of controlling costs. The first is one of language. So many cases for expenditure are confused by jargon. It may require considerable courage and patience to make the expert restate his arguments in clear and simple terms so that an ordinary business man can make a commercial judgement. If a Finance Manager allows himself to be 'blinded by science' he will soon lose grip of the whole cost situation. The second is the unscrupulous use of the anxiety of every airline official to do nothing that will jeopardise safety. A casual reference to the safety factor can change the merit of a case so much. The obvious temptation to take advantage of it should place the Finance Manager on his guard.

It is a hard and lonely task arguing against the expert and the exponent of the safety angle. If the finance man turns out to be wrong he will never be forgiven. But someone has to stand up and represent the commercial point of view.

Costs of airport and navigational services

Although these are not a high percentage of total costs they are difficult to control. The governments that impose them are often unwilling to consult airlines before raising charges. Understandably airlines dislike this situation as they may find themselves paying for things they do not want. For example, the décor of some airports is more lavish than airlines want, because the government wishes to make a showpiece of the airport in the interests of national prestige. Or an airport may be designed in such a way that it makes the cost of handling traffic unnecessarily high. Secondly, governments make it difficult to budget for increases by raising charges at short notice. It may take an airline a year or two to raise its fares, but a government can raise its costs with less than a month's notice.

Airlines almost always have to pay landing fees for the use of runways, taxiways, ramps, runway lighting, and emergency services. Some authorities also charge for those parts of terminal buildings that airlines share. These charges are contentious because airlines have little or no say in the design or cost of these areas. Thirdly, airlines pay rent for offices, check-in areas, freight sheds, maintenance bases, etc. Governments sometimes attempt to cover the cost of navigational aids for approach, landing and take-off. In the early 1960s airlines began to face the prospect of charges being raised to cover navigational facilities. At certain airports fuel taxes are levied to help defray the cost of airport and navigational services. At others the government makes a levy on passengers' use of its services, as distinct from the airlines' use of facilities.

What costs are included when assessing landing fees differs from government to government. Some include the 'technical' services (communications, meteorological and navigational) provided at the airport, others do not. Some governments do not take into account interest on capital invested in an airport; others do. Some governments recognise that the costs of military use of an airport should not be borne by civil aviation, and some of them believe that the community should share the costs of benefits that an airport brings them (e.g. promoting industry, trade and tourism, providing employment and raising land values). This belief that the community should contribute to the costs of an airport may cause a local authority to give tax concessions, land grants or even capital grants.

The revenue from concessionaires is at some airports an important factor in reducing costs to the airlines. At the major United States airports concessions of all sorts—car parking, restaurants, shops, banks, car hire, etc.—bring revenue to benefit the airport authority and thus the airlines.

It has been suggested that there should be one standard charge for the use of all airports. This has been resisted on the grounds that services vary from airport to airport, and it would be unrealistic to divorce charges from costs. A common basis for charging landing fees was according to the gross take-off weight of aircraft. This was because a fully-loaded aircraft on take-off has the maximum need for runway thickness and length. A practice then began of calculating so that rates, per thousand pounds of all-up weight, increased with the size of aircraft. This was to reflect the requirements of heavier long-range aircraft for stronger and longer runways. At some airports this principle gives rise to surcharges for long-range flights and rebates for short-range flights.

Most airlines have opposed another alternative, i.e. that of 'capacity to pay'. This would use capacity, instead of weight, as a measure of the earning potential of the aircraft. Opposition is grounded on the fact that 'capacity to pay' is not related to revenue, but to profit. Services that produce most revenue may be least profitable.

Where a government makes a separate charge for navigational facilities it may charge a flat amount per flight through its airspace, or through a control zone for which it is responsible. Sometimes a government relates such a charge to the distance the aircraft flies through the area it owns or controls. Sometimes such charges are related to aircraft weight, or to both weight and distance flown.

Financial accounting in an airline

Financial accounting is the name given to the conventional procedures for recording assets, and the receipts and payments, occurring in the course of business. These procedures are designed to safeguard the assets, provide a control on receipts and payments, and to furnish periodically the results of the business.

Financial accounting helps not so much in the *making* of managerial decisions as in their *implementing*. Once a depreciation policy has been made, the financial accountant will see that it is observed to the letter. Once an operating plan is approved the financial accountant will ensure that his records faithfully record the working of the plan.

Although the statements of the financial accountant are usually about *what has happened a while ago*, this does not mean that these statements are no help in planning, motivating, controlling and contracting. History provides valuable guide lines for current managerial action. A careful reading of accountancy history will make a wiser man of any manager.

Having said this, however, it is not unfair to regard financial accounting as the watchdog of the investor and the public rather than the manager.

Management accounting

The airline finance manager has a vital role in assisting managers of other parts of the organisation to carry out their tasks. He does this by giving *accounting information*, which makes a timely contribution to the data used in the managerial activities of planning, motivating, controlling and contracting.

The information for planning purposes may be provided as a matter of routine or upon special request from a manager. In the former category are the usual annual budgets, continual aircraft type costings and route analyses. In the latter category come requests for special costings. For example, management might ask for an estimate on the profitability of certain all-freight services, or the cost of issuing a ticket, or the cost of training a steward.

Information for managerial control purposes is usually issued on a routine basis. The two most important instruments of this nature are the revenue and expenditure budgetary control reports, that are issued periodically to enable managers to see how actual results compare with expected results.

Budgeting

One of the most telling exercises of general management is in the annual examination and reconciliation of the budget proposals of specialist managers. Budgeting procedures differ from airline to airline, both from the point of view of thoroughness and sequence, but basically the following steps should be taken.

Each specialist manager should begin to discover, some time before he is due to submit his budget, the consequences for his own organisation of the physical plans of the airline. That is, he must ask himself what he has to do, say as a result of the airline having to change its route pattern. Having made up his mind on what *his* physical task will be in the light of the *overall* physical tasks he must then decide what funds he needs. This is an exercise in getting the best value for money.

At this stage he may obtain some guidance from general management in the shape of an assumption built into a cost/revenue estimate for the budget year. This may indicate, for example, that general management have assumed in their estimates that he will need to increase his expenditure by 5 per cent in order to carry out his revised task. His detailed workings may appear to invalidate the assumption, and then he will have to argue a case for altering the estimates.

Finally, all the proposals for expenditure are collated and compared with revenue estimates. General management then has to grapple with the problem of squaring proposed expenditure with estimated revenue. This almost inevitably involves knocking down some proposals, mediating between those contending for limited funds, and ending up unpopular with everybody. It is an unenviable job.

Budgetary control (revenue and expenditure)

Budgeting is mostly concerned with the managerial activity of planning. Budgetary control is a special part of the managerial activity of control. The essential aim of budgetary control is to give managers information about their actual performance, in terms of money spent and money received. This enables them to compare actual performance with budgeted performance. The information should be given promptly enough for managers to be able to take corrective action if necessary. So that comparisons can be made quickly the feedback on actual performance should be cast in the same form as the budgeted performance.

Finally information for budgetary control should enable general management to perceive whether or not subordinate managers are taking effective measures to correct deviations from planned revenue and expenditure.

CHAPTER XIV

PURCHASING MANAGEMENT

The importance of skilful purchasing

Depreciation costs are usually a small proportion of overall costs, and this reduces the significance of the price at which aircraft are purchased. The effect of an addition of 10 per cent to the capital cost of aircraft, say through weak bargaining on the part of an airline, may be demonstrated as follows:

TABLE 17. *Effect of an addition of 10 per cent to the capital cost of aircraft.*

1st situation

Assume a fleet cost of £50m. depreciated over 10 years to a book value of nil.

Annual depreciation charges	= £5m.
and Other costs	=£45m.
Overall annual expenditure	£50m.

2nd situation

Assume a fleet cost of £55m. depreciated over 10 years to a book value of nil.

Annual depreciation charges	= £5·5m.
and Other costs remain at	=£45m.
Overall annual expenditure is now	£50·5m.

Thus an increase of 10 per cent in capital cost of the fleet has occasioned a 1 per cent increase in overall annual expenditure.

Despite the fact that additions to the capital cost of aircraft have a much less than proportionate effect on overall annual expenditure the quality of aircraft is so vital to successful operation that their purchase is a responsibility assumed directly by general management, and not left to specialist purchasing management.

The problems of purchasing for the needs of an airline are different from those encountered in businesses where the cost of raw materials is highly significant. A few pence on the price of a pound of sugar may make a tremendous difference to the costs of an industry using it as its main raw material. Quantities bought at a price a fraction too high per unit can spell ruin. In airlines the raw materials are passenger and freight, and these are not 'purchased' in the usual sense of the word. Most airline purchasing is of equipment, where the critical factor is the performance of what is bought, rather than the price at which it is bought. This idea must not, of course, be carried too far. As can be seen from Fig. 41 maintenance and overhaul costs may be as high as 8 per cent, and of these as much as three-quarters may be purchases of equipment; fuel and oil is another 9 per cent, accommodation 3 per cent, and so on. All in all, the sheer volume of purchasing makes its management of considerable significance.

TABLE 18. *Illustration of type of data on which judgement of aircraft performance is made (assuming an aircraft utilisation of 2,000 hours per annum)*

Aircraft Type		A	B	C	D	E	F
Purchase Price							
Purchase price of aircraft	£m.	1·5	2·0	1·9	0·9	1·9	1·3
Purchase price of spares	£m.	0·25	0·4	0·3	0·2	0·4	0·2
TOTAL Purchase price	£m.	1·75	2·4	2·2	1·1	2·3	1·5
Size of Aircraft							
Mixed-class seating nos.		78	124	89	63	117	76
All-tourist seating nos.		95	143	106	69	129	85
Freight capacity lbs. (after all tourist seats filled)		—	9000	2850	1500	2632	1010
Unavoidable Costs							
Interest on Total Purchase Price	£hr.	33	44	43	21	42	28
Depreciation	£hr.	93	125	122	59	120	79
Insurance	£hr.	25	32	31	15	31	21
Crews	£hr.	39	42	39	35	42	39
Maintenance and R & D	£hr.	76	110	92	54	110	61
Total unavoidable costs	£hr.	266	353	327	184	345	228
Avoidable Costs							
Fuel	£hr.	51	85	70	38	76	54
Landing fees	£/Landing	42	90	53	26	93	39
For 500 st.m. Stage							
Block time	hr.	1·3	1·3	1·2	1·4	1·3	1·4
Total costs that vary with aircraft type	£	450	660	530	330	640	430
Costs in pence per aircraft mile		216	316	254	158	307	206
Cost in pence per seat mile (mixed-class seating)		2·8	2·5	2·9	2·5	2·6	2·7
Cost in pence per seat mile (Tourist seating with freight)		2·3	2·0	2·3	2·2	2·3	2·4

The sort of data that is used to guide managements' assessments of aircraft 'quality' is illustrated in Table 18. It must be stressed that this data 'guides' and does not 'determine'. The problem is to isolate costs that vary significantly with aircraft type. There is usually room for argument as to which costs do, in fact, vary with different types of aircraft. Furthermore, to the cost data must be added assessment of the 'attractiveness' or otherwise of the aircraft.

The contract for the purchase of new aircraft

If an airline decides to buy a new (i.e. tailor-made) aircraft, a high degree of skill is called for on the part of the purchasing manager to draft a contract that will give protection from costly consequences of such a venture. For example, the period between the ordering and delivery of new aircraft is often so long that management has time to have several changes of mind on the specifications. In the case of the Britannia, BOAC had to re-negotiate the contract for purchase no less than five times.

Manufacturers usually cover themselves in the contracts for rises in wages, cost of materials and the cost of modifications, required by the airline. It is important for an airline to obtain such protections as penalty clauses for late delivery, and for 'short performance'. An example of the latter is where the speed of the aircraft turns out to be less than was specified in the contract. Arrangements are sometimes made to pay for new aircraft in stages. For example, progress payments may be certain percentages payable:

On signature of the contract.
At the end of every six months after signing the contract to a maximum of six such periods.
On taking the fuselage out of the jig.
On completion of the inner main planes.
On completion of the fin-tail planes.
On completion of the main nose and chassis.
When the engines are received at works.
On completion of power plants.
On completion of outer main planes.
On completion of ailerons and flaps.
On completion of elevators and rudders.
When the aircraft is complete to engine test.
On completion and acceptance.

The major items of purchasing

The following are the major categories of material purchases in airline operation:

(*a*) Aircraft, aircraft equipment, spares and furnishings.
(*b*) Hangar, workshop and tarmac equipment for the maintenance of aircraft.
(*c*) Land, buildings, interior equipment and furnishings.
(*d*) Printed material and stationery.
(*e*) Uniforms.
(*f*) Catering stores and equipment.
(*g*) Ground transport equipment.
(*h*) Fuel and oil.
(*i*) Ground communications equipment.

The volume of purchasing

The volumes of purchasing in major airlines require sizeable organisations to deal with them. The following table indicates the amount of work that was done in a recent year by a department (employing over 100 staff) purchasing only aircraft, aircraft accessories and ground communications equipment, for a fleet of approximately 100 aircraft.

Total number of suppliers	2,377
Total number of orders	50,559
Average number of orders per supplier	21
Total value of orders	£13,234,936
Average amount spent per supplier	£5,568
Average amount spent per order	£261

To show that these figures are not dominated by a few large purchases the table below gives every case where more than £100,000 was spent with a single supplier in the course of the year.

TABLE 19. *Airline purchases*

Categories of purchases	No. of orders	Total value to nearest £1,000
		£
Aircraft frames and spares	187	220,000
	596	260,000
	423	110,000
	94	180,000
	1,855	400,000
Instruments	27	270,000
	14	110,000
	127	370,000
	822	490,000
	77	150,000
Engines	298	250,000
Propellers	325	180,000
Tyres	473	220,000
Ground communications equipment	250	300,000
		3,510,000

The aims of a purchasing organisation

The aims of the purchasing component of airline organisation are to buy equipment in such a manner that:

(*a*) The right equipment is available at the right time in the right place; and
(*b*) The equipment is bought at lowest price; and
(*c*) In considering lowest price account is taken of storage costs, interest charges and organisational processes.

This simple statement of aims contains implications of the difficulties of this branch of management. The aims plainly are in conflict. To make sure equipment is available at the right place at the right time means that its delivery should not be left to the last moment. Yet to obtain delivery before the time when something is needed involves storage charges. This adds to the cost of equipment. Obviously skill is required to draw the line between economies of purchase and the operational dis-economies of not having equipment when it is required.

The aim of getting equipment at the right time is difficult enough without having to consider price. It involves what are called lead times. These are the periods between order and delivery needed by each supplier. Lead times differ from supplier to supplier and from commodity to commodity. Some suppliers are more reliable than others in keeping to their declared lead times. In general the longer the lead times an airline can afford to give its suppliers, the lower will be purchase prices. This is because orders placed a long time in advance of the date on which delivery is required enable the supplier to plan production to take place in the cheapest way. In pursuing an aim to order equipment well in advance of the need for it, purchasing management is likely to come into conflict with the planning processes of other departments. In fact, the chance of managing purchasing well is reduced by constant changes of plans in operating departments.

The arguments for and against a single purchasing organisation

Four of the ten airlines illustrated in Figs. 20 to 29 each do their purchasing in no less than four organisation components, another four do it in three, and two in two. If we set aside the purchasing (buying advertising and agents' services) in marketing departments, we have two airlines that have centralised equipment purchasing, and the other eight that have not centralised it.

The arguments for centralising are:

(*a*) By centralising purchasing a sufficiently large organisation can be created to take advantage of the benefits to be derived from specialisation.

For example, reporting to the General Manager, Purchases and Stores, Trans-Canada Air Lines were the following senior officials:

Contracts Administrator.
Economic Analyst.
Manager, Aviation Fuel Supply.
Project Co-ordinator,
and Director, Purchases and Stores.

The Director, Purchases and Stores, had reporting to him the following:

Officials	*Assisted by*
Manager, System Inventory	Inventory specialist and inventory analyst.
Supervisor, Performance Analysis	Performance analyst.
General Purchasing Agent	Buyers, warranty administrator and surplus sales administrator.
Supervisor, Administrative Services	Personnel assistant, customs and transportation specialist, and supply procedures planner.
Stationery Storekeeper	
Supply Managers, Dorval, Winnipeg, Malton, Vancouver and London, Eng.	Office manager, technical assistant stores, purchasing agents, foreman stores, inventory manager.

(*b*) The knowledge to be gained from experience of dealings with suppliers is not scattered throughout the airline, but is collected in a single department.

(*c*) The airline speaks with one voice to each supplier.

(*d*) A single purchasing department has quasi-monopolistic power in its dealings with suppliers.

(*e*) A single purchasing department can enjoy the economies of scale in record-keeping, accounting, storage, security, etc.

(*f*) A single purchasing department can take advantage of the economies of bulk buying.

The arguments against centralising are:

(*a*) To allow large quantities of materials to be bought by one man is incurring the risk of making big mistakes.

(*b*) While centralisation enables an airline to benefit more fully from *buying expertise*, it also makes the *expertise of the user* one stage removed from the supplier. For example, the engineer specialising in the use of test equipment who wants to buy something may go to a buyer who then goes to a firm specialising in the manufacture of test equipment.

(*c*) A centralised purchasing department is liable to incur unnecessary delivery costs because of the distances comprising an airline network. In other words the extra costs involved in making small local purchases may be more than offset by the costs of transport from a single supplier to points distributed over a wide area.

The tasks of a purchasing department in an airline

The tasks of a purchasing department in an airline are typically as follows:

Ordering—including negotiating terms of contract, placing orders, checking on deliveries and remedying failures to meet contracts.

Analysis—keeping records on prices, examining materials, studying markets, analysing prices and storage charges, and controlling variations from specifications.

Accounting—checking invoice quantities and prices, ensuring that the right discounts have been allowed, and correcting wrong charges.

The disposal of unwanted equipment.

Customs clearance of incoming and outgoing company equipment.

Accepting delivery—recording deliveries, checking that consignments are in accordance with orders both in quantity and quality, and where necessary arranging for expert inspection.

Storage and security.

Issuing of equipment from stores.

Delivery of equipment to shops and offices.

Making periodical physical inventories of stores stocks.

Arranging the shipment of stores.

Airline planning and purchasing management

Fundamentally the role of purchasing management in an airline is to provide at least part of the equipment and raw materials element in the other components of the organisation. The demand for equipment and raw materials is, of course, dominated by the annual operating or fleet plan, so purchasing departments can usually use these plans to forecast their own activities. For example, the fleet plan can be used for forecasting the amount of each type of fuel that will have to be bought for use at each station. This forecast, together with the information supplied by stations on their refuelling service needs, can be used as a basis for re-negotiating contracts with fuel companies.

Company planning should enable the purchasing manager to plan his purchases over the long-term. This means that the purchasing department can then buy in bulk to meet short-term orders from the other departments. For example, all the spares needed for a certain aircraft type could be bought at one time, rather than buying an initial quantity and adding to it later. This might bring about savings in spite of increased storage charges.

In general it is true that better planning leads to better prices; and better planning reduces the number of occasions on which an airline has to resort to the costly procedure of emergency buying.

CHAPTER XV

PRODUCTION MANAGEMENT

What is 'Production' in an airline?

To answer this we may first state the characteristics of production, and then identify those activities in an airline that have these characteristics. For example, production may be defined broadly as an act of change: we may then regard all acts of change in an airline as part of production.

Production may be defined more precisely as changing the condition of a person or thing from one of less value to one of more value, as evidenced by someone's willingness to pay for the change. Most of the activities in an airline are 'productive' in this sense. There may be changes that are valueless, and therefore 'unprofitable' (i.e. without gain), but these should be exceptional in a well-run business. Thus, from this point of view, accountants, buyers, engineers, pilots, salesmen and personnel officers can all be said to engage in production.

How is it then that any activity can be singled out and given a Production label? The author has dealt with this question at some length in a previous work,[1] but briefly it is useful to regard Production (with a capital P): (*a*) as the *residue* from all the common productive activities that make up a business, and (*b*) as the most *businesslike* of all the productive activities. Production in this sense comprises all those activities that cannot be labelled finance, purchasing, marketing, personnel or development. It is what is left over after all the other major specialisations have been identified. This leads us to the next point. The techniques of financing, purchasing, marketing, and so on are similar from one business to another. But production is different from one business to another. An airline is recognisable, not because it keeps accounts, buys materials, or advertises, but because it carries people and goods in aircraft.

This reasoning may be useful to establish a basis for the divisions in overall organisation. Certain features are common among the

[1] *Fundamentals of Management*, p. 153 et seq. W. S. Barry. George Allen & Unwin, 1962.

residual activities; they are watched by customers; timing is of prime importance in them, and so on. This suggests that the whole of Production should be headed up by one man reporting to the managing director. But the argument is still insufficiently complete to eschew the confusion that arises from the use of the term production with a small 'p'.

The trouble is that the word is used as a label for three aspects of the activity described above. Firstly, production is used to describe achievement. In this sense production means *the gain in value* brought about by change. It is used as a synonym for 'product'. The product of transport is primarily the arrival of passengers or goods, so it may be argued that there is no production unless this is achieved. Secondly, production is used as a label for the *process* that achieves profitable change. It is used as a label for the process of 'carriage', by which the products of 'arrivals' are secured. There is a *direct* relationship between these two aspects of production and while the distinction is useful, confusion of the two is not serious. The danger lies in the use of the word production as a label for a third aspect. This is where the word is used as a label for *process-plus-waste*. All processes of production involve waste. It is impracticable to work the elements of organisation continuously and 'productively'. Inevitably lathes will turn awaiting work; men attend their benches awaiting work, aircraft fly around the skies empty. Process-plus-waste bears no direct relation to the product, and confusion can be dangerous. Process-plus-waste is referred to in an earlier chapter as utilisation. The danger is that, in accepting waste as inevitable in the production process, we may lose sight of the need to minimise it.

Airline products

Airline products are the arrivals of passengers, freight and mail (collectively known as traffic) at the right place on time. There are not just a few types of product, but rather an infinite variety. Products are differentiated basically by each arrival having associated with it certain variables that alter its value in the eyes of the customer. Every arrival is associated with distance from the point of departure. Generally speaking the greater the distance, the greater the geographical controls to overcome, the greater the value in the eyes of the customer, and the greater the cost to the airline. Every arrival is associated with times of departure and arrival. Certain times have more value in the eyes of customers than other times. Arrivals are associated with the process in what are, to the customer, 'conditions of carriage'. Certain conditions of carriage make arrivals more valuable than others in the eyes of customers.

Divisions of Production Management

A practicable division of production management that is reflected in numerous organisations, is into the three aspects of passenger and freight control, aircraft movement control, and maintenance control. These may be defined as follows:

Passenger and Freight Control

Is imposed on the embarkation and disembarkation of passengers, and the loading and unloading of freight, from ground installations to aircraft and vice versa; it may also be regarded as including the care of passengers and freight on-board vehicles.

Aircraft movement control

Is imposed on the movements of aircraft from terminal to terminal in accordance with flight plans.

Maintenance Control

Is imposed on the task of keeping terminals, aircraft and navigational aids in good order, either by the prevention or speedy remedy of breakdowns.

The term 'traffic' is sometimes used to describe activities falling within the purview of passenger and freight control as defined above. But at other times 'traffic' is used to cover aircraft movement control as well, and at times to cover all aspects of production. The terms 'operating' and 'operations' are sometimes used to describe activities falling within the purview of aircraft movement control, as defined above. But at other times 'operating' and 'operations' are used to cover passenger and freight control as well, and at times to cover all aspects of production. For this reason the terms have been avoided here.

Co-ordination of Production Management

The three aspects must be dove-tailed by the time an aircraft is due to depart. A serviceable aircraft must be provided by the maintenance department, a competent crew by the flight department, and a properly attended group of passengers for embarkation, and cargo and mail for loading, at the same time. The big question is at what level of authority should these aspects be co-ordinated? Is the production task a real enough entity to be represented by one man in the top rank of specialists? Should the managing director himself co-ordinate the activities of three specialists dealing in different aspects of production? Or should they be co-ordinated at a level below the managing director, so that they present a united front? Should the conflicts between groups of widely different skills be resolved by the managing director or before they reach him?

At one end of the spectrum we have companies like Trans-Canada Air Lines that in 1961 had co-ordinated all three with a Senior Vice-President, Operations, who reported to the President (Fig. 29). At the other end we have companies like British European Airways that in 1962 had a Traffic Director, a Flight Operations Director and a Chief Engineer reporting to the Chief Executive (Fig. 23). In the middle we have companies like KLM that co-ordinated two aspects under a Vice-President, Operations, leaving the third to report separately to the President via a Vice-President, Engineering and Maintenance (Fig. 25).

A not unusual answer to the question raised above is that even though it may be argued that passenger and freight control is part of the production process, it is so important to marketing, by nature of the industry, that it must be co-ordinated with marketing at a level below the managing director. Thus British Overseas Airways in 1961 had a Commercial Director co-ordinating both these functions (Fig. 23).

Co-operation in the production field

Co-operation among airlines occurs in the three aspects of production, viz. aircraft movement, passenger and freight and maintenance control. There are cases in which airlines of more or less the same size have pooled their production resources. Scandinavian Airlines Systems and Swissair made such an arrangement in the early 1960s. There are other cases in which a large airline has co-operated with a smaller one, as with BEA and Olympic Airways, and BEA and Cyprus Airways.

Measures of production

The significance of ideas on what is and what is not production is highlighted when we attempt to measure it. If measures of production are not to include the waste referred to above, they must be confined to activities that secure arrivals over a given period of time. The value of simply counting arrivals is limited since not all arrivals are similar products. Arrivals are differentiated by distance from the departure point. An arrival 500 miles away from the departure point is probably valued more highly than one 300 miles away. True measures of production must not only take into account the fact that nothing is produced unless arrivals are secured, but also the different distances that are associated with various arrivals.

The most comprehensive measure is that of Revenue Tone-Kilometres (RTK) or Load Ton-Miles (LTM), which is paying load in tons × the distance it is carried. If the LTM measure is used miles must be defined, e.g. as statute miles of 1,760 yards. In either case distance must be defined, e.g. that based on Standard (Great Circle) distances between airports. Tons must also be defined, e.g. short tons of 2,000 lb.

Besides this comprehensive measure the following are commonly used for various forms of traffic:

(i) Passengers carried (omitting consideration of distance).
(ii) Revenue passenger-miles.
(iii) Mail carried in tons (omitting consideration of distance).
(iv) Mail ton-miles.
(v) Freight carried in tons (omitting consideration of distance).
(vi) Freight ton-miles.

Measures of aircraft movements *per se* are not true measures of production; they are measures of process-plus-waste. For example, capacity ton-miles measures the *capacity* for the payload of the aircraft, measured in short tons, multiplied by the miles flown. Tonne-Kilometres available is a similar measure in which Kilometres are used instead of miles. The usefulness of the measure of aircraft movements (or utilisation) is that, by comparing it with LTM or RTK, management can find out how much aircraft movement is wasted because of lack of raw materials (i.e. passengers and freight).

Journey lengths and flight stages

An important variable in the production-effort involved per passenger-mile flown is the average journey length. The longer the journey the greater are the number of miles over which to spread selling, embarkation and disembarkation efforts. Another important variable is average stage length. Journey length is the average distance between points of embarkation and disembarkation of passengers and freight; stage length is the distance between airports of *aircraft* departure and destination. Problems increase if journey lengths do not coincide with stage lengths.

The handicap of producing short-haul arrivals

Passengers travelling short distances prefer to avoid night departures and arrivals, because of surface transport and accommodation difficulties. They do not usually mind flying through the night on long journeys. Passengers travelling short distances need the inducement of lower fares to persuade them to travel by night, but there are limits to the reductions that airlines can make in night fares. The costs of night services may be higher than those of day-time services. Night duties may be paid at overtime rates, or attract shift pay. Crew utilisation drops because of restrictions on night work, and so on.

If aircraft are taking off and landing every hour of their working life, as they may have to do in a short-haul airline, aircraft utilisation is inevitably low. Crews who have to spend 'duty-time' on the ground making the arrangements connected with each flight will be under-utilised from the point of view of hours spent flying. Fuel consumption per mile-flown increases with the number of take-offs and climbs made per 100 miles of flight. The shorter the distance between stations the higher is the staffing and equipment ratio per route mile for passenger and freight, aircraft movement and maintenance control. Marketing costs, reservations costs, etc., are higher per seat-mile as the length of a journey decreases. It costs just as much to do the paperwork for a passenger flying from London to Paris as it does for a passenger from London to New York.

MAINTENANCE CONTROL

The need for maintenance—preventive and remedial

There are five main ways in which the need for maintenance of aircraft arises.

Preventive maintenance

(*a*) Normal wear and tear occurs in working parts.
(*b*) Deterioration occurs in equipment whether it be standing still or working. This deterioration is a result of environmental factors such as atmosphere, and may, therefore, be seen as a product of time.

Remedial maintenance

(*c*) The sudden failure of materials is caused through their being subjected to periodic stresses and strains. For example, material fatigue may result from the shock produced in aircraft landings.
(*d*) The inherent characteristics of equipment may make its behaviour unpredictable, and therefore unreliable. Thus an intricate piece of machinery may suddenly fail through malfunctioning of the parts, which in turn may result from faulty design or manufacture.
(*e*) Accidental damage may occur, in which equipment is subjected to conditions, such as collision, that were not intended to be part of their use.

Remedial maintenance and standby aircraft

Management's main objective is to control maintenance in such a way that it has the least adverse effect on the productive capacity of equipment. This means planning to maintain aircraft during periods when they are not wanted on service. Plans will be based on normal wear and tear, and deterioration (i.e. the need for preventive maintenance). Sudden failure, and the need for remedial maintenance, usually requires management to provide standby equipment. Some airlines keep between 8 and 10 per cent of each type of aircraft in reserve, to put on the line if aircraft in service suffer sudden failure.

To provide standbys to meet needs for remedial maintenance poses problems. If 10 per cent is the optimum for aircraft in reserve what if the operation calls for the use of only five aircraft? The choice may be between nothing and a 20 per cent cover. This is a more serious problem for the small operator. A small line with only two or three aircraft has to face the possibilities of leaving passengers stranded or provide an uneconomic 30 per cent to 50 per cent reserve. The small airline with inadequate financial reserves, cannot afford to lock up capital, and there is a constant temptation to bring reserve aircraft into full service. There may be conflict even in large airlines between general management and maintenance control over the question of encroachments on aircraft reserves.

Planning preventive maintenance

The pattern of preventive maintenance is affected by aircraft type and traffic. A high-cost aircraft may have to be flown during daylight hours to attract high-paying traffic. It may, therefore, have to be maintained at night. A low-cost aircraft may be used profitably to carry low-paying traffic by night, and employ otherwise idle maintenance equipment by day. Most passengers prefer to fly by day, whereas most freight is conveniently carried by night. These facts may enable management to plan a programme of maintenance spread over 24 hours. This makes for economical use of hangars, workshops, and repair and overhaul equipment.

Certain systems give rise to 'peaks', and do not make the best use of operatives and equipment. This can be illustrated by plotting a maintenance schedule for one aircraft. It is assumed that maintenance is carried out by four programmes, or 'checks'. Each programme involves more components than its predecessor, and takes longer to complete. Assuming that Checks 1 to 4 take place after 200, 1,500, 2,100 and 2,900 flying hours, and that they take 10, 60, 80 and 150 hours respectively to complete, the schedule may be represented graphically as in Fig. 44. For simplicity this pattern excludes checks that have to be made after a certain amount of time has elapsed, whether the aircraft has flown or not.

This is what is happening on a special time scale, i.e. hours flown. It is not what is happening in the real time scale at the maintenance base. We have to add the natural time scale as in Fig. 45 to show that.

The problem is basically the product of:

(*a*) Periodicity of programmes for each aircraft type (expressed in hours flown, or time elapsed); and

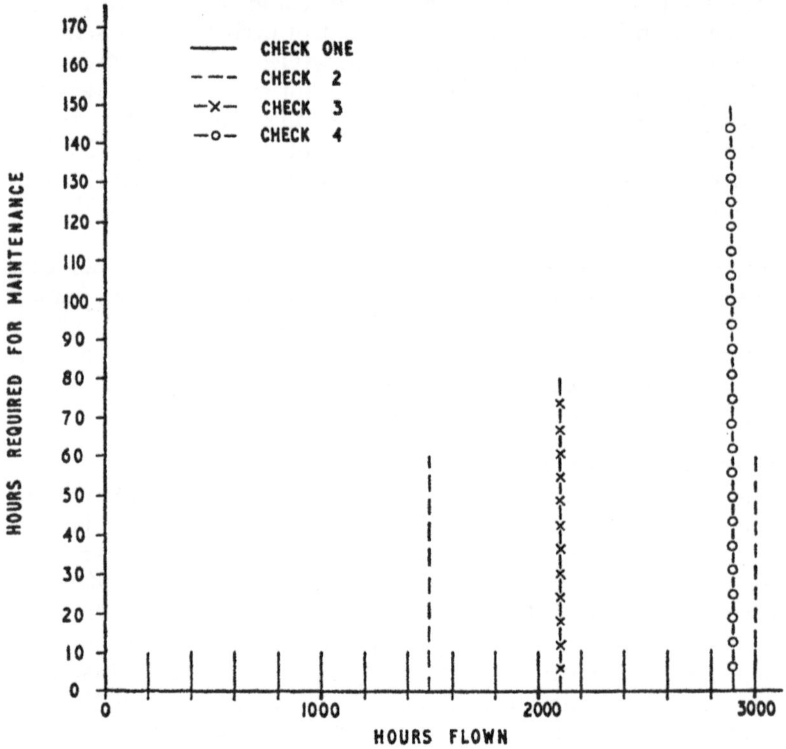

FIG. 44. *Showing a possible maintenance pattern for one aircraft: hours flown × hours required for maintenance*

(*b*) Rate of utilisation of each aircraft; resulting in;

(*c*) Time of acceptance of each aircraft into the maintenance base; and

(*d*) Duration of each type of maintenance check.

Making full use of organisation for maintenance

Management's main objective in maintenance control is to ensure the least adverse effect on the productive capacity of equipment.

The second objective is to carry out the programme at least cost, by fully using the organisation. Overheads will thus be spread over the maximum number of checks, and each check will bear a minimum share of the overall cost.

Assuming that the organisation, doing the maintenance of the one aircraft referred to above, were capable of handling only one aircraft *at a time*, then the utilisation of the maintenance organisation by operating only one aircraft would be just over 9 per cent. In 5,500 hours of maintenance (elapsed) time we have:

$$\begin{aligned} 15 \times 10 \text{ hours} &= 150 \text{ hours spent on Check 1s} \\ 2 \times 60 \text{ hours} &= 120 \text{ hours spent on Check 2s} \\ 1 \times 80 \text{ hours} &= 80 \text{ hours spent on Check 3} \\ 1 \times 150 \text{ hours} &= 150 \text{ hours spent on Check 4} \\ \text{Total} &= 500 \text{ hours spent on all Checks} \end{aligned}$$

It is tempting to conclude that a fleet of 11 aircraft would make the most of the organisation. But this would be wrong because long checks are interspersed among short ones. Every so often a single aircraft occupies the organisation for 150 hours making the scheduling difficult, and reducing the maximum utilisation of the organisation.

Limitations of a maintenance organisation

The limitations of a maintenance organisation are:

(*a*) The overall number of operatives employed;
(*b*) The number of operatives possessing particular (specialist) skills.
(*c*) Effectiveness of planning.
(*d*) Amount of hangar space available.
(*e*) Amount of workshop space and tools available.
(*f*) Availability of spares.

Compromises in maintenance planning

As aircraft become more complicated, and checks bigger, planning difficulties increase. So some airlines simplify the problem by spreading some of the bigger checks over a small number of equal doses. The penalty for doing this is that some components have to be dealt with before their proper time; but this disadvantage is outweighed by the simplification in planning, and by the gains from keeping aircraft flying in the daytime.

In one airline a Check 4 for a jet aircraft is planned to take 14 days. General management decided that the airline could not afford to have these aircraft idle at weekends when they would earn most

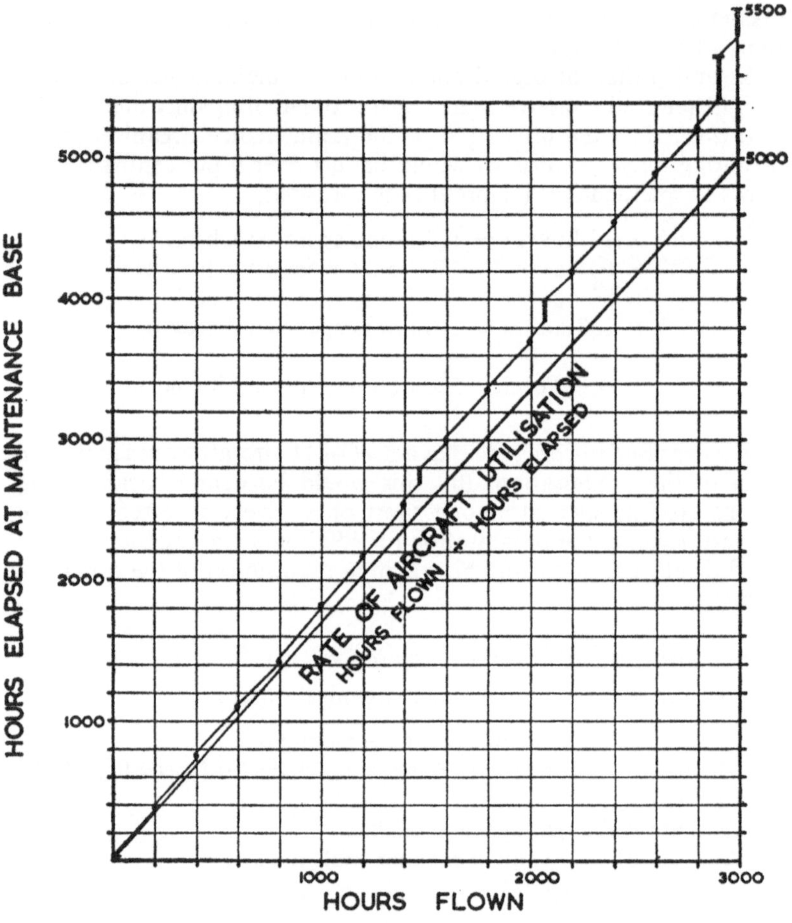

FIG. 45. *Showing maintenance base loading for a single aircraft*

money. So Check 4s were chopped up and spread over the other checks, so that no one check took more than 5 week-days. In another case it was decided that a freighter could not be freed for more than 8 hours in every 24, so maintenance had to be arranged in 8-hourly doses. These cases illustrate a trend in which airline management was breaking away from the technical optimum for maintenance (which had hitherto dominated its operations) in favour of the marketing optimum.

Inspection

One of the most effective managerial controls on the quality of work done by an aircraft maintenance organisation is achieved by Inspection Branches. Although Inspection Branches are usually closely integrated with the 'doing' part of the maintenance organisation, to ensure that the work of inspection does not impede production, the Chief Inspector usually regards himself accountable to the national authority for safety standards. Chief Inspectors usually have the right of direct access to the Managing Director, so that in cases of conflict between inspection and production, the inspection point-of-view can be fully represented at the highest level.

The Chief Inspector has one of the most difficult managerial tasks in the airline. He has to play his part as a loyal member of the airline management team, and yet have the integrity to be awkward when the occasion calls for it.

State control on maintenance standards

Airline managements usually have to conform to standards of maintenance and 'airworthiness' laid down by government authority. In the United States the Civil Aeronautics Board is such an authority, in France it is the Bureau Veritas, and in England it is the Air Registration Board. Inspection Branches usually constitute the main link between the government authority and the airline.

'Base' and 'on-line' maintenance

The big tasks in aircraft maintenance are almost always undertaken at a main base. The siting of main bases has an important effect on the economics of maintenance. The problem is to reduce 'dead' flying (i.e. in which no paying passengers or freight are carried) by aircraft that become 'unserviceable', and must be returned to base for attention. By 'unserviceable' we do not mean unable to fly; we mean not in a fit state to carry its proper load.

Sometimes a big maintenance job has to be undertaken away from main base, because an aircraft cannot be flown before it is repaired. Otherwise on-line maintenance is confined to small checks and the replacement of parts that have become defective en route.

General ideas of 'airworthiness'

The concept of 'airworthiness' is useful to management in the task of striking a balance between the demands of safety and the economy of an airline. It provides a standard without which extreme views could not be held in check. Admittedly it is undefined, but this is not a fatal flaw as one might expect. To make something fit to travel through the air is a commonsense aim, and eschews the extravagances of perfection. Something that is *fit* to do a job is suited to the circumstances of the case; it *answers the purpose*. The purpose of an aircraft travelling through the air is to take people safely to their destination at a price that they can afford to pay.

By and large the managerial approach to establishing airworthiness is empirical. It is based on observation and experiment. Management gives first place to experience, and second place to the knowledge of principles. This is one reason for saying that the industry works at the boundaries of knowledge, much of what is done is imperfectly understood. But it is enough that it works. Interestingly this lack of knowledge of principles in many areas makes the 'proving' processes of the industry elaborate and painstaking. No piece of equipment is thoroughly trusted because it is *theoretically* sound. Equipment has to earn the trust put in it. At first it acquires little, it is expected to fail at any moment; then with experience the belief in its reliability grows, and this belief is quantified by extending it reliable life in terms of working hours.

The effect of maintenance on utilisation

The time needed for maintenance is only one of the factors that limit the utilisation of aircraft. By 'utilisation' we mean here the time an aircraft spends flying on service. Utilisation is not necessarily profitable but it provides a yardstick to measure the effect of maintenance. Other factors affecting utilisation are:

(*a*) Time spent preparing for flight, e.g. refuelling, embarking and disembarking, loading and unloading;
(*b*) Time spent in reserve, as standby for other aircraft going unserviceable;
(*c*) Time during which aircraft are not commercially usable, e.g. it may not be possible to sell seats on aircraft flying in the early hours of the morning.

The effect of maintenance on aircraft utilisation is illustrated by Fig. 46 showing the utilisation of certain jet aircraft during a summer month in 1963. The utilisation for the month has been expressed as daily averages.

The balancing of hangars, workshops and stores

In most big organisations equipment is divided into three:

Hangars: these usually house whole aircraft to enable work to be done under cover. Aircraft are stripped and re-assembled in them.

Workshops: components are stripped, tested and, if necessary, repaired in workshops. Here faults are rectified as distinct from merely removing and replacing components.

Stores: these are where aircraft spares are kept.

These three sections are closely related, and skill is required in balancing the demands made on each. Management will balance these demands at a level that calls for minimum holdings of spares. Nevertheless, spares holdings of between 20 per cent and 40 per cent of the value of a fleet are not uncommon.

Let us assume that the mainplane of a certain aircraft takes 10 days to overhaul, and that two routine checks have been established, one of 5 days and one of 14 days. If the mainplane is overhauled during the 14-day check it can be overhauled *in situ*, in the hangar.

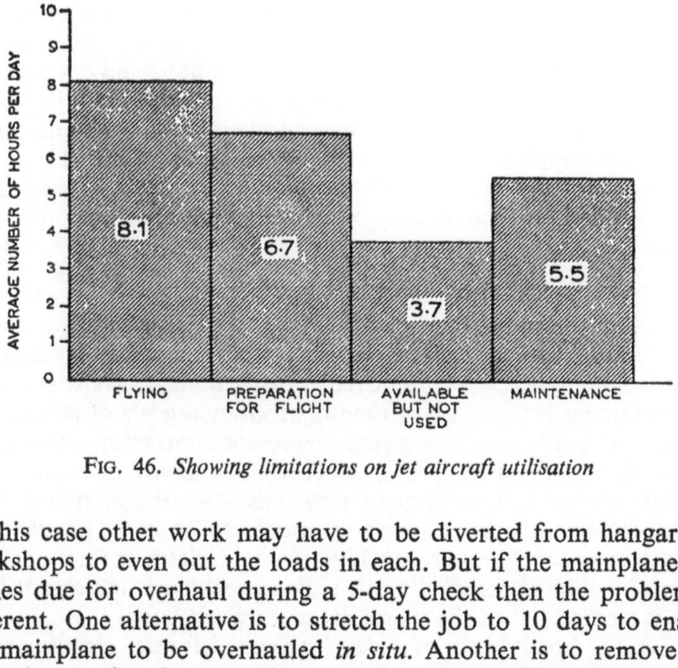

FIG. 46. *Showing limitations on jet aircraft utilisation*

In this case other work may have to be diverted from hangars to workshops to even out the loads in each. But if the mainplane becomes due for overhaul during a 5-day check then the problem is different. One alternative is to stretch the job to 10 days to enable the mainplane to be overhauled *in situ*. Another is to remove the mainplane and replace it with a spare from stores. Then the overhaul can be done in the workshops, but the stores have to carry a spare mainplane. These are the sort of considerations that management must weigh carefully in their efforts to balance the load of the three sections.

'*Main units*' *and* '*components*'

The concept of a main unit as a bundle of parts called components has been well-used. Aircraft used to be referred to as 'bundles of components flying around in close formation'. The concept was useful because the components had 'lives' independent of the main unit. The hours of life varied for each component according to its reliability, position and importance. There were few main unit characteristics to discourage the idea. They did not suffer from being regarded as bundles of components. The constant stripping and tampering with main units, to get at small components did not appear to upset the working of the whole unit.

With the coming of jet aircraft the situation began to change. Main units acquired characteristics that made it undesirable to break joints between one component and another any more than was necessary. In some cases breaking the joints could increase the probability of fatigue. Aircraft began to have 'systems', that were easily upset by tampering with their parts. Indeed the electronic systems and controls of subsonic aircraft made them 'whole' aircraft and it is doubtful whether the concept of main units and components having separate existences continues to be as useful as it has been. It remains useful to purchasing management as it is still necessary to balance supplies of main units and components. The main importance of this change was that maintenance had henceforth to be controlled in such a way that stripping of main units was minimised.

Maintenance by organisation or contracting

It has been estimated that, of the total cost of *overhauling an engine* in an airline's own workshops, the cost of raw materials, in the shape of replacements for parts removed, can be as high as 70 per cent. The remainder is made up of the organisational costs of labour and equipment. This represents a high degree of contracting, and a low degree of organisation. The specialisation involved in engine construction makes it necessary in most cases to obtain spares from manufacturers. Charges for spares appear to be high, but whether they are or not they represent a high raw material cost for an airline. The proportion of contracting in engine overhaul is increased if the work is carried out in the manufacturer's workshops.

A typical breakdown of total (engine, airframe, electrics, etc.) maintenance costs is as follows:

TABLE 20. *Breakdown of total maintenance costs*

		Per cent	Per cent
By organisation:	Operatives	33	
	Equipment	12	
	Inspection	6	
		—	51
By contracting:	Raw materials		22
	Overhauls—engines	14	
	—others	13	
		—	27
			100

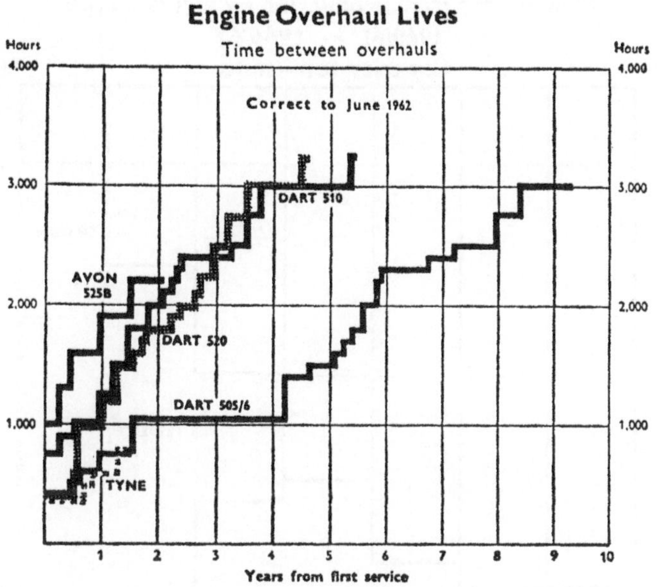

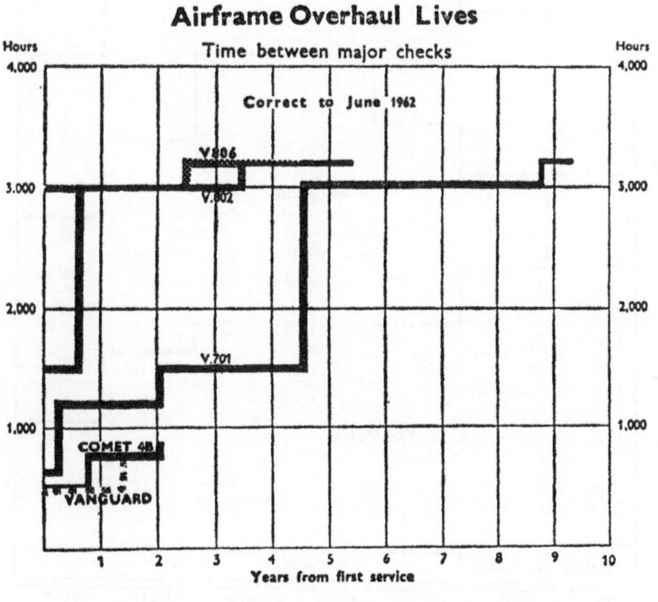

FIG. 47. *Efficiency Indicators: Engine overhaul lives*
Airframe overhaul lives

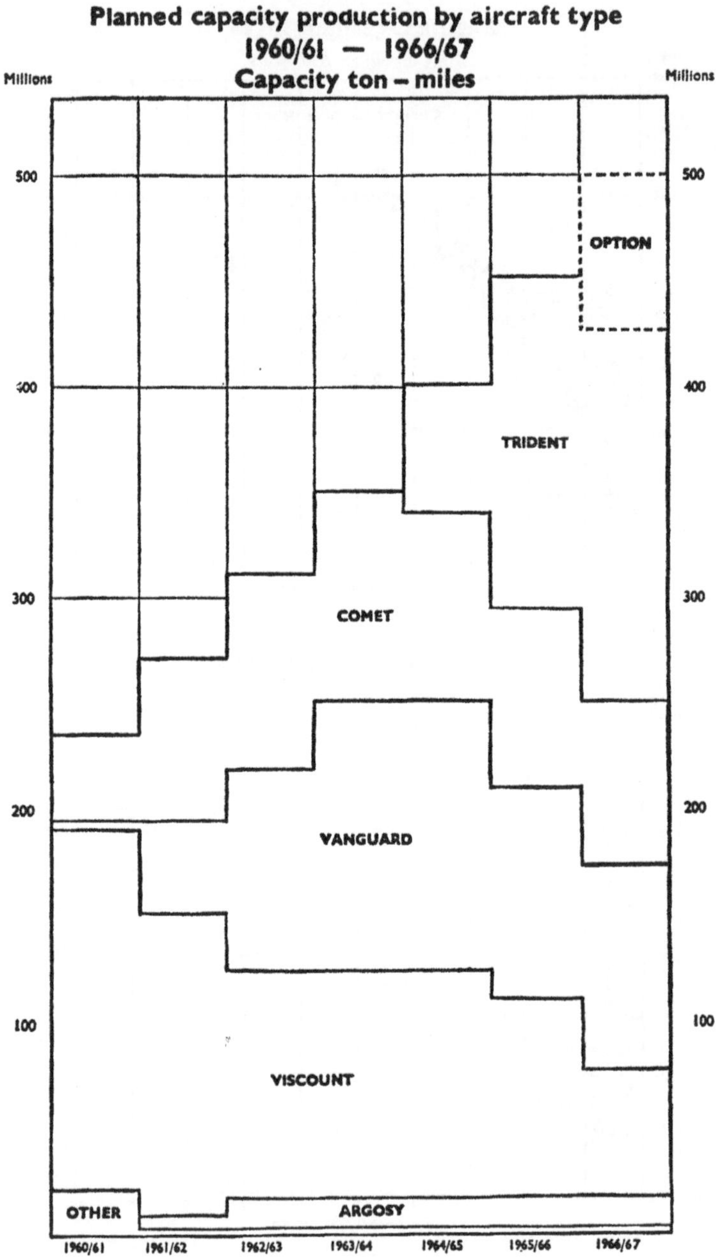

FIG. 48. *Planned capacity production by aircraft type*

Factors that enter into decisions whether to organise or contract maintenance are:

(*a*) When an airline has bought new and relatively untried equipment it may send this to the manufacturer to enable the latter to become familiar with likely defects.
(*b*) Some forms of equipment require exceptionally expensive testing apparatus, perhaps kept in a clean, dust-free, atmospherically controlled chamber. In this case the manufacturer may be able to provide these facilities more economically than the operator can.
(*c*) In some cases the number of components that have to be dealt with do not justify an airline's acquisition of testing apparatus.
(*d*) The spares' float necessary if an airline is to do its own overhauls may make the cost uneconomic.
(*e*) Where the maintenance organisation is not fully used it may pay the airline to do more work within.

AIRCRAFT MOVEMENT CONTROL

Schedules Planning

Aircraft movements are controlled to achieve the aims of safe, punctual, comfortable and cheap flights. But these aims are not equal in importance. Safety comes before everything else. Punctuality and comfort must be sacrificed if necessary and no reputable airline will lower its safety standards in order to reduce its costs.

Assuming the over-riding importance of safety we can establish an order of priorities in the aims of aircraft movement control. Firstly it must aim to fulfil the long-term fleet plan as long as it is economically sound. Aircraft movements must be controlled to cover all costs (under a standard costing procedure) in the long run, and to provide the margin of profit envisaged.

Long-term schedules-planning aims to control aircraft movements so that they will secure the maximum economic advantage. The maximum use must be made of aircraft by the optimum distribution on routes. The demand on a certain route may call for only two hours' flying a day from an aircraft that could fly eight hours. The aircraft must then be moved from the one route to another to obtain good use of it. The success of the movement from route to route depends upon their being in the right place at the right time. Often this is rendered impossible by the pattern of demand. For example, the traffic flow on a certain route may be concentrated on a 0900 hours departure from point A and a 1800 hours return from point B. To make use of the intervening hours may then require a journey on which the aircraft flies empty.

Short-term operational control

The next important task in controlling aircraft is to set up a day-to-day watch on movements to ensure that they are as far as possible in accordance with the schedules plan. Where it is no longer possible to operate to schedule, then movements must be controlled to derive the maximum economic advantage from the changed circumstances. Management has to have a different approach to short-term operational control from that which it has to long-term schedules planning. The latter calls for decisions that take all costs into account. Short-term operational control calls for decisions based on marginal costing. From the point of view of the manager faced with making a decision on the movement of a diverted aircraft, a great number of costs have already been incurred, and could not be reduced by cancelling a flight. A schedules planner can often make substantial economies by reducing the frequency on a certain route. But once the organisation has been set up to provide a given standard of service it is not possible to make significant economies by the cancellation of services at short notice. About all that can be saved by cancelling a flight already planned is on petrol, landing fees and possibly crew allowances.

Day-to-day movement control must therefore be flexible enough to make the best of a bad job. Diversions from plan are usually uneconomic to some extent. The immediate job is to minimise the losses. This can be done by obtaining the maximum contribution to costs already incurred, and does not necessitate covering all costs. Finally we must emphasise that the point of view of short-term operational control would be disastrous in the long term because total costs would not be covered by decisions based on marginal costs.

Notams

Individual airline managements are unable by themselves to collect, arrange and distribute on time all the information that is required for the safe movement of aircraft. Airline pilots obtain a vital part of the information they need from 'notams' (an abbreviation of the phrase 'notices to airmen'). The form of international notams is generally supervised by the Aeronautical Information Services Branch of ICAO. Notams are usually produced as daily bulletins at about 0900 hours, and aircraft commanders examine them as a routine part of their pre-flight preparations. Any amendments needed after printing are provided for separately so that information can be fed in hourly.

A notam may be originated and issued whenever the following information is of direct operational significance:

(*a*) The establishment or withdrawal of electronic and other aids to air navigation and aerodromes.
(*b*) Interruption or return to operation, change of frequencies, change of identification, change of orientation (directional aids), change of location, power increase or decrease amounting to 50 per cent or more, change in broadcast schedules or contents, or irregularity or unreliability of operation of any electronic aid to air navigation, and air-ground communication services.
(*c*) Interruption of or return to operation of aerodrome lighting system.
(*d*) Establishment, withdrawal or significant changes made to visual aids.
(*e*) Occurrence or removal of temporary obstructions to aircraft operations in the manoeuvring area.
(*f*) Presence or removal of hazardous conditions due to snow, ice or water on the movement area.
(*g*) Establishment, withdrawal or significant changes made to procedures for air navigation services.
(*h*) Presence of airborne hazards to air navigation.
(*i*) Military exercises or manoeuvres affecting air navigation.
(*j*) Major changes to search and rescue facilities and services available.
(*k*) Interruption or return to operation of hazard beacons and obstruction lights marking obstructions to air navigation.
(*l*) Changes in entry regulations requiring immediate action.
(*m*) Erection or removal of obstructions to air navigation.
(*n*) Establishment or discontinuance (including activation or deactivation) as applicable, or changes in the status of prohibited, restricted or danger areas.
(*o*) Occurrence or correction of major defects in the movement area.
(*p*) Interruption or return to service of significant units of airport rescue or fire fighting facilities.
(*q*) Interruption or return to service of refuelling services.
(*r*) Air displays or mass movements of aircraft.
(*s*) Availability of new maps and charts.
(*t*) Changes in legislation requiring immediate notification.
(*u*) Any other significant circumstances.

Air Traffic Control

'In the history of most forms of transport there is a point where the gravest risk becomes one of collision between vehicles. This point is reached as the number of vehicles grows, and the frequency of journeys increases to such an extent that the distance separating each vehicle is no longer enough to leave matters safely in the hands of the man steering the vehicle. This has now happened with air traffic.

The skies are no longer the vast empty spaces that confronted the early aviator. They are now so full of aircraft that it is necessary for pilots to put themselves under the care and protection of authorities who police the skies. ATC exists for the orderly conduct of air traffic so that collisions may be avoided.'[1]

ATC is an aspect of aircraft movement control in which individual airlines have little say. Furthermore, it is an aspect in which little regard is paid to profitability. It is exercised almost exclusively in the interests of safety. The overall effects are, of course, necessary and beneficial. Occasionally they are deleterious to the economies of airlines. The delays from ATC figure prominently among the 'unavoidable' handicaps to punctual departures and arrivals.

The characteristics of demand increase the problems of ATC. When traffic is concentrated in short periods the congestion of aircraft makes their separation and speedy handling more difficult.

The economic disadvantages of air traffic control

The economic disadvantages caused by air traffic control are mainly of three sorts:

(*a*) Delays to the arrival and departure of aircraft cause loss of goodwill and diminish revenue; such delays derive from the inadequacy of runways to deal with traffic at peak periods, and from the overloading of controllers of blocked airspaces. Modern aircraft fails to gain full advantage from being faster because block-to-block speeds are increased proportionately less. Re-equipment may thus bring increased costs without corresponding increases in revenue.

(*b*) The circuitous nature of controlled airways causes flights to be longer than they would otherwise be, thus adding to costs of operation.

(*c*) Jet aircraft may be held at low altitudes at which they consume fuel at a high rate.

Channels of communication between management and aircraft crews

Because only a proportion of the flying staff are on duty at any one time, management's surest way of ensuring that everyone receives the same instructions is to put them in writing. Most airlines consolidate their written instructions into *Operations Manuals*. These should be arranged to ensure that someone wishing for information on a subject does not have to refer to an unreasonable number of parts of the manual. They should be clearly written and well-indexed. The style should be concise and should avoid unnecessary jargon. Above all, statements must not be ambiguous.

[1] *The Language of Aviation*, p. 151. W. S. Barry. Chatto & Windus, 1962.

Operations manuals are an embodiment of (permanent) *Standing Instructions.* In order to maintain the comprehensive nature of Operations Manuals the Standing Instructions they contain must be cancelled, modified or added to from time to time. Manuals are usually made up in a loose-leaf form so that they may be changed more easily. In their attempt to produce a comprehensive volume of instructions managements face a serious dilemma. Should they aim to be so complete that instructions cover every conceivable situation, or should they cover only those situations where doubt might exist as to the correct procedure? If they aim to be complete and a crew member does not depart from the book, the latter cannot be held to blame for an accident. Management has to accept responsibility for behaviour that is in accordance with its own instructions.

In practice airline managements do not attempt to provide for all eventualities in their instruction. Indeed most Operations Manuals are prefaced by a disclaimer of completeness. Usually some reference is made to the need for leaving a number of matters to commonsense, and the discretion of the crew member.

Control procedures usually include some provision for instructions given to cover a temporary situation, and which will no longer apply when the situation has changed. *Temporary instructions* should be identified as such, and should be removed as soon as they no longer apply so that they do not clutter up the volume of permanent instructions and create the danger of misleading. The shortest of temporary instructions are those covering situations contained within a single flight. These flight notices must again be clearly identified from the point of view of the flight to which they refer, to remove any danger of their being misapplied.

Flight Plans

One of the most important managerial controls is that of requiring an aircraft commander to file a flight plan. This partly overcomes the problem of obtaining a 'feedback' on aircraft movements. In making his flight plan an aircraft commander states his intentions in advance of take-off. Flight plans usually show such details as the identity of the pilot and his aircraft, the time and point of departure, proposed cruising altitude and airspeed, proposed route, destination, estimated time of arrival, the serviceable radio equipment the aircraft carries, and the frequency of its transmitter if it has one, and the alternative airport it will go to if it needs to divert from the original. It is then assumed that if an aircraft commander has to depart from his plan after take-off he will report this fact so that after making the necessary alterations management will once again have the whole picture. Management is able to check a captain's intentions before he leaves the ground, and, if it wishes, to give its approval to the method of carrying out each flight. It also receives a negative feedback in the shape of reports of deviations from plan.

Sometimes flight plans are partly prepared by a planning section attached to management. In these cases the area of decision left to the individual aircraft commander is reduced. Captains do not like to have their responsibilities diminished in this way, but the preparation of flight plans may relieve them of routine elements that waste their time on the ground. The preparation of flight plans compels an orderly approach to the problems of establishing objectives and to means of achieving them.

In-flight communications

A refinement in managerial control over aircraft movements is by means of communication with the aircraft commander in flight. Although developments in radio telephony have made this possible, all problems are not solved merely by establishing a company frequency. However many radio frequencies are set aside to deal with aircraft movement control, a pilot has only one pair of ears, and his ears are busy most of the time listening to messages from Air Traffic Control. Company directions for the economic disposition of aircraft cannot be allowed to impede the flow of navigational and meteorological information into the control cabin.

The volume of information pouring into the eyes and ears of aircraft crews is by itself a problem. There is a danger that at times it will be humanly impossible to accept all that is presented, and that vital information may be excluded. The pressure is relieved by enabling information to by-pass the pilot, and to be fed directly into automatic equipment. The limits of automation have not been reached, and the full automatic control of aircraft from take-off to touch-down is within the bounds of possibility.

The expense of maintaining individual airline communication-networks is considerable. Certain economies have been achieved by airlines sharing networks like SITA in Europe.

Establishing standards of performance

Both airlines and governments play important parts in establishing good standards of performance for aircraft and their crews. Governments' surveillance of materials and processes in the manufacturing of aircraft aims at promoting safe movement for passengers and third parties. Their periodic examination of medical fitness and competence of the human beings who operate the aircraft has the same end in view. Broadly speaking the attitudes of airline managements are related to government standards in one of two ways. An airline may regard the standards established by governments as the maximum concession that can be made to the requirements of safety, because of conflicting economic interests. In other words governments can be trusted to establish standards that satisfy all reasonable demands for safe flying, and it is the job of the airline to make an economic proposition out of those standards. Another airline may regard government standards as minimal, indicating danger points below which disaster may occur and for that reason giving insufficient margin of safety for day-to-day use. This view often derives from a belief that government concern does not extend beyond the safety of third parties, and that airlines themselves must look to the safety of their crews and passengers.

The soundness or otherwise of these two attitudes is, of course, a matter of fact. Some governments may set dangerously low standards and some airlines may set unreasonably high standards. The latter failing is by no means impossible in an industry that employs so many people who are dedicated to technical perfection.

The process of establishing standards of performance is rationalised by relating it to the limitations of men and equipment. For example, company regulations on such matters as maximum speeds, cruising speeds, rates of climb and descent, approach speeds, V_1, V_2 and V_R speeds are not arbitrary, but are disciplined by the nature of the aircraft to which they apply. Similarly an airline sets up a critical height of say 200 feet, at which a pilot must be able to see the runway clearly to be able to land, by having regard for the time it takes aircraft crews to stop a descent and do an overshoot. In fact, the minutia of 'management' regulations are recognised for what they are, that is to say, the expression of the disciplines of a craft.

Maintaining standards of performance

It is one thing to 'motivate' the performance of crews by making statements on standards, and another thing to exercise 'control', by obtaining feedbacks on actual performance so that corrective action can be taken if necessary. Just as the fact of a man's having passed a driving test does not guarantee that he will always perform to the standards exhibited under test, so the competence of flying staff does not automatically control their performance. The main problem for management is to provide the supervision necessary for the control process. They would not wish nor think it necessary to apply the same degree of supervision that would be found in a factory. Great stress is laid on the personal responsibility of aircraft commanders. Generally they are men of the highest integrity who can be trusted to do their best, even when not being watched. On the other hand, management can never relax its vigilance nor yield its own mastery of the situation.

Some airlines have established a measure of supervision by carrying out a series of 'checks'. Route-checking is carried out by line captains who observe the performance of a crew from the beginning to the end of a flight, and talk over the conduct of the flight with them. Other airlines have considered the possibility of installing a 'management' pilot permanently in the control cabin to assume a role akin to that of a captain of a ship, who does not himself touch the controls. In other cases a limited 'monitoring' procedure is adopted in which at critical stages one pilot 'monitors' the work of another.

While supervision is difficult management have other means of obtaining 'feedbacks' on the conduct of flights. Radio-telephone conversations and voyage reports give some sort of picture of what is going on in control cabins.

Training

Training may be recognised as the *whole process* by which aircraft crews become *competent*. In practice managements usually use the word 'training' for that part of the process carried out in formal instruction. Training is usually regarded as an activity that takes place off-the-job. Experience on-the-job is then regarded as the other way of becoming competent.

If training is not thought of as an integrated process of instruction on-the-job and off-the-job, in both classroom and control cabin, training and experience may easily become regarded as indirectly related means of achieving the same ends. In other words management may think that the more training a man has the less experience he will need to become competent and vice versa. The claims of each may begin to conflict if they are backed by different people. This would be a mistake if there were one 'best' mixture of off-the-job and on-the-job instruction. Such a situation is not unlikely. It would appear reasonable to suppose that the best training consists of a judicious mixture of two sorts of instruction.

While training may be recognised as a process for becoming competent it is less easy to see it as ensuring that people behave according to their competence. Yet in the airline industry training must contribute to developing right attitudes to the use of skills, because of the difficulties of supervision mentioned earlier. The objectives of training cannot be restricted to the attainment of technical competence, that management then controls by normal supervision. Aircrew training must include in its objectives the attainment of an attitude of self-criticism, that will make every member his own supervisor.

Training must also induce habits that will survive emergencies. There are times when aircrew need to summon additional resources.

Because of the nature of their work these must come from within themselves, and some activities must be entrusted to habit to enable the mind to concentrate on critical points.

Reporting procedures

The efficiency of aircraft movement control depends partly on the quality of the reporting procedures established by management. Because of the difficulty of supervision management must rely on the reports it obtains from aircrew for the 'feedback' necessary for control. The filing of a flight plan amounts to a captain giving a report of his intentions. The captain again may give a report if he has to deviate from plan. He may report any untoward incident or adverse weather. He may report on the conduct of his crew, and on the performance of the aircraft. All these reports can be pointers to the way things are going, but their value depends on the manner in which they are prepared. If management do not insist upon high standards for the reports made to them they are in effect allowing their picture of events to become distorted. Clear and accurate reporting is not something that a man can learn overnight. Management should insist that it is practised throughout a pilot's training syllabus. For this reason it is wise to see that instructors in all subjects are articulate men, not selected merely for their technical competence.

Analysis of delays in aircraft movements

Many airlines analyse the causes of delays to aircraft movements to assess relative importance. Most analyses take account of many factors, including unserviceable equipment, weather, surface transport, customers and immigration and so on. Some airlines take care to assess the impact of air traffic control. In United Airlines a member of the crew has to furnish details of delays in a form constructed as follows:

A. The Departure section accounts for delays incurred while taxi-ing and/or climbing.
   (1) *Field Traffic.* Delay while waiting to cross runways or waiting for other aircraft.
   (2) *ATC Clearance and Instrument Procedures.* Delay on ground awaiting ATC clearance or release, and excess time required to perform instrument departure procedures.
   (3) *Other.* Warming engine, burnout, deviation from taxi-time allowance, etc.
B. The Cruise section accounts for deviations from scheduled cruise time.

(1) *Wind Factor and Altitude/Route.* Time deviations from schedule due to these factors based on wind component built into the schedule.
(2) *Turbulence and Weather/Detour.* Delays due to operating at reduced power because of turbulence, and delays due to re-routing to avoid weather.
(3) *Mechanical.* Delays due to aircraft mechanical irregularities.
(4) *Temperature.* Difference from forecast, affecting turbine performance/speed.
(5) *Other* (special).

C. The Arrival section accounts for delays incurred during arrival, letdown and taxi-in.
(1) *Holding Account Weather.* Time holding while waiting for weather improvement to landing minima.
(2) *Time to Alternate.* Time en route deviating to alternate in excess of flight plan, calculated from departure, holding, or en route fix.
(3) *ATC Clearance and Instrument Procedures.* Delays incurred awaiting approach or landing clearance, and excess time required to perform instrument approach procedures.
(4) *Field Traffic.* Delays while waiting to cross runways or waiting for other aircraft.
(5) *Ramp Congestion.* Delays account ramp traffic on holding for gate space.
(6) *Other.* Waiting for flagman, deviation from taxi-time allowance, etc.'

Data extracted from the completed forms is sent to Denver, where it is analysed by computer.

Reporting Accidents and Incidents

The words 'accident' and 'incident' refer to an occurrence outside the normal course of events. The word accident is usually used for occurrences that are at least tinged with the idea of disaster, and incident is used for any occurrence viewed as a separate circumstance. The reporting of accidents and incidents plays an important part in the practice of *management by exception.* In the managerial control process more often than not action is called for only when there is a deviation from plan. Thus managers are concerned primarily with occurrences that are not according to plan, and call for action on their part. This practice relieves them of the burden of examining great numbers of routine reports of normal functioning.

Once again a critical aspect of the managerial task is entrusted to other people. It is because management cannot be completed without contributions from aircrew, that the latter tend to be regarded as part of the management team of an airline.

PASSENGER AND FREIGHT CONTROL

The control of passengers and freight is fundamentally the control of the supply, flow and processing of the raw materials of the airline industry. Characteristically the function involves 'display' and so is of interest to the marketing side. The production processes experienced by customers, and particularly by passengers, are an advertisement.

The major tasks involved in the passenger and freight control aspect of airline production are as follows:

	Passenger and Freight terms	*Passenger terms*	*Freight terms*
1.	Use of timetables		
2.	Route determination		
3.	Services extra to carriage		
4.	Bookings on other carriers		
5.		Reservations	Securing space
6.		Tariffs	Rates
7.		Tickets	Waybills
8.	Load control		
9.		Embarkation and disembarkation	Loading and unloading
10.		Personal baggage handling	
11.	Communications along routes		
12.	Corrective procedures		

All these tasks require practical skills, and some of them social skills of a fairly high order. They should be taught and seen in the light of the intention of this aspect of organisation, which is the care of customers and their property.

Timetables

Timetables are important documents. They represent a channel of communication between airlines and customers. They should be the means by which airlines tell their customers about the timings, quality and costs of the services they offer. Even though a service is a good bargain there will be little demand for it unless potential customers are told about it. All the skills of communication should be devoted to the preparation of timetables. The selection and arrangement of material, the layout, colouring and emphases should all contribute to the making of a didactic instrument.

It is difficult to make timetables look simple. It is difficult to make them look attractive. Yet they must be made to look both inviting and easy to understand. A good deal more study of customer reactions to timetables is required before managements get anywhere near these ideals. The first step to take is to ensure that customers are provided with timetables drawn up specially for them, and not for the use of airline officials.

Since timetables are key documents ideally all members of airline staff should be familiar with them, so that no opportunity is missed to convey the information customers need. Those members of staff dealing with the public should have a working knowledge of timetables. A member of airline staff should not be concerned only with the timetable of his own company. He must be prepared to assist a passenger with the timetables of other companies.

Route determination

In many cases there are a number of routes that a passenger could take to reach his destination. In some cases there is one route that is in his best interests, for reasons of time, or cost, or scenic attraction. Here the carrier has a clear duty to act for the benefit of his customer. Occasionally it is a matter of indifference to the customer and the carrier may legitimately persuade him to fly a route that is to the former's advantage. For example, a certain route may give the carrier doing the booking a greater distance on its own services. If every airline trains its booking clerks to obtain the maximum company advantage, regardless of the interests of customers, the reputation of the whole industry will suffer. On the other hand, no single airline can be allowed to consistently take unfair advantage. Only if every management insists on fair practices can there be a sound basis for the exercise of legitimate skills in route construction.

Services extra-to-carriage

Services extra-to-carriage include a wide variety of incidentals such as the provision of food and beverages, and the sale of cigarettes, liquor, perfumes and so on. They also include such courtesies as public-address announcements during flight and the personal attentions of ground and air staff. The results of surveys indicate that passengers do not put these services high in their list of priorities in what they look for in good airline service. But surveys usually tell us what passengers think when they are coolly reflecting on experiences put into proper perspective. Experience suggests that passengers' views on the quality of a flight are very much coloured by the impressions created by services extra-to-carriage. The importance of controlling the quality of these services is enhanced by the fact that the area of effective competition in air transport is so drastically reduced by international regulations.

Bookings on other carriers

An airline cannot be managed as an isolated phenomenon beginning and ending at its routes' extremities. Embarkation is not the beginning for its passengers, nor disembarkation the end. The need to recognise the importance of the relationship between surface transport and air transport in the carriage of freight is dealt with in the next chapter, but here we must note the requirement for all employees to appreciate that there is a difference between a customer's total transport demand and the amount that is supplied by air. Aircraft are not like omnibuses that go from door to door. More often than not they fly from one fairly inaccessible airfield to another. Moreover, even the biggest airlines are relatively incomplete systems. They give scant coverage by any reckoning.

Unless management succeeds in inculcating a sense of the dependence of its own airline's success upon other carriers, both air and surface, it will run a constant risk of making faulty commercial judgements. The goodwill of customers will also be affected by any apparent disregard for their wider interests. Consequently the passenger and freight control sections of most airlines provide a specialist 'interline' service at airport sales offices and town terminals.

Reservations

A. J. Burkhart[1] said, 'Characteristically, an airline holds its own entire stock of seats for sale, and makes them available on application by the retail travel agent. The latter does not demand stock for retail sale until the passenger is already demanding a seat from him. The reservations systems of an airline, which provide this access to stock, have as their main function the rapid and easy supply of unsold seats to the retail outlet, whether this is a travel agent's or the airline's own sales offices. All seats are sold firm and reserved, although a particular seat in a particular aircraft may not be allocated until the passenger boards the aircraft.'

This line of thinking is connected with the fact that most airlines associate reservations systems with the marketing function. By referring loosely to the airline product of arrivals, in terms of aircraft seats, it is possible to imagine a stock of 'products' available for distribution. But it should be remembered that at the time of making a reservation the seat concerned has not yet taken to the air on the service concerned. It would be more logical to talk in terms of

[1] 'Advertising and Marketing in the Airline Industry', *Journal of Industrial Economics*, November 1962, Blackwell.

pre-empting a seat to be produced in the future, rather than distributing a seat from stock produced in the past.

However, this is still confusing. The airline product is 'arrivals'. The seats and space freight flown around the sky should be regarded as equipment in use. Whether that equipment is productive or not depends on whether it is used on raw materials, i.e. passengers or freight. Reservations, therefore, are of equipment and not of stock.

The word reservation conveys the idea of keeping something for a certain purpose (in the case of a seat—for the use of a certain person). This, however, is much too passive a notion of what really happens in making airline reservations. Here it is a matter of allocating a passenger to a certain flight (after seeing that there is room for him), and then guiding him by various means to that flight. In the circumstances 'passenger-allocations' would be a more meaningful term than reservations. Seen in this light the task of reservations properly belongs to the function of passenger and freight control.

The arguments that 'reservations' are part of the process of production in no way invalidates Burkhart's additional point that 'reservations systems exist, not ultimately for the convenience of the passenger but in order that the airline may secure a high load factor (the percentage of capacity on offer which is sold at the time of departure). There exist a variety of penalties which can be (but rarely are) imposed on passengers who make a reservation and fail to take it up—such passengers are known graphically as 'no-shows'. The reservations systems allow flights to be cancelled if there are few or no passengers for them or extra services to be added at periods of peak demand. Further, the airline's own offices have an opportunity to sell seats not already sold by retail travel agents. Space in aircraft is a highly perishable commodity and the reservations system of an airline exists to ensure that, when the doors are closed, the aircraft takes off with the highest attainable load.'

The view that 'reservations' are a matter of process of production is supported by the fact that passengers can be just as happy with and as successful in obtaining the product of arrival without a reservations system. Given that there are sufficient flights to ensure that everyone waiting can obtain a seat there is no need to allocate passengers to a particular flight. At worst this might mean that an extra flight would have to be arranged for a single passenger. Management has to make up its mind whether the expense involved in this would be greater than the cost of a reservation system.

Undoubtedly a reservations system affords a considerable measure of passenger and freight control. Without it the flow of passengers into an airport would be unregulated, and might therefore be unpredictable and erratic. An important task in most businesses is that of regulating the flow of raw materials to match the capacity of equipment. Unless the flow is self-regulated the abandoning of managerial control will give rise to serious production problems.

Tariffs and rates

Although correct tariffs and rates must be established at the point of sale, the matter is not then finished. In business where there is a simultaneous exchange of money for goods or services, the act of exchange fixes the price for once and all (except on occasions of misunderstanding and fraud). In air transport the situation is different. Money is usually paid by the customer ahead of production, and when the time comes for the delivery of the product of arrival, he may by force of circumstances or by oversight receive something different from what he has paid for. For this reason it is important for certain employees working in the passenger and control function to have an expert knowledge of tariffs and rates to ensure, if possible, that customers get what they have paid for, and if not that charges are properly adjusted.

Tickets and waybills

Tickets and waybills are valuable control documents in the handling of passengers and freight. Their intelligent use can provide management with the means of making rapid summaries of the processing situation before flight. Ticket counterfoils give the number of passenger arrivals, the number of pieces and total weight of baggage, numbers to each destination and so on. Counterfoils that are mislaid can cause delay to flights. Passenger and freight control cannot be complete without the ability to amend tickets and waybills to provide for changed circumstances such as re-routing.

Load control

Weight limitations differ from one type of aircraft to another. How much can be lifted depends first of all on the power of the engines. The landing weight of each type of aircraft is further limited by critical structures such as the aircraft's undercarriage. Then the length, thickness, materials and construction of the runway produce another limit on the amount that can take off and land on it.

Load control sections of the passenger and freight control function have to ensure that aircraft and their loads do not exceed these limits. The task is crucial because decisions must be made within a relatively small proportion of all-up weight, and to be profitable aircraft must be flown close to operational limits. The weight of the aircraft is fixed; a certain number of crew must be carried; and the amount of fuel depends upon the total weight, the distance it has to be carried, and meteorological conditions.

Besides ensuring that the total weight of the aircraft is within the landing weight, load control staff must also see that the load is distributed properly about the centre of gravity.

Aircraft loads must be controlled with extreme accuracy, but the time in which to achieve that accuracy has to be kept to a minimum because it is waiting time for passengers. Management's aim is to leave as little as possible to do after a flight is closed. As much as possible is prepared before closure time, and the remaining tasks are simplified and standardised to promote speed and accuracy.

Embarkation and disembarkation

This has to be controlled in such a way that passengers, cargo and vehicles are not endangered. The movement of traffic from terminal buildings to aircraft is a source of danger to the latter. Vehicles on the apron can cause accidents to passengers unless the movements of both are regulated. Finally embarkation and disembarkation has to be achieved with the minimum delay as costs increase with the time taken, mainly through keeping aircraft idle.

There are problems connected with the loading and unloading of freight. Loading must be controlled so that delays are not caused by freight required at a first port of call being stowed behind freight not to be unloaded till later. Heavy weights must not be stowed on top of fragile pieces, and the whole load must conform to the balance and trim requirements of the aircraft.

Personal baggage handling

Loading and unloading passengers' baggage calls for careful control. Mistakes that seem trivial to an airline official appear to be very much more serious to a man whose comfort and convenience may be seriously disturbed for days. These belongings are personal and necessary. Baggage should be handled as carefully as if it were part of a person.

Communications along routes

The task of keeping an aircraft full on a long route with many intermediate stops is complicated. Passengers may have to be disembarked, and freight unloaded at each stop. The seats and space that are vacated must be filled if possible. Arrangements to do so are made on the basis of information available a short while before take-off. These arrangements often have to be altered because the passengers and freight at take-off are not quite what was expected a few hours earlier. Last-minute cancellations and reservations upset the picture in the hands of stations some hours before the arrival of the aircraft. The situation has to be controlled by means of rapid and reliable communications to enable stations to be warned of changes.

The problem is not just that of keeping aircraft full. It is also a question of keeping facilities matched to needs. An aircraft that is diverted might find a station understaffed for the sudden influx of traffic, unless it has had time to call in reserves. Also provisions must be made to adjust the in-flight services to changes in traffic.

Corrective procedures

Passenger and freight control must include a range of procedures connected with the explanation, settlement and perhaps correction of service failures. Drills must be established to deal with such eventualities as delayed flights, diversions, accidents and so on.

Aircraft for freight-carrying

It is reasonable to suppose that tailor-made aircraft ease the tasks of loading, carrying and unloading freight. There is less reason to suppose that by making the task easier it would thus become more profitable. While outlay to make aircraft more appropriate for passenger transport may be justified partly on the grounds of reduced operating costs (e.g. with increased speed and consequent greater utilisation), and partly on the grounds of increased revenue (because of greater passenger-appeal), the same does not hold for cargo aircraft. Firstly the demand for air freight services is not as responsive to advances in aircraft design as is the demand for passenger transport. This in turn means that it is harder to realise the efficiency that derives from increased speed. Faster aircraft covering more ground in a day require more freight to keep them going profitably, and if the freight is not forthcoming they cannot be regarded as more efficient. Speed, *per se*, has little appeal to the shipper as long as his goods arrive during business hours on the planned delivery date. Similarly while the potential efficiency of cargo aircraft rises as their size increases this potential cannot be realised unless there is sufficient traffic.

Although the world freight market grew rapidly in the 1960s, it was still too small to support the purchase of more than a few big jets. This meant that no production run could be long enough to be economic, unless manufacturers of airframes geared their production to dual purposes. For years members of staff responsible for freight handling had been complaining that they had to use equipment originally designed for use by passengers, and that the marginal modifications could not fully take into account the physical characteristics of cargo. Yet in 1962 Seaboard World Airlines were specifying as a requirement for the turbo-jet replacement of the turbo-prop CL-44 that it should be convertible for passenger use either in whole or in part. In British European Airways at about the same time requests were also being made internally for the modification of their Argosies from specialised cargo to convertible aircraft. Until the market is developed it will not permit the introduction of optimum production units.

Pre-arranging loads

The task of fitting a number of ill-assorted packages into a rigid container like that of an aircraft hold, to optimise the use of the space is time-consuming and costly. A big part of the cost arises because the aircraft has to remain idle while loaders experiment with ways of packing freight into the hold. One solution to the problem would be to have a close-fitting container that would slide in and out with full loads. In this way all the packing could be done while aircraft are airborne. The handling of whole freight-hold loads presupposes the existence of adequate trucks and hoists.

Airlines have moved only part of the way to satisfy this concept. They have begun to use a number of containing and retaining devices that enable them to pre-arrange loads and fill a certain amount of space. The most commonly used retaining device is known as the pallet. Pallets are flat wooden platforms that slide along the floors of freighters with consolidated loads fastened to them. They were first used in the mid-1930s, but it was not until airlines faced in the 1960s the over-riding necessity of keeping expensive jet aircraft on the move that their use was extended. In the intervening years the loss of payload caused by using pallets was reckoned to more than offset any gains in aircraft utilisation.

CHAPTER XVI

MARKETING MANAGEMENT

The nature of a market

The 'market' for an air transport service may be considered to have two aspects. Firstly, there is the demand within the market. Secondly, there is the area over which that demand exists. The word 'demand' is being used here in the way that economists use it, that is to say, as embracing the quantities that would be demanded throughout a range of prices. Demand is always *at a price* and may or may not change with every price. Current demand (i.e. at current prices) for air transport seldom matches supply; either too much or too little 'capacity' is provided. Current demand exists, and is exercised within the limits of supply. There is a 'potential' demand that could be made 'current' by price changes.

Demand can vary by responding differently to changes in price. Sometimes a small decrease in price will cause a big increase in demand. Sometimes a big decrease in price will cause only a small increase in demand. Price should be understood not as an *absolute sum* of money, but as *a ratio* of quality and quantity of service exchanged for a sum of money. Thus, even though the 'fare' between say New York and Chicago did not change the 'price' could be changed by improving the speed or convenience of carriage. Price is indicated by the term 'tariff' and not by the term 'fare'.

The area over which demand exists is classified into 'off-line' sales areas, and 'on-line' sales areas. For example, Europe would be regarded as an off-line sales area by a United States domestic carrier.

Physical limitations on marketing

The activities of marketing management are limited by the aircraft seats and space for freight on offer. This is in turn determined by:

(*a*) The size of the fleet (in terms of the overall number of seats);
(*b*) The opportunities of chartering additional aircraft; and
(*c*) The amount of *fleet-time* that is scheduled for sales (i.e. alongside the alternative demands for embarkation and disembarkation, preparation for flight, maintenance and standing in reserve).

The way in which marketing management can bring about an increase in the supply of seats and space for freight to meet rising demand is as follows:

(*a*) By the purchase of additional aircraft;
(*b*) By the addition of seats to existing aircraft to make what is referred to as high-density configuration, and by the maximum utilisation of freight-holds;
(*c*) By the charter of aircraft; and
(*d*) By pressing for reductions in time spent on out-of-service activities (flight preparation, maintenance, etc.).

Aims in marketing

Because of short-term limitations on the supply of seats and space for freight, the aims of marketing management should not be to raise demand to the maximum. This has happened. On some routes demand has been stimulated to outstrip supply. This causes an airline to lose goodwill, and in a sense it is marketing for competitors. Success in marketing is indicated by the extent to which it can sell seats and space for freight up to, but not beyond, total capacity. Conversely, the number of unoccupied seats and empty freight space on the aircraft is a measure of failure for marketing management.

Market potential

Market 'potential' from the point of view of the management of an airline may be restricted:

(*a*) By IATA fixing fares and rates for its routes; and
(*b*) By governments' agreeing traffic rights, frequencies and capacities on routes. Apart from government and IATA restrictions, all airlines do not begin with equal market potentials. Certain areas have powers to produce and attract more traffic than other areas, by virtue of size and sort of population.

Economic limits on marketing

Certain economic 'laws' of supply and demand operate in the airline market despite the apparently rigid controls of the international cartel, and governments' bilateral agreements. The profitable exchange, from an airline point of view, of arrivals for money depends upon the following conditions of supply and demand:

Supply

(*a*) The cost of supplying various quantities of arrivals, according to whether,
(*b*) Unit costs of the supply of arrivals are constant, rising or falling.

Demand

(*a*) The number of arrivals that will be bought at various prices, according to whether,

(*b*) The rise in price will cause a less than proportionate fall in demand, a proportionate fall in demand or a more than proportionate fall in demand.

Conditions of passenger supply and demand cannot be equated at a practicable level for journeys less than a certain distance. This distance varies from one part to another, but in well-developed communities it would appear to average around 250 miles. Minimum journey length is usually one of the clearest limits to profitable marketing.

Theory of demand for air transport

A study was completed in 1950[1] and another in 1954[2] to establish some of the factors that affect the demand for air transport. In general these studies assessed the importance of density of population, occupational characteristics, distances between cities, natural obstacles to competing ground transport, atmospheric obstacles to flying, and a number of management factors such as shape and lay-out of routes, frequencies and timings of services, etc. While not all these factors can be measured accurately a knowledge of the variables involved is a *sine qua non* in any attempt to weigh up markets. The conclusions of these studies may be stated briefly as follows: the demand for air transport between any two points is partly determined by:

(1) The sizes and densities of the two populations. Demand tends to increase directly with increases in the combined sizes and densities.

(2) The distance between them. Up to a certain point demand tends to vary inversely with the distance between them. As distance increases demand decreases. This principle probably does not apply to distances less than 100 miles, because of the inconvenience of air terminals compared with those of road and rail.

(3) The natural obstacles to ground transport and their effect on the time saving of air transport. Straight flight has on average a 20 per cent advantage over land distances between the same points. Exceptional obstacles like lakes and mountains may increase the disparity between land and air distances.

(4) The natural obstacles to flying, and their effect on the regularity

[1] *Effective Community Air Traffic Potential*, U.S. Department of Commerce, Civil Aeronautics Administration.

[2] *Air Transport in the United States*, W. S. Barry. Thesis, University of London.

and reliability of air transport. If an airport cannot be used for a number of days because of bad weather, people tend to be discouraged from booking by air.

(5) The occupation of the people who inhabit the areas served by air. Different occupations give rise to variations in purchasing power. It has been established, for example, that in the USA, marketing towns usually generate more passengers than the average industrial town.

(6) The number of neighbouring towns. If there are only two towns in the area most of the traffic will go from one to the other. If a third town exists the traffic from any one will be shared to some extent by two neighbours, instead of going wholly to one another.

(7) The shape and layout of routes, frequencies and timings of services. For example, basically circular and parallel layouts suffer certain disadvantages that basically straight line and radiating layouts do not. Up to a certain point traffic tends to increase more than proportionately with increases in frequency of service. Certain timings are usually more 'saleable' than others.

The significance of IATA in marketing management

IATA stands as an expression of the fact that the marketing of air transport must be rationalised by (*a*) there being only one price in the market at any one time, and (*b*) the fixing of this price by all the interested parties meeting at one place and at one time. Thus an individual airline cannot pursue the management strategy of lowering price to increase demand. This also means that individual airlines cannot manipulate price to relate it closely to considerations of cost and profit.

The history of attempts to introduce new classes of service provides evidence of the conservatism and cartel-like nature of IATA. The association has tended to restrict the growth in variety of services, e.g. neither tourist nor economy class was approved when first suggested by Pan American, and they were unable to obtain any support at the 1963 IATA meeting for proposals to carry passengers across the Atlantic for a Thrift class fare of $160 (£57) compared with the Economy class fare of $250 (£88). This resistance was probably due to the fact that changes of class of travel often called for changes in equipment. Some airlines were not equipped to cater for a lower class of service. For example, an airline proposing lower fares for propeller-driven aircraft met opposition from airlines that did not have any.

The threat of not reaching a decision on fares in traffic conferences tends to strengthen the voices of small airlines. Sometimes one small airline can influence the market against the interests of all the major carriers. If IATA did not succeed in fixing fares then they would have to be fixed within the governments' bilateral agreements. This would open up the possibility of one operator flying with a lower fare on a certain route. Most airlines are unwilling to run such a risk. The airline asking for lower fares is always a threat in a disagreement, so it usually wins the day. This tends to keep fares down to a level regarded by some operators as uneconomically low. The usual argument that IATA is a cartel keeping fares artificially high is, therefore, an over-simplification.

The normal process of fare-fixing in IATA is that each airline in turn says what fares it would like to have in the coming year. The public debate, and the behind-the-scenes consultations that then follow, result in shifting of ground, compromise and horse-trading, until a position is reached that commands unanimous approval. The costs of obtaining unanimity in IATA Traffic Conferences are considerable. Airline officials must spend a great deal of time and effort thrashing out ideas and positions well ahead of Conferences. The managements of individual airlines are often called upon to abandon what they regard as optimum marketing positions, and to accept compromises. The hard professional bargaining that goes on, is seldom related to considerations of cost and prolongs uncertainty to the last moment.

The need for governments to ratify IATA decisions only occasionally affects them. Governments' powers of ratification spring from the fact that they give effect to IATA decisions by their concluding bilateral agreements incorporating them. In principle price-fixing in the industry is closely tied to obtaining rights to fly, but in practice governments rarely disagree with IATA proposals. So what IATA agrees to is in almost all cases what the customer pays.

Divisions of the World Market

IATA is responsible for a conceptual division of the world airline market into three. Europe, and Africa is one; the Americas form another; and the rest of the world the third. These divisions are more a matter of convenience than a product of the logic of the marketing situation. The arbitrary definition of marketing areas enables decision-making to be less wasteful of the time of airlines not interested in a particular area. There are separate Traffic Conferences for each area, and consequently a separate fare-fixing body for each. Only those airlines operating in an area are allowed to partake.

Airlines marketing agents

IATA airlines are obliged to employ only IATA approved agents for the sale of their tickets. These agents in turn may sell airline tickets for IATA members only. An airline that had not applied for membership of, or had been expelled from IATA would thus be denied a great number of sales outlets.

The retailing of 'arrivals' through *agents* rather than retail *principals* makes airline marketing different in character from that of most manufacturing industries. A travel agent does not buy for himself a number of airline seats and cubic feet of space for freight, in order to sell arrivals to his customers. Most of the time he does not 'charter' equipment, and therefore does not share in the risk of being left with unused 'perished' services. This throws the task of the *short-term* clearance of services back on to the airline. They have to provide a customer-by-customer reservations system to provide the agent with ready access to services. While this is only a short-term difference, because in the long run all producers must pay the penalty for no-sales, it is significant. For this reason the travel agent's return of 7½ per cent commission is small compared with the retail principal's profit. The latter's profits are, in part, payment for risk.

When an agent does take a bigger risk, airlines give him a bigger commission. Some of the larger agents, with representatives distributed over a wide area, do more than produce a selling-service for airlines. They may 'construct' or make complete arrangements for holidays that include travel by air. Agents earn a higher commission on the air travel element of these 'inclusive' or 'packaged' tours, in recognition of the risk involved in their marketing. The larger agents also charter whole aircraft and bear the risk of having unfilled seats. They pay the airlines on a whole aircraft basis and hope to make a profit higher than 7½ per cent by reselling individual seats.

The way that airlines handle their relations with travel agents can make a considerable contribution to success in marketing. On the other hand, if handled badly agents can be a drain on airline resources and a barrier to successful selling.

The division of the market into 'international' and 'cabotage' routes

International and cabotage routes are usually considered separately when marketing policies are framed. Cabotage routes are those 'wholly within one state or between that state and an overseas colony or territory'. Cabotage routes include domestic and colonial routes. International routes must be considered within the framework of IATA resolutions, whereas policy on cabotage routes is mainly effected by the airlines' own governments. Tariffs on cabotage routes are often either fixed by them or subject to their approval. Some people hold the opinion that government intervention here is unnecessary, as the best check on tariffs is the competition of road and rail transport. There was, however, an interesting situation in England in the early 1960s where the nationalised airlines were looking to a Ministry for their fare proposals, knowing that the Ministry had no legal right to demand that the airlines sought their approval.

Cabotage routes are sometimes parallel with international routes. This means that there may be competition between the two. The cabotage operator can undercut the international operator since the latter is tied by IATA and the former is free. For this reason it was agreed that international passengers may not be accepted for carriage on cabotage routes. This rule was sometimes broken, and consequently the offending airline obtained an unfair advantage.

Feeder Services

Some airlines operate routes that do not by themselves make profits, but which 'feed' passengers and freight into routes that do. These airlines may calculate that the gains from traffic fed into the profitable routes exceed the losses made on feeder routes. It is also frequently assumed that traffic derived from feeder routes would not travel at all if the latter did not exist.

Airline specialisation in particular markets

Airlines may be 'world' airlines, serving the capitals and other big cities of countries where there is a demand for air transport. Or they may be less-than-world airlines, serving the major cities within an area. The commonest examples of the latter are the domestic carriers of countries like the USA and Australia, but we also come across the occasional carrier with an arbitrarily defined market such as that of British European Airways. The market of a world airline is *extensive*, in the sense of being widespread, but with the demand not fully exploited in any particular area. For example, the world airline tends not to exploit the demand for short journeys within a limited area. The market of the less-than-world airlines is *intensive* in the sense that its traffic is more concentrated, routes are shorter, and the demand within the area is fully exploited.

Airlines confining their operations to either an extensive or intensive market can be said to specialise because the characteristics of each call for different production and marketing organisations. We should note in passing that not all world airlines could be said to specialise in extensive marketing, as they engage marginally in intensive marketing. Thus many trans-Atlantic carriers also attempt to pick up local European traffic. The possibilities of specialisation do not end, however, with the difference between extensive and intensive operations. Within the field of intensive operations there are still further specialisations. For example, domestic trunk-lines may be separate from feeder services, scheduled services from charter services, passengers from freight and so on. Certain specialisations can also occur in extensive operations, particularly in the separation of passengers and freight.

Progress Indicators for marketing management

Figs. 49–52 show some typical charts used by airline marketing managers to indicate the results of their efforts. These progress indicators suggest that what is happening to the world airline industry is taken as a yardstick against which to measure the performance of an individual airline. If an airline does better than the world average in, say, traffic growth, and load factors, then there is cause for satisfaction and vice versa. They also reveal interest in the overall air-share of travel markets, besides the conventional comparisons in traffic from one period to another.

Marketing management and load factors

An airline's load factor is partly the result of general management's skill in matching the supply of aircraft to the demand for them, particularly where demand fluctuates widely. The contributory skills of marketing management lie in estimating accurately and in detail the amount and nature of demand, and in supporting an effective reservations system. But besides the influence that marketing management has on load factors we must also consider the influence that load factors have on the difficulties of marketing. Skill is needed *to achieve* the load factor that is set as the objective. Skill is required *to decide* on the right load factor as the objective. The load factor aimed at can make a considerable difference to the task of marketing.

The basis for determining the load factor to be aimed at on each route is the probability at each load factor of a customer's not being able to obtain the service he first asks for. Calculating the probabilities is a matter for operational research, but deciding on an acceptable risk is a matter for the commercial judgement of management. If too high a load factor is insisted upon customers will tend to regard the service as poor, just as they would if they had to wait for service in a shop. If too low a target is set the customer will be pleased, but the costs of supplying the service will be inordinately high.

The possibility of maintaining high load factors and at the same time giving a good service is diminished where average bookings are not made singly, but in groups. The possibility is increased where the volume of demand on a route is high, and where the aircraft flown are large. Where demand is high, frequent services can be supplied. The consequences of not being able to give the customer what he first asks for is not so serious if he can be offered something

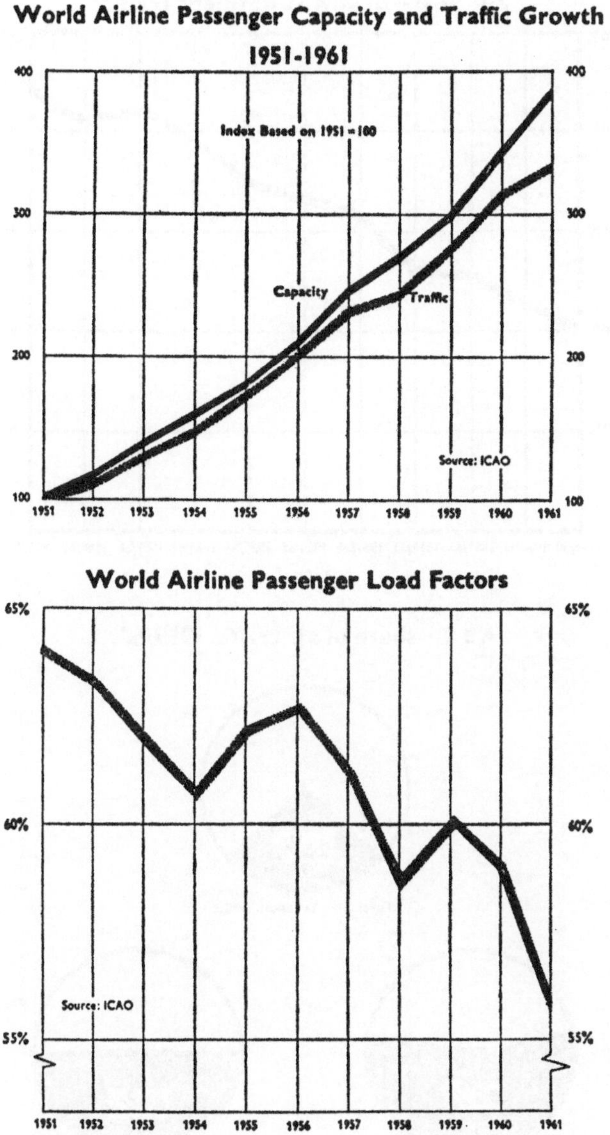

FIG. 49. *Progress Indicators: World Airline Passenger Capacity and Traffic Growth World Airline Passenger Load Factors*

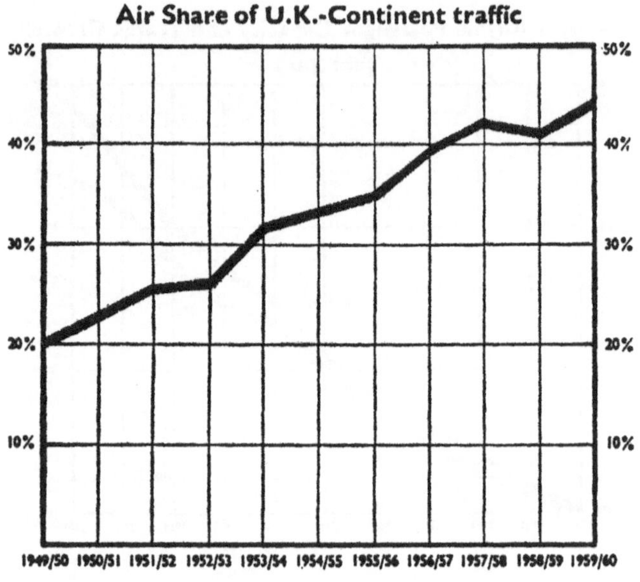

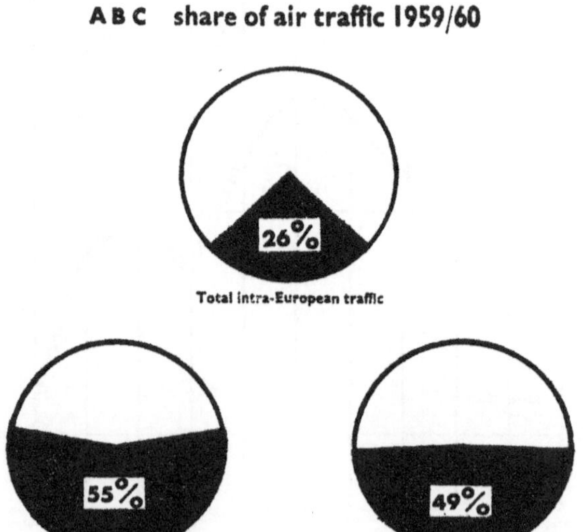

FIG. 50. *Progress Indicators: Air Share of UK–Continent Traffic ABC share of air traffic 1959/60*

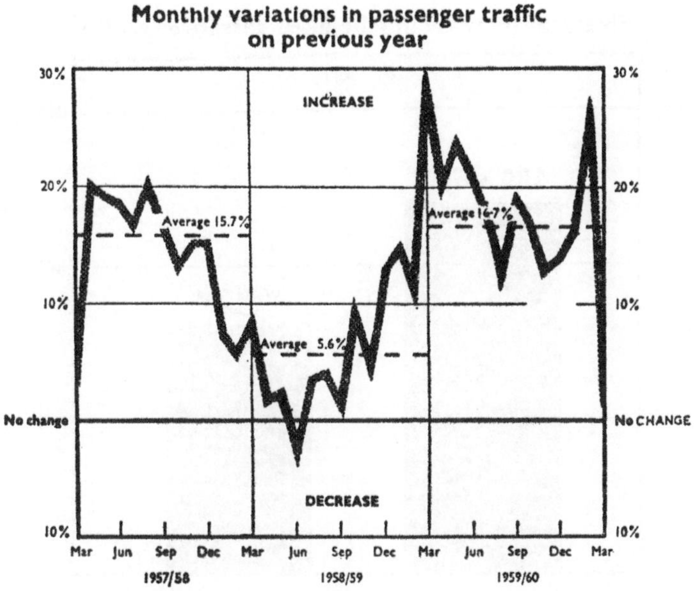

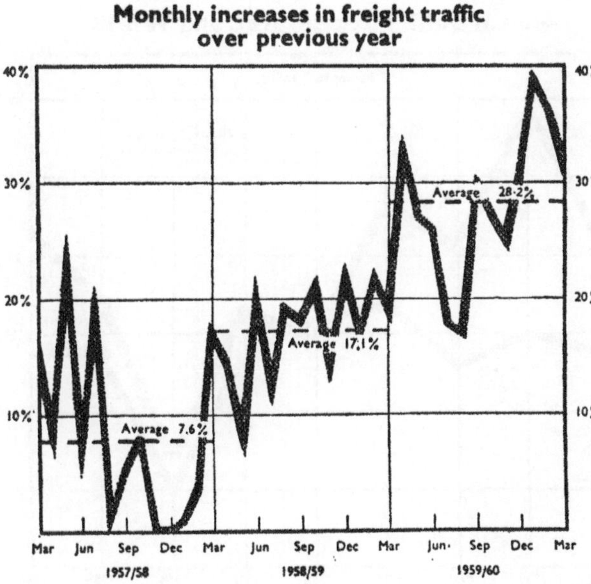

FIG. 51. *Progress Indicators: Monthly variations in passenger traffic on previous year*
Monthly increases in freight traffic over previous year

Five-year increase in scheduled passenger traffic

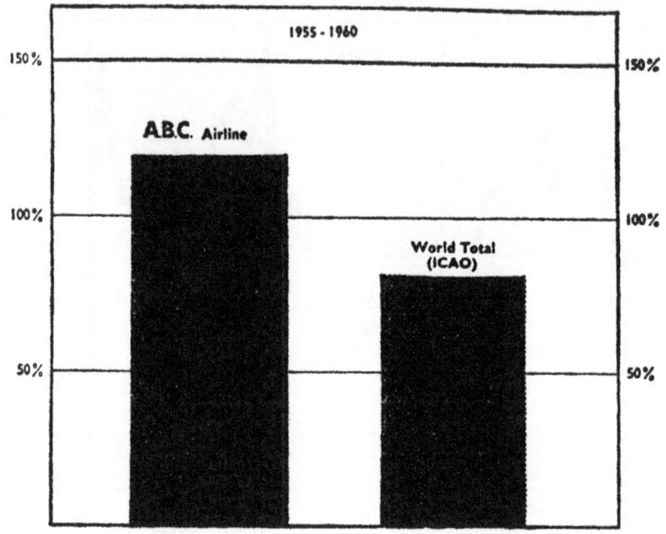

Annual traffic increases ABC and World

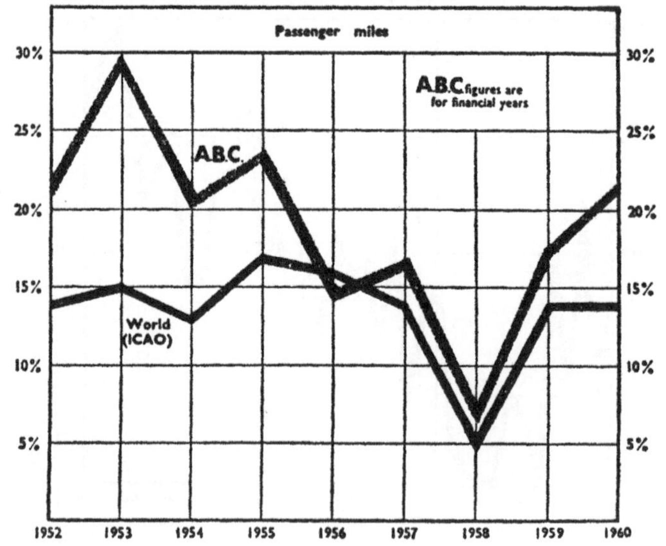

FIG. 52. *Progress Indicators: Five-year increase in scheduled passenger traffic Annual traffic increases ABC and World*

close to it. If aircraft are large, a high load factor will still leave a considerable amount of space available. For example, a 90 per cent passenger load factor in a 150-seater aircraft would still leave 15 empty seats on average.

Marketing management and equipment

From the point of view of marketing managers the equipment (aircraft and ground installations) their airlines employ should ideally match up to the following specifications:

(*a*) Equipment should contribute to the marketing manager's 'display' efforts.
(*b*) Equipment should be sufficiently adaptable to be able to deal with all sorts of 'raw materials'.

The term 'display' is a technical term used in marketing to label the channels through which information is passed from producers to customers. The conventional channels used in 'display' are posters, newspaper advertisements, pamphlets and so on, but it should not be forgotten that impressions about an airline are derived from aircraft performance and interior décor, and from sales and check-in clerks. As we have seen much of the process of production in air transport is 'display', so that besides the behaviour of equipment, the marketing manager is concerned with the behaviour of operatives. But no matter how good is the latter, it cannot overcome crippling handicaps of the former.

One of the greatest problems in marketing is to maintain an even flow of the different sorts of raw materials (various classes of passengers, mail and freight) so that equipment can continually produce arrivals at various destinations. In practice, of course, no airline ever achieves an even flow among the numerous kinds of traffic. More passengers may travel during summer than winter, during day than night. First-class travellers may not wish to travel at all at the 'awkward' hours; tourist travellers may have a strong preference for weekends. Shippers may send freight in one direction, but have nothing to send in the opposite direction, and so on. If equipment is absolutely specific to different kinds of traffic (say first and tourist class passenger and freight) the marketing manager must devote great effort to reshaping the natural tendencies in demand to suit the needs of his airline equipment. If, however, the equipment is adaptable some of these energies can be released for other purposes. If an aircraft can be converted from a passenger carrier to a freighter or vice versa in a few minutes; if the proportion of space for passengers and freight can be altered, selling becomes easier. This means not only having aircraft that can be altered easily, but also that can fill up with one type of traffic (e.g. passengers) without having to carry around deadload capacity for another type of traffic (e.g. freight).

Price and the concepts of 'fares' and 'tariffs'

Price is the amount paid for a product of a certain quality and quantity. Price is a ratio and not a fixed amount. Thus, if the distance between A and B is 100 miles, and the distance between C and D is 200, and the fare from A to B is £10 and from C to D £20, then the price is the same for each journey.

The term tariff is usually used by airlines to mean price in this sense, so that different fares may be based on the same tariff. The ratio of money to product is not just a matter of money to journey-miles. Because the conditions under which a person travels affect his view of the value of a journey, price can be increased by worsening conditions of travel, and price can be reduced by improving conditions of travel. Thus, in order to control price, or tariffs as distinct from fares, IATA must control the quality of services given while travelling, as well as the amount of money paid per mile travelled.

Price policies and marketing

It is wrong for management to take the view that framing price policies is not part of their job. While it may be true that no airline is likely to persuade IATA to support its particular policy in every detail, IATA decisions on price are produced from the interplay of the policies of individual airlines. The price policies of many airlines contribute to the making of price policies for the whole industry.

(*a*) *Relating prices to costs*

There was no major change in US policy on domestic fares from the time of passing the Civil Aeronautics Act, 1938, down to 1962. Fares continued to be charged at a constant rate per mile, and set a pattern for the industry. They took no account of the differences in costs of production between short haul and long haul, nor between routes supporting small scale production and those supporting large scale production. There were good reasons for this. Up to the middle of the twentieth century the industry had little reliable information on the costs of providing various types of service. The perplexity of US railway management in the face of an intricate tariff structure warned airlines of certain dangers. At the same time the need to do something in a hurry was relieved by preparedness of government to pay subsidies for services that were not profitable. But by 1950 these reasons were beginning to fade. Costing systems had been refined to a point where they were providing indisputable evidence of cost differences. The industry was already sampling the fruits of varying tariffs. Governments were declaring their unwillingness to go on paying subsidies indefinitely. Although a formal reshaping of the US domestic fares policy has never taken place, prices have been adjusted to some extent to reflect differences in costs. Cheaper 'cabin' services were introduced on long hauls and on routes supporting large-scale production. The trouble remained that coach fares were related to a first-class fare structure that did not recognise differences in costs. The CAB also introduced in 1962 a $1 surcharge on all fares, and later a $2 charge. These surcharges had the effect of giving slightly higher returns on the more costly short-haul routes.

While it is now generally agreed that the prices charged by airlines should cover their overall costs in the long run, people do not agree on the need for prices on a single route to cover costs on that route in the short run. In other words, some people think that it is not necessarily bad business to allow the losses on one route to be offset against the profits on others. They take the view that unprofitable routes can often be nursed into profitability with subsidies from other routes, and that these subsidies are really development costs. On the other hand, most people would agree that if a community insists on having an air service on a route that can never be profitable (and these cases may be few), its government should pay a subsidy to meet the losses.

The economist's argument against 'cross-subsidation' (as the offsetting of profits on some routes against losses on others is sometimes called) is that it causes operatives and equipment to be deployed in a manner contrary to the preferences of consumers. If a route is unprofitable then clearly consumer preference for it is not strong enough for a sufficient number of people to want to pay a price equal to the cost of travelling on it. But the development of traffic on these routes in little demand is encouraged by lower fares than would be charged if costs had to be covered. On the other hand, the development of traffic on routes in much demand is retarded by higher than necessary fares to pay for losses elsewhere. These tendencies prevent airlines from enjoying the full economies of large-scale production. The economic argument for 'cross-subsidisation' is that by giving a route a shot in the arm, demand will be artificially raised to a level at which costs of supply are reduced, and supply and demand can be equated at an economic price.

(*b*) *Discriminating markets by prices*

Salesmen are said to prefer having one tariff rather than several on a route. Their task is less complicated and they can concentrate their efforts. A single tariff, however, presupposes a single product, i.e. only one sort of arrival. Unfortunately customers may not regard night arrivals as being the same sort as day arrivals, or weekday arrivals as weekend arrivals, or summer arrivals as winter arrivals. They may not be willing to buy the quantities jointly supplied unless there is a different tariff for each.

By increasing the number of tariffs an airline can increase the number of markets for its products, and thus the overall volume of demand. This in turn will increase the use of equipment, and may reduce unit costs. As prices become more discriminating the difference between the standards of luxury and spartan services should increase, and services at extremely popular times should be matched by those at extremely unpopular times.

(*c*) *Changing prices to equate supply and demand*

Demand for air transport like demand for most other products varies from one period to another. Personal incomes change, tastes change, and even the psychological atmosphere of spending changes. On the other hand, the supply of air transport is not easy to change in the short run. The only means of equating supply and demand in the long run is by adjusting prices. If this is not done, there must be recurring cycles of under-utilisation and over-capacity. On the few occasions that the industry has attempted to adjust prices it has assumed that demand is inelastic, and has raised prices to compensate for falling demand, only to find that demand responds to price and falls still faster.

(*d*) *Elasticity of the demand for air transport*

Some authorities hold the opinion that a 5 per cent decrease in fares would not increase demand significantly within a market. They estimate that something of the order of 15 per cent to 20 per cent is required. A price reduction of this magnitude, they point out, would probably raise break-even load factors to an impracticable level. A workable break-even load factor is generally regarded as about 65 per cent.

The fact is that we know very little about the elasticity of demand for air transport. We have had too little experience to judge from, and research is made difficult by the continual changes in factors other than price. It is not easy to isolate the effect of price changes.

Effects of competition and collaboration in marketing

Marketing managers generally look at the pros and cons of competition and collaboration with a different point of view, from that of, say, production managers. To marketing managers competition represents an opportunity for expansion. While there are competitors there is traffic to be taken away from them. Another company's share of the market is a pool that can be drawn on by harder selling and better service. To production managers all too often competition appears as a risk of waste. Competitors are people who take away traffic from aircraft that would otherwise fly full. With competition the volume of demand for the services of each carrier may not be sufficient to allow them to raise production to that level where it can be carried out at minimum cost. This would be the case where an airline was working under decreasing costs.

This dilemma arises because competition stops short of price cutting. If there were no price fixing by IATA a marketing manager whose airline was working with decreasing costs could happily attack his rivals' share of the market by lowering price. If this manoeuvre were followed by all competitors reducing prices, overall demand in the market might increase and overall supply might be at reduced costs.

Conversely, marketing managers tend to look on collaboration as an activity that can easily blunt the keen edge of aggressive marketing. Yet most of them admit the necessity of pooling agreements on certain routes. Once again this outlook derives from the knowledge that competition cannot be carried to normal business extremes.

Partly because they believe that demand on particular routes does not increase *pro rata* with increasing frequency of service and total capacity offered, European airlines have agreed to 'pool' revenues earned on a number of routes. By these agreements they aim to match frequency and capacity with the level of demand established primarily by price-fixing and advertising. One of the effects of these agreements is to reduce the incidence of day-to-day competition and to replace it by the periodic competition that expresses itself whenever agreements come up for renewal. From the marketing managers' point of view this has certain advantages. The neutralising of the day-to-day operations enables him to collaborate with his rivals in the task of raising total demand on a route. He does this by advertising, and otherwise promoting sales jointly with the so-called 'parallel' operator, and by co-operating with tourist boards at both ends of a route.

Suggestions for opening up the market

Airlines are constantly receiving suggestions for new routes. Government officials, industrialists, and traders are prominent among those who make these suggestions. They only occasionally help the airlines. They are less objective than the continual surveys made by airline market research organisations.

Market research organisations

A market research organisation should report on the likelihood of a new route being profitable. This follows from its function, to discover what markets there are open to the products of a particular airline. It must look for markets for travel by day and by night, by weekday and weekend, to Athens, to Rome, by first-class, tourist class and economy class. It must determine the strength of demand at various prices.

Information about 'markets' is gained through information about people. Managements must seek to identify their customers. They should have enough information to be able to pick out the one person in ten (or whatever the proportion) who travels by air. Otherwise airlines cannot address themselves to their customers continuously and with certainty. To be sure to be able to find people and communicate with them we must know something of their habits. We must know such things as where they live, what they read, what they listen to, what they work at, and so on.

This line of enquiry should lead on to the discovery of those people who do not yet travel by air, but who would do so if there were some change of circumstance. These findings should reveal the reasons why they are not travelling at the moment, and the changes that would be required to induce them to travel. For example, there may be a number of 'potential' customers waiting for the opening-up of a new destination. Others may be waiting for a drop in price.

The third area of knowledge to explore is that of the attitudes of both customers and potential customers towards the services supplied, and their views on the improvement that should be made. They should be asked whether the timings and frequencies of services suit them, whether conditions of travel are comfortable enough, ground services efficient enough, etc. If customers or potential customers regard any of these aspects of service as being unsatisfactory they should be asked what they would regard as a desirable standard.

The attitudes of customers and potential customers will be affected by the services offered by competitors. Airlines must compare and contrast their own standards with those of competitors. To be able to do this they must establish an order of preference. Some features of service may be incompatible. It may be impossible to cut down the period between check-in and departure, and at the same time maintain punctuality. In a recent survey arrival on time proved to be the most sought-after feature, and refreshments the least sought after.

Finally, with the information on the identity of customers, and potential customers, customers' attitudes and priorities, and the standards of competitors, management must decide on the best way of selling the services on offer.

Market research is conducted by means of personal interviews, telephone enquiries, mail enquiries and by questionnaires distributed on aircraft. Questionnaires must be designed to eliminate bias, and a reliable sample of the population must be chosen for study.

Market research is more important for air transport than for most other industries. Many vital management decisions take years to come into effect, so it is necessary to forecast the circumstances that will obtain when they do come into effect. It is usually a costly matter to change a decision such as that of aircraft purchase when it becomes apparent that long-term market forecasts are wrong. The need for accuracy in forecasting is emphasised by the slender margin of profitability of even prosperous airlines. The penalties of failure are magnified by the fact that vital decisions affect whole fleets of aircraft, rather than single aircraft. Long periods between making decisions and implementing them is not confined to the purchase of aircraft. In many countries the time that elapses between deciding that a new route should be opened, and obtaining domestic licences and traffic rights can be years.

Finally, market research must not be restricted to finding out what will be the future *demand* in the market. It must also provide facts on the future *supply* in the market. If demand doubles in ten years, but supply trebles, the declining share of market available to each carrier must be taken into account when assessing the effect of a rise in total demand. The main hazard in airline operation is that the total supply of aircraft will exceed demand. It is possible to reach a position in which aircraft are too big and require too long a haul.

Marketing prospects for air freight

The marketing prospects for freight are spoilt on the one hand because transport by air appears to be more expensive than transport by any other means. They are enhanced on the other hand by advantages that produce savings for the shipper. While the costs to shippers are clear for all to see in a published schedule of rates, the savings are little understood and open to argument. The greatest prospects lie in persuading shippers *to recognise* these savings.

A promising outlook exists in what might well be referred to as transport revolution. The growth in recent years of trade in machinery and other goods requiring replacement of parts has given rise to a considerable movement of spares. Producers are beginning to appreciate the importance of servicing their products in the hands of the consumer. They can be persuaded to recognise air transport as the most efficient means of servicing products in all corners of the globe.

The problems of marketing freight services

One of the handicaps encountered by cargo sales managers is that passenger services dominate the thinking of the world's major airlines. The interests of the few all-cargo carriers are squeezed out by this concentration of effort. Yet it would be rash to deny the possibility of abrupt increases in the demand for the transport of freight by air.

It was customary in the two decades following the war for cargo men to attribute most of their troubles to the lack of specially built all-cargo aircraft. These aircraft began to appear in the early 1960s and it became apparent that they would not immediately solve all the problems besetting the marketing manager. The Flying Tiger Lines' new Canadair CL-44 aircraft soon showed about a one-third reduction in flying costs, and promised further economies with mechanised loading and unloading procedures. British European Airways' Armstrong-Whitworth Argosies provided opportunities to reduce costs and extend services. But in neither case did the hoped-for upsurge in demand appear. Indeed in a statement made by Seaboard World Airlines in 1962, concerning the introduction of turbo-jet all-cargo aircraft, it was said after stressing the low available ton-mile cost, and completely mechanised loading system, that a third advantage would be the ease of conversion for passenger use. Seaboard believed that they would need passenger revenue initially to cover operating costs.

It is reasonable to suppose that the freight market is more sensitive to the cost of air transport than is the passenger market. Cargo traffic is different from passenger traffic in that the former is governed more strictly by business considerations. Even with business-passenger traffic there is a considerable margin of consumer-satisfaction. Very few businessmen will carve their air journeys down to the bare bones of economy. But the shipper tends to look at cost and disregard other features, as long as they meet his minimum requirements.

This attitude on the part of shippers should influence the freight-marketing strategy of airlines. First there is a need to adjust rates to exploit demand more fully; secondly, marketing management must set out to change traditional attitudes to transport costs by giving shippers a comprehensive view of the costs of materials movements.

The delicacy required in fixing cargo rates, to take into account the value of commodities and the cost of carriage, and the particular advantages and disadvantages of air transport, cannot survive in the normal atmosphere of IATA negotiations. The procedures for fixing cargo rates should be divorced from those for fixing passenger fares so that, for example, experiments on the cargo side are not frustrated by the unanimity rule applicable to the passenger side. It would also help if the negotiation of cargo traffic rights were divorced from the negotiation of passenger traffic rights so that cargo services could be taken out of the passenger strait-jacket. A new concept of free-ranging fleets serving 'areas' rather than routes, is needed to fully develop the demand for freight services.

A systematic study of the movement of materials (called 'Rhocrematics' by S. H. Brewer of Washington University) may do much to bring reason to bear on the traditional attitudes that handicap the carriage of goods by air. This approach to the logistics of distribution suggests that while the total costs of distribution (covering the flow of goods from plant to user) may represent half the total costs attaching to products, *transport costs* are usually only a small part of *distribution costs*. In particular it emphasises the *costs of possession*, in the shape of costs of interest, storage, insurance and obsolescence. It also focuses attention on the distribution costs of crating, damage and revenue lost from slow delivery. Air transport could, by making inroads into these distribution costs, bring about a change in the significance of its own rates. Marketing management must be prepared to educate industrialists on this subject.

The proper perspective for the transport of freight by air

An advertisement appeared for The Flying Tiger Lines, in which a picture of New York's Times Square at night bore the caption 'End of the Tiger Runway'. This emphasised the vital role of surface transport in the process of 'air' transport. Airline managements and governments have made strategic errors on the passenger side of the industry by failing to recognise the importance of the relationship between surface transport and air transport. Hence we have the situation in which a passenger struggles for an hour and a half to reach an airport to take a half an hour's flight. But the dangers of allowing passengers to 'find their own way to airports' are much less than the dangers in allowing the same laissez-faire approach to air cargo.

The role of 'forwarders' in cargo marketing

We have already seen that the air freight market is distinguished by the facts that shippers have developed the habit of buying transport at lowest possible prices and that the freight market is spread over wide areas, and not concentrated in towns in the same way as passenger traffic. A higher proportion of cargo than passenger sales would be 'off-line' in a well developed industry. Thirdly, air freight may well be offered in thousands of penny packets, that are valuable in total but costly to handle individually. Forwarders claim they can reduce costs to a competitive level, give a wide sales coverage and consolidate traffic to enable airlines to make profits.

In the United States air freight 'forwarders' are regarded as common carriers. Their tariffs must be approved by the Civil Aeronautics Board and published. They issue their own waybills; their responsibility for loss or damage extends from the point of collection to the point of delivery. This is how they stand in relation to their own customers, to the people who own the cargo that is to be moved. But to airlines they are shippers. This means that having completed all the formalities and documentation for customers, forwarders then have to go through much the same procedure with the airlines. Forwarders may cause duplication of effort that can be avoided only by airlines giving them special recognition and accepting their documentation for the air trip.

Forwarders increase the problems of airlines by aiming to achieve the maximum consolidation of freight daily. This causes cargo shipments to be concentrated into a few hours at night. This situation might be eased by airlines charging shippers on a weight-per-day rather than on a weight-per-shipment basis. Perhaps the ultimate solution in the United States is to abandon the practice of treating forwarders as common carriers and to establish them as recognised agents of the airlines working on a commission basis.

Advertising

Airline marketing managers are not able to display their wares to potential first-time buyers. The situation is different with second-time buyers who have 'experience' of flights to do the work of display. But the potential buyer of air transport has not the same opportunity of examining what he is thinking of buying as has the potential buyer of a manufactured article on sale in a shop. Airline marketing managers have to resort to notional representation of their product. Their display is an idea and not the product itself. The main problem is that air transport provides a variable mixture of consumer satisfactions, including those of 'process of production' by carriage, and a 'product' of arrival and it is consequently difficult to fashion a comprehensive notional representation.

In advertising the marketing manager must allow that the product is arrival. His display should include destination. In fact, a great number of airline posters are predominantly destination displays. There is the danger that this will help competitors serving the same destinations, so a clear message to travel by a certain carrier must be built into the picture.

The clarity of the image produced by reference to a carrier on a predominantly 'destination' poster will depend on what has been referred to by one airline as its 'corporate identity'.[1] This immediately recognisable identity can be built up only by a consistent and coherent 'house-style'. Every aspect of display encountered by the customer from the first time he considers air transport should bear the hallmark of the airline's official design policy.

[1] An occasional paper—Advertising Manager BEA. No. 8. 'The corporate identity of an airline'. An address read before the Council of Industrial Design Congress 1961 by A. H. Milward.

It is not easy to ensure that all sections of a large organisation thoroughly understand and act in accordance with a design policy. Considerable success was achieved by British European Airways through its publishing a Manual of Design to guide officials in every corner of its network. The manual specifies the correct trademarks of the airline, down to details of colours, proportions and so on. It also illustrates the use of trademarks and their colours in the design of working units like sales offices, airport check-in points, aircraft, etc.

The mandatory and educative influence of a design policy should be evident in every aspect of customer service. But it should go beyond this and permeate every managerial decision, especially when they impinge on other sorts of external relations. For example, the way the annual report and accounts are presented, invoices are designed, and the way employment booklets are prepared, all contribute to the corporate identity of an airline.

There is more room for misunderstanding, and consequent dissatisfaction where products are represented notionally than where they are actually displayed. Even when advertising is not careless and inherently misleading a customer may imagine he is buying something different from what he gets. Airlines must keep an eye on customer complaints touching on this matter. There are a number of strategic decisions concerning advertising that must be made by management. First they must decide how much money to 'appropriate'. There are no clear guides to the amount that should be spent. There is no formula to tell management how much return it will get for a certain expenditure. It is virtually impossible to isolate the effect of advertising, and every pound spent on it after a certain point will have to be taken from some other branch of expenditure. Secondly, management has to decide where to do the advertising. They must balance correctly their spending on display at the focal points of the airline network and at the extremities. If the balance of spending is wrong it may well result in a disparity between traffic in one direction and the other. Deciding what towns to advertise in is not enough: management must also decide whether to advertise in people's places of work, their places of pleasure, or their homes. The third strategic decision is that of the *media* to be used for display in the *places* that have been decided upon. Various places may call for different media for the best result. Television may be the best means of getting into homes, newspapers into offices, posters into holiday resorts and so on. The advertising in each place by each means is subject to its own graduation of returns. The onset and pace of diminishing returns will differ from place to place and from means to means. The fourth strategic decision is that of timing. A small amount of advertising that is well-timed can be more effective than a large amount that is ill-timed. For example, holiday advertising must coincide with holiday planning, and not with going on holiday: advertising a new route cannot wait until the route is opened, yet it is wasteful to begin too far ahead.

The place of advertising in the overall marketing policies of airlines is somewhat unusual. There are grounds for doubting whether advertising can create brand preference. The fact that air transport is something that is, in general, not purchased frequently makes it difficult to build up loyalties to a particular airline. Yet some airlines have spent no less than 10 per cent of a year's revenue on advertising. This is because individual airline managements are denied the most effective means of changing volume of demand, that is, by altering price through a change in fares. Advertising is seen as a means of altering price (remembering this is fundamentally a *ratio* between what is spent by the consumer and what he gets in return), by persuading people that the airline product is worth more than they thought. By enhancing air transport advertising will, in effect, lower its price in the eyes of customers. That this is a marginal process compared with changing fares and rates is suggested by the differences in European and American practices. The former have, in fact, obtained agreement within IATA for a range of fares that enables them to tap a number of levels of demand. For example, tourist fares for London to Rome in the summer of 1963 varied from £36 5s 0d (for night flights from Monday night to Friday morning, at the beginning or end of the summer) to £39 11s 0d, £41 4s 0d, £49 8s 0d and £61 0s 0d for return tickets valid for a year. On the other hand, the Civil Aeronautics Board has not encouraged United States' airlines to develop similar fare differentials. Thus we find US airlines spending between 5 per cent and 10 per cent of their revenues on advertising against a European average of between 2 and 3 per cent.

There are two other factors circumscribing managerial decisions on airline advertising. The first is the territories at each end of a route are seldom equal in importance. Some airlines have main bases in a hinterland giving rise to considerable traffic. Others must concentrate on attracting traffic from other sources. The second is that since the industry has no retail stockists, the airline has to address the consumer directly with his advertising.

Finally, airlines are faced with the problem of ensuring that the fruits of their advertising are garnered at the point of sale. A well-conducted advertising campaign can easily be turned to no account by the indifference of sales clerks and travel agents.

The organisation of marketing

The marketing activities referred to in this chapter are not always in the organisation of a single marketing manager, reporting directly to the President or Managing Director. Very many airlines do have a recognisable marketing division of overall organisation, but there are some that separate the activities and co-ordinate them at President level only. For example, American Airlines (Fig. 54 et seq.) have a Vice-President managing an advertising organisation, and a Vice-President and General Manager managing a sales and services organisation both reporting to the President.

The differences of opinion on how marketing should be organised reflect not so much the different circumstances of each airline, as the dilemma that faces the whole industry. As in all so-called 'service' industries, the process of production is a secondary product. The marketing manager must be concerned with the way that customers and their goods are 'carried' in the process of achieving primary intention of 'arrival'. For this reason some airlines choose to integrate closely the two aspects of 'sales' and 'services' under one head, and to separate the conventional display activity of advertising.

No one can be sure which is better—to integrate all marketing activities, or to integrate sales with after-sales services. Both methods of organisation can be made to work. There are profitable airlines on both sides of the fence.

The critical issue is this. Does the close integration of certain aspects of marketing and certain aspects of production make the co-ordination of the three aspects of production more difficult? There is no getting away from the fact that the activities that immediately precede a culminating act of take-off constitute a unified operation—unified by circumstances and not by any man-made organisational device.

CHAPTER XVII

PERSONNEL MANAGEMENT

The role of personnel management

Personnel management is to do with fairness. It is to do with ordinary workpeople's notions of justice, and what is right and what is wrong. It is to do with the claims of the persons rather than the money and materials, concerned in a business. Personnel management is not, however, a 'soft' form of management, any more than judges who also deal in fairness are 'soft' members of the civil administration. The idea that personnel management means softness to workpeople is wrong for a number of reasons. Firstly, it is concerned with fairness to the employer as much as with fairness to the employee. Secondly, it is concerned with employees' claims that may conflict with the claims of other employees, and softness to one group of employees may be injustice to another. Thirdly, the tempering of the strict demands of justice, which is occasionally the work of a personnel manager, is a positive contribution to human relations that does not merit the description of softness.

Because managers specialise in finance, production, marketing and so on, it follows that someone must specialise in personnel. By dividing up to obtain the advantages of specialisation management inevitably incurs some disadvantages. Among these is the preoccupation with processes of say production or marketing. By being preoccupied with technical processes the specialists are unable to devote enough attention to the human aspects of management. In a business sense it may even be wrong to expect, say, a brilliant aircraft designer to spend much of his time settling human affairs. Delegation of human administration is exemplified in a number of occupations: lawyers, medical men and academics have their specialist administrators.

Then again, if a business organisation is divided up it is impracticable to allow each manager to be 'fair' to his own operatives. Every alteration in the conditions of workers in one department of an organisation reflects on the conditions of workers in other departments. While it is practicable for management to be departmental in their thinking on machines and processes, they must deal with human sections within the context of the whole organisation.

The work of an airline Personnel Department

The following are aspects of employment commonly dealt with in the Personnel Departments of airlines:

1. Staff engagement, transfer and termination procedures—preparation of service agreements, medical examinations, references, selection procedures, probation periods.
2. Procedures for temporary absences from work—e.g. annual leave, compassionate leave, sickness and accidents.
3. Procedures for dealing with prolonged illness, and death of staff.
4. Pension schemes.
5. Promotion procedures—notifying vacancies.
6. Procedures for giving references for ex-employees.
7. Conditions for part-time employment.
8. Conditions for the employment of aliens.
9. Regulations for retirement of staff.
10. Publications describing conditions of employments.
11. Emoluments—overseas allowances, separation allowances, travelling, accommodation, car allowances, travel concessions, entertainment expenses and medical expenses.
12. Disciplinary procedures.
13. Staff assessment procedures and awards of pay increments.
14. Regulations for wearing uniforms and protective clothing.
15. Negotiation of basic rates, proficiency pay, premium rates, bonuses, overtime and shift pay.
16. Provision of welfare services in cases of hardship.
17. Provision of facilities for recreation.
18. Training and education.

Personnel problems characteristic of airlines

The following aspects of airline operations give rise to characteristic personnel problems:

(i) The wide variety of skills employed;
(ii) The need to deploy simultaneously social and mechanical skills of a high order;
(iii) The wide fluctuations in the amount of work to be done from one period to another;
(iv) The geographical spread of employees;
(v) The employment of 'other nationals';
(vi) The need to maintain a 24-hour service;

(vii) The need to retire certain categories of staff at an early age;
(viii) The need for a constantly effective disciplinary code;
(ix) Differences in the nature of service in the air and on the ground;
(x) The economic vulnerability of an airline;
(xi) The optimum size of airline organisation.

The wide variety of skills employed

Highly organised airlines (i.e. those that put relatively little work out to contract) employ people on tasks calling for the exercise of considerably varying degrees of skill. In a catering organisation they may vary from a simple domestic task to preparing hundreds of aircraft meals a day. In the engineering field they may vary from cleaning an aircraft to improving engine performance. They may vary from a routine clerical task to cost accounting. Catering, accountancy, piloting, communications, electronic data processing, and property maintenance are but a few examples of the wide variety of skills required in a sizeable airline organisation.

These differences in the skills of employees are often reflected in their styles of living, eating habits, manner of communication, leisure pursuits and so on. These in turn provide a variety of 'outlooks', on the amenities provided. In short it makes it difficult to please everyone. Consequently it is not uncommon for airlines to have to provide separate amenities for different groups, for example, by having several grades of cafeteria and restaurant service.

A wide variety of skills also makes it difficult to apply the principle of equal pay for equal work. Admittedly this principle is hard to adhere to anyway. The interests of business often demand that wages are geared to the economist's 'scarcity' value rather than the personnel manager's 'effort' value, although the latter is claimed to be the more equitable. This claim is based on the assumption that a person endowed by birth and circumstance with skills he cannot be said to have fully earned is entitled to recompense for them. Be that as it may, in accordance with the principle of equal pay for equal work, wage differentials should match skill and effort differentials. The practical difficulty comes in measuring the distinctions. Why, for the sake of argument, should a pilot get four times the pay of a skilled aircraft mechanic, and a salesman get double that of a check-in clerk? While commonsense tells us that differences there must be, notions of fairness are not satisfied by any of the bases yet established for discriminating one job from another. Until a satisfactory measure is found, every increase in the number and variety of skills merely increases the problems of creating a 'fair' wage structure.

The need to deploy simultaneously social and mechanical skills of a high order

A pilot has an exacting mechanical task to perform: at the same time he is responsible for seeing that his passengers feel well-cared for. A reservations clerk must see that his ticketing and tariff calculations and route construction conform to numerous IATA and company regulations, and at the same time remain attentive and courteous to the customer. An airport clerk must ensure that all his actions conform to the regulations of his own company and those of the airport authorities, designed for the prompt departure and safe arrival of aircraft. But in attending to the programmes of aircraft he must never lose touch with the feelings of waiting passengers.

Mechanical craftsmanship and human sympathy are the warp and weft in the texture of many an airline job. These threads are seldom well-matched in the nature of men. The important and difficult problem of integrating craftsmanship and sympathy must be considered when preparing any syllabus for training.

The wide fluctuations in the amount of work to be done from one period to another

We have already noted that the ups and downs in airline activities cause serious economic problems. Because demand fluctuates from season to season, from weekday to weekend, and from day to night, neither the human nor material resources of organisation can be used to maximum effect. At times they tend to be over-worked and at other times under-worked. To this picture of economic waste we must add the important touches of the strains of concentrated activity and enforced idleness.

Personnel management should adopt one of two policies. Either it should decide that short period of strain followed by short periods of recuperation is an acceptable pattern in the employment of some categories of staff, or it should decide to promote all practicable means of levelling up the day's work for each individual.

By pursuing the former policy there is little doubt that in most cases an agreeable rhythm of work and rest can be achieved. There are, however, inherent dangers in the system. Firstly, idleness can be demoralising. The experience of many airline personnel managers is that trouble brews up when business is slack. A recent investigation into the attitudes of ex-apprentices in one airline revealed that one of their strongest dissatisfactions was with 'so much hanging around doing nothing'. In fact, unless men are so exhausted that they sleep, they cannot be kept idle. They will find something to do, even if it is only drinking cups of coffee or tea, smoking and talking. So if there are to be 'idle' periods some sort of provision ought to be made for them. Not enough thought has been given to the furnishing and equipping of 'waiting' rooms for staff on-duty. They usually appear to have got into the hands of staff by accident, and to have been furnished by scrounging. It is possible, of course, that by making 'waiting' rooms too comfortable, men will be distracted from their work.

The second inherent danger, in accepting that idle periods are reasonable, is that of failing to maintain a sufficient degree of alertness. Men who have just tumbled out of the relaxing environment of a rest room may not be geared up to deal with a critical situation. Experienced mountaineers have found that frequent rests in a day's climb reduce the efficiency of their performance considerably. The need to 'get into one's stride' and to 'warm up' is supported by physiological studies that have produced output curves rising slowly at first, and then more steeply. While this fact may be more important to the athlete than to the airline official, it is not without significance to the latter.

Since there is little evidence of harmful effects resulting from the bursts of activity called for at busy periods, the best personnel policy is probably to promote means of employment during what would otherwise be idle periods. The first field to examine is that of job specification. The clear definition of an employee's task is useful in a number of ways, but it has its drawbacks and one of these is the *restrictive* nature of the definition. Vested interests soon become entrenched along the lines of demarcation. Those inside the boundary will not step beyond it without more pay. Those outside will not permit what they regard as encroachment on other people's preserves. Job demarcation is easier to prevent than to cure. Heed should be taken of the plight of the British Dock Industry, that in the middle of the century with nearly a hundred types of job had hundreds of men idle who could not be fitted into vacant jobs.

If an official can move, for example, from check-in to passenger escort, and then to embarkation it may be easier to keep him busy than if he specialises on one of these tasks. There is much to be said for allowing officials to see passengers through from beginning to end of the preparations for flight. In a sense this makes for specialisation in passengers, rather than in a particular process.

Finally, the fluctuations in work-load that are so common in the industry afford opportunities for maintaining a high standard of training. Management must, however, be prepared to employ modern training techniques such as programmed instruction, use of tape recorders, projectors and so on. This may require a considerable investment of money, but the results would justify it.

The geographical spread of employees

In trying to be fair, in the payment of employees, personnel management has to look beyond what the economist calls the 'nominal' wage. A man's nominal wage is simply stated in terms of dollars, pounds or francs, or whatever currency he is paid in. The nominal wage has no intrinsic value. As a statement it has little significance until we know what can be bought with the money. This value of nominal wages is referred to by economists as 'real' wages.

If an airline paid the same nominal wage to all its employees over its whole network it would soon learn that the nominal wage would not buy as much in one part as in another. It would, in fact, end up with many degrees of 'real' wages, paid for the same work, and this would be inconsistent with good personnel policy. The cost of living may vary considerably from one spot to another within one country; thus living in a town may cost more than living in the country, and living in one town may cost more than living in another.

It would cost a Frenchman, stationed in Lagos, more to educate his children to the standard enjoyed by the children of his colleagues in Paris, than if he were stationed in Paris. It might cost more for a man stationed in Moscow to buy fresh vegetables than his compatriots would have to pay in, say, Amsterdam. Certainly the costs of housing, clothes and medical care differ considerably from one country to another.

There are a number of commonly employed devices for levelling up real wages. Many airlines supply accommodation (a house or a flat) as part of the emoluments of overseas employment. Many also arrange for local medical services to be made available, free of charge, to their expatriate employees. Provisions of this sort prevent discrepancies from arising, from the point of view of the individual employee. To compensate for differences in the costs of food and clothing, most airlines establish a complex structure of allowances. Again, many airlines make substantial grants to enable the children of their expatriate staff to be educated in the home country. One way and another airlines succeed fairly well in their adjustments of real wages.

Insuperable difficulties often occur in attempting to equate the pay of employees of different nationalities. Germans, Italians and Frenchmen must be paid in accordance with complicated labour laws that leave airlines very little room for manoeuvre. Russia dictates the sum that must be paid to Russian employees and so on. Although airlines can do little about equating terms and conditions of employment of other nationals with those of their own, they can often do something to ensure that each 'foreign' airlines in, say, Rome pays approximately the same rates to the Italians they employ.

Airline staff abroad

Members of staff employed outside their native lands work and live under peculiar difficulties. Extra pay by way of allowances, rent-free homes and boarding-school education for their children may partly compensate for, but not eradicate, their problems. And envy of these material advantages all too often robs them of the sympathy of those at home.

Because these people are 'fit' to represent their companies abroad, they are usually well fitted to take advantage of the wide variety of cultural opportunities usually available to them in their homelands. Language difficulties may severely reduce their ability to enjoy similar opportunities in a foreign country. The faculty of communication in its highest forms, tooled with precision and rich in nuance, is a prerequisite for a full life. To be deprived of linguistic maturity is no less a hardship than losing a limb. This by itself is enough to drive exiles into the small society of their compatriots, and into a way of living that divides them even more firmly from the people of the country in which they live.

In some cases the position of expatriates is made even worse by the tendency for those at home to suspect as 'going native' any attempts to live in Rome, as the Romans do. An airline man abroad is between two worlds. He should retain a headquarter's outlook, and at the same time adjust himself to the mental climate of the community in which he lives. This is a balanced position that few achieve.

Going abroad to work inevitably results in a loosening of some of the ties back at home. This process of erosion threatens the day of the exile's return. He is fortunate if he has a house to go back to, and a job he can fit into, and friends who have not forgotten him. Some airline managements tend to push uncomfortable thoughts of this sort into the background, to leave them unspoken, or muted by the exchange of pleasantries as the exiles cross their paths from time to time.

Airlines should carefully determine their personnel policies to avoid the danger of this sort of predicament. The possible alternatives are:

(i) To leave it to the expatriates themselves to apply for a transfer each time they wish to move to another posting abroad, or to be repatriated;
(ii) To post men to a foreign country for a lifetime's career;
(iii) To post all executives for at least one short tour abroad, but not expecting anyone to make a home abroad;
(iv) To staff foreign stations entirely with their own nationals.

Of these alternatives probably the first gives rise to the most personal problems, and the last gives rise to the least personal problems. Management must, of course, weigh commercial considerations against personal ones.

The employment of foreign staff

Paying the right rate for the job in comparison with home-based staff is not the only important personnel problem involved in the employment of foreign staff. The second major difficulty is that of providing a satisfactory career prospect for them. Most of the top posts in any airline call for permanent residence near headquarters in the airline's homeland. Even if there are no labour laws preventing a foreigner from obtaining a permanent post there are obvious social and domestic handicaps. Often the delicate use of language required of the occupants of top posts eliminates those who do not speak like a native. Then trade union pressures and political considerations may make it more difficult for the foreigner. Finally the foreigner is less likely to be in the right place at the right time—a piece of good fortune that is an ingredient in most successful careers.

There are even arguments against an airline's appointing a foreigner to command an overseas station or area. For example, the representative of Aer Lingus in France must bridge the gap between two economies, two lingual areas and two cultures. Very rare is the man who can give equal support to the traffic of ideas from both sides. If bias there must be, then it is probably better for the Aer Lingus representative to be more accessible to ideas from Dublin than those from Paris. This is only a matter of emphasis, but it is often important enough to tip the balance in favour of appointing a man from the home country.

A tacit acceptance seems to have developed among airline staffs of the position that high office can be obtained only in one's national airline. Thus a German national who serves with an American airline in Hamburg will one day transfer to Deutsche Lufthansa if he has ambitions to obtain a post above the middle ranks. Personnel policies are probably wisely based on this acceptance.

An international outlook for home-based staff

International airlines have the problem of inculcating, in their home-based staff, a sympathetic outlook on the attitudes and customs of foreign colleagues and customers. It is all too easy for an Englishman sitting in London among thousands of his English co-workers to slip into the habit of regarding his airline's French, German and Dutch employees as Englishmen under a different name. Or it is not uncommon for the head office staff of an airline with stations in the under-developed countries to regard local staff as somewhat sub-human. In a hundred small ways rancour and resentment can be caused among foreign employees by the insular outlook of home-based staff.

Widespread insularity in outlook can also, of course, be extremely damaging to customer relations. An airline that expects all its customers to conform to the eating, drinking, smoking and other social habits of its own country will in time alienate the good will of other nationals. There is already a strong enough tendency for people to travel by their own national airline in order to enjoy a sympathetic environment. This tendency should not be reinforced by the stupidity of refusing to recognise other people's way of life.

Part of every airline's educational effort should be to teach the differences in the *modi vivendi* of their more important groups of customers. This teaching will be of little value if it is superficial: it must be a serious attempt to develop genuine sympathy.

The need to maintain a 24-hour service

There are three good reasons for having shift work in airlines.

(*a*) Airline organisations have to employ very expensive equipment. Airliners now cost between one and two million pounds. In order to earn its keep, expensive equipment must be kept working.

(*b*) The airline production process is not one that can be contained between the hours of nine to five. A maintenance programme cannot be suspended at the blast of a whistle. Aircraft cannot be landed on the stroke of the hour. Although air transport cannot properly be considered as a continuous process, in the way that steel, oil, chemicals and papermaking industries are, it has some of the attributes of momentum in common with them.

(*c*) Since the delivery of the airline product immediately follows the process of production, demand for the former controls the timing of the latter. It is passengers and shippers who say when aircraft shall fly. And in saying when aircraft shall fly they consequently dictate the hours of maintenance.

In acknowledging the economic necessity of shift work we must not blind ourselves to its undesirable physiological and social features. According to the experts the human body has a diurnal rhythm. This involves factors such as blood pressure, pulse and breathing rate, and gland action. Research has shown that the body is at its most efficient at about 6 p.m. and least so at about 3 a.m. Research has failed to show that night workers are more prone to accident or illness, but it has shown that night workers suffer from loss of appetite and weight. They also sleep badly during the day.

Unfortunately neither the family nor the community can be expected to adjust themselves completely to the pattern of shift work. Children cannot be switched over to night living. Wives cannot provide meals day and night. Shops, banks, post-offices, libraries and cinemas will not provide a 24-hour service. Doctors and dentists continue to go to bed at nights. The unchangeable pattern of domestic and community life tends to establish the shift-worker in a position of being odd-man out.

It is easy for airline managers who do not work shifts to lose touch with the men on the shop floor who work for them. For this reason managers who are responsible for shift workers should spend some time with men working outside the normal daylight hours. Also personnel managers administering to bodies of shift workers should ensure that their services are available to all shifts. Personnel management has usually to undertake the delicate task of ensuring that 'shift pay' does justice to the worker who suffers from shift work and to the employer who cannot, by the nature of his business, avoid it.

The need to retire certain categories of staff at an early age

Personnel management policy must take account of the fact that there is a danger that certain airline jobs will not be done well by persons over a certain age. For example, it would not be unreasonable to argue that generally women over 35 years of age would be likely to find the duties of cabin staff too onerous. Again it would be reasonable to suppose that generally men over the age of 55 would not be good pilots.

Why generalise on the matter? Why not deal with each case individually and retire such people only when it is found that they are 'beyond' it? The suggestion is superficially attractive. It has the merit of being more flexible than a rule applied without regard to individual circumstances. Yet individual treatment can cause more suffering than the most impersonal regulation. The weakness of the individual approach to the problem lies in its personal nature. One man has to judge when another has reached his limit. This is distressing for he who judges, and like a sentence for he who is judged. The impartial application of a regulation enables management to avoid condemning the individual and saves the individual from being told he is no longer adequate for the task.

The fixing of the right retiring age for a group of staff is an important task. It is important to those retiring. A mistake of a few years may make it difficult for them to begin other work, or it may unnecessarily restrict the size of a pension. On the other hand, a mistake may deprive a company of many years of useful service from well-trained and experienced staff. Or it may involve the company in the risk of employing staff who are physically unreliable.

The need for a constantly effective disciplinary code

Airline organisation must be sustained by an effective disciplinary code. The procedure to be followed in the case of an alleged breach of regulation should be designed to avoid the danger of its being repeated before a verdict is reached. For this reason employees are often suspended from duty pending the results of an enquiry. Enquiries must be thorough not so much to establish blame, but determine causes and to avoid repetition.

Suspension from duty pending the results of an enquiry, lengthy enquiries, delays in promulgating findings and the danger of legal prosecution, all place strain on the individual. The burden is inevitable in an industry that involves public safety. But it places a duty on the shoulders of personnel management. The individual must not be allowed to suffer unnecessarily by the length of process. His interests should not be completely sacrificed to those of society. The individual should not become a scapegoat for the mistakes of management. In short it is encumbent on personnel management to afford the individual adequate protection against the powerful social forces that begin moving against him when something goes wrong. This is not to say that the individual must be sheltered from the consequences of established guilt. It is a matter of seeing that he does not suffer unduly in the process of establishing his innocence or guilt.

Differences in the nature of service in the air and on the ground

T. T. Paterson in his descriptive summary of the problems at a certain wartime fighter station said:[1] 'In the officers' mess flying men segregated themselves from non-flying men, and the latter split into occupational groups—controllers, aerodrome control officers, and administrative officers. The pilots' conversation, when analysed, showed that they tried to place the blame for the accidents on the airfield, non-flying officers, weather and bad luck. But these were merely rationalisation, attempts to explain something they could not understand. Analysis of the conversation of all officers suggested that the groups placed themselves in a scale of prestige, the pilots being highest. The non-flying groups accepted the scaling as it applied to other groups, but not to themselves. Three forms of behaviour seemed to be peculiar to Bogfield. The non-flying men referred to groups higher in the scale with expressions epitomised in "Who do they think they are?" Junior officers among the pilots had

[1] *Morale in War and Work*, T. T. Paterson, Max Parrish 1955.

little respect for senior ranks among non-flying men. The pilots had a marked disinclination to fly.'

Unfortunately this sad state of affairs is easy to reproduce in an airline. In some ways the circumstances of an airline are more favourable than those of an air force, for the development of such problems. Military aircrews and ground staff usually live alongside each other, and share duties common to all officers. Airline crews arrive at an airport in time to prepare for a flight and leave as soon as it is completed. They may have very little to do with ground staff. They even tend to live in districts away from those containing the average 'ground' official. As high income earners they tend to congregate in the better residential areas.

This problem is not new to the transport industry. The seafarers and landlubbers in trading companies were at loggerheads for centuries. This did not matter so much when sailors could survive for months on their own, cut off from the landsmen at base. The aircraft pilot is, however, continuously dependent upon men on the ground. Installations on the ground are as important to him as the engines on his aircraft.

So the hurt pride, suspicions and resentments that are produced by the 'separation' of flying and non-flying staff can be damaging to efficiency. Some separation is inevitable by the very nature of the situation, but much can be done by good personnel policies to avoid making matters worse. A certain amount of joint training helps to bring the two sides together. Common amenities for eating and recreation may reduce feelings of apartheid. Above all, management should ensure that neither 'side' receives more favourable treatment than the other. In its dealings concerning both flying and non-flying staff, management requires to exercise the wisdom of Solomon.

The economic vulnerability of an airline

In many industries, if the operatives go on strike for a week, their employers will lose approximately one-fiftieth of their annual production. In some airlines, if operatives choose the right week, for the loss of a week's pay they can cause the loss of one-twentieth of the annual revenue. This is because the demand for air transport is not evenly spread throughout the year. By striking at certain periods employees can cause disproportionate losses.

Also the industry is vulnerable because production cannot be made up to any extent by working overtime when a strike ends. Some industries can make good all the production lost through a strike by redoubling efforts on the return to work. But a day's loss of flying is more or less gone forever.

This results in a weakness in bargaining position. Airline

negotiators are under constant pressure to keep the airline going during critical periods. Union negotiators are usually well aware of their anxieties and occasionally are tempted to take advantage of the situation. If management once gives way to pressures of this sort, it is asking for further trouble. Union leaders usually respect those managements who deal with their claims on their merits, and do not resort to expediency.

The size of airline organisations

The following table shows the average numbers of staff employed by 10 major airlines during 1962:

TABLE 21. *Average numbers of staff employed by 10 major airlines during 1962*

Air France	BEA	BOAC	KLM	PAA	QEA	Sabena	SAS	Swiss-air	TWA
25,000	16,200	22,100	17,400	23,300	6,700	7,700	12,900	7,700	20,700

The evidence produced by social scientists suggests that the behaviour of members of large organisations is less favourable than that of members of small organisations. In big units there are more disputes, absences without leave, sickness and risk of accident. In general, the bigger the organisation the less attached people are to their colleagues and their work.

R. W. Revans said, 'the cruellest problems of big modern organisations are the problems of change'. He was referring to the strain imposed on human beings by the rapid changes demanded by technology. This often changes methods, materials, designs, policies, skills, perceptions and values, overnight.

It is encumbent on large organisations to minimise the stagnation of authority, and the deadening effect of standardisation. They must equip their employees with the means of learning to adjust to change. This means not only teaching them new mechanical skills to replace obsolete ones, but also about their new place in a changed organisation. It means not only teaching them about changes in policy, but also about the way they should modify their behaviour to meet changed circumstances.

Selection procedures in airlines

At the time of writing it could cost up to £8,000 for the initial training of a pilot, and as much as £10,000 to convert them from one type of aircraft to another. The apprenticeship training of an engineer could cost up to £2,500 and the apprenticeship training for non-technical staff a similar sum. It could cost up to £200 to train a stewardess, who might stay for only a year. The total bill for training an airline staff of 20,000 will probably be running between £1½ million and £2 million a year.

Training costs depend to a considerable extent on the aims and success of staff selection procedures. An airline can aim to select skilled staff requiring the minimum of training; or it can aim to select unskilled staff requiring considerable training. In the latter case the airline might expect to recoup part or whole of the training costs from the difference in pay for skilled and unskilled workers. Without going into the pros and cons of either approach, we can see the need to have clear aims at the selection stage: otherwise selection and training efforts will be at variance.

In the airline business there are a number of tasks that call for endowments[1] that are capable of little or no development by training. For example, a pilot must have good eyesight and muscular co-ordination and freedom from certain physical defects. He must be endowed with a certain minimum level of intelligence, verbal, numerical and mechanical ability. Without these endowments no amount of training will produce a good pilot. Staff dealing with the public must have a pleasing appearance. Engineers must have considerable mechanical aptitude and so on.

The fact that certain endowments are absolutely necessary for the successful performance of a number of tasks means that airlines must equip themselves with fairly refined selection techniques. Many airlines took advantage of the advances made during the Second World War in the selection of army, navy and air force officers. Using these techniques as a starting point they have developed procedures that are tailored to the needs of all categories of staff.

However, much remains to be done. The amount of thought given to the aims of selection has not kept pace with that spent on techniques. So we occasionally come across the case of a man selected with precision on the basis of characteristics that are irrelevant to the requirements of his post. On the other hand, there is the opposite danger. If all staff were matched too narrowly to the requirements of their job on entry, it might be difficult for them to move from one job to another later in their careers. This touches on the issues of generalist and specialists dealt with in Chapter 10.

The costs of inadequate training

The results of inadequate training are reflected in both revenues and costs. The losses incurred are difficult to identify, and all too often they are glossed over as unavoidable costs of production. For example, the costs of rejects of repaired equipment, or baggage wrongly routed are commonly regarded as operating costs as long as they do not much exceed the average for the industry. Indeed

[1] *Fundamentals of Management*. p. 108.

we are so accustomed to see the performances of one airline measured by comparisons with other airlines that we tend to overlook the fact that this way of measuring efficiency is not very useful for other than competitive activities (such as gaining a share of a market).

On the revenue side, inadequate training may prevent an airline from satisfying all the demand that exists for its services. Or it may reduce demand by reducing the quality of the product (and in effect raising its price). Almost every member of staff can affect the image of the services offered to customers.

On the cost side, inadequate training may prevent an airline from optimising the use of its equipment. Wrongly used equipment either fails to bring about the essential change of production, or else calls for too high a proportion of operatives to equipment. Inadequate training may also increase the cost of recruitment and remuneration. Inflated recruitment costs, in advertising, travel, subsistence and selection, and inflated salaries are often due to competitive bidding for trained personnel because of an airline's inability to train effectively.

Training for cost control

We have already mentioned in Chapter XIII the difficulties in controlling costs in airlines. At the same time the narrow margin of profits in the industry makes it necessary to exercise the strictest control on costs. This may be achieved partly by a budgetary control system and cost accounting, but it can never be completely effective unless all personnel fully sympathise with its purpose. An airline must establish an acute sense of cost through all ranks of staff.

The training and education of maintenance engineers

We have already referred to the importance of the skill of airline maintenance engineers. Aircraft are exceptional vehicles in that they are operated close to the boundaries of human knowledge. Airlines cannot afford to build in extravagant safety margins, and the costs of maintenance figure high in the total bill of airline costs.

Many of the world's major airlines employ graduate engineers. Some of them accept men with traditional academic disciplines, while others are insisting on training and education geared more closely to airline industrial needs. In general the subject of engineering is treated too much as an applied science, touching but briefly on the play of human judgement. Nor do the traditional disciplines deal adequately with economic dispositions, managerial processes or organisation principles.

The areas other than these which need most attention in the training and education of maintenance engineers for airlines may be summarised briefly as follows:

(1) Language—an airline engineer must be able to convey his thoughts to colleagues who are not engineers.
(2) Statistical techniques—a number of new techniques have been evolved that may prove to be of great usefulness in maintenance control.
(3) Organisation and methods techniques—maintenance engineers need to appreciate the possible gain from O. & M.
(4) Data processing (including electronic data processing).
(5) Fundamentals of management.

Training 'programmes' instead of 'courses' for 'non-technical' staff

Training for these staff should be planned not as a series of *courses*, but rather as a series of *programmes* or *schemes*, each training programme consisting of a number of layers. For example, those staff not going through an apprenticeship scheme would have a programme of this sort arranged for them.

1. Preparatory on-the-job study (illustrated by a SAS scheme (1961) of providing pre-course material, in which the student is given a number of questions to explore, with the help of his supervisor).
2. A training course, either local or centralised.
3. Follow-up 'on-the-job' study, possibly including correspondence courses (such as these arranged by KLM (1962)).
4. Follow-up or refresher courses (of which a good example was the Sabena scheme (1962) for traffic staff, with refresher courses after one or two years' service, and then at three-yearly intervals).

Other layers might consist of more specialised training courses, such as when a change in procedures is made (for example, the introduction of an electronic reservations system), or when it is desired to teach an additional skill (for example, a supervisor might be sent on an instructors' course).

Levels of training for non-technical staff

The training of non-technical airline staff should be conducted at the following four levels:

1. Introductory Training

   This should be common to all non-technical staff, and should be given not later than when a recruit joins an airline. SAS began their introductory training programme (1962) two or three weeks before an employee joined them, when they sent out a 78-page booklet prepared by their Sales and Station Training Unit entitled 'This is Your Company'. Two full days should be devoted to background or fundamental information about the air transport industry and the company.

2. Basic Training

This should begin immediately after the introductory training, with on-the-job training followed, after one or two months, by a basic training course. The length of basic training should depend upon a number of factors—the education level of the employee, the nature of his duties and so on—but it would probably last from one to two years. The training should be broadly based, in furtherance of the policy of generalisation with, perhaps, three programmes—one for people employed on passenger sales and service, another for cargo people, and a third for aircraft and load handling personnel (where there is direct entry to this sort of work). People employed on space control are normally recruited from within the industry and would, therefore, receive basic training in either passenger or cargo work. People recruited for sales promotion work should be given an accelerated basic training in passenger or cargo work (or a combination of the two) before beginning their sales promotion training.

3. Advanced Training

At this level, training should be more specialised and should be aimed at producing people who, so far as their day-to-day jobs are concerned, can be expected to work without supervision. This level should be reached by all staff wishing to make a career in the air transport industry. Only when the advanced training programme has been completed should an employee be regarded as 'fully trained'; then he would be a person of some experience, with responsibility for answering queries from or checking the work of people who have reached only the basic level (but not for supervising them or organising their work). An individual's authority should be related to the amount of training that he has received; so, for example, only someone who has completed the advanced aircraft and load handling training programme should be permitted to sign a load sheet.

4. Supervisory Training

At this level, training should become more generalised—at least in so far as its technical content is concerned—covering the range of work to be dealt with at a particular location. The 'leadership' element in supervisory training would be common to all. Supervisory training should begin when an employee has been identified as a potential supervisor. One of the 'layers' of this training might well be a period as understudy to a supervisor, but no-one should be promoted without undergoing some training first.

The way to construct a syllabus for training non-technical staff

The mere listing of subjects in various training programmes is of little use, as one programme ends up looking very much like another.

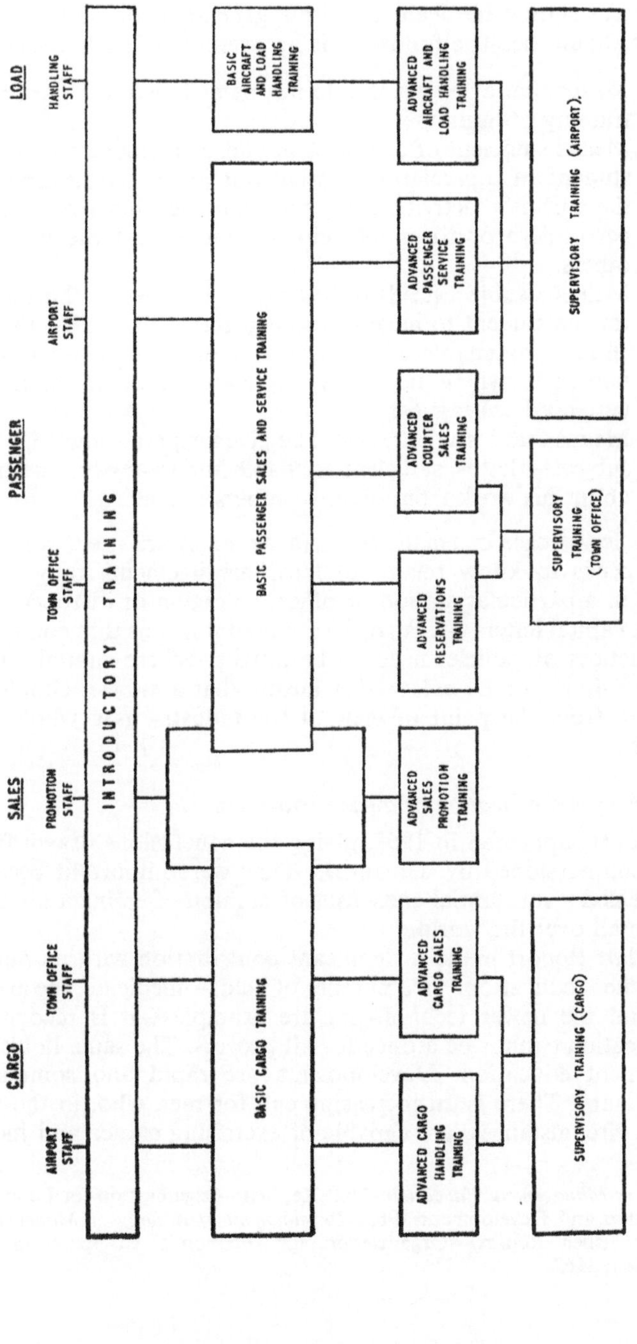

FIG. 53. *A plan for training non-technical personnel of airlines*

It is better to find a way of indicating the thoroughness with which each subject should be dealt, and how general to the industry the coverage should be. The following is an example of such a scheme:

O	Means that a subject should not be included in a particular training programme.
A,A,a	Means sufficient of a subject should be included to give the student an appreciation of what is involved in this aspect of the airline's activities, to help him get his own job in perspective or to enable him to understand the work of others.
W,W,w	Means a subject needs to be covered sufficiently thoroughly for the student to have a working knowledge of it—that is, enough to enable him to do his day-to-day work with reference, where necessary, to manuals or to more experienced colleagues.
E,E,e	Means that a student should be given expert knowledge of a subject—that is, sufficient to enable him to answer questions about his work from other members of staff.

Where lower case or small letters (a, w, or e) are used, what the student needs to know relates to local arrangements only (what happens in a particular station or office, or region or district).

Where capital letters (A, W, or E) are used it means that company-wide practices or policies need to be taught. Where capital letters *in italics* (*A*, *W*, or *E*) are used it means that a subject should be dealt with from the point of view of the industry as a whole (see Table 22).

The training and education of airline managers

Two Reports appeared in 1963, giving the conclusions drawn from studies commissioned by the OECD.[1] They were important because they revealed a substantial consensus of opinion of eminent authorities from all over the world.

The Platt Report made a significant contribution with its notion of permanent education. In a number of fields—medicine, the armed forces and the newer technologies are examples—it is recognised that education cannot be a once-for-all process. The same holds for management education. Developments are rapid and sometimes revolutionary. There is an increasing call for men who, in the face of novel circumstances, are capable of exercising choice and judgement.

[1] *Issues in Management Education* (Platt Report)—Organisation for Economic Co-operation and Development 1963; *Development of a Body of Management Teachers* (Fisher Report)—Organisation for Economic Co-operation and Development 1962.

TABLE 22. *Illustration of method of constructing a syllabus*

	INTRODUCTORY TRAINING	BASIC TRAINING			ADVANCED TRAINING							SUPERVISORY TRAINING		
		Cargo	Passenger and Sales Service	Aircraft and Load Handling	Cargo Handling	Cargo Sales	Sales Promotion	Reser-vations	Counter Sales	Passenger Service	Aircraft and Load Handling	Cargo	Town	Office
PRACTICAL SKILLS														
Common:														
Timetables	O	W/*A*	W/*A*	W	E/*W*	E/*W*	E/*W*	E	E/*W*	E/*W*	O	*E*	*E*	*E*
Route construction	O	W	W	W	E	E	E	E	E	E	o	O	O	O
Communications	O	W	W	W	W	W	W	W	W	W	W	E	E	E
Other airlines' procedures	O	w	w	w	w	O	O	O	O	w	w	w	O	w
Space Control	O	A	A	A	O	O	O	E	O	O	O	w	w	w
Emergency procedures	O	A	A	A	W	W	W	W	W	W	W	E	E	E
Passenger:														
Ticketing	O	a	W	a	O	O	W	E	E	W	O	O	E	W
Tariffs	O	O	W	O	O	O	W	E	E	W	O	O	E	W
Passenger Handling	O	a	W	a	O	O	W	W	W	E	W	O	W	E
Baggage handling	O	a	W	a	O	O	W	W	W	E	W	O	W	E
Services extra to carriage	O	O	W	O	O	O	E	E	E	E	O	A	E	E
Reservations	O	O	W	O	O	O	A	E	W	W	O	O	E	W
Cargo:														
Airway bills	O	W	a	O	E	E	W	A	O	O	O	E	O	O
Rates	O	W	O	O	E	E	W	A	O	O	O	E	O	O
Cargo handling	O	W	a	a	E	E	W	W	O	A	w	E	O	W
Services extra to carriage	O	W	a	a	E	E	E	E	A	A	O	E	W	A
Securing space	O	W	O	O	E	E	A	E	O	O	O	E	O	O

The pattern of working life is increasingly coming to be seen as the continuous inter-action of experience and education. Underlying this is the notion of education as a permanent process, demanding the ability to draw on the lessons of experience and a readiness to renew knowledge and understanding.

Basic education will never be enough. There will always be the need for short, intensive courses, both of a specialist and general nature, to introduce men to new developments and to prepare them for higher responsibilities. Such courses though can be only a partial substitute for the intellectual foundations which a sound basic education should provide.

The stimulus to self-development is crucial. The individual must be encouraged to play an active part in his own growth and maturity. Courses must be carefully designed and timed if they are not to induce a passive attitude in the minds of the participants, if they are to avoid being haphazard, intermittent and ill-related to the interests of participants. Only then will value be obtained from opportunities provided at appropriate points during a man's career to enable him to rethink his past experience, to come abreast of new thought, to gain insight into wider problems and issues.

Such a conception has profound implications. It entails a reconsideration of the traditional view that the education received through childhood and adolescence is an adequate preparation for the rest of life.

The organisation of firms will have to be suitably adapted. A view is emerging that the employing organisation has an educational function during adulthood corresponding to the role of the school and the university in early life. Practitioners everywhere will require to recognise their role as educators. The educational function will become more broadly defined with the responsibility for education more generalised.

A few airlines have established Staff Colleges in which some of the soundest work in the field of management education has taken place, because they did not have to flounder in the intellectual disarray of general business management. It is important to decide at what points to end general studies of management and to begin studies of general transport, and to go on finally to airline management.

The Fisher Report made the following important points, concerning the teaching of management:

(i) It is vitally important to establish for students a conceptual framework for the whole management process. (This the author attempted to do in a previous volume.[1])

(ii) Promising new research techniques should be used to find

[1] *Fundamentals of Management.*

generalisations about the management process and managerial behaviour, but the use of these techniques pre-supposes a well grounded basic education which alone can show up the operational limits.

(iii) Different programmes must be adapted to the different levels of responsibility which mark out the career of a manager.

(iv) Active pedagogical methods are of predominant importance in all teaching.

This last point is elaborated in the next section dealing with simulation in management training.

Finally, the Report strongly recommends that all those who take part in 'in-company' management training and development should also have administrative responsibility and opportunity for consultancy or research work. And these men are well placed to conduct some of the research that is badly needed.

The use of simulation exercises in management training

Many airlines use business 'games' in their management training programmes. Trans-Canada Air Lines was among the first to use a 'simulation of an airline situation'.[1] The idea was developed further by British European Airways in 1963. The essential features of the similar organisations of three airlines were set up in a mathematical model, programmed for an Emidec 1100 computer. Each simulated airline had a fleet of ten jet and twenty turbo-prop aircraft; each aircraft was identified by registration letters, and had its own record of flying hours and maintenance. The fleets competed for first and tourist class passengers on six routes of varying lengths, with fare differentials and incentives for off-peak travel. The proportions of first to tourist class seats were changeable for each aircraft over a range of six configurations.

Each company aimed to obtain its capital at lowest cost and in general to pursue an optimum financial policy, to purchase equipment in such a way that both shortages and excessive storage charges were avoided, and to pursue a personnel policy that produced neither high turnover rates nor 'featherbedding'. Crews had to be provided, and each aircraft maintained strictly in accordance with a cycle of 'checks', while allowance had to be made for some unscheduled maintenance, arising from component failures. Adequate resources had to be devoted to passenger services, marketing and development.

Each simulated airline was managed by a group of about eight, who fed decisions for a quarter's operations into the computor twice daily. This gave them practice in the managerial process of planning,

[1] *Management Games*, Kibbee, Craft and Nanus, Rheinhold, 1961, p. 274.

motivating, controlling, and contracting, and involved them in the difficulties of assessing the significance of variables at work in the airline business. They were brought close to the problems of co-ordinating specialist managers. Above all, the exercise provided illustrative material for use in discussion, and a basis for examining assumptions critically.

CHAPTER XVIII

THE MANAGEMENT OF RESEARCH AND DEVELOPMENT

The fundamental role of research and development in airlines

Airlines are similar to other sorts of business in being constantly subject to change. In fact, the rate of change in the first few decades of the industry was exceptional. This was due to developments in aircraft design and construction, the results of which extended to all parts of the industry. Developments in aircraft came about partly through the ambitions and efforts of designers and constructors, partly through the competitive spirit and vision of airline operators, and partly through the readiness of customers to switch demand to the latest and the newest.

There are two main sorts of innovation that occur in airlines. The first consists of changes to improve the quality of the product. The second consists of changes to improve the processes of the business so that they become cheaper without affecting the quality of the product. The first sort of improvement is to increase revenue: the second sort is to reduce costs. Research and development can be directed to achieve either one, or both, of these. It aims to improve the profitability of an airline by constant innovation.

Research is the searching for the truth about persons, things, situations and processes. A piece of research is directed to *the discovery* of facts. The techniques of enquiry in industrial research are somewhat different from those employed in scientific or literary research, but are nonetheless effective. Once research has established the facts it often points the way to developments that are practicable. Thus research and development go hand in hand.

The meanings attached to the terms 'research' and 'development' in aviation

1. Fundamental research is carried out at universities to establish the scientific laws governing the conduct and interaction of the atmosphere and aircraft. It takes place in a variety of disciplines such as aerodynamics, fluid mechanics, metallurgy and so on.

2. Industrial research is carried out by manufacturers to establish the characteristic behaviour of equipment (particularly aircraft) over a range of conditions of speed, loading, atmosphere, etc.
3. Operational research is carried out by airlines to establish the optimum use of equipment under operational conditions.
4. Pre-delivery development is carried out by the suppliers of equipment from experience gained in the use, testing and adjustment of prototype and production models.
5. Pre-operational development is usually carried out by airlines from experience gained in the use, testing and adjustment of production equipment working under near operational conditions.
6. Operational development is carried out by airlines from experience gained in the use, testing and adjustment of equipment working under full operational conditions.
7. Commercial research is usually carried out by airlines or their agencies to discover the strength of demand, and the factors giving rise to that demand.

Distribution of R & D activities in airlines

The need for research and development is not confined to aircraft. Airport design and operation, air traffic control, scheduling of aircraft, rostering of operatives, spares holdings, office systems, marketing and organisation could be improved by research into their problems. In the infancy of the industry most of the funds available were devoted to aircraft whose performance lay right at the heart of successful airline operation. The fifteen years, from 1945 to 1960, saw an increase in average cruising speed from about 150 m.p.h. to about 600 m.p.h., but during the same period there were no serious prospects of aircraft being able to operate economically except close to the limits of their performance.

This tendency to concentrate R & D resources on aircraft is more marked in airlines that buy 'new' aircraft. Recently designed and relatively untried aircraft are bound to have teething troubles so that any airline taking on such an aircraft is obliged to incur development costs. These are offset by the commercial advantages that are derived from superior equipment.

Certain development costs must be incurred whether a new type of aircraft (from the point of view of an airline) is relatively tried or untried. These may be described as introduction or preparatory costs. The pre-operational development costs referred to above are for untried aircraft.

Introduction costs include:

(*a*) Keeping watching brief on manufacturers during periods of design modification and construction.

(*b*) Setting up maintenance organisation ahead of the delivery of aircraft (which may be delayed).
(*c*) Setting up a flying organisation ahead of the delivery of aircraft.
(*d*) Maintenance and flying organisations during the training period following the delivery of the aircraft, and before operations begin.

Many airlines include market research among their research activities. This is not, of course, the sort of research carried out by the physical scientist, but employs the techniques of the social scientist.

The decentralisation of R & D activities

One of the difficult decisions that general management has to make concerning the organisation of research and development is in determining the extent to which it should be *decentralised.* The problem is best put this way, if there are gains to be had from specialisation and if this is assisted by centralisation. General management might accept that there is a prima facie case for centralisation to ensure that the arguments for decentralisation are weighty enough.

Decentralisation does not preclude managerial specialisation. Many airlines employ a number of R & D managers. For example, it is not uncommon to find a data processing manager, a commercial research manager, a flight research manager, a traffic-handling procedures development manager, a personnel development manager, and an organisation and methods manager. The dangers in having so many R & D organisations in an airline are that there will be duplication of effort and that the requirement for a number of specialists may be met by diluting the skill deployed. Long training and special ability are indispensable in producing a man capable of employing the techniques of first-class research and development workers. Most countries are short of men with such qualifications and airlines are not usually in a special position to attract them.

Against the arguments for having expertise in R & D in airline management we must consider those for having industrial expertise. Is it more important to have, say, a commercial research manager who knows the airline business inside-out, than to have a man academically sound in his methods but unfamiliar with the milieu in which he exercises them? The question poses a real difficulty. Of course, the research worker must have a thorough knowledge of his subject. If he is given sufficient time he is usually able to acquire it; and this is the crux of the matter. Management sometimes cannot afford to wait until a professional research worker learns to fly, or to be an accountant, before he solves certain problems.

That each department of an airline usually has some sort of

research and development organisation is, therefore, not surprising. What is surprising is to find that, say, data processing and commercial research are carried out by separate organisations in the same department.

Governments and R & D

Many governments assist research and development for both military and civil purposes. While their main interests are usually on the military side, many of them are also interested in promoting civil aircraft construction to support military production and for export. Even if civil needs are regarded as secondary they may still benefit from the military. So one way or another aircraft constructors usually obtain government help with R & D ahead of airline orders. Sometimes if airline orders do not appear to be forthcoming a government will withdraw its support from a project. In other cases there may be a complete change of policy. In Britain up to the late 1950s, the government met the costs of basic research for the design of civil aircraft, and then changed its policy of one of placing the onus for this expenditure on the aircraft constructors. The governments in some other countries oblige constructors to include an R & D levy in the price they charge customers, and the governments are reimbursed from sums so recovered.

Precepts for airworthiness governing aircraft development

Jerry Lederer's Flight Safety Foundation, in one of their publications gives seven precepts for airworthiness that airline managements pay regard to, in their development work. These are:

(i) Parts or components of the aircraft other than the basic structure should be designed to fail with safety.
(ii) The structure and its components should be designed to encounter, with safety, the impact of objects, the rough handling by men and the effects of natural phenomena which are likely to be met with in service.
(iii) The procedures for adequate maintenance and operating practices established by the designer should be consistent with average human effort, ability and attitude.
(iv) The aircraft and its components must be protected against the effects of normally inadvertent or uncontrollable human errors or carelessness.
(v) The structure and its components shall be compatible—one part with the others—from the standpoint of durability, deflections, wear, and the danger of one creating a hazard by proximity to other parts.

(vi) The structure and its components, especially moving parts, should be protected against the effects of environment likely to be encountered in service such as vibration, dust, great pressure differentials, oil mists and temperature extremes.

(vii) Through no fault of the designer, all of these may fail to prevent an accident, therefore, the seventh and final precept is that the aircraft should be designed to give occupants reasonable assurance of protection in accidents which are considered to be survivable.

Engineering R & D in airline organisation

Many airlines have a component of organisation engaged in research into and development of airframes, engines and instruments. The activities of such departments vary from airline to airline, and the range of tasks is likely to be greater if an airline introduces 'untried' aircraft into service. The sort of work done in a large engineering R & D department is as follows:

(*a*) Preparing and examining *speculative* proposals for future airframes, engines, and instruments;
(*b*) Preparing *outline* requirements for new aircraft;
(*c*) Preparing operator's *specification of requirements* for new aircraft;
(*d*) Examining *outline and detailed proposals* made by aircraft constructors;
(*e*) Keeping informed on the research undertaken in universities and other institutions for research, including the research departments of aircraft constructors;
(*f*) Studying the pre-delivery development undertaken by aircraft constructors;
(*g*) Undertaking certain pre-operational development of new aircraft;
(*h*) Undertaking certain operational development of all aircraft in the fleet: involving numerous studies to establish the optimum use of airframes, engines and instruments under operational conditions.

In general engineering R & D departments aim to reduce costs of operation by improving the performance of all aircraft equipment, and by reducing maintenance costs. They also aim to increase the earning ability of aircraft by improving their 'product'. Thus they aim to improve speed, safety, comfort and so on.

Improving aircraft movement control

Flight research and development organisations aim to improve the equipment and services available on the ground to assist the safe, punctual and regular movement of aircraft. They also aim to improve the equipment carried on the aircraft and linked with that on the ground. In pursuing these aims they must not make the operation of aircraft uneconomic, by adding too much to the weight of equipment they have to carry.

These airline departments are not often directly responsible for the supply of ground equipment and services. This is usually the responsibility of State authorities. So results in this area must be achieved largely through submitting 'requirements' to governments, either directly or through IATA and ICAO. Work on aircraft equipment takes the form of 'requirements' to aircraft and engine manufacturers, and to the manufacturers of auxiliary equipment.

The constant improvements in air traffic control, navigational aids, crash equipment and apron parking methods are due partly to the efforts of government agencies and partly to the efforts of the airlines. The constant improvements in control cabin layout, and the aircraft end of navigation and communications systems are due partly to the efforts of manufacturers and partly to the efforts of airlines. The strategic decision facing airline management is that of determining the extent of resources that it needs to devote to keeping governments and manufacturers on their toes.

Improving passenger and freight control

There are three main ways in which passenger and freight control can be improved. They are:

(*a*) In the procedures for handling passengers, mail and freight; and
(*b*) In the equipment that is used in the handling procedures; and
(*c*) In the buildings and areas involved in traffic handling.

Improvements may either reduce costs by introducing more efficient methods, or increase revenue by introducing methods that increase the convenience and comfort of passengers.

Often an individual airline requires co-operation to bring about improvements. For example, valuable developments have come from the work of IATA Committees to establish common handling procedures. Before standardisation European carriers had to deal with ten different loadsheets in handling each other's flights. Other advantages have come from what airlines call 'facilitation'. This means the progressive easing of bureaucratic controls on the movement of traffic. The main bogies have been customs and immigration authorities, but some countries have now set an example that must one day be followed even by the most reactionary authorities.

Developments in the equipment used for traffic handling procedures include improvements in check-in desks, conveyor systems for baggage, loading trucks, aircraft access points, ground transport, etc. In this field airlines have freedom to make their own developments. However, this does not mean that equipment becomes markedly different from airline to airline. Any airline that gains a lead with a piece of new traffic handling equipment will soon find it copied. It is difficult to keep ideas secret in an international industry.

The development of airport buildings and apron areas concerns airport authorities. But few airlines are willing to leave the initiative for such development with the 'supplier'. This is a reasonable attitude because the airline, as the *user* of airport facilities, is in the best position to know where improvements need to be made. Developments in airport buildings have included such measures as the introduction of the 'finger-and-gate' system of access to aircraft, two-level layouts for incoming and outgoing traffic and mechanised baggage handling.

The need for research and development in the traffic handling field is no less important than in aircraft performance. The build-up of traffic at the major airports of the world can be accommodated only by improving the procedures, equipment and buildings on limited sites.

Improving maintenance control

Research into and development of maintenance procedures may produce substantial economies. That there is room for improvement in individual airlines is indicated by the fact that the expenditure on maintenance expressed as a percentage of traffic has varied as much as 5 per cent from one airline to another. A low-cost airline will spend about 18 per cent of its traffic revenue against about 23 per cent by a high-cost airline. As a percentage of total annual operating costs, maintenance of equipment may vary from about 13 per cent to 27 per cent.

Maintenance strategies have been changed greatly during the short history of the industry. These changes have not been at the same pace among all airlines, nor even consistently gone in the same direction; nevertheless, certain broad trends are discernible. In the early days there was a tendency to give maintenance the priority implicit in the idea that maintenance departments 'sold' whatever hours they could to the airline, to use as best it could. The maintenance function was organised for the convenience of maintenance. Flying hours were a residue after maintenance had been well-planned to suit an 'efficiently' run maintenance base.

Later strategy swung over to the idea that maintenance should be done in the hours left over after aircraft had flown the best commercial hours. Thus maintenance became the residual activity, and commercial needs took priority. At first there was resistance to the change, on the grounds that an absolute rise in maintenance costs consequent upon maintenance procedures having to be geared to the fluctuating nature of demand was a dis-economy. Subsequently people realised that it is not the absolute cost of maintenance that is important, but the relative cost. So if the concentration of maintenance in off-peak hours gives rise to increased costs because of poor production-flow, but at the same time gives rise to increased revenue because more capacity is available at the right time, the *relative position* may be better.

The idea that maintenance should not set the pace for all other operations brought about some interesting developments. Instead of arranging the various 'checks' on the basis of maintaining the greatest possible number of time-expired components at each check (to give the longest working life for each component), some airlines began to equalise the work involved in each check. In this way individual aircraft are more regularly available for service, and scheduling is made easier. Secondly, some airlines developed the practice of doing maintenance more expensively at night in order to leave aircraft free to earn more revenue in the daylight hours. These are only two illustrations of developments.

Some airlines are developing in ways that reduce their dependence on contractors. They are equipping themselves to do repairs and overhauls that would otherwise have to be sent back to the manufacturer. New test equipment, such as X-ray apparatus, and engine test beds, is reducing the number of unnecessary operations in stripping down and sending components away from base. Operational research with linear programming and queuing theory, and the use of critical path techniques, has begun to rationalise the programming of modifications and unscheduled maintenance. All in all the field of maintenance continues to be rewarding for the efforts put into R & D.

Market research

Airline market research is conducted not only for the purpose of discovering the facts about a current situation so that it can be exploited fully as it stands, but also to discover opportunities for development. An important part of the market research function is, of course, to feed data in a routine manner into those components of organisations engaged on planning and those engaged on the managerial control processes. An equally important function is, however, to provide ideas for innovation and to promote development. Furthermore, research must attempt to determine the results of innovation to see whether it has changed a situation for better or for worse.

Fundamentally the importance of market research to airlines lies in the fact that it is an activity designed to discover the truth about the *behaviour of the raw materials* of the industry. This sort of discovery has been important in manufacturing industries and theoretically would appear to be no less important in service industries. Secondly, airline market research sets out to discover the truth about the behaviour of competitors.

Research and Development in the personnel field

There are many aspects of the recruitment and employment of personnel that call for the sort of research carried out by social scientists. Valuable work has already been done by occupational psychologists in the field of selection and training, and the mental climate of the working environment. Airlines have not been slow to take advantage of the results of this research. Many of them use advanced techniques in the selection of their staff, particularly flying staff. Training has benefited from the work of educational psychologists, and airlines were among the first industrial organisations to make use of programmed instruction.

Work has been done on the human factors contributing to safety in the air. Attempts have been made to measure the work-load in the cockpit. Studies have been completed on the fluctuations in the work of telephone sales clerks, the relationship between stewards' initial training course examination results and their subsequent performance on the line, and the effectiveness of an airline apprenticeship scheme. To conduct their personnel research, some airlines employ small research units composed mainly of social scientists; others rely on the work of universities, consultants and other research agencies.

Development in the personnel field takes various forms. It may be an improvement in the working environment, or procedures may be altered to make a task easier or more interesting. A wages structure may be altered to provide more incentive to good workers. Promotion prospects may be opened up. Careers may be planned; more opportunities given for training and generally more scope provided for employees to lead satisfying lives. The men and women in an airline deserve just as much attention from the 'innovator' as do aircraft and airports.

Data processing

The revolution in data processing brought about by the arrival of the modern digital computer has had as profound an effect on the airline industry as on any other. The original intention was to use computers to explore the characteristics of mathematical systems that could not be explored by existing analytical techniques. In aerodynamics and meteorology, to name but two branches of science closely affecting air transport, the systems of differential equations were penetrated by computers to depths hitherto unknown. At the same time even more massive mathematical problems were being thrown up for treatment by computers, in the field of linear programming and the construction of dynamic models to aid management decisions.

If a 'model' or copy of a situation is programmed for a computer the reactions of its elements can be studied by making the computer imitate the behaviour of the dynamic elements. This sort of computer simulation has been used by airlines to study the economics of standby aircraft. Models have also been used to study, during management training courses, the major variables in the airline management task. Among further possibles uses are studies in airport and airway congestion, stock control and purchasing policies.

Of course, not all data processing is for research and development. Airlines are able to make as much use of the everyday applications of computers to business. Many airlines have automated a great amount of routine calculation associated with the collection of revenue and the payment of wages. But large-scale data-processing contributes something to development by releasing energies that would otherwise be devoted to routine tasks, and enabling them to be turned to prospects of improvement.

Development of clerical systems

It is a common fallacy that airline organisations are numerically dominated by flying staff and engineers. In fact, many airlines employ more 'clerical' staff than either flying staff or engineers. For example, one airline employing a total of 17,000 employees has 4,500 clerical staff, 3,000 engineers and 2,000 flying staff (pilots and cabin crew). Clerical staff are usually closely associated with the managerial 'control' process and are found in large numbers in financial control, traffic control, maintenance control, etc. Most clerical activities may be classified as either communicating or recording. Plans, policies, practices, decisions, instructions and information are communicated and recorded by means of letters, memos, telephone calls, teleprinter tape, invoices, financial summaries and so on.

All airlines are likely to find room for improvement in their clerical systems. The improvements may not always result in savings in clerical staff, equipment or materials; they may indirectly affect the efficiency of aircraft movement or traffic handling or maintenance. Often the effectiveness of a physical operation is influenced by the associated clerical procedures.

Special techniques have been devised to examine and discover the reality that lies behind clerical methods and procedures. For example, the technique of flow charting can show a clear picture of the movement of pieces of paper and reveal weakness in a system. The research conducted on clerical systems aims to discover and eliminate duplication, unnecessary raising and movement of paperwork, and unnecessary copying. It also aims to discover and eliminate procedures that have become an end in themselves, bearing little or no relation to the objective of an airline. Improvements may range from small changes to complete reconstructions of systems. Sometimes it is a matter of redesigning forms; sometimes it is a matter of installing a computer. The effectiveness of clerical activity is, of course, affected by the layout, temperature, humidity of buildings, and particularly offices. Research sometimes reveals the need to reconstruct the physical environment in which this sort of work is done.

Airlines are apt to under-estimate the importance of clerical systems. This is because of the impressive nature of their flying and engineering problems. Offices seem remote from the atmosphere of hangars and workshops, cockpit and cabin. And the people in them tend to get relegated to a sort of second league that is not expected to play the same standard of game. This attitude is dangerous. Innovation is as vital to the office as it is to any other part of an airline.

Work study

'Work study' is the name given to the search for better ways of doing things in industry. Of course, the search is as old as industry itself, but the techniques for conducting it are comparatively new. Work study is primarily concerned with the way that *people* do jobs, rather than the way that *equipment* functions, although at times the two cannot be considered apart. It has refined techniques for analysing *movement* and the measurement of work by the *timing* of jobs and parts of jobs.

These two techniques labelled 'motion-study' and 'time-study' have at times been used in a dangerously self-contained manner. The examination and timing of bodily movements is basic in work study, but the findings must then be related to the context of industrial and social environment in which the movements are performed. For example, it is no good 'rationalising' the movements of a counter-sales clerk if by doing so we strip him of the element of grace and charm that is pleasing to the customer. Work study must be sufficiently broad in scope to include all the important factors bearing on a work situation.

The air transport industry cannot afford to neglect the contribution that work study can make to its economy. Labour costs form a high proportion of airline direct or running costs, and human productivity is thus important. All useless, inept and fruitless effort must be eliminated. This calls for careful study of situations. The best way of doing passenger check-in, or aircraft loading, or whatever it is, must be established. Then procedures must be standardised on the basis of the established best method. And training must be similarly based.

New thinking in management

Research and development is being applied to the processes of management. An excellent summary of the advances in thinking is supplied in Appendix I of the Report of the Organisation for Economic Co-operation and Development on 'Issues in Management Education' 1963 (pages 84–88) quoted, *in extenso*, in Appendix I of this book.

Part III

The Individual Manager

CHAPTER XIX

THE INDIVIDUAL MANAGER

Managerial Specialisation

The management of most airlines have readily appreciated the benefits to be gained from managerial specialisation. The degree to which many of them have gone is well illustrated by the organisation directory of American Airlines set out in Appendix II. Here we see passenger sales management specialised into interline, military and government, travel agency, commercial, convention and group sales. Maintenance management is specialised into maintenance personnel, production and material control, general production, production engineering, inspection and flight test. The flying organisation is divided into operations, training, performance, administration, planning and manning, dispatch, crew scheduling and recruitment.

The organisational advantages of managerial specialisation are not achieved without some cost to the individual manager. Many managers in marketing find it irksome to have their careers confined to one department by the skills required for careers in flying, engineering, finance, personnel and so on. They find the position even more intolerable if pilots and engineers are allowed to invade their preserves along a one-way channel. Indeed it is the exclusive nature of flight and engineering management that characterises special management in every department. Few people are prepared to accept that their job can be done by anybody right away, whereas other jobs call for long training and special skill. These restrictive factors and attitudes, that make for career 'preserves', permeate into all corners of managerial structures. Thus the credit card accounting manager finds it said that he has not enough experience to become the passenger revenue accounting director, or the passenger refunds manager.

To be trapped in a narrow specialisation, without hope of escape: this can be terribly distressing. Every manager should be prepared to face temporary losses of expertise in his organisation, in order to improve the prospects of his subordinate managers. The short-term loss in efficiency is likely to do far less damage to his organisation than the long-term stultification of hope and interest.

Change and the individual manager

The airline business as a whole has been subject to frequent changes throughout its short history. Aircraft speeds have gone up in leaps and bounds. Engines have been radically redesigned. Improvements have been made in airport design: maintenance procedures are better; computers have been introduced to deal with reservations. These and numerous other developments constantly change the face of the industry. How do these rapid changes affect the individual manager?

It is not uncommon to find men who have managed over a half a dozen flights using progressively different types of aircraft, in the course of their managerial careers. It is not unusual to find men who have managed the maintenance of about a dozen different types of aircraft in their time. These men have had to change their technical ideas about every two years. They are steeped in change. In their working lives the prospect of change continually overlaps with current practice. They are not the men to lag behind it.

The men who are more likely to be overtaken by technical developments are those who might reasonably regard their skills as timeless. The skills of the accountant, of the personnel manager, of the lawyer, of the doctor, of the architect are not radically affected by technological change. For this reason we may find that some individuals fail to make even the marginal adjustments that almost certainly will be required of them. Thus an industrial relations officer may continue to conduct his negotiations at a tempo appropriate to the piston-engine era long after jet engines have been introduced. An architect may continue to design buildings to last fifty years long after it is apparent that they will be useless in ten.

The individual manager who must consciously foster thought of change is the man who on the surface appears to be least affected by it. Otherwise, while he remains in his quiet backwater, the fierce current of progress will sweep by him, and he will understand less and less of what he sees beyond his own small stretch. There are airline accountants who know nothing of the problems of flying modern aircraft. They were good men in the days when there was little they could not tell you about the small fleet of propeller aircraft. But nostalgic memories are not sufficient to sustain the efficiency of an accountant, or an airline lawyer, or an airline insurance manager.

Pride in the system

Once an airline gets going it begins to take on a life of its own. The daily cycle of operations, the seasonal pressures and reliefs, and the annual ups-and-downs compel devotion regardless of ultimate aims. The immediate purpose of 'keeping things going' is satisfying enough. An airline is a voracious animal, devouring the efforts of its servants; and willing servants at that. What is there about transport that stirs up inordinate feelings of pride in its prime, and in its last throes a desperate sentimentality? Why are vehicles regarded with respect and even reverence, and afforded the care and attention we normally reserve for living creatures?

It may be because man sees his transport vehicle as an extension of his very self. It may be because of the dramatic quality of an instrument of safe carriage. Men commit their lives to vehicles. Whatever the reason, pride in the system is a force to be reckoned with in any transport business.

It has its good side. This pride sustains the individual manager through wearisome hours, moments of anxiety and through those discouraging spells that seem to be a feature of most transport undertakings. Pride in the system encourages him to place the demands of the service above his own personal convenience. Above all, this pride has helped in establishing the splendid traditions that are woven into the history of the industry.

The danger is that this pride will blind the individual to the need for change. It is hard to believe that a sweetly running aircraft that has served an airline faithfully for a number of years has to go to the scrap-heap. Or that a route that has been sustained by the unstinting labours of station staff, and an overworked sales force should be abandoned. Even to alter an airline system fractionally provokes some individuals to accusations of wholesale dismemberment.

The 'safety-angle'

The dramatic nature of an airline crash tends to cast an unhealthy spell over the minds of airline officials. Of course, air transport is inherently dangerous, and that fact must never be forgotten. Of course, airlines are obliged to put safety first. But airlines are not the only form of business which have obligations that conflict with economy. Good manufacturers are constantly taking expensive precautions to avoid poisoning their customers. The manufacturer of electrical apparatus must always spend money to ensure that he does not electrocute his customers. Even the toymaker must make an effort to prevent the seemingly harmless from becoming lethal.

It is true that the precautions that airlines have to take to ensure safety are usually more elaborate than those taken by the manufacturer. Thus there are more opportunities for error: thus there is need for more extensive vigilance. On the other hand, the airline product is produced and consumed in a well-controlled environment. The customer is surrounded by professionals.

This is worth saying, because having emphasised safety airline managers must then put it in perspective. Thinking about safety does not preclude them from thinking about profitability. Safety and profitability are just as compatible objectives in airlines as they are in any other business. By all means have safety first, but make sure that profitability is second.

The individual manager must not allow the 'safety angle' to become an automatic let-out from the hard thinking that is usually necessary in reconciling the conflicting claims of safety and economy.

Professionalism

Airline organisations are usually sufficiently big, and the work they have to do sufficiently complex, to need the services of professional men. The American Airlines' directory (see Appendix II) shows the employment of professional accountants, economists, organisation and methods officers, operations research workers, insurance officers, lawyers, property experts, engineers, teachers, personnel officers, medical officers, etc. Most of these men have the standards of their craft set outside the airline organisation. The accountant will probably have qualified by passing the examinations of an accountants' association. The lawyer is probably subject to a legal council and the medical officer to a medical council. The engineer is probably a member of his Institute, the economist of a learned society and so on.

Individually they will have two standards to work to; one established by their professional training, and the codes of whatever association they belong to; the second established by the business they have chosen to serve. This dual element in the working life of a manager can give rise to strain because professional standards are not always easy to square with business standards. The former tend to a perfection that leaves costs as a secondary consideration. Occasionally we may find the professional quite unwilling to compromise on what he regards as ethical, or scientific or academically sound, or whatever else is his canonical prescription. Business standards, however, are characteristically a matter of compromise.

Business is essentially a balancing of a number of efforts, at a level below the maximum of each, because of the scarcity of resources. This reconciliation of optima is achieved among the primary functions of finance, purchasing, production, marketing, personnel, research and development, by the authoritative relationships among general and special management. The advocacy of special managers is resolved into the best interests of the business by the judgement of general managers. There is no court of appeal beyond the general management of the business. General management and no other represent the best business interests of the undertaking.

If a professional man feels he cannot compromise his professional standards even within the authoritative framework of business, he ought to stay outside of business and provide his service on a contractual basis. If he agrees to go into a business organisation, he should be prepared to give that organisation his loyalty.'[1]

Conclusion

We have seen that there are a number of features of the air transport industry that tempt individual managers into unbusinesslike attitudes. Over-specialisation, resistance to change, excessive pride in the system, too much emphasis on the safety angle and professionalism, all have one thing in common: they are centred on the organisation. They are not directly concerned with the customer.

The most powerful corrective for the thinking of any manager, in any branch of the airline business, is to take time off from his particular preoccupation to consider the point of view of the customer. In the midst of the absorbing details of this complicated business, it is salutary to remember that the industry will always begin and end with the customer.

[1] *Managing a Transport Business*, W. S. Barry, George Allen & Unwin, 1963.

APPENDIX I

NEW THINKING IN MANAGEMENT

(from *Issues in Management Education*, a Report by the Organisation for Economic Co-operation and Development)

1. CYBERNETICS meaning 'steermanship' was chosen by Norbert Weiner in 1948 to cover all aspects of 'communication and control in the animal and the machine'. Cybernetics looks not so much at what a thing is, as at what it can do and what are the possible ways in which it might behave.

The essential concepts of feedback and servo-mechanism link the key ideas of self-regulation and of homeostasis, a term denoting to biologists a state of balance of an organism. A vocabulary and set of concepts have been developed to express in unified form diverse types of systems in terms of 'connectedness' and 'interaction'.

Cyberneticians classify systems as 'deterministic' or 'probabilistic'. Both can be of varying degrees of complexity. The difference can be illustrated by comparing the simple deterministic on-off control operation of a thermostat with say the variety of chance factors governing the flow of customers through a supermarket.

A company is an exceedingly complex 'probabilistic system'. It is not an organism in the physiological sense but it behaves like one in its communications, feedback and control mechanisms, interacting with its environment, growing or decaying organically in response to internal and external pressures.

2. DECISION THEORY seeks to develop the most rational procedures for choosing between alternative courses of action in situations of varying degrees of uncertainty. Inspection schemes based on sampling represent 'decision models' which incorporate within them the acceptable level of risk of error.

There are methods, mainly mathematical, which provide a means of choosing a course of action which keeps to the minimum the risk of maximum loss—the 'minimax' principle. Other approaches to decision theory employ logical analysis to move from problem to solution by methodically predetermined steps.

3. ECONOMETRICS. The problems in measuring and predicting the outcome of interactions between economic forces are difficult. The number of variables involved is large. Controlled experiment is usually impossible.

Econometrics uses mathematical and statistical analysis to bring out the interdependence and complexity of the many factors which determine prices, costs, etc., and to demonstrate the repercussions that a change in one factor can have on the others.

4. ERGONOMICS, studying man-machine systems as an entity, aims to fit the job to the individual in a way which ensures that the mental and physical demands of the job are within the capacities of normal people.

In the main it relies on contributions from physiologists, who study energy expenditure, muscular fatigue, relations between work and environmental conditions (temperature, humidity, air movement, noise) and from experimental psychologists concerned with such problems of perception and recognition as the difficulties of translating sense data into action.

5. GROUP DYNAMICS attempt to analyse the behaviour of individuals in groups.

Formal relations cannot alone satisfactorily regulate the varied interactions between people. Insight into social phenomena and processes and sensitivity to the emotional aspects of social relations are necessary if co-operation is to be secured.

Seminars designed to develop social skills allow participants to experiment under skilled guidance with social situations resembling those which occur in the working environment. There are other simpler methods (e.g. role playing, the incident method and the business game) which seek the same purpose.

6. HEURISTIC denotes an approach to problem-solving which utilises experience in a step-by-step procedure, where the next move towards the solution is systematically determined in the light of experience gained from earlier choices successful or otherwise.

It constitutes a process for progressively clarifying issues too complex or too indeterminate for a straightforward application of scientific method. Heuristics may show how rigorous scientific proof can be construed for issues which at first sight offer no such prospect. By analogy, it may be seen as serving the ends of rigorous scientific theory in a manner akin to that of scaffolding erected prior to the erection of a building.

7. INFORMATION THEORY. In coming to decisions and seeing that they are implemented, management depends on the selection, collection, transmission, processing, evaluation and presentation of information.

Information theory attempts to:

(*a*) Measure the amount of information carried by a given message or messages, a function of such factors as clarity and brevity of the matter transmitted, the percipience of the recipient, the speed of transmission;
(*b*) Assess methods of coding, i.e. the kind of language and vocabulary used;
(*c*) Define the value of a given message to the recipient;
(*d*) Compute capacities and relative efficiencies of communication channels and networks.

At first an engineering field, it now commands the attention of psychologists, sociologists, experts in linguistics, logicians, physiologists, neurologists, mathematicians and specialists in communication. Information theory may come to have an important influence on the character of management activities, as developments in data processing point to new patterns of thought and action.

8. INPUT/OUTPUT ANALYSIS. The mathematical economist Leontief is credited with the original attempt to analyse the economy of a country or an industry in terms of a system of inputs and outputs.

By way of analogy, a river system draining a watershed takes in spring and surface water and discharges into the open sea. The internal combustion engine takes in fuel and air, which it converts into power and output.

The description and analysis of an economy or an industry by the systematic tabulation of inputs and outputs can lead to models which are useful in clarifying inter-relationships and in improving the methods by which problems of an applied economic character are tackled.

9. MANAGEMENT SCIENCE. In the plural this term would embrace those scientific disciplines relevant to management as a field of study. In the singular it denotes the attempt to fuse such contributions into a new and distinctive science of its own.

A parallel has sometimes been drawn with medicine, in a sense a science in its own right, yet which relies on many other sciences, while art continues to play a decisive part in practice.

10. MODELS are simplified representations of the essential aspects or properties of an object or situation. Science differentiates between:

(*a*) ANALOGUE models which may be a simple graph representing the relation between two variables, though still powerful enough to predict changes between the two. A more complex analogue would be a computer programme representing relationships in an economic system.
(*b*) SYMBOLIC models where magnitudes and interrelationships are represented by symbols, often mathematical, which can then be manipulated for analytical and prediction purposes.

The process of abstraction necessary to design models, particularly of a symbolic kind, calls for considerable powers of imagination and insight. A model which attempts to represent reality in its precise detail would become so complicated that the scope for manipulating it purposefully would be seriously impaired. Some simplification is therefore inevitable. Parallels with reality must then be drawn cautiously.

11. OPERATIONAL (or OPERATIONS) RESEARCH brings to bear on complex business problems rigorous scientific thought, and especially the skills of quantitative analysis.

The approach is to formulate the problem in logical terms, construct a model, usually mathematical or symbolic, to represent the situation under study and produce solutions in terms of the model. Judgement on the applicability of the solution rests with the management, since criteria and scales of value are usually involved and these are matters of managerial policy. However, quantification even of the so-called 'management imponderables' is sometimes possible.

Techniques developed by Operational Research can provide answers to some quite complex problems. References to some of its methods are appearing increasingly in the literature of management.

(*a*) Linear programming refers to a group of mathematical methods which allow problems containing many interacting variables to be solved, for example the proportions in which resources available at different cost should be compounded to maximise profitability.

The 'transportation method' and the 'simplex technique' in particular, have been used in various forms to determine the optimum use of steel processing facilities, the most economic coal purchasing programmes, and many similar problems in a wide variety of industries.

(*b*) Queueing problems arise whenever demands exceed the rate at which the service required can be provided.

(i) Waiting line problems are concerned with the optimal number of service points or rate of arrival of demands, or both (e.g. the number of ships awaiting berths, or of people kept waiting when buying tickets, the arrival of customers in a retail store, the calls made on tool and material stores). The aim is to determine the amount of facilities which will minimise the total caused by 'waiting times';

(ii) Sequencing problems place the emphasis on the order or sequence in which demands are to be met. The facilities are fixed but the sequence of servicing is subjected to control by scheduling. A typical problem is the sequence of processing of orders through a machine shop.

The mathematics of queueing theory are more complex than those employed say in linear programming but may be simplified by use of the 'Monte Carlo' technique.

(*c*) 'Monte-Carlo' simulation. Strictly speaking any model simulates a real situation. The term has, however, taken on a more specific meaning for the somewhat unconventional 'Monte Carlo' type of models.

As an example, the problem of minimising stockholding costs without allowing the percentage of sales lost to rise as a result of being out of stock, is essentially a queueing problem but can be handled more simply by:

(i) Recording frequency of demand over a period;

(ii) Recording replenishment periods or 'lead times' for receiving stocks from suppliers;

(iii) Running the model on a computer for say 10,000 weeks for assumed inventory levels against typical patterns of weekly demands and periodic replenishments.

This will yield a curve showing lost sales at different inventory levels.

12. ORGANISATION THEORY examines the relations in which the parts, factors or people stand to one another and to the objective in working towards a common goal. In developing its conceptual models it uses such terms as:

Bureaucracy, to describe the formal allocation of authority and responsibility as well as the prescribed channels of communication and action.
Hierarchy, to express the level at which the individual or part is located relative to the whole.
Line and staff, to differentiate those who have the executive authority and do the primary work for which the organisation has been set up from those who advise them or provide them with a serivce.

A typical field for research is found in the conflict between the goals of the formal organisation (the bureaucracy and the way in which its parts interact) and those of the informal organisation which develops between people to express their individual goals.

13. SYSTEMS ANALYSIS. 'Systems' are complexes of elements which interact. The term 'system' therefore can cover a wide range of phenomena. Some are conceptual, others physical. There are philosophical systems, number systems, communication systems, educational systems, weapons systems, etc. Boulding, an economist, has developed a hierarchy which ranges from static through clockwork to social systems.

A biologist, Ludwig von Bertalanffy drew attention to the fact that problems of balance or growth in systems concern scientists in many different fields and advanced a case for a general systems theory.

The relationships between the inter-dependent parts of a system are its organisation. It is necessary to study not only isolated parts and processes, but the organic relations that result from dynamic interaction and make the behaviour of parts appear different, according to whether they are studied in isolation or as a whole. This thinking is reflected in 'Gestalt' psychology and in modern group concepts in the social sciences.

Some leading management researchers hold the view that the comparative study of systems in various fields may lead to a dynamic conceptual framework that will prove capable of accommodating the complex interactions inherent in the management process.

APPENDIX II

THE ORGANISATION STRUCTURE OF AMERICAN AIRLINES

American Airlines is regarded as the second biggest carrier of the USA. In 1962 it served over 50 points in the US, as well as Mexico City and Toronto, with a fleet of 176 aircraft, performed a total of 844,646,000 ton-miles, representing progress over 1958 of 37·4 per cent and an average annual increase in the last five years of 9·6 per cent. Financial results in 1962 showed a net profit of $7,098,000 or 1·5 per cent on revenues as against 2 per cent in 1961, 3 per cent in 1960, 5·6 per cent in 1959 and 5·1 per cent in 1958.[1] The detailed organisation of this large, successful airline is shown, by kind permission of the Company, in the following Figures 53 to 74. Level of titles shows only reporting relationships and has no significance with regard to the importance of positions.

[1] *Bulletin de l'Institut du Transport Aerien*, Paris. June 1963.

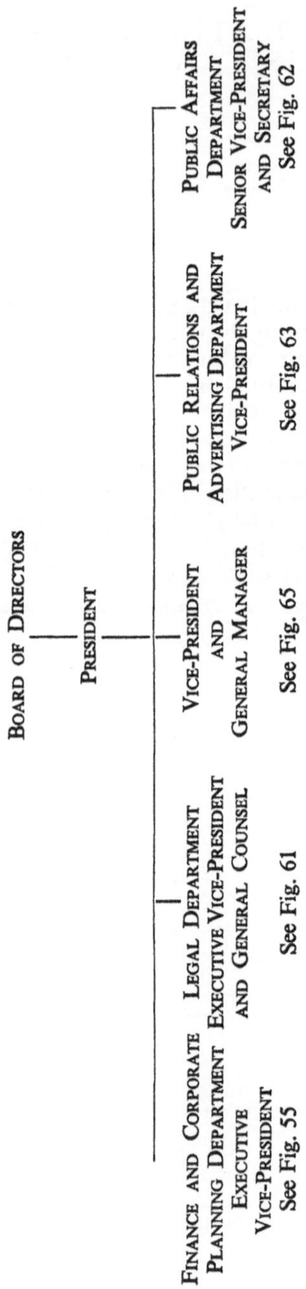

FIG. 54. *American Airlines Overall organisation*

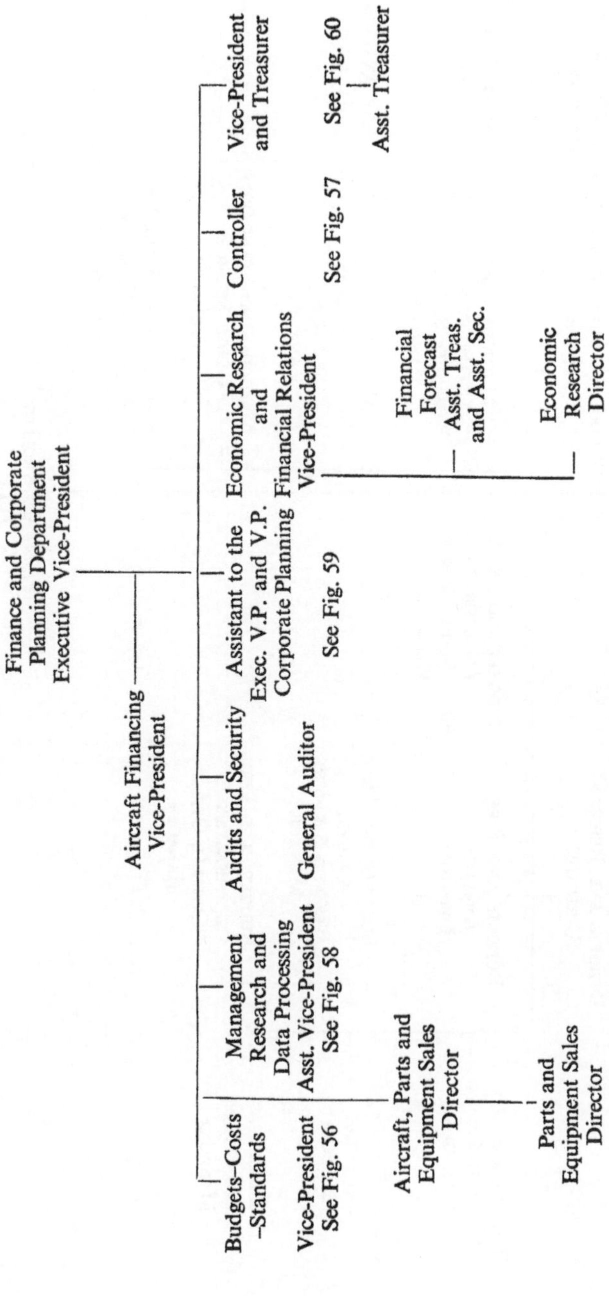

FIG. 55. *American Airlines Finance and Corporate Planning organisation*

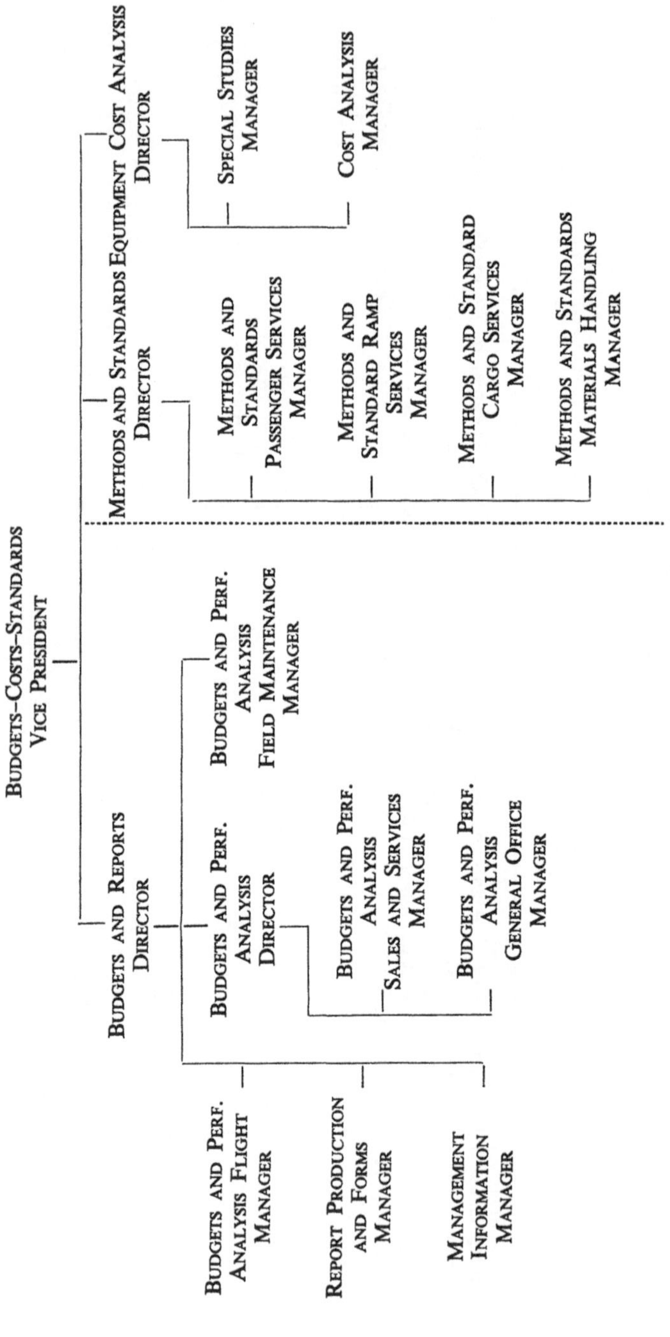

FIG. 56. *American Airlines Budgets–Costs–Standards organisation*

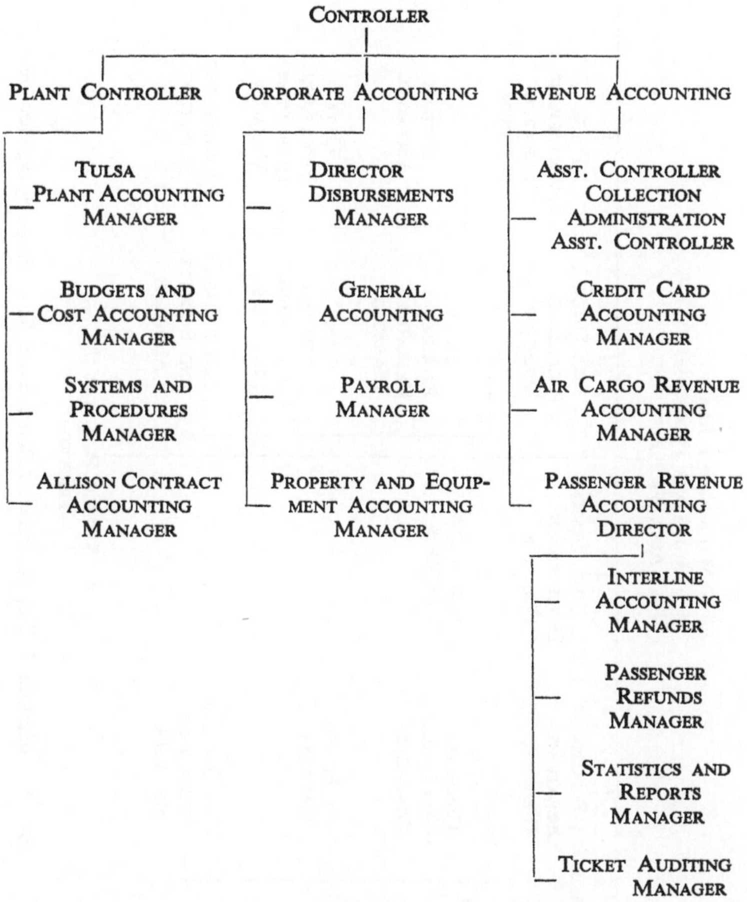

FIG. 57. *American Airlines Controller's organisation*

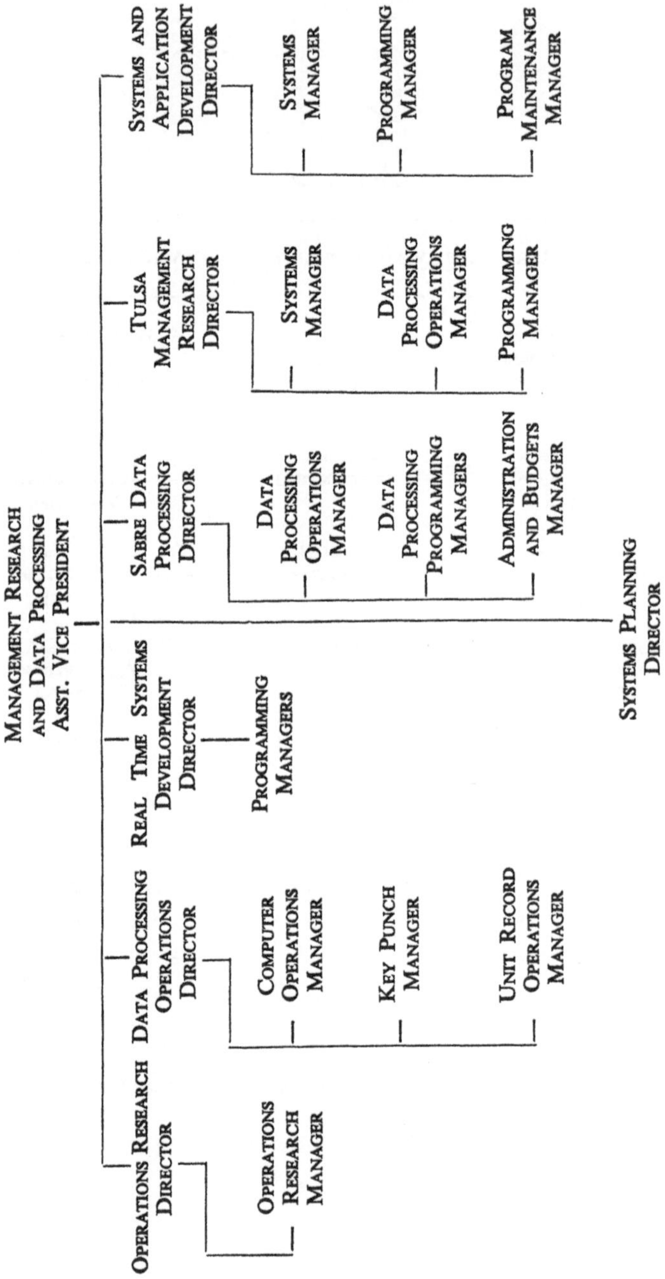

FIG. 58. *American Airlines Management Research and Data Processing organisation*

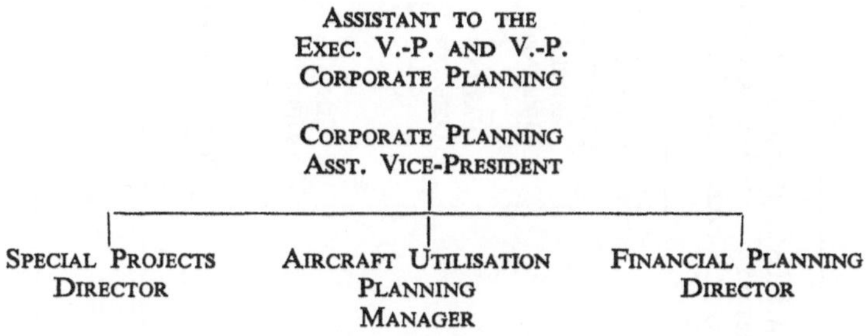

FIG. 59. *American Airlines Corporate Planning organisation*

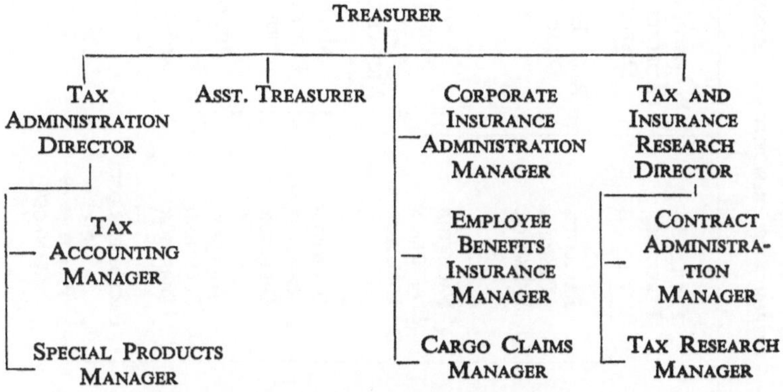

FIG. 60. *American Airlines Treasurer's organisation*

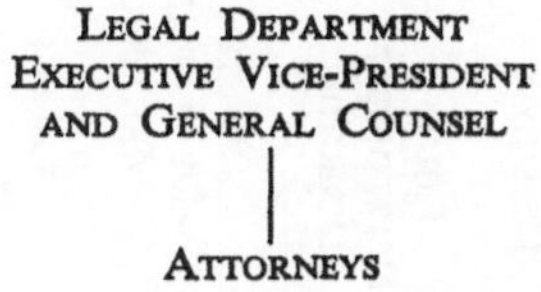

FIG. 61. *American Airlines Legal organisation*

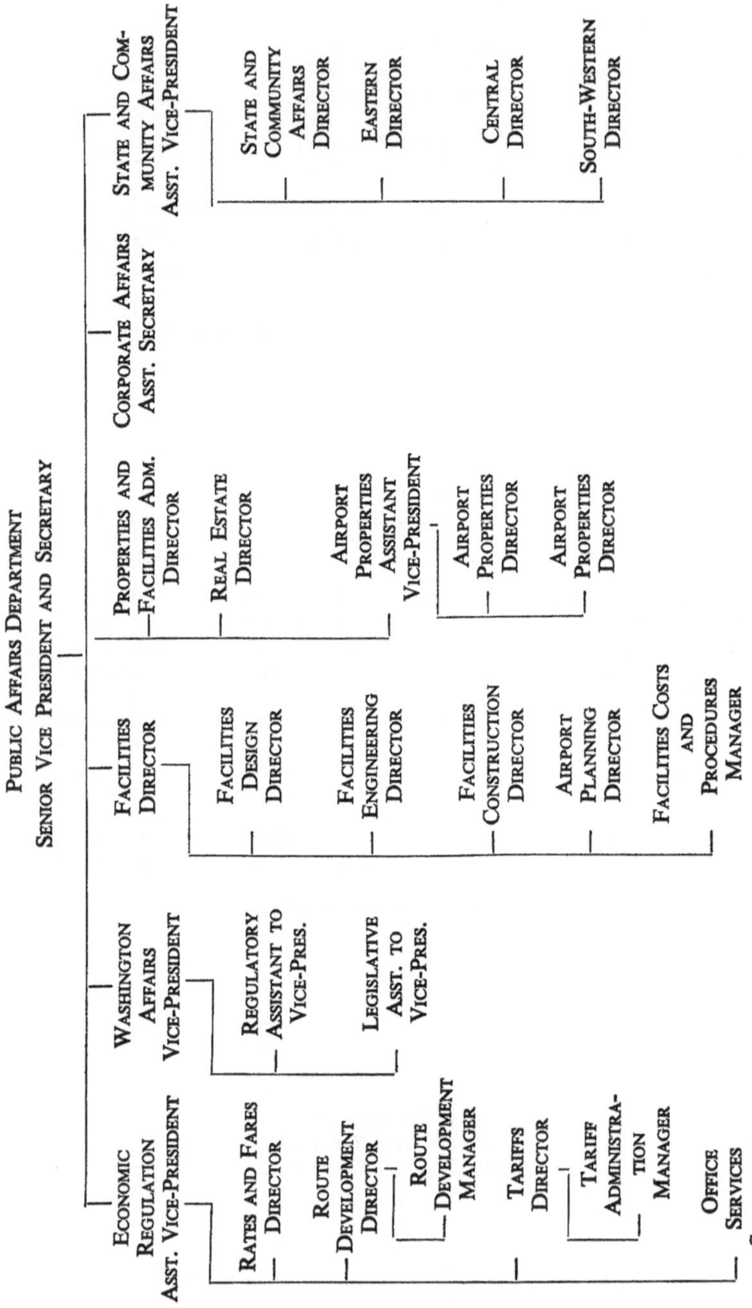

FIG. 62. *American Airlines Public Affairs organisation*

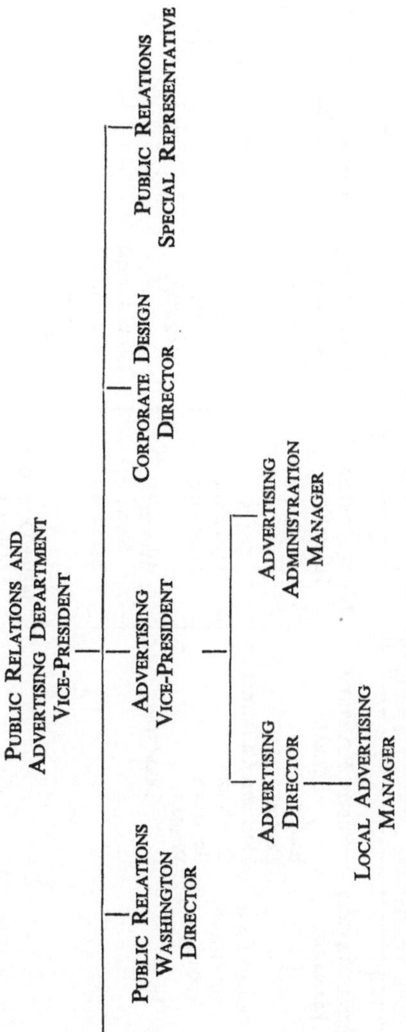

Fig. 63. *American Airlines Public Relations and Advertising organisation*

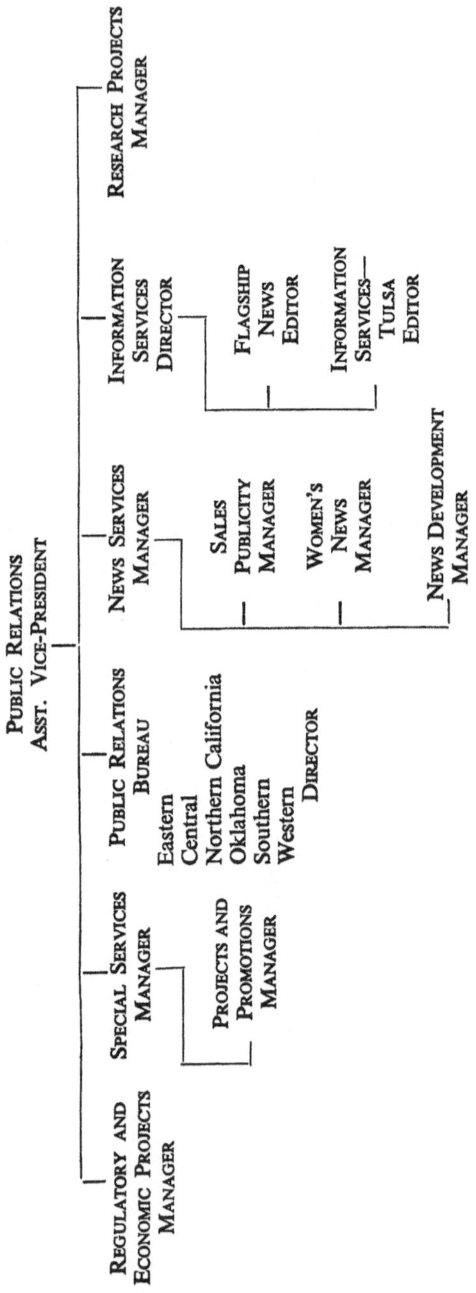

FIG. 64. *American Airlines Public Relations organisation*

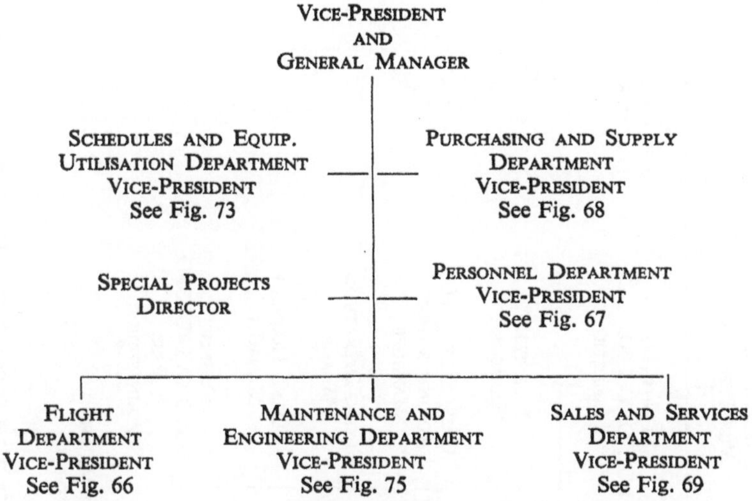

FIG. 65. *American Airlines Vice-President and General Manager's organisation*

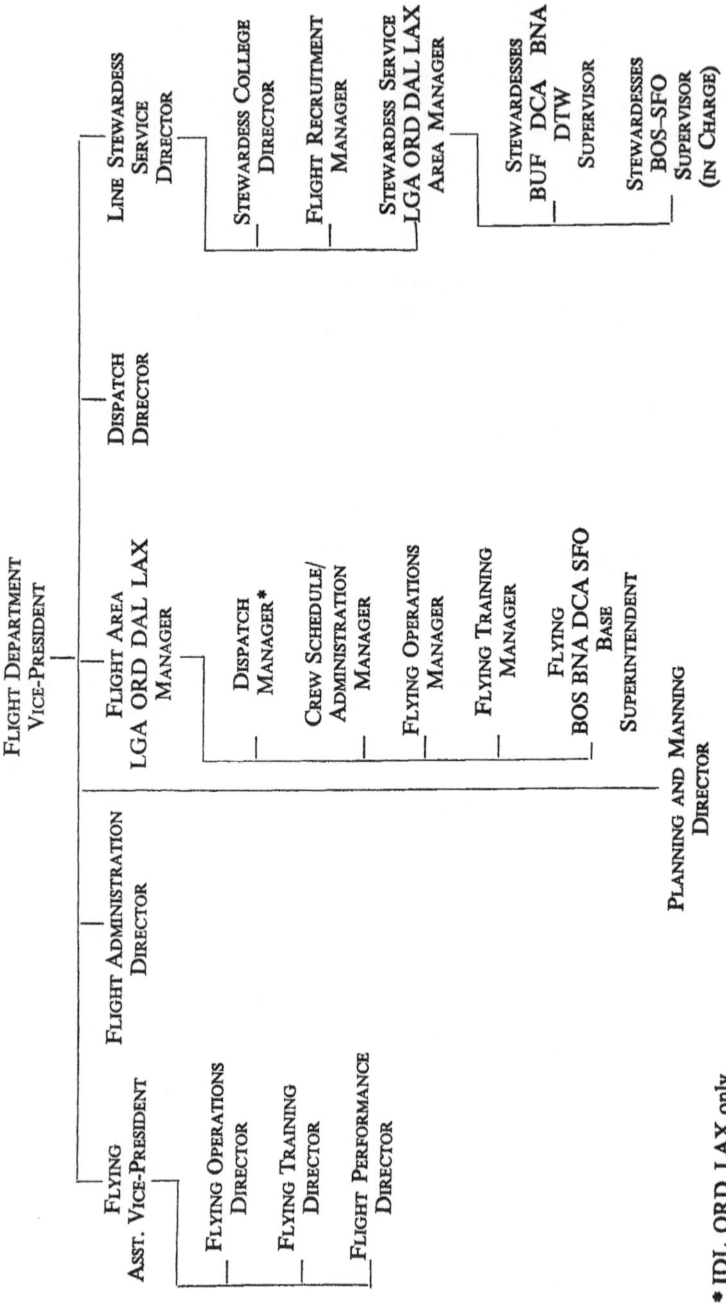

* IDL ORD LAX only.

Fig. 66. *American Airlines Flight organisation*

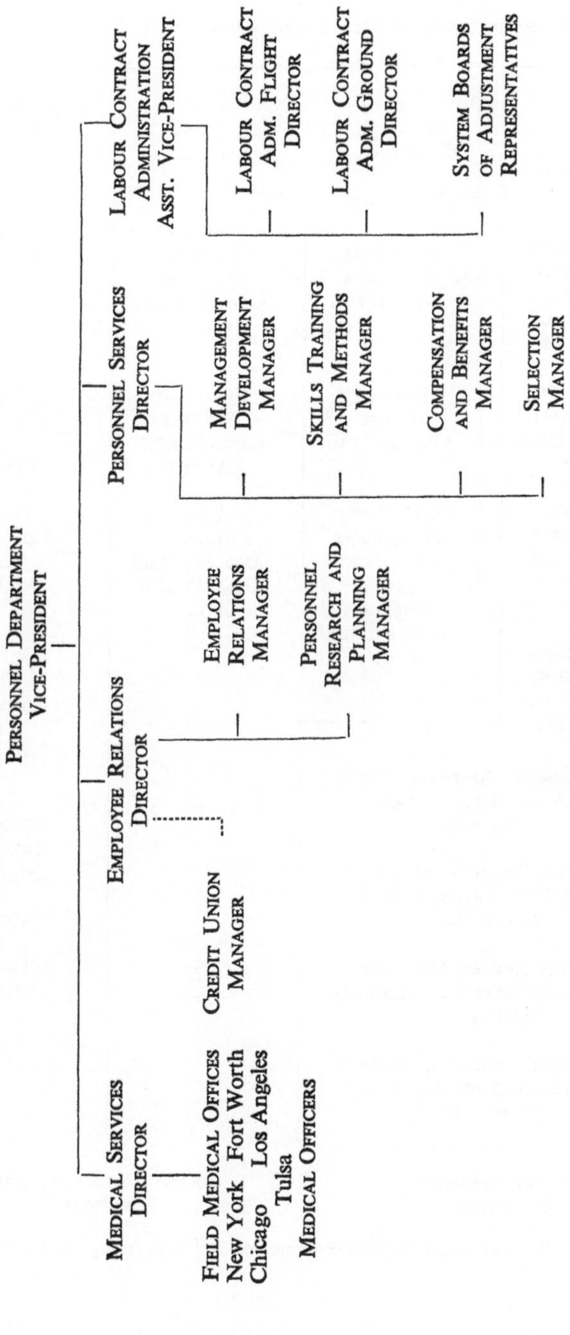

FIG. 67. *American Airlines Personnel organisation*

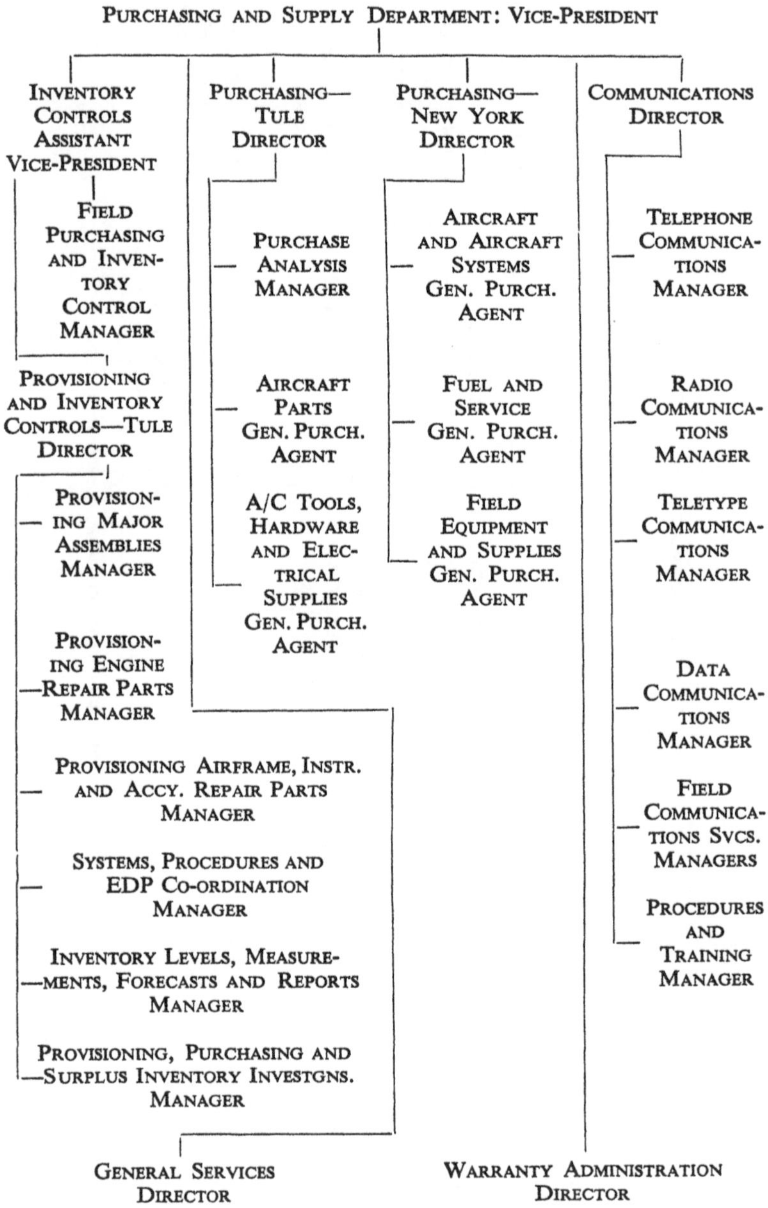

FIG. 68. *American Airlines Purchasing and Supply organisation*

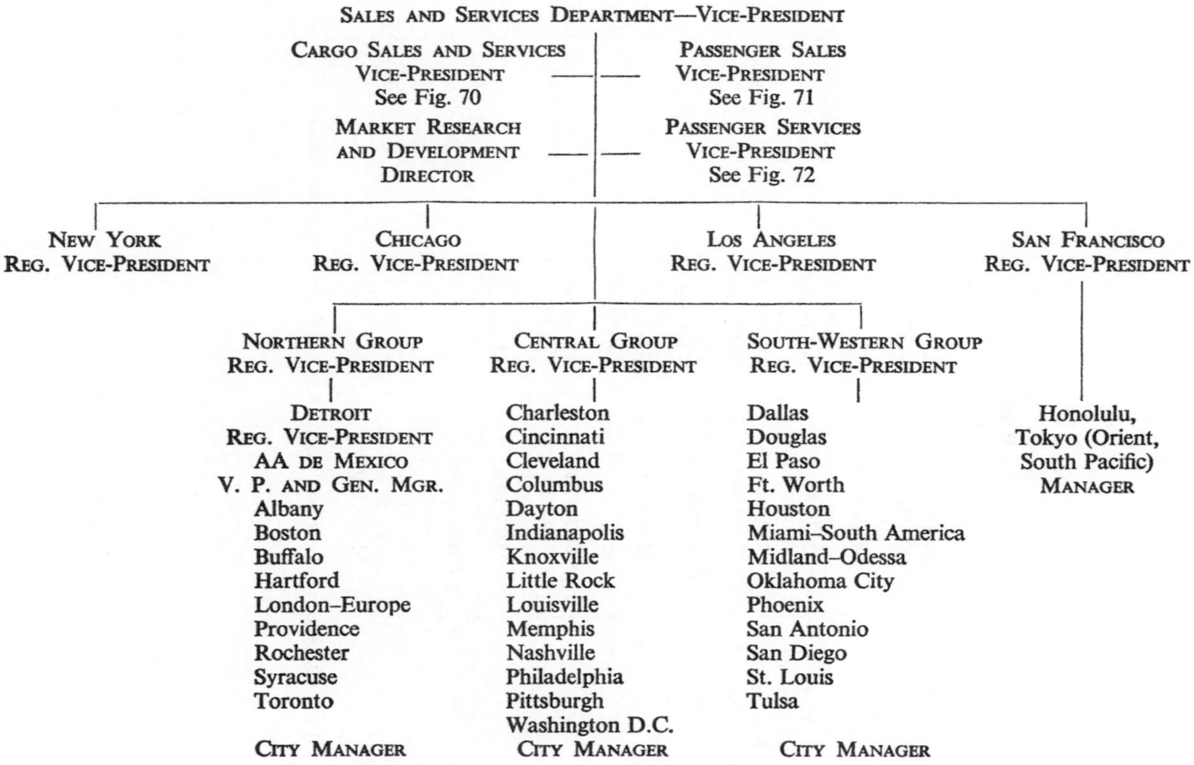

FIG. 69. *American Airlines Sales and Services organisation*

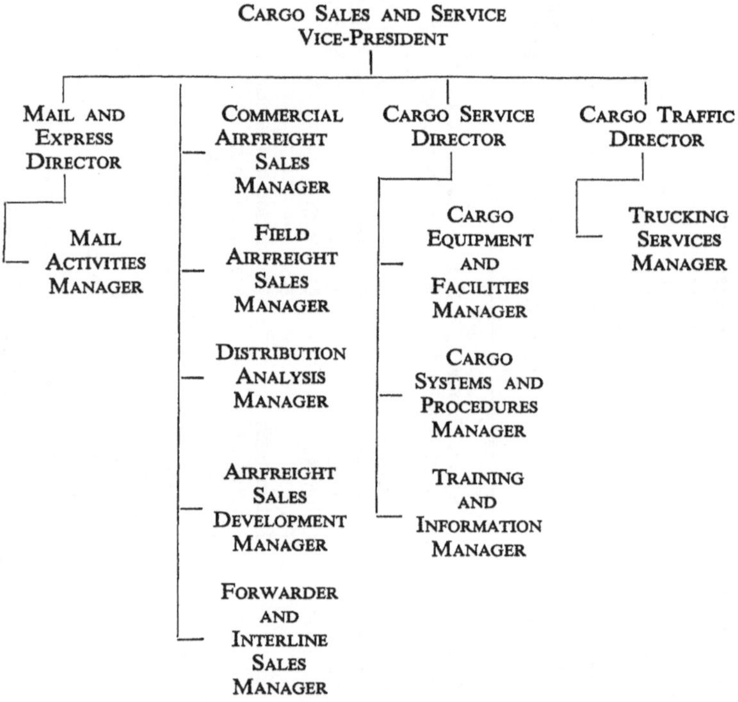

FIG. 70. *American Airlines Cargo Sales and Services organisation*

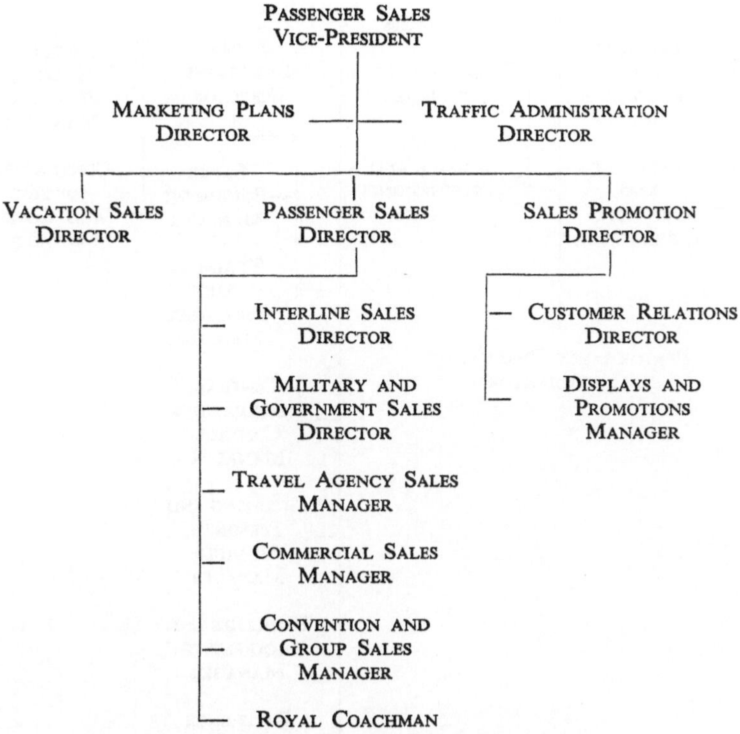

FIG. 71. *American Airlines Passenger Sales organisation*

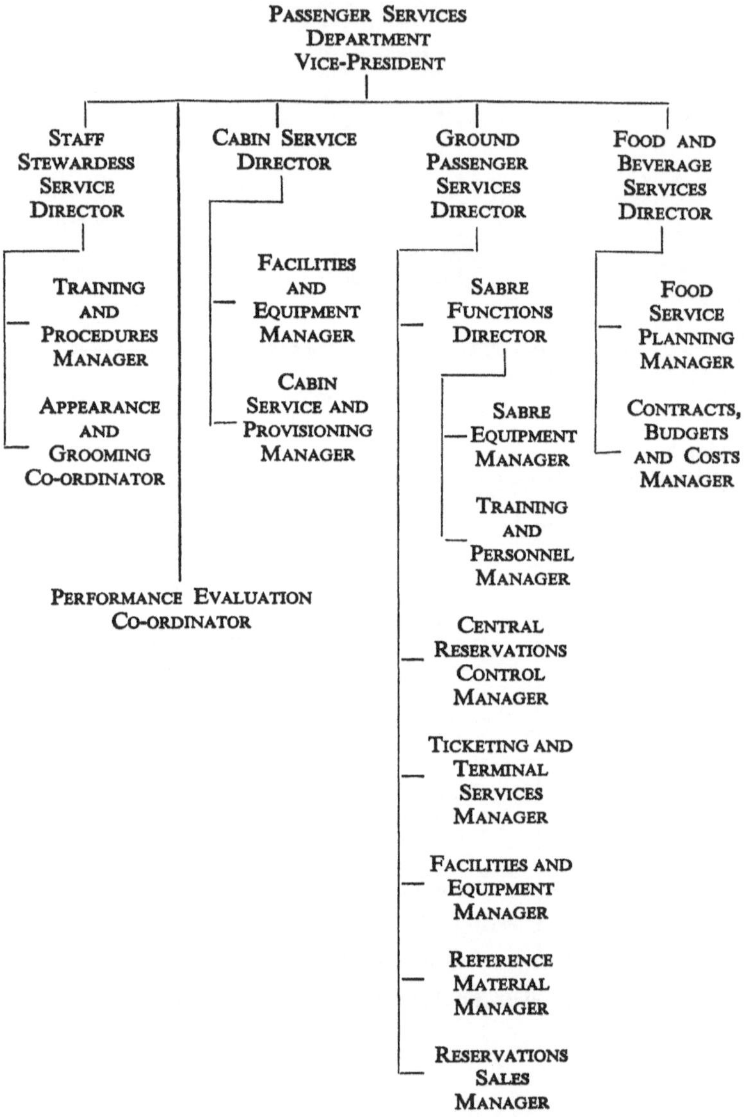

FIG. 72. *American Airlines Passenger Services organisation*

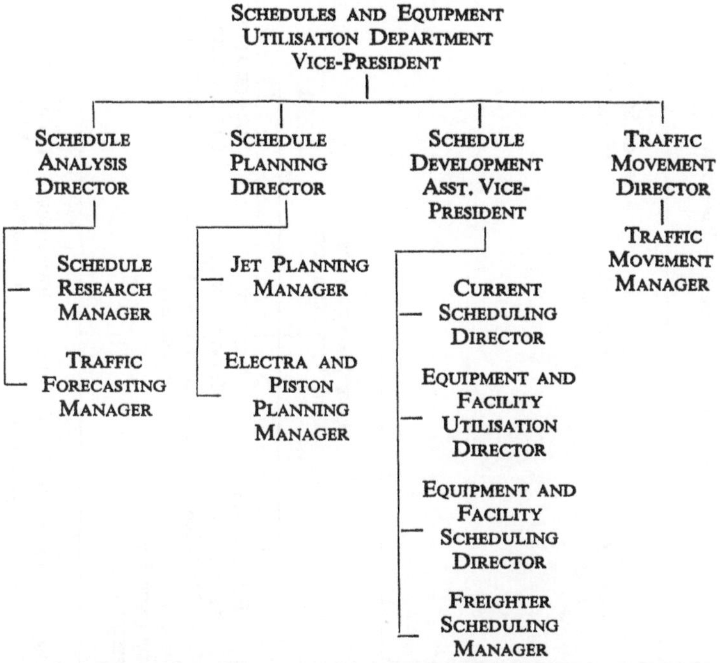

FIG. 73. *American Airlines Schedules and Equipment Utilisation organisation*

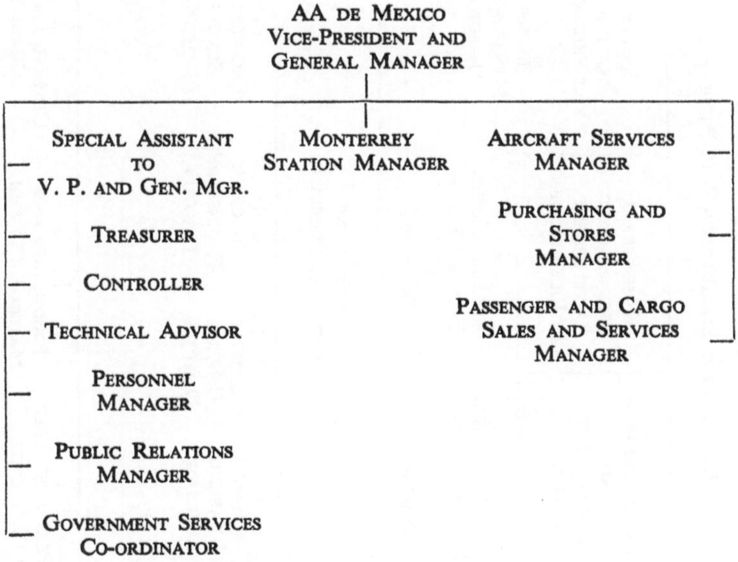

FIG. 74. *American Airlines de Mexico organisation*

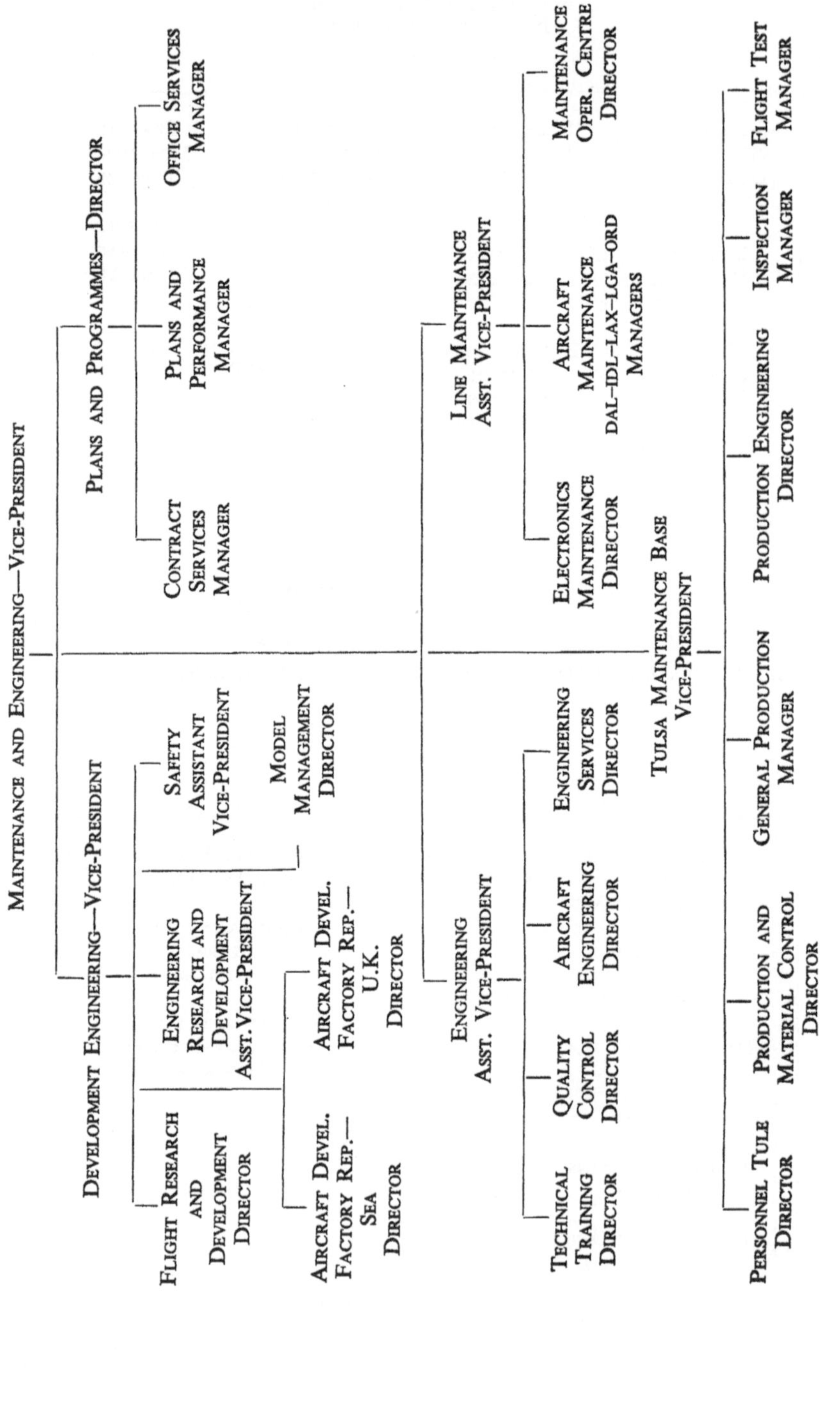

Fig. 75. *American Airlines Maintenance and Engineering organisation*

INDEX